DATE DUE

DE 1 8'98			
Sept 5			
AP 3 02			
OO 24 02			
NO			
AP 9 05			
AP 1 7 06			

DEMCO 38-296

Iraq

CSIS Middle East Dynamic Net Assessment

Iraq

Sanctions and Beyond

Anthony H. Cordesman
and Ahmed S. Hashim

WestviewPress

A Division of HarperCollins*Publishers*

Copyright © 1997 by Anthony H. Cordesman

Published in 1997 in the United States of America by Westview Press, 5500 Central Avenue, Boulder, Colorado 80301-2877, and in the United Kingdom by Westview Press, 12 Hid's Copse Road, Cumnor Hill, Oxford OX2 9JJ

Library of Congress Cataloging-in-Publication Data
Cordesman, Anthony H.
  Iraq : sanctions and beyond / Anthony H. Cordesman and Ahmed S. Hashim.
    p. cm.
  Includes bibliographical references (p.   ).
  ISBN 0-8133-3235-4 (hc). — ISBN 0-8133-3236-2 (pbk.)
    1. Iraq—Politics and government—1979–   2. Iraq—Foreign
relations—1979– I. Hashim, Ahmed S. II. Title.
DS79.7.C67 1997
956.704'3—dc20   96-46046
                                            CIP

This book was typeset by Letra Libre, 1705 Fourteenth Street, Suite 391, Boulder, Colorado 80304.

The paper used in this publication meets the requirements of the American National Standard for Permanence of Paper for Printed Library Materials Z39.48-1984.

10   9   8   7   6   5   4   3   2   1

Contents

Tables and Illustrations

Maps

Acknowledgments

This volume is part of a six-volume series reporting on a dynamic net assessment of the Gulf. The project was conceived by David Abshire and Richard Fairbanks of the Center for Strategic and International Studies and is part of a broader dynamic net assessment of the entire Middle East.

The authors would like to thank Kimberly Goddes and Kiyalan Batmanglidj for their research and editing help in writing this series, and Thomas Seidenstein and David Hayward for helping to edit each volume.

Many US and international analysts and agencies played a role in commenting on drafts of the manuscript. So did experts in each Southern Gulf country. The authors cannot acknowledge these contributions by name or agency, but they are deeply grateful. The authors would also like to thank their colleagues at the CSIS who reviewed various manuscripts and commented on the analysis. These colleagues include Richard Fairbanks, Arnaud de Borchgrave, and Co-Director of the Middle East Program Judith Kipper.

Anthony H. Cordesman
Ahmed S. Hashim

Iraq

1

Introduction

Iraq's current regime presents unambiguous security threats to the other states of the Gulf and to the West. While Iran's regime may offer some hope for constructive engagement, Iraq is virtually certain to be a revanchist and aggressive state as long as Saddam Hussein is in power. Even if Saddam and his coterie should fall from power, their immediate successor will most likely consist of another Sunni authoritarian elite, made up of other members of the Ba'ath party, senior military officers, or a combination of both.

It may well be a decade before any political transformation occurs in Iraq that produces a stable, moderate government. In the interim, Iraq may go through several short-lived regimes and even civil war. Its politics are likely to remain the politics of violence, many of its future leaders are likely to seek revenge for the Gulf War and its aftermath, and its political elites are likely to reassert Iraq's search for hegemony in the Gulf and seek to become the leading regional military power.

This does not mean that Iraq cannot change, and should not be encouraged to change. It does not mean that sanctions and isolation are the only way of dealing with Iraq, or that Iraq's people should be punished indefinitely for the actions of its leaders. It does mean, however, that the Gulf and the West must be realistic in shaping their policy towards Iraq, and must have a realistic understanding of its current regime and military potential.

The Policy Options for Dealing with Iraq

The West and the other states in the Gulf must find ways to live with Iraq, seek to moderate the conduct of its regime, and create a climate for positive political change. The basic issue for policy is how this can best be done. There are several major policy options that the West, other Gulf states, and other nations can pursue:

1

- Lifting political and economic sanctions under conditions that leave Saddam Hussein and the Ba'ath elite in power, and which effectively recognize that Iraq will not fully comply with the terms of the UN cease-fire.
- Continuing the present UN sanctions that isolate Iraq politically and cripple its economy, in order to force Saddam Hussein from power and to create a successor regime that will be less aggressive and willing to trade changes in the regime's behavior for a lifting of sanctions;
- Lifting all or most political and economic sanctions in return for a large degree of Iraqi compliance with the terms of the UN cease-fire, requiring full Iraqi compliance in providing reparations and the recognition by Iraq of its new borders with a sovereign Kuwait, but leaving Saddam Hussein and the present regime in power;
- A step-by-step lifting of political and economic sanctions under conditions which trade specific changes in the conduct of Iraq's regime for each step in reducing the present sanctions, while leaving Saddam Hussein and the present Ba'ath and military elite in power;
- Seeking to create an alternative "centrist" regime that is still based on the Ba'ath, Sunni elites, and/or the military, but drives Saddam Hussein and his coterie from power by maintaining a mix of sanctions, using other economic and political pressures, using covert action, and persuading neighboring states like Turkey and Jordan to support such a "peripheral strategy";
- Adopting a "peripheral" strategy that combines sanctions with covert action, which attempts to mobilize the Kurds and Shi'ites against the central regime, and which seeks to persuade neighboring states like Turkey and Jordan to support such a "peripheral strategy" and;
- Pursuing an individual national policy towards Iraq that seeks to maximize political and/or trade benefits in dealing with Iraq, regardless of the character of its regime and its conduct towards other states.

The UN is still committed to a policy of sanctions, but it is clear that there no longer is such a degree of international unity in pursuing this policy.

- Some states—such as Kuwait, Saudi Arabia, Britain and the US—continue to favor a hard-line approach because they believe it is impossible to deal with Saddam Hussein's regime. Even Kuwait and Saudi Arabia, however, did not fully support the US during the Kurdish crisis of August–September, 1996.
- Other states, including major outside powers like France and Russia, believe that sanctions now harm Iraq's people without offering any

guarantee of changes in its leadership or the character of its regime. They are more concerned with debt repayment and resuming trade, arms sales, and other economic relations than with containing and deposing Saddam Hussein.

- Other nations support the containment of Iraq's military build-up but oppose continuing with sanctions that cause massive hardship for Iraq's people and block oil exports, other trade, and investment. These states include many Arab, European, and Asian states friendly to the US, as well as friendly Gulf states like Oman, Qatar, and the UAE.

- There are also a number of developing states which believe that the UN resolutions now take the form of an oppressive or "neo-imperialist" interference in the national affairs of Iraq. Still other states pursue a policy of covert opportunism, laying the ground work for future economic ties and arms sales to Iraq.

These divisions within the international community create growing uncertainties as to whether a policy or strategy that relies on sanctions can be successful. In spite of continuing discoveries that Iraq has lied to the UN about its holdings of weapons of mass destruction, a combination of legitimate humanitarian concerns and Iraq's oil wealth and economic potential make it doubtful that a sanctions policy can remain in force for more than a few more years. One can never underestimate Saddam Hussein's unique ability to alienate world opinion, but policy must begin to look at other options, including how to live with Iraq on different terms.

Key Policy Complications in Dealing with Iraq

Finding such a new strategy for dealing with Iraq will not be easy. There is no question that Saddam Hussein and the present Iraqi regime are repressive and represent a serious threat to regional peace. At the same time, there are a number of other variables that must be considered in trying to shape such a policy towards Iraq, and in developing a consistent and workable policy approach to deal with the Iraqi regime:

- *The humanitarian issue is very real, and raises growing questions about how much an entire nation can be punished for the actions of an authoritarian elite.* Iraq is a nation of over 20 million people, with a high birth rate, and a population that is two-thirds non-Sunni Arab. The UN sanctions have begun to inflict so much hardship on Iraq's people that they threaten widespread malnutrition. Most of the costs of these sanctions are being paid for by Iraqis who are victims of Iraq's authoritarian leadership.[1]

- *The Gulf and the West must live with the Iraq that UN sanctions are creating.* The suffering caused by UN sanctions is creating broad Iraqi resentment of the US, Kuwait, and Saudi Arabia—who are now seen as largely responsible for the continued enforcement of sanctions. The resulting revanchism may well survive Saddam Hussein, and could play an important role in shaping Iraqi politics and actions for several decades.

- *The terms of the cease-fire accords call for massive Iraqi reparations and offer no clear path to stable peaceful relations.* Coupled to the impact of sanctions over the half-decade since the cease-fire, a literal enforcement of current reparations agreements is certain to increase Iraqi revanchism, just as the "economic consequences of the peace" following World War I helped create the extremism that destroyed the Weimar Republic and brought the Nazis to power.

- *There are many well-educated and moderate Iraqis, but there is no meaningful moderate political opposition with any popular standing.* Iraq has long been an authoritarian state ruled by small, violent, ruthless factions within its Sunni minority. It has no tradition of legitimate representative government, or of providing representation that reflects the ethnic and sectarian differences within its population. Further, Saddam's alliance with the Kurdish Democratic Party in September 1996 allowed him to drive most of Iraq's weak opposition elements out of the Kurdish exclusion zone in Northern Iraq. It is easy to talk in vague terms about the emergence of a more representative regime, but there is no real political base for such change.

- *Iraq is a deeply divided nation that could be torn apart by civil war.* Recent CIA estimates indicate that 63–68% of Iraq's population is non-Sunni (60–65% Shi'ite) and that 20–25% are non-Arab (15–20% Kurdish).[2] These sectarian and ethnic divisions within Iraq have already created a separate Kurdish entity in Northern Iraq and a civil war between the Kurdish factions in this entity. They have led to civil war between the Iraqi regime and some of its Shi'ites. Any policy towards Iraq must deal with the Kurdish question, and the risk of Shi'ite separatism.

- *The Kurdish question cannot be dealt with as an Iraqi issue alone.* It affects Iran, Syria, and Turkey, countries with sizable and restive Kurdish minorities.

- *Iraq cannot be dealt with in isolation from Iran.* A weak, divided Iraq might lead to Iranian efforts to divide or absorb part of Iraq. At the same time, there is always the risk that Iraq may be willing to strike a "devil's bargain" with Iran, and that both nations may act in unison to threaten the Gulf or try to break out from containment.

- *Iraq is a major oil power with vast oil reserves that have a major impact on world energy supplies.* Virtually all projections of future energy balances call for large-scale Iraqi oil production to ensure an adequate world supply of oil and to keep oil prices moderate. The US Energy Information Administration (EIA) projects Iraqi oil production at 4.4 million barrels per day (MMBD) in 2000, 5.4 MMBD in 2005, and 6.4 MMBD in 2010. These projections would make Iraq the second largest oil producer in the Gulf, providing nearly 7% of all world oil production.[3]

A Lack of Present and Future Consensus

Iraq is a case where all the available policy options have powerful negatives. No policy can avoid the contradictions inherent in choosing between the near-term security provided by sanctions and containment, and the resulting costs in terms of Iraqi revanchism and human suffering.

There are several small, moderate, and democratic Iraqi opposition movements, but they have little power or internal influence in Iraq. Iraq's politics are highly nationalistic and violent in character, and they are the politics of small competing Sunni power elites and clan groupings. Even if Saddam falls, his most likely successor would be another small autocratic elite. The military remains the second most powerful element in Iraq, and seems likely to be the only real rival to some new Sunni "extended family." No policy can expect to produce a moderate regime quickly or to reconcile Iraq's ethnic and sectarian divisions.

There also is little meaningful chance of forging a high degree of lasting unity among Western, Gulf, and other nations that deal with Iraq. The United States and its allies can influence the policy of other states, and may be able to shape much of the outcome of debate within the UN, but it cannot count on the full support of many of its allies. Policy towards Iraq will inevitably become steadily more adversarial as nations increasingly divide over the enforcement of sanctions and the level of military containment.

This makes the choice of policy options particularly difficult for the US, Saudi Arabia, and Kuwait—the nations that face the most direct threat from Iraq. The fact that no policy towards Iraq can bring total consensus or result in a clearly predictable end game is scarcely an argument for appeasement. The fact that there are no good alternatives to Saddam Hussein does not mean that some alternatives would not be better. As a result, the US, Saudi Arabia, and Kuwait will almost certainly be forced to take a harder line towards Iraq's present regime than other states. This may increase the divisions between their policies and those of other states, but such divisions may well be a necessary element of any valid policy in dealing with Iraq.

Policy and the Role of Analysis

No amount of analysis can resolve these problems and provide easy answers to choosing the right strategy towards Iraq. Analysis can, however, provide insights into the key factors and contradictions involved. It can help the policy-maker find the proper balance between efforts to contain Iraq and efforts to ease the plight of the Iraqi people, and to evaluate the potential for change within the Iraqi regime and Iraqi politics. Analysis can also provide important insights into Iraq's strategic future. It can look beyond political rhetoric and examine the details of Iraq's present and possible military capabilities and the threats Iraq can and cannot pose to other nations in the Gulf.

The analysis in this paper focuses on the following issues:

- The current political situation in Iraq, and the prospects for political change.
- The problems posed by ethnic and sectarian divisions in Iraq, and the creation of a Kurdish enclave.
- The current economic situation in Iraq, and the impact of sanctions.
- Current energy developments within Iraq, and the strategic impact of Iraqi capability to resume oil and gas production.
- Iraq's external relations, and the threat it poses to its neighbors.
- Iraq's role in supporting terrorism and extremism.
- Iraq's efforts to rebuild its conventional military forces, and the threat this poses to the region.
- Iraq's efforts to rebuild its ability to manufacture and deliver weapons of mass destruction.

The conclusion to each chapter makes specific recommendations for policy action, but the primary focus of this analysis is to provide an improved basis for understanding current developments in Iraq and what given policy options can and cannot hope to accomplish. A simple and consistent policy may look desirable on paper, but it will rapidly fail under the pressure of events. Iraq is not a short-term problem. Indeed, it may be optimistic to think in terms of a decade of deterrence, low level conflict, and constant uncertainty.

Iraq is a game of three-dimensional chess in which each piece is a separate player, and not a game of checkers in which the US or any other nation can control the board against a single opponent. There are many actors on the board with their own motives, rules, and moves. Any policy that tries to be rigid in the face of both the uncertainties in Iraq, and the moves of other players, is almost certain to fail.

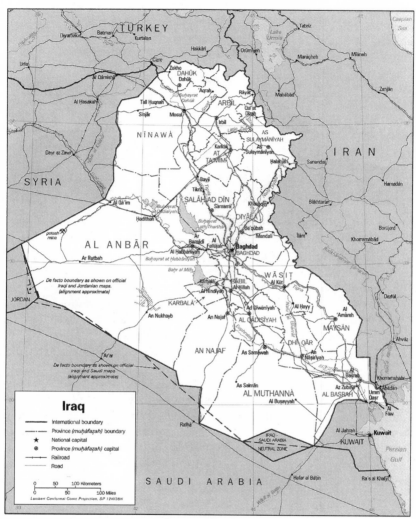

MAP ONE   Iraq. *Source:* US State Department.

2

Internal Political Developments Since the Gulf War

Saddam Hussein has survived Iraq's defeat in the Gulf War, and more than half a decade of post-war sanctions. He and his supporters have managed to suppress almost all active dissent, and have caused a new series of post war clashes between Iraq and the West. They have survived more than half a decade of sanctions, and agreed to an oil deal with the UN in 1996 that has relieved much of the economic pressure upon the regime. Saddam may remain one bullet away from a new "election" to the "presidency," and may have become more isolated from many of his traditional supporters, but he and his immediate coterie continue to rule, and Iraq's government is as repressive as ever.

Any strategic analysis of Iraq must, therefore, begin with Saddam Hussein and the present Ba'ath elite. As long as they are in power, Iraq is almost certain to be revanchist and aggressive in character. This revanchism and aggressiveness may not lead to overt Iraqi use of military forces against other states, or to large scale conflicts, but it is almost certain to lead to constant Iraqi tests of Western resolve, and new Iraqi efforts to intimidate the Southern Gulf states.

Internal Political Developments Since the Gulf War

The cease-fire in the Gulf War initially seemed to promise a very different future. The terms of the cease-fire set forth in UN Security Council Resolution 687, which was adopted on April 3, 1991, called for an Iraq that would accept peace with its neighbors, and which would be subject to powerful international controls.

Resolution 687 required Iraq to:

- Recognize the adjusted Kuwaiti-Iraqi border,
- Accept a UN guarantee of the border,

- Allow the UN to establish a peace observer force in a zone along the Iraqi-Kuwait border 10 kilometers in Iraq and 5 kilometers in Kuwait,
- Reaffirm its commitment to the Chemical Warfare and Nuclear Non-Proliferation Treaties,
- Allow the UN to inspect the destruction of all biological, chemical, and nuclear weapons, long-range ballistic missiles, and related facilities, equipment and supplies,
- Accept liability for Kuwait's losses,
- Accept liability for all pre-war debts,
- Return or account for all Kuwaiti prisoners, and
- Renounce terrorism.

At the same time, UN Security Council Resolution 688, called for major improvements in political liberalization and human rights. The resolution, which was adopted on April 5, 1991, declared that the UN Security Council was gravely concerned by the repression of the Iraqi people, and the massive flow of refugees into neighboring countries, which threatened the peace and stability of the region. It condemned the actions of the Iraqi government, and called upon it to end its repression, to allow immediate access for humanitarian agencies to all those in need throughout Iraq, and to respect the human and political rights of Iraqi citizens. In addition, it called upon the Secretary General to pursue humanitarian activities in Iraq by using the relevant agencies of the UN, and to address the critical needs of Iraqi refugees. The resolution demanded that Iraq cooperate with the Secretary General in his endeavors.

If Iraq had complied with the terms of Resolutions 687 and 688, and other relevant UN resolutions, it would soon have become a very different country. In practice, however, Saddam Hussein and the ruling elite of the Ba'ath Party made every possible effort to avoid such compliance. Iraq's state-controlled media continued to assert Iraq's claim to Kuwait. Iraq resisted every effort to constrain Saddam's regime, and to limit the government's control over its Shi'ites and Kurds. It resisted UN efforts to destroy Iraq's weapons of mass destruction, and challenged UN efforts to provide relief to Iraq's Kurds and Shi'ites wherever possible.

The first signs of Iraq's determination to challenge the UN emerged even before the UN voted on the final terms of the cease-fire agreement. On March 5, 1991, two days after the initial agreement to halt the fighting, Saddam Hussein appointed his cousin, Ali Hassan al-Majid as Minister of the Interior. Majid had helped lead the suppression of the Kurds in 1988, and his appointment was clearly designed to help Saddam take a hard line in suppressing the Kurdish and Shi'ite uprisings that took place once the fighting halted in Kuwait.

In the weeks immediately following the cease-fire, Saddam demonstrated both his strength and his rejection of the spirit of the cease-fire accords. He ruthlessly put down a Shi'ite uprising in the south—which was centered around Basra and Najaf, but encompassed most of the south. He was equally ruthless in putting down a major Kurdish uprising in the north. In both cases, he was rapidly able to reconstitute the instruments of state power that had given him control over Iraq for more than a decade before the Gulf War, and the small military forces that Shi'ite and Kurdish ethnic groups were able to muster proved no match for Iraq's main force combat units.

Once Saddam suppressed these uprisings, he began a broader political struggle with the UN over the issue of sanctions and humanitarian aid. He refused to accept the terms offered in UN Security Council Resolutions 706 and 712, which would have allowed Iraq to begin exporting oil under UN control and monitoring.[4] Instead, Saddam used his security apparatus to harass the UN and maintain control over the Iraqi people. He also used his control over Iraq's budget, and financial and business infrastructure, to force a level of austerity on his people that allowed him to reconstitute and maintain much of his military machine. At the same time, he attempted to undercut support for sanctions by exploiting the human cost of the UN sanctions, and highlighting Iraq's potential value as a trading partner.

The Informal and Formal Basis of Iraq's Power Structure

Saddam did not reassert power by being loved or popular. While Saddam has probably put more effort into establishing a personality cult than any other contemporary leader in the Middle East, Iraqi popular support for this cult is more an illusion than a reality. This became clear immediately after the Gulf War when Kurds, Shi'ites, and Sunni military deserters were seen defacing and destroying posters and statues of the Iraqi ruler in riots approaching raw fury. Even in the Sunni parts of Iraq, many Iraqis privately expressed profound bitterness over Iraq's defeat. They felt that Saddam had badly miscalculated in invading both Iran and Kuwait, and blamed him for squandering Iraq's resources and wealth during both the Iran-Iraq War and the Gulf War.

Saddam was able to stay in power because of his immense power over Iraq's political leaders and ruling Sunni minority. He used this political power to quickly purge potential rivals, remove disaffected officials and commanders, and remove uncertain loyalists. He used it to make other changes in Iraq's political and military leadership designed to ensure that no opposing centers of power existed within the Ba'ath, the government, the security services, and the military. And, he used his family, tribe, and friendly clans to help secure his power.

Saddam also used his control over key state institutions like the security forces, the army, and the state-controlled media. He used force wherever this was desirable. At the same time, he used the power of government to provide economic incentives for his supporters, and to deny economic resources to the Kurds, hostile Shi'ites, and other opponents.

He also used his control over institutions like the media to stress the "need" for his leadership in the face of Iraq's new difficulties. As one paper put it: "the years of war with Iran have proven the soundness of the conclusion that Iraqi dignity, future territorial integrity are contingent upon maintaining the leadership of Saddam. . . ." Saddam was described as the "honest struggler," and the symbol of Iraq's achievements, having made a "qualitative leap" by bringing Iraq out of its backward existence to an era of military strength and scientific progress. The Iraqi media then drew the conclusion that Iraq could only regain its former strength under Saddam's leadership.

In short, Saddam exploited both a permeating *informal* political structure of power based on ethnicity and ties of kinship and long-standing friendships, and a vast *formal structure of* power based on state institutions. An understanding of these power structures is essential to understanding Saddam's survival after eight years of conflict with Iran and after the Gulf War. It is essential to understanding why Saddam may survive several more years of UN sanctions, why it is so difficult to change the fundamental character of Iraq's regime through any measure short of direct invasion. And, it is essential to understanding the strengths and limitations of a "centrist" strategy towards Iraq, and the limitations of any "peripheral strategy" which is not based on civil war.

3

The Informal Politics
of the "Center"

Saddam Hussein—and those around him—base much of their power upon an informal and highly personalized domestic political structure which draws on support from Iraq's Sunni minority, which makes up 32% to 37% of the total population.[5] The key clans and families within the Sunni heartland—which is composed of the four provinces of Baghdad, Takrit, Mosul and Ramadi—form the bedrock of this political power structure although it also includes some proven Shi'ite and Christian loyalists.

Iraqis refer to this aspect of Iraqi politics as the "center," which is both a geographic term denoting the Sunni Arab heartland and the capital Baghdad (whose population is actually 40%–50% Arab Shi'ite and Kurd), and a political, socioeconomic and cultural area that is largely Sunni and which has the nation's highest standard of living, economic development, urbanization, and education. The "center" is home to the vast majority of Iraq's large middle-class professionals and intellectuals.[6]

Sunni Popular Opinion and the "Center"
Immediately After the Gulf War

Saddam was able to draw heavily upon support from the "center" after the Gulf War. He drew upon broad support from the Sunni Arab minority, which included many of the middle class professionals in urban areas. He also drew on support from major tribes such as the al-Bu-'Assaf, al-Halabishah, al-Janabi, al-Bu-Fahd, al-Ma'adid, al-Mahamidah, al-Jumaylah, al-Sa'dan, al-Bu'Isa, al-Mawali, al-Bu-'Alwan, al-Bu-Nimr, Shammar and Dulaim all of which are to be found in Al Anbar province. In addition, he drew upon the group of "Takriti" clans of which Saddam and his family are members, and upon support from his extended family.

Saddam was able to obtain relatively broad support from Iraq's Sunnis for a number of reasons:

- The Sunni heartland felt little sympathy for the rebels in the north and south during the insurrections following Desert Storm. The rebels in the Shi'ite south were perceived as being inspired by Shi'ite Islamists with ties to Iran, and as being determined to establish an Islamic Republic modeled on Iran. This goal was viewed as little more than treason by many Sunni Iraqis, and was opposed by many Shi'ites as well. Similarly, the Kurds were seen as putative separatists that had betrayed Iraq during the Iran-Iraq War and were doing so again. Further, many educated Iraqis saw even Kurdish autonomy as a threat to central control over the oil-rich Al-Tamim province.
- Many Sunnis and more secular Shi'ites in the "center" had a genuine sense of commitment to the Ba'athist goals of secularism and modern economic development within the framework of national unity, even though most had no deep ideological commitment to the Ba'ath party. The "center" perceived the Shi'ites and Kurds, and many of Iraq's outside opposition groups, as threats to these goals or as allies of the West and the nations that had "opposed" Iraq during the Iran-Iraq War and Gulf War.
- Some in the "center" felt that if Saddam's regime collapsed, Iraq might unravel or they would come under Shi'ite control. They accepted the "legitimacy of the worst alternative."
- Finally, the pervasive presence of the intelligence, security and military in the "center" further discouraged overt opposition and all but the most determined insurrectionists and coup plotters.

Sunni Popular Opinion and the "Center" Since the Gulf War

These Sunni groups do not offer Saddam and his coterie the same security today, and this may offer the West and Southern Gulf states an opportunity to exploit a strategy focused on political change. The Iraqis in the "center" have grievances and problems which have grown steadily worse in the years that have followed the cease-fire.

No accurate statistics are available on the Iraqi economy since the Gulf War. There are many estimates, but outside observers have little ability to collect or verify data, and the Iraqi government has fluctuated between making exaggerated claims that Iraq can recover and survive the sanctions, and efforts to propagandize and exaggerate the very real human suffering in Iraq in an effort to get UN sanctions lifted.

It is clear, however, that Iraqi living standards have declined precipitously since 1990, and that this decline has reached the "center" as well as

Shi'ite and Kurdish areas. Prices have increased sharply while wages and salaries have not risen for the past six years. Poverty is widespread even in Sunni areas, and much of Iraq's prosperous middle class has been wiped out. Many Iraqis have had to sell off or pawn their valuables, and take second jobs—driving cabs or hawking their wares on the streets.

More and more of the lower classes are relying on the state for their basic nutritional needs, or are on the edge of falling below subsistence. As early as 1991–1992, then Minister of Commerce Mohammed Mahdi Salih claimed that the rationed food products provided by the government could furnish only 55% of the calories required for proper nutrition. There is no way to validate this statement, but virtually all observers agree that Iraqi levels of nutrition have dropped steadily in the four years that have followed.

Efforts to stabilize the Iraqi Dinar (ID) between mid-1994 and spring 1995 collapsed in the summer of 1995 and the exchange rate fell by 23%. The Iraqi Dinar, which had been close to 3.5:$1 in 1990, plunged to ID 1,600:$1 and prices reached new heights. News reports indicated that one egg cost as much as 80 Iraqi Dinars—or $258 at the official exchange rate—and the government was forced to introduce yet another series of price controls and rationing measures to try to halt the rise in the price of basic goods.

In spite of increases in wages, price controls, and special privileges, few in the "center" have been immune to these economic pressures. Ordinary Sunnis have suffered almost as much as urban Shi'ites. Many Sunni, pro-regime professionals, technocrats, teachers, Ba'ath functionaries, and journalists have been reduced from moderate wealth at the time of the cease-fire to hardship and then to poverty. Even many of the "elite" within the Ba'ath and military have been forced to sell much of their wealth.

Further, it has become steadily harder for even privileged members of Iraqi society to leave the country, and new control measures were announced in mid-1995. These measures included a dramatic increase in the fees payable for all Iraqis wishing to travel abroad. The required fees have risen from ID 6,000 to ID 200,000 in less than a year for normal adults. The fees for highly qualified professionals, including university professors, scientists, and engineers have been raised an additional ID 5 million, as part of the government's effort to halt the "brain drain" following the war. This restriction has had a serious financial impact on the "center," and other middle class Iraqis, because Iraqi émigrés are no longer able to send money to their family members, money that has greatly helped those still in Iraq to survive.

There is no way to gauge how much these economic forces have undermined Saddam's support relative to the power base he could rely on immediately after the Gulf War. It is also important to understand that much of the resulting hostility is directed at the US, Kuwait, and Saudi Arabia—rather than the regime. Nevertheless, reports from visitors to Iraq indicate that the "center" feels a growing bitterness towards Saddam and the regime as a result of the steady erosion of Iraq's wealth and power.

Anecdotal reports indicate that many Sunni Arabs have lost patience with the government's repetitive propaganda claims that Iraq must pay a material price for standing up to the 'imperialist' and 'Zionist' enemy and that Iraq is maintaining its honor and pride. This theme of "pride" over wealth is one that Saadun Hammadi first advanced following his elevation to the post of Prime Minister in March 1991:[7]

> The citizen in Iraq and the Arab homeland and the free Muslims and free people in the world will see that Iraq has paid a price for a just and a noble aim: namely, resisting imperialism, Zionism, and the old system. A just struggle for this cause or any other serious cause is not expected to be without a price.

Rhetoric, however, is no substitute for food, shelter, savings, and security. Further, the regime's current propaganda line contradicts much of the propaganda that it used to gain the support of the "center" in the late 1970s and early 1980s. The Ba'ath then told Iraqi "centrists" that the people of Iraq must judge the Ba'ath by its material achievements for the country. It is not surprising, therefore, that many Sunni Iraqis reacted with anger or despair to Saddam's initial statements that Iraq could survive for a long time under sanctions, and that this anger and despair grew worse with time.

Iraq's acceptance of the terms of UN Security Council Resolution 986 in April 1996 created an oil-for-food deal that has relieved some of these pressures, but the immediate impact of the agreement between Iraq and the UN will be limited. The agreement only allows Iraq to sell $330 million worth of oil a month for a period of six months, and less than half the proceeds will go to provide food and medicine in the areas under Saddam Hussein's control. Another 30% will go to war reparations, 15% for food and medicine in the semi-autonomous Kurdish region, and 10% to pay for the costs of UN operations in Iraq. A total of about $106 million a month will not give Saddam much with which to reverse the impact of a decade of war and a half a decade of sanctions in the in the areas under his control.

Further, more is involved than economics. No Iraqi in the "center" can ignore the calamitous decline in social and moral mores, the rising crime, price gouging, open prostitution, widespread corruption, a decline in civic virtues and the decline in the enrollment of Iraqi youth in schools. Even if Iraqi Sunnis and other supporters of the Ba'ath are willing to live with the present conditions, they are likely to be less willing to live with the cost to the future. Education has disintegrated. Parents can no longer afford to send their children to school, instead they are sent to beg or steal. This has become a norm in a state which once had stiff sanctions against such behavior.[8]

Growing Alienation and the Death of "Reform"

The "center's" reaction to the failure of political reform since the Gulf War is more uncertain. Few Iraqis in the center seem to demand or desire Western-style democracy, but many have long indicated they would like more liberalization and less state interference in their lives. There are also reports of growing resentment among Iraqi Sunnis of the arbitrariness, oppression, corruption, and lack of public accountability enforced by Saddam and senior Iraqi officials.

It seems likely that many Sunnis remember that Saddam Hussein had promised political reform following the end of the Iran-Iraq War, and that none of these promises have been kept. The government never went beyond symbolism in implementing its postwar promises of political liberalization—which included providing new political leadership, allowing the creation of political parties, and allowing a freer press. In March 1991, Saddam declared that the leadership's commitment to building a "democratic society based on constitution, law, institutions, and (party) pluralism . . . is an irrevocable and final decision." Official speeches were heavy with promises of democracy, political and administrative reform, and an end to nepotism.

Saddam took some highly visible steps that made it seem like he might act upon these words. In March 1991, he appointed a well-known Shi'ite Ba'athist and American-educated economist named Saadun Hammadi as Prime Minister, and charged him with implementing reform. Hammadi was a veteran politician with diplomatic experience. He had been Minister of State for Foreign Affairs, and in June 1989 was appointed deputy Prime Minister in which post he was tasked to deal with economic affairs, including Iraq's post–Iran-Iraq War revitalization.

The fact that Hammadi was given the post of Prime Minister was seen as significant, because hitherto it had always been held by the President, Saddam himself. Saddam was seen as having decided to delegate some authority to trusted followers, including granting them the authority to implement political programs. Hammadi was very much a part of the Ba'ath power structure—but he had repeatedly expressed the belief that Iraq would move slowly but surely from the dominance of the revolutionary phase of political life, under which Iraq had existed since 1968, to constitutional politics characterized by the rule of law. According to one source, "he (Hammadi) absorbed a commitment to democratic ideals that makes him unique in Iraq's top echelon," while studying agricultural economics at the University of Wisconsin.

The Iraqi government also announced political reforms which included the implementation of a constitution drafted in 1990, creation of a free press, eventual abolition of the supra-legal Revolutionary Courts charged with trying crimes against the state, eventual abolition of the Revolutionary Command Council, and the establishment of a multi-party system. On March 24, 1991, Iraq announced its tentative acceptance of Kurdish autonomy. On May 8, 1991, Iraq announced that the ruling Revolutionary Command Council (RCC) of the Ba'ath would be abolished and replaced with a more democratic government. In March 1991, it declared an amnesty for deserters who were not officers. The coverage of this amnesty was expanded on July 21, 1991.[9]

These reforms are precisely the kind of reforms that Iraq should adopt in the future, but Saddam's promises soon proved to be little more than a political ruse designed to reduce foreign criticism and disguise the government's violent suppression of Shi'ite and Kurdish resistance. As the regime became more secure, it turned back to oppression, and this oppression began to affect the "center" as well as the "periphery."

The new multi-party law passed by the National Assembly on August 24, 1991 is a good example of the hollow nature of Iraqi political reform. The initial draft of the law dropped a provision banning any party whose ideology was inimical to Ba'athism, but insisted that all parties "should value and be proud of Iraq's heritage, glorious history, and achievements attained by national struggle; particularly by the great revolutions of July 14, 1958 and July 17–30, 1968," which overthrew the monarchy and brought to power the Ba'ath party respectively. It was then changed so that parties could not be founded on the basis of sectarianism, apostasy, regionalism, or anti-Arabism. Provisions were added so that only the Ba'ath party was allowed to engage in political activity within the armed forces. As a result, the new law had no real meaning by the time it was passed on September 3, 1991.

In various speeches during 1991, Saddam made it clear that Western-style democracy and other forms of political liberalization were not welcome in Iraq and that Iraqis who adhered to it would not be allowed any leading positions in the political, social, and cultural domains. Further, Saddam and the Ba'ath leadership proceeded systematically to purge the "center," the military, and the Ba'ath. They suppressed any real dissent, violated the civil rights of Iraqi citizens, as well as put additional military pressure on the Kurds and Shi'ites.[10]

Hammadi was removed from office on September 13, 1991, at the height of the Ba'ath party's 10th regional (Iraqi) congress, which had supposedly been convened to elect new members. There were reports that Hammadi had fallen victim to the party's "old guard" because it feared for the party's already tenuous position, but these reports seem to have had little validity. The Ba'ath leadership no longer had the power—assuming it ever had had it—to force the removal of Hammadi if he had had Saddam's support. Instead, Hammadi received an overwhelming vote of no confidence. Only 27 delegates out of 261 voted for him during the elections for the regional command, leaving him a humiliating 39th out of 42 possible candidates.[11]

Saddam proceeded to demonstrate that senior government posts were directly under his personal control. He appointed another Shi'ite, Mohammed Hamza al-Zubaydi—a former minister but a political lightweight—as Hammadi's replacement. The 1991 Ba'ath party congress, dubbed the Congress of Reconstruction and Jihad, then endorsed the principle that the Ba'ath party should have total control over Iraqi political life. It re-elected Saddam as Secretary General of the Regional Command Council, and Saddam's closest associates retained their posts.

Since that time, Iraq's ministers have been "lightning rods" rather than leaders. Al-Zubaydi lasted until 1993, and then was removed as a convenient scapegoat on the grounds he had failed to deal with Iraq's worsening economic fortunes. He was replaced by Ahmad Hussein al-Khodeir, who was himself forced out in May 1994—after Uday Hussein blamed him for the Iraqi Dinar's worsening plight.[12] Saddam then took back the post of Prime Minister, and supposedly the task of dealing with the crisis in Iraq's economy. However, Saddam has since regularly blamed subordinate ministers for Iraq's problems. He has tightened his control over the politics of the "center," while maintaining his strategy of making other government leaders the scapegoats.

Given this background, it is not surprising that many Sunnis increasingly react to the actions and statements of ministers and government officials with apathy and cynicism. This trend was apparent in 1993, when one of Iraq's leading intellectuals and poets—Jabra Ibrahim Jabra—said, "We are not concerned with democracy right now. We need a peace, then we need stability and then we can talk about political liberalization."[13] It has grown more apparent with each year that has followed.

Many of the reporters the Iraqi regime allowed into Iraq in 1995 to observe a referendum on whether Saddam should remain in power concluded that few educated Iraqis believed the referendum had any meaning, or believed Saddam's promise that there would be meaningful elections for the National Assembly in 1996. In fact, Iraqis in the center seemed to believe they would have to live with a steadily more intrusive government, one that attempted to regulate virtually every aspect of their day-to-day economic behavior, and one that would do less and less to preserve them from poverty.

At the same time, such trends do not seem to threaten Saddam or offer any clear alternative. The "center" may want an end to sanctions, to government oppression, and even to Saddam and those around him, but no popular forces have emerged within the "center" that have been able to take on organized political form. The "center" does not have any domestic alternatives to Saddam, or any reason to support outside political movements like the largely Shi'ite Iraqi National Congress.

The Sunnis in the "center" still have reason to fear the consequences of any change that threatens Sunni political dominance. Further, the "center" has little reason to admire or trust the West or other Arab states. The Sunni elite consists largely of technocrats, professionals, military officers, and party functionaries who have no reason to share the West's commitment to political ideals such as liberal democracy or see the Gulf monarchies as a superior form of government. Many in this elite also see the West—and particularly the US—as responsible for the deliberate and methodical destruction of Iraq as a modern regional power. Even Iraqi Sunni intellectuals who admit their opposition to Saddam in private are often far more nationalistic—and "anti-colonial" and "anti-imperialist"—than pro-reform and pro-democracy.

Problems with the Key Clans

Saddam is experiencing growing problems with the key clans in the "center" which may pose more of a threat to his rule. The politics of the "center" are far more dependent on the loyalty of key clans, tribes, and families than on public opinion. Experts like Charles Tripp have noted that Iraqi politics are the politics of *patrimonialism* wherein a community of trust (*ahl al-thiqa*) follow or trust a leader who emerges from within the community. The patrimonial leader's position is based on his ability to distribute tangible and concrete material rewards, on his control of instruments of state, and on a variety of personality characteristics such as charisma and ruthlessness that enable a patrimonial leader to maintain authority. These factors explain why many of the leading Sunni clans stayed loyal to Saddam through the Iran-Iraq War and the Gulf War, and they have been as important in securing his power as the more formal instruments of state control.

The leader's position is also dependent on the "unquantifiable ties" of kinship that bind the community to the patrimonial leader. These ties range from immediate family ties to shared clan, tribal, religious, geographical, and ethnic identity.[14] Saddam Hussein has long been as dependent on a small coterie of Sunni clans and personal supporters as he has upon the loyalty of the "center." Support from regional-clan and familial kinship groups has been one of his most effective means of conserving power.

Since 1994, however, Saddam has had increasing problems with even his most loyal clans and closest supporters. Dissatisfaction spread widely among several key Sunni tribes by 1995. For example, there were strong indications that Saddam was having growing problems with the Juburi clan. The Juburis are centered around Mosul and Hilla, and had collaborated with Saddam's tribe for many years, and a number of Juburis had reached senior positions in the armed forces and internal security apparatus.[15] Nevertheless, two senior officers from this tribe: Major-General Salem al-Bassu, deputy commander of the air force, and Major-General Hasan al-Haj Khader, air force director of operations, seem to have made coup attempts against Saddam in 1993.

Another Sunni clan of federation, the Al-Duris, had presented problems since early 1994. Two senior Ba'athist officials from the Al-Duris, Abdel Rahman al-Duri and Khidr Abed al-Aziz al-Duri were arrested in mid-1994 ostensibly for objecting to Saddam's demand that his son, Uday, be considered for the post of Defense Minister.[16] Another Duri, Saber al-Duri was divested of his power. Several Duri officers were purged at the same time from the military. Izzat Ibrahim al-Duri, the most senior member of the clan in office continues to hold the title of Vice-President, but has no real executive power.[17] Moreover, his health is bad and the execution of members of his clan has reportedly had an adverse impact on him.

The powerful Al-Dulaim tribal confederation has traditionally been a strong supporter of Saddam Hussein. The Al-Dulaim clan is based in Al-Anbar province, in the Sunni heartland, which Saddam declared was the 'white province' because of its complete loyalty during the March 1991 rebellions. The Al-Dulaimis are important for other reasons. The Takritis—the al-Bunasser clan from Al'Auja—are an offshoot of the Dulaim tribal confederation. Al-Anbar province dominates the trade and commercial activity of sanctioned Iraq, and it is the Al-Dulaim who control most of this activity and trade with Jordan, and across Jordan with the outside world. Finally, the Al-Dulaim clan is so large that the tribe extends across the desert into Syria.

In May 1995, opposition within the Al-Dulaim clan reached the point of serious revolt. This revolt took place in the town of Al-Ramadi in the overwhelmingly Sunni Arab governate of Al-Anbar. It was triggered by the delivery of the mutilated body of Major-General Mohammed Masloum al-Dulaimi to his family. Dulaimi had attempted a coup in November 1994, and Saddam had reacted with characteristic swiftness and exacted ruthless retribution. He executed the would-be coup maker, and the general's body was delivered mutilated to his family in a characteristic display of the brutality the security services have used to try to intimidate Saddam's opposition. The revolt was followed by an uprising which spread to the military installations in Abu Ghuraib, outside Baghdad. It was suppressed and 120–130 army officers were executed.

Other problems occurred in Samara, another major Sunni Arab town, during the summer of 1995. According to some reports, 43 leading personalities from the town, including many from the powerful Samara'i family, were arrested. They were accused of trying to organize an assassination attempt against Saddam. Among the arrested were two Air Force generals: Yunis Atallah al-Samara'i and Yasin Jasim al-Abboud. There are many other less reliable reports of opposition within "centrist" tribes and clans.[18]

These developments offer some hope that a "centrist" opposition could still arise against Saddam from within the key clans in spite of the lack of organized "centrist" political movements and institutions. Once again, however, there are problems for a "centrist" strategy. First, the longer Saddam succeeds in suppressing such opposition, the weaker the power base will be for creating a stable successor. Second, none of the clan or tribal opposition to date seems "moderate" or "reform" oriented. A different mix of centrist clans or tribes might prove to be more pragmatic, but it is unclear that it could reach a lasting accommodation with Iraq's Kurds or Shi'ites by peaceful means or would abandon any of Saddam's ambitions for a greater Iraq that it was not forced to abandon.

Problems in Saddam's Family and Coterie

Saddam Hussein's ability to secure his rule through nepotism and personal patronage at the highest level of state power is reinforced by his ability to surround himself with relatives or friends from Takrit that form part of his extended family. These members of Iraq's ruling elite are bound closely to Saddam, and allow him to extend his personal rule throughout the military, the security services, the Ba'ath, and the government.

Saddam has long placed members of his Beijat clan in key positions in the governing system. Early in his rule, he gave senior positions to members of the Tulfah family, but this branch of his clan has faded into obscurity because of a lack of outstanding male members and their loss of influence following the death of Defense Minister 'Adnan Khayrallah Tulfah in 1989. Saddam has recently relied more on the Ibrahims (his half-brothers), and the Al-Majids (his cousins from his paternal side of the family). Until recently, this small group of Takritis had become so preeminent that it would have been difficult to see how a non-Takriti regime could have been established without a major coup or civil war.

In the past, Saddam has been able to count upon the loyalty of these Takritis for a number of reasons: The kinship ties between them, the material benefits and power he has given them, and their role in creating a strong and powerful Iraq—one where they benefit from corruption and a phenomenal growth in wealth. The Takritis have learned to fear Saddam's personal ruthlessness, and Saddam's actions have shown even his closest associates that they can lose power or die as easily as Hussein Kamel. At the same time, they have good reason to fear his fall. They know that that if Saddam goes, whether by their hands or the hands of non-Takritis, they may also fall, and do so at the cost of their lives. As a result, the Takritis face a Hobson's choice: Many increasingly fear Saddam and want him out of power because his presence endangers them and their gains, but they also fear what could happen to their gains and their lives if they remove him.

The Takriti threat to Saddam has also been diminished by the fact that neither the Takriti clan at large, nor Saddam's immediate kin group, constitutes a monolithic bloc. Saddam has probably encouraged some family rivalry and rifts by using his ability to grant and withhold positions and favors, but he has found his "family" to be as difficult to manage as Napoleon found his own fractious family.

At the same time, there has been constant in-fighting among the Takritis, and Saddam has long had to intervene to reconcile the conflicting ambitions and greed of this group. One of the first Takritis to fall from grace was General Hardan al-Takriti, a Ba'athist, a popular and charismatic army officer, and a principal instigator of the July 1968 coup. He was dismissed in October 1970.

Another noteworthy example of such infighting was the temporary decline in the role of the Ibrahims—Saddam's half-brothers. This decline occurred at about the same time as the death of Subha Tulfah, the mother of the Ibrahim brothers as well as of Saddam.[19] Saddam removed Barzan al-Tikriti from the job of intelligence chief, and then removed Barzan and Watban from senior positions in 1983.[20] In 1989, he had a falling out with his Defense Minister, 'Adnan Khayrallah, whose sister Sayidah is Saddam's wife. It was reported that the Tulfahs were infuriated by Saddam's taking on of a mistress, Samira Shahbandar—whom he reportedly married. Not long after Khayrallah died in a helicopter accident under 'mysterious' circumstances.

This family strife has also become progressively more serious since the Gulf War. Before the war, Saddam was able to deal with most such infighting by dealing with individuals, rather than groups. He had little reason to fear a major split in his extended family, or that such feuding would become a potential threat. Since the war, Saddam has experienced growing problems with the al-Majid clan and even with his own sons.

The first major sign of these problems surfaced on November 6, 1991, when Saddam removed Hussein Kamel al-Majid, his cousin and son-in-law from the post of Defense Minister, and replaced him with Interior Minister Ali Hassan al-Majid, another paternal cousin and Hussein Kamel al-Majid's cousin.[21] Ali Hassan al-Majid had led the repression of the Kurds in 1988. Saddam also temporarily closed down *Babil*, the newspaper published by his elder son, Uday.

This shift was unexpected because Hussein Kamel al-Majid had risen rapidly in the regime in previous years. Kamel had led the build-up of Iraq's military industries and weapons of mass destruction programs as Minister of Industries and Military Industrialization. Some experts feel Saddam's action was the result of a rift within the two main branches of Saddam's clan—and intelligence reports surfaced later that rival security forces of Ali Hassan al-Majid and Hussein Kamel al-Majid had clashed when Ali Hassan replaced Hussein Kamel al-Majid. Others feel that Saddam needed firmer military support and that Kamel's youth, and lack of formal military training and experience, seem to have created friction with senior military officers.[22]

At the same time, Saddam increased the role of other members of his tribe and extended family. He placed members of the Ibrahim and Majid branches in senior security positions. On November 13, 1991, he appointed a maternal half-brother, Watban al-Tikriti, to replace Ali Hassan al-Majid as Interior Minister. He appointed Barzan al-Tikriti (another half-brother) as Iraq's Permanent Representative in Geneva and a foreign affairs adviser to Saddam. He appointed Sabawi al-Tikriti as head of the General Intelligence Service.[23]

Saddam also tried to heal whatever divisions had led him to fire Hussein Kamel al-Majid from the post of Defense Minister. On December 4, he increased the power of Hussein Kamel al-Majid and then appointed him as a presidential adviser on February 13, 1992. Al-Majid retained his rank of Lieutenant General and the privileges of a Cabinet minister in this role, and was later restored to his role in charge of Iraq's defense industries. At roughly the same time, Saddam allowed *Babil*, to resume publication with Uday as editor. The first new issue described a cordial lunch attended by Saddam and other major members of the Tikriti clan.

Even so, major new signs of trouble emerged in May 1995 when Saddam shifted his half-brother Watban Ibrahim al-Hasan from the post of Interior Minister to the symbolic post of presidential advisor. In spite of the Interior Ministry's importance in internal security matters, he assigned the post to a relative unknown, Mohammad Zimam Abdel-Razzaq, an intelligence and security official.[24] It is not quite clear why Watban was dismissed. Some reports conclude that Saddam had taken behind the scenes control of the Interior Ministry because of the deterioration of the economic situation.[25] Some reports argue that Watban had mishandled the Al-Ramadi disturbances. Others argued that Watban had ran afoul of Uday Hussein. There were also reports that Watban's demise symbolized the eclipse of the Ibrahim branch of the family and the return of the Al-Majids to the limelight.

The Defection and Death of Hussein Kamel al-Majid

These latter reports were soon proven wrong on two counts. In mid-July, Ali Hasan al-Majid was replaced as Defense Minister by General Sultan Hashim Ahmad, a professional officer who had served as the Army's chief of staff since April 1995. Then, on August 7, 1995, Lieutenant-General Hussein Kamel Hasan al-Majid defected to Jordan. He defected with his brother Lieutenant-Colonel Saddam Kamel al-Majid, who was also married to one of Saddam's daughters and with 16 other members of the Majid clan. This was the most important defection of a senior Iraqi during Saddam's years in power.

At the time Hussein Kamel Al-Majid defected, he was 41 years of age and a case study in Iraqi nepotism. He was born in the same village of Al-'Auja, outside Takrit, as Saddam. He first rose to prominence and power in the mid-1980s when he emerged as a bodyguard for Saddam. He then married Saddam's oldest daughter Raghida, and in 1985, Saddam put him in charge of military procurement from foreign suppliers. He is also the cousin of Saddam, being the son of Saddam's uncle Kamel Majid.

When the Ministry of Military Industrialization was created, Hussein Kamel al-Majid became its head. It was in that role that Kamel built up his reputation as the managerial and organizational talent behind Iraq's chemical, biological, ballistic missile, and nuclear programs—although all of these programs had commenced well before his rise. Hussein Kamel proved relatively efficient in acquiring the technologies needed for the nuclear program by setting up an international network of front companies channeling dual-use technology to Iraq. As a result, Saddam also appointed him as Minister of Industries in 1987, and Hussein Kamel was charged with the role of implementing the privatization process launched by the government.

Although Hussein Kamel was a man with no military experience, he was first appointed Colonel and then given the rank of Major-General in April 1991. Following the Gulf War, Kamel was made a Lt. General and was made Defense Minister between April 1991 and September 1991. He was removed in November 1991—possibly for the reasons discussed earlier or because he failed to rebuild the armed forces or to deal with the low-level insurgency in the south. He was made presidential advisor, however, and was replaced by his cousin, Ali Hasan Al-Majid.

After another cabinet reshuffle, Hussein Kamel was appointed Minister of Industries and Minerals. He was also made the chairman of the Higher State Engineering Effort Commission, a large inter-ministerial body created in March 1991, and tasked with the supervision of reconstruction. He and his brother also played a role in setting up and controlling the Amn al-Khas (Special Security Force) which was directly attached to the president's cabinet.[26] In short, as a true insider, Kamel was privy not only to the secrets of Iraq's massive weapons of mass destruction programs, but as a member of the innermost circle of power he knew intimately the workings of one of the most secretive governments in the world.[27]

Hussein Kamel's defection showed that Saddam could no longer trust even the closest members of his family and almost certainly represented a serious psychological blow to the Iraqi ruler. At the same time, the defection was the product of personal feuds, and not of any opposition to Saddam's rule or policies. Although Hussein Kamel claimed that he defected because he had lost confidence in the regime and in its political stability and because he wished to bring about change in the discredited political system, his real reasons were very different.

- First, Hussein Kamel's relationship with Saddam's oldest son, Uday, had deteriorated dramatically since 1994. They had struggled over material rewards, power, prestige and money.[28] It also seems likely that Uday—whose greed for power and money is legendary—had tried to move in on Kamel's turf in the domain of military industries and control of the limited oil exports allowed Iraq under sanctions.
- Second, Hussein Kamel, who at the time of his defection was Minster of Industry and Minerals and Director of Military Industrialization, seems to have been convinced that sooner or later he would lose his power and possibly even his life. In May 1995, his uncle Watban was dismissed as Minister of Interior and in July 'Ali Hasan al-Majid, one of the most powerful Takritis, lost his post as Minister of Defense. Both men were replaced by non-Takritis. Kamel implied that these cabinet reshuffles had an impact on his decision to defect, as did a reported shoot-out on August 7 between the followers of Uday and the recently fired Watban Ibrahim, following a gathering of members of the Takriti clan during which Saddam's half-brother reportedly criticized both Hussein Kamel and Uday.
- Iraqi government and media statements described Kamel in biblical terms as a "Judas," rather than as any kind of opposition leader. A

typical statement reads as follows, "Just as Judas—who physically resembled Jesus in Saddam's mind—betrayed the Messiah, so did Kamel—who resembles Saddam—commit an act of betrayal."[29]

The regime did its best to ensure that the defection was described as treason to Kamel's family, as well as treason to Saddam and the state. Kamel's uncle, the once-powerful Hasan Ali al-Majid declared: "this small family (the al-Majids) within Iraq denounces his cowardly act and strongly rejects the treason, which he has committed and which can only be cleansed by inflicting punishment on him in accordance with the law of God. . . . His family has unanimously decided to permit with impunity the spilling of (Kamel's) blood."[30]

In effect, Hasan al-Majid announced that the Majids would not, in accordance with tribal custom, revenge themselves on anybody who killed Kamel. Iraqi officials also proceeded to accuse Kamel of being a corrupt individual who had absconded with millions of dollars of state money, as well as of being a spy for the Central Intelligence Agency.[31] Further, given Kamel's position in the regime the defection caused tremendous "political panic" in Baghdad, in the words of Rolf Ekeus, the head of the United Nations Special Commission overseeing the destruction of Iraq's weapons of mass destruction.

The end game of the defection was typical of Saddam Hussein. The government arrested scores of mid-level military and civilian officials for their association with the defectors. Saddam then conducted a series of negotiations with his daughters and their husbands which ended in promising a pardon. On February 20, 1996, Hussein Kamel and his brother, Saddam Kamel, returned to Baghdad after being granted full formal pardons by Saddam Hussein and the Revolutionary Command Council.

While they were met by Qusay at the border and were escorted to a villa, their pardons were short-lived. The next day, the state 'granted' divorces to their wives, Raghad and Rana. Three days after their divorce, the two Kamel brothers were dead, along with their father, sister, and another brother by family members from the wider al-Majid clan. Hussein Kamel and Saddam Kamel were killed in a shoot-out at the house of Hussein Kamel's father. The al-Majids then claimed that they had decided to kill them, in spite of their official pardon, because they were dishonored by the Kamels' treason.

It is inconceivable that the murders of the defectors could have been undertaken without being sanctioned by the regime. The killing of the Kamels at the hands of their own clan was a political fiction that allowed the Iraqi leader to say that he did not go back on the official pardon that he had granted them, while at the same time exacting vengeance. In fact,

Saddam stated several months later that, "Had they asked me, I would have prevented them, but it was good that they did not."[32]

Iraqi Vice-President Taha Yasin Ramadan declared at the time of the killings that the "state had no say in the matter of his (Hussein Kamel's) killing. It was the will of his family." He then seemed to invent a new definition of pardon when he declared that "pardon is not a right that belongs to traitors. It is a right that belongs to those who err or lose their way, but not to those who sell their country and its destiny."[33]

The participation of members of the government at a *state* funeral for two of the members of the al-Majids who led the assault on the Kamel family also indicated Saddam's satisfaction that the punishment had been meted out and family honor retrieved. On the other hand, the opposition groups claimed that the deaths of the Kamels were followed by wider purges and executions of members of the al-Majids and the killing of Hussein Kamel and Saddam Kamel's children, Saddam's own grandchildren.[34] These claims have not been substantiated and may be part of the external opposition's strategy of painting the Takriti regime in the worst possible light.[35]

Why the Kamels chose to return remains a mystery. Hussein Kamel's arrival in Amman in August was regarded by many as the beginning of the end for Saddam Hussein's regime. Hussein Kamel was seen as the source of information not only on Iraq's residual weapons of mass destruction, but also on the inner workings of the Ba'athist political elite. More significantly, he was perceived as the potential architect of a "palace coup" against Saddam Hussein. However, this perception was flawed from the start, left unsaid was the question of how a "palace coup" plotter could succeed if he were 600 miles away.

Furthermore, Kamel's suggestion to Western intelligence officials that the best way to unseat Saddam Hussein was to arm and train an army inside Jordan to move on Baghdad under allied air cover, indicates that he was scarcely the prime candidate to manage a palace coup.[36] In fact, if Hussein Kamel, a senior member of the regime and part of the Takriti ruling family, could not unseat Saddam Hussein, it was doubtful that it would be any easier for others. Moreover, the suspicion and distrust of Kamel on the part of the opposition forces contributed to maintain his status as a pariah in Amman. Not surprisingly, Western states and Jordan began to lose interest in Hussein Kamel. This took place notwithstanding the latter's attempts to raise his profile and improve his image by the creation of the still-born "Higher Council for the Salvation of Iraq."

Hussein Kamel's failure to rally Iraqi opposition forces ultimately did little more than provide the impetus for King Hussein of Jordan to take an *active* role to bring some semblance of unity to the dispersed

Iraqi opposition. In turn, this more active Jordanian posture contributed to Hussein Kamel's decision to return. He had expressed extreme displeasure with King Hussein's project. First, he felt he was being further marginalized. Second, he disagreed with the federal or confederal nature of the project. Third, he objected to the inclusion of "Iranians," by which he meant Shi'ite Islamists based in Iran. Furthermore, sources in the Middle East believed that Hussein Kamel feared that King Hussein would allow Iraqi opposition groups to bring war crimes charges against him for his activities in Iraq over the years as a leading henchman of Saddam Hussein.[37]

In conclusion Kamel's political marginalization in Amman and his increasingly tense relations with his hosts, his discomfort with a life of exile, his inability to be taken seriously by other regional powers, especially Cairo and Damascus, and his belief that he could return unscathed because of his marriage to Saddam's daughter led him to take the fateful steps back to Baghdad.

Reports of Other Divisions Within Saddam's Family

Hussein Kamel's defection was followed by rumors about the loyalty of Saddam's half-brother, Barzan al-Takriti—Iraq's ambassador to the UN in Geneva. Barzan had written some extraordinary pieces on the deterioration of the Iraqi state, of the Arab world, the decline of Arab nationalism, and on international affairs generally in recent years, particularly in regards to the factors behind the collapse of the Soviet Union. Although it is difficult to discern what led to his writing, it was commonly accepted that in many of the pieces he was engaging in thinly veiled criticism of the Iraqi regime. Barzan's importance lies not in the fact that he is Iraq's ambassador to the UN but more in his control over Iraq's secret finances. According to some reports Barzan oversees a complex web of undercover and dummy companies which have in excess of $20 billion in hidden investments.[38]

During August 1995, several sources in the Middle East reported that Barzan al-Takriti had refused a direct order to return to Baghdad, that he had asked for political asylum in Switzerland, and/or that he had sought refuge in an Arab country. These rumors came to an end, however, after a remarkable interview that Barzani gave on August 31, 1995. Barzan denied that he had broken with Baghdad, but he dismissed the importance of Hussein Kamel and indicated his growing disenchantment with some other members of the ruling family.

Barzan, who is Kamel's uncle, described Kamel as "an impetuous, rough and aggressive boy who knows nothing of civility."[39] He also said that Kamel could not be seen as a legitimate alternative to Saddam:[40]

In Iraq there are Arabs and Kurds, Sunnis, Shi'ites, Christians and Yazidis, many minorities. What legitimacy does Hussein Kamel have to gather the country around him? There is a deep chasm between him and the Iraqi Kurds. . . . How could the Iraqi Shi'a cooperate with him when he was the one who attacked the tomb of the Imam Hussein bin 'Ali?

Barzan dismissed Kamel's claim that Iraq was about to invade Kuwait and eastern Saudi Arabia out of hand:[41]

I have only heard this story from him, and the western countries know that six years of sanctions on Iraq have affected its forces and its infrastructure. And even if it were still capable of attacking a small country like Kuwait, Kuwait has international alliances to protect it. Simple logic refutes these allegations.

Barzan's commentary on the state of affairs in Iraq, particularly the mind of Saddam and the meteoric rise of the leader's son, Uday, was even more striking. He dismissed rumors that the Iraqi leader was seeking political asylum in Egypt, and confirmed the general perception of Saddam as a man who is determined to stay the course or who would rather go down fighting than flee:[42]

President Saddam Hussein is not the sort of man to seek political asylum or to accept to live outside his country. Nor will he abandon his responsibilities and lay them on the shoulders of others. And if he relinquishes power, the situation will only worsen. The regime will not fall, and even if he is on his own and down to his last bullet, President Saddam will continue to resist.

Barzan poured scorn on Uday Hussein's pretensions and ambitions:[43]

Iraq is not a monarchy with a son or brother succeeding the king, it is a republic ruled by a revolutionary party. . . . I do not know if Uday is preparing himself or not. But each man should know his values and abilities if he is to avoid having many problems. Problems arise from people who do not know their true caliber. . . .

Uday: The "Son of Pericles"?

Hussein Kamel Hasan al-Majid's reports that he feared for his life because of Uday's unpredictable behavior, and Barzan's contempt for his nephew, highlighted the problems Saddam has in dealing with his oldest son, in finding a successor, and in relying on nepotism as a substitute for a broader base of power. Uday Hussein's is now thirty years old, and seems to be the closest thing Saddam has to an heir apparent. There is a broad consensus in the Middle East, however, that Barzan's description of Uday is largely correct and that Uday is a thug who lacks Saddam's shrewdness, cunning, political savvy, ruthlessness, or conspiratorial mind—all of which are essential to survive in Iraqi politics.

The bloodiest reports of Uday's conduct centers around an incident in 1988.[44] According to a number of reports, Uday bludgeoned to death Saddam's trusted and loyal bodyguard Kamel Hana Gegeo. He did so in a fit of rage over the fact that Kamel Hana Gegeo arranged for Saddam to meet a new mistress, who later became his second and most influential wife. Saddam is reported to have been outraged by the murder of Gegeo and to have threatened to execute his son, although he then exiled him to Europe. After several years, however, Saddam forgave Uday, allowed him to return from exile, and to establish his own power base and wealth.

By 1990, Uday owned a chain of money-making food processing firms. He moved on to head the Iraqi Olympic Committee, the Football (soccer) League, the Iraqi Union of Journalists, the Union of Writers, and Iraqi Students Union. He took control of two papers, *Babil* and *Al-Rafidain*—and used them to run articles critical of government officials and ministers like Information and Culture Minister, Hamid Youssef Hammadi, who displeased Uday or Saddam. Uday became even richer after sanctions were imposed through his control of hotels, night-clubs, transportation centers, and the food smuggling business. He is the most prominent member of a parasitic class of Iraqis who have become fabulously wealthy because of their ability to make money through sanctions-breaking.

Saddam also increasingly involved Uday in intelligence and security matters. In late 1994, Uday was given command of a new praetorian security detail, called Saddam's Feda'iyeen (Saddam's Commandos) made up largely of teen-age toughs. This security detail now has near carte blanche. Uday reportedly used this force in mid-June to help put down the allegedly serious revolts or mutinies prompted by the Dulaimi dissatisfaction. The more power and wealth he amassed, the more brutal and greedy Uday became, and more often than not, his prime victims were not ordinary Iraqis—they often had nothing to give him—but members of the ruling elite.

Uday bullied or brutalized other members of the Takriti ruling family—as well as other regime officials, and used his control of the media to wage vitriolic campaigns in print against men he dislikes. These targets included his half-uncle, Watban Ibrahim who became Interior Minister in 1991 and was in overall charge of internal security. In 1994, Uday began to use his newspaper Babil to attack Watban. Watban then lost his position as Minister of Interior in late May 1995.[45] It also seems possible that Uday was responsible for the abrupt removal of Oil Minister Safa Hadi Jawad al-Habubi and for the fall of Defense Minister Ali Hasan al-Majid.[46]

Qusay and the Hope of Dynasty

Saddam does have another younger, quieter, and far more effective son, Qusay, 28, who controls the Special Security Organization, which overseas all of the intelligence and security services of the regime. In contrast to his pathologically murderous older brother, Qusay, who shuns the limelight, is almost invariably reported as a more serious and responsible individual. Complicating Saddam's political power over his family are reports of tensions building up between the two brothers over control of the myriad number of security services. Saddam may have been alluding to this still latent rivalry in a speech immediately following Kamel's defection. He recounted the story of Cain and Abel, and said Cain,

> erroneously imagined that he had rights over his brother based on avarice, jealousy and envy, and not based on God's laws. So his avarice killed him when he was deprived of prestige, right, honor and kinship through killing his brother. Thus, he became a wrongdoer.[47]

Saddam seems to have little practical hope of ever founding the equivalent of a political dynasty and may find it difficult to use his extended family as a secure asset in the future. It seems likely that Saddam has little hope that any of his sons could survive him in power for more than a few months, and it is more likely that the politically active members of his family will die if Saddam does, or be driven into exile. Famous fathers often breed infamous sons.

Current Trends in Iraq's Informal Power Structure

The main short-term impact of Saddam's problems with key clans, Kamel's defection, and the furor over Uday, has been to make Saddam reach out to other sources of support from within his coterie and reverse his growing dependence on his family. Saddam sought to do this in several ways.

- He curtailed Uday's visible political role and forced him to tone down his considerably flamboyant lifestyle.
- Saddam reduced the visibility and power of Takritis in the state apparatus and widened the ruling elite's power base by appointing older Ba'ath party members and non-Takriti technocrats to positions of power.[48]

- Saddam made new efforts to create the illusion of democracy. In 1995, he organized a massive national referendum to try to demonstrate that he was still in control and he still had the support of Iraq's people. This referendum did not permit any opposition to run, it simply asked the question, "do you want Saddam to remain President for another seven years?" Citizens were given a choice of voting for or against an extension of Saddam Hussein's rule for 7 years, and no other questions were included on the ballot, nor were there any political debates or campaigns. Voters were obligated to identify themselves on their ballots. The actual vote was held on October 15, 1995, and Saddam demonstrated that his police state was fully intact. Over 99 per cent of the electorate reportedly voted, and 99.96 per cent approved the extension of Saddam's presidency.
- Saddam promised in the fall of 1995 that there would be new elections for the National Assembly in 1996. In March 1996, the government held the fourth and largest parliamentary elections in Iraq's history. The highly publicized campaign had a number of "independent" candidates, and reported voter turnout reached 93.5%. However, both Ba'athist and independent candidates were screened in advance for loyalty to the regime and for their support of the principles of the July 1968 Ba'athist revolution. The Ba'athists won 169 seats and the now somewhat "worn" Sa'adun Hammadi was elected Speaker of the new National Assembly. However, the 250-seat Iraqi National Assembly is a political fiction which is completely subordinate to the executive branch.

These cosmetic exercises have not changed the realities of Iraqi politics. Iraq's overall process of political repression and human rights violations have grown even worse during 1995 and 1996, and there is no real prospect that the regime will take measures like moving the country away from "revolutionary" towards "constitutional" legitimacy. There is equally little prospect of a freer press, multi-party pluralism, a more independent National Assembly, and the disbanding of the Revolutionary Command Council.

This makes the mid-to-long-term impact of the recent trends in Iraq's informal power structure hard to determine. There is no guarantee that Saddam's declining support in the "center," with the clans, and with his extended family will bring Saddam's downfall. The "center" still lacks any clear alternative to Saddam. Blood feuds in ruling clans and extended families have been the rule, rather than the exception, for thousands of years. Rulers as diverse as Octavian, Genghis Khan, Napoleon, Louis XI, Stalin, and Hitler all survived such "family" problems. Now that the has accepted the terms of UN Security Council Resolution 986,

Saddam has at least a reasonable chance of surviving several more years of the impact of the remaining UN sanctions, and such a policy could simply end in increasing the revanchism and resentment within the "center." Saddam's acceptance of the terms of UN Security Council Resolution 986 has also given him some relief from the impact of economic sanctions.

At the same time, Saddam does seem to be growing weaker over time. He scarcely seems likely to pursue real reform, and his recent efforts to expand his power base are unlikely to bring him real loyalty or support from the center. They may, however, isolate him more from key clans, and some members of his extended family. This may make it progressively harder for Saddam to avoid the backlash from his defeat in the Gulf War and UN sanctions, make coup attempts somewhat more likely, and increase the probability of more assassination attempts.

What is less clear is that any change in leadership in the "center" of this kind will alter the ruthless, authoritarian character of Iraqi politics and whether there are ways that outside powers can exploit the trends undermining Saddam's control over the informal mechanisms of power. A new Iraqi ruling elite may be somewhat more pragmatic in character, and may turn inwards to deal with the problems posed by Iraq's present economic crisis, the Kurds, and the Shi'ites. Such a regime, however, is still likely to perceive itself as surrounded by enemies, and therefore maintain a high level of military spending.

Further, any new "centrist" regime must deal with the threat posed by internal ethnic and sectarian conflict, and with the fact that Iraq's strategic position is exposed in many ways. It is likely to see the growing military capabilities of Iran and Turkey as a threat, and to see the West and Southern Gulf states as, at least potentially hostile countries. It is unlikely to trust Iran, which has a 1,448 kilometer land boundary with Iraq. It is likely to feel it must compete with its Gulf neighbors for a share of oil revenues, and compete with Iran in developing weapons of mass destruction. As a result, future Iraqi regimes are likely to continue to seek weapons of mass destruction as long as any other state in the region possesses them—including Israel.

Implications for Western and Southern Gulf Strategy

This analysis of Iraq's informal power structure indicates that the prospects for rapid, fundamental changes in the character of Iraq's regime are anything but good. Saddam's recent history in manipulating Iraqi politics is as strong an argument against any strategy that attempts to accommodate Saddam as is his past. Regardless of any agreements other nations may reach with Saddam, his behavior will only be as restrained as it is forced to be and if Saddam becomes more secure within Iraq, he is likely to translate this security into new foreign adventures.

At one level, one may argue that virtually any leader other than Saddam is likely to be better and worth seeking. Nothing about Saddam's history indicates that he will be safe to deal with, or will ever be more moderate than he is forced to be. A strategy of living with Saddam can only work if it is a strategy in which the illusion of better relations is mixed with a strong US presence and power projection capability, firm deterrent action by the Southern Gulf states, and efforts to insure that Iran remains a counterbalance to Iraq. No successor to Saddam can quickly acquire the same personal authority. Most successors will probably be less revanchist and extreme in character, more willing to concentrate on Iraq's internal problems, and less willing to indulge in foreign adventures. Most successors are also more likely to rely on a coalition of factions and have less freedom of action.

At another level, the previous analysis indicates that any successor to Saddam that is not the product of civil war is likely to be an authoritarian Iraqi nationalist, and is likely to pursue many of Saddam's ambitions—at least covertly. Such a "centrist" leader may initially use the language of moderation and democracy, but such rhetoric is likely to prove as hollow as Saddam's, and such a leader will only be "pragmatic" to the extent he is deterred by Iraq's neighbors and the West.

At least in the near-to-mid-term, the trends in Iraqi internal politics seem likely to be a struggle for power by the same factions within the Sunni elites in the "center" that brought Saddam and his coterie to power. Saddam's ruthlessness since 1979 has scarcely helped train moderates or technocrats, and his purges and executions since the end of the Gulf War have ensured that only the most ruthless rivals can survive. As a result, even if sanctions succeed in bringing down Saddam, a strategy of living with his successor will probably be equally dependent on the illusion of better relations, a strong US presence and power projection capability, firm deterrent action by the Southern Gulf states, and efforts to insure that Iran remains a counterbalance to Iraq.

The very nature of Iraqi "centrist" politics also ensures that outside powers cannot count on Saddam's fall and that they have little flexibility in trying to select some other "centrist" that will displace him. There are no visible "centrists" outside powers can approach without making them targets for Saddam's security forces. There may be an opportunity to support a well organized coup or assassination attempt, but this means tacitly accepting the coup leader as Iraq's next ruler.

As a result, any strategy based on using the "center" to replace or moderate Saddam may well mean living with an elite that is incapable of putting lasting pressure on Saddam to change or of finding any replacement for Saddam that will be a radical departure from a personalized authoritarian regime.

What can be done is to create a clear set of incentives and guidelines that will both set rules for the future behavior of Iraq's rulers and encourage the fall of Saddam. The problem with the present policy of sanctions is that it has no clear end game, offers no incentives, punishes the ordinary Iraqi far more than the elites responsible for Iraq's actions, and sets only vague rules for the future. What is needed is to make it clear that the UN will be far more willing to lift sanctions on favorable terms if Saddam goes, and that debt relief, a forgiveness of reparations, a forgiveness of war crimes trials, and trade and investment, will be dependent on Saddam's departure and the conduct of a successor regime.

The US, Kuwait, and Saudi Arabia must face the fact that trying to force democracy on Iraq while mixing war crimes trials with massive reparations is simply a formula for another war. They must be clear that no effort will be made to try to interfere constantly in Iraqi "centrist" politics, and that the "rules" for better relations are limited to demands Iraq can meet. These include full recognition of Kuwait and the new border with Kuwait, a settlement with the Kurds that offers them protection and at least cultural autonomy, and Iraq's agreement to continuing UN inspection over a period of years to limit sharply or prevent Iraq's re-emergence as a power capable of using weapons of mass destruction.

At the same time, other Western states and other Gulf states must have no illusions. The word "containment" may be unpopular, but military containment will be needed until a new regime of a fundamentally different nature emerges in Iraq. The forces that have led to the Iran-Iraq War, the Gulf War, and an Iraq on the edge of becoming a nuclear power will not vanish with Saddam. There also is little near-term prospect that any Iraqi regime drawn from the "center" will support political reform, human rights, and liberalization, or that these goals are ones that outside powers can realistically hope to force on today's Iraq.

4

The Formal Politics of Iraq's Instruments of State Power

Saddam and the present Ba'ath elite exert control over a number of strong instruments of state power. These instruments include the Revolutionary Command Council, the Ba'ath Party, the security services and the military. Saddam and his coterie can exert control over these instruments through both a formal administrative structure, and a series of informal personal networks. Like Iraq's informal political structure, these instruments of state power help to preserve Saddam Hussein's rule and make it difficult for any rival other than another Sunni authoritarian elite to come to power.

The Revolutionary Command Council

The Revolutionary Command Council (RCC) is the supreme-decision making institution in the country. In practice, the RCC is a small close-knit body which includes Saddam Hussein and his close associates. It is also a self-appointed body which appoints its chairman. The chairman of the Revolutionary Command Council is Saddam Hussein, who is also President, Prime Minister, the Secretary-General of the Regional Leadership of the Ba'ath, i.e., head of the Iraqi Ba'ath party, and Commander-in-Chief of the Armed Forces.

The Revolutionary Command Council is under the total control of Saddam Hussein and his immediate supporters. Its decrees are issued under Saddam's name and it has the power to appoint the cabinet under his direction. It is a typical ruling body for an authoritarian state that combines the ability to rule through a personal elite with an integrated line of control over party, government, military, economy, and security forces.

Saddam's ability to combine the political leadership of the Ba'ath, the leaders of government, and the military into one body whose actual day-to-day membership in dealing with any issue is under his direct control is another factor that allows him to maintain power and survive. Similar bodies in Nazi Germany and the Soviet Union helped preserve the power of Hitler and Stalin, respectively, and have allowed other dictators to integrate personal rule into the administrative structure of the state.

The RCC does, however, make it difficult for outside powers to deal with Saddam or any dictator that rules a similar body. First, it allows the leader to effectively bypass any apparent reform within the formal structure of government. If Saddam chooses, he can appear to permit reform within the Cabinet or National Assembly and still use the other instruments of state power to maintain control. Second, any "centrist" coup or change in government that retains the RCC or its equivalent, also retains an authoritarian instrument of power that it is virtually certain to abuse. Few "centrist" groups are likely to abandon the RCC—even if they rename it. The RCC is another aspect of Iraq's political structure that makes it likely that any successor to Saddam—short of one brought to power by a civil war—will be similar in character.

The Ba'ath Party

Like the Revolutionary Command Council, the Ba'ath Party of Iraq has shifted from a pan-Arab socialist party to become an extension of the Iraqi Sunni ruling elite. In the 1960s, the Ba'ath had many of the characteristics of a genuine popular movement and a Sunni-Shi'ite partnership. Indeed, the founder of the Iraqi branch of the Ba'ath party, Fu'ad al-Rikabi, was a Shi'ite who controlled an organization made up almost entirely of Shi'ite relatives and classmates. His successor, 'Ali Salih al-Sa'di was another Shi'ite from the working class neighborhood of Bab al-Shuyukh in Baghdad. Most of his supporters were petty gangsters from the same neighborhood.

This situation changed radically by 1968, the time of the second Ba'athist coup. The role of Sunnis in the Ba'ath Party had risen sharply while that of the Shi'ites had precipitously declined. This decline can be explained by a number of factors. First, following the collapse of the first Ba'ath regime in 1963, the Arab nationalist regime of Abdel Salam 'Aref hunted Shi'ite Ba'athists with more vigor and brutality than it did Sunni Ba'athists. This focus on hunting down the Shi'ites, rather than Sunnis, was a result of both the traditional discrimination against Shi'ites, and the fact that the Sunni Ba'athists who were being hunted down were from the same families, clans and tribes as the men in the security and intelligence services who were hunting them down. The Departments of Interior and Security were filled with functionaries from Al-Ramadi and the Sunni quarters of northern Baghdad, who made far less effort to find their Sunni "cousins."

Since 1968, the policies of the Ba'ath Party has also been reshaped by Saddam Hussein's reinterpretation of Ba'athist ideology. This took the form of pragmatism in the 1970s and 1980s, and opportunism in the mid-1990s. Saddam has done much to de-legitimize Ba'athist ideology. He has never been an ideologue per se, but rather a quintessential political organizer, a conspirator and a man of action. He has seen the party's ideologues, particularly those on the left, as a threat and has done much to drive them from power and to replace the Ba'ath Party's original ideology.

Saddam was also responsible for the emergence of an 'Iraqi-first' ideological framework at the expense of pan-Arab nationalism—a basic principle of the Ba'ath. As part of his efforts to unite Iraqis of all ethnic and sectarian backgrounds, Saddam developed the idea and practice of a Mesopotamian and Iraqi identity that was both Arab and non-Arab, and Islamic and non-Islamic. He not only transformed "Ba'athist socialism" into "state opportunism," he made the Ba'ath party into a cover for Iraqi nationalism.

Saddam accelerated this trend during the Iran-Iraq war when Iraq was fighting for sheer survival. From 1982 onwards, he tied Iraq's role in the Iran-Iraq War to Mesopotamia's long history of warfare with the Iranian plateau and the tacit revival of the Caliphate in Baghdad. He accused the Arab world of failing to support Iraq in the struggle against a "hated" Persian enemy. At the same time, he faced the irony that Syria—the birth-place of modern Arab nationalism and of Ba'athism—supported Iran. He also faced a situation where the conservative Arab Gulf states never fully endorsed Iraq's invasion of Iran, gradually cut their aid, and insisted that Iraq accept loan agreements that saddled it with billions of dollars in debts.

After the Iran-Iraq War, Saddam struck another blow to the Ba'athist edifice. He began to dismantle the huge and inefficient socialist infrastructure within the Ba'ath party and the Iraqi government and to implement a massive program of privatization and of opening up the Iraqi economy to foreign investment. The fact that Iraq's economic reform program failed to produce any significant success by the time Iraq invaded Kuwait did not prevent Saddam's efforts from cutting back the Ba'ath Party's huge administrative structure, as well as the bureaucracy, a situation which adversely affected the lower middle class which serviced the state sector.

The Ba'ath party suffered a further loss of morale and prestige during the rebellions following the Gulf War. Party officials and functionaries were not prepared for trouble, and many were either killed by the rebels or panicked and fled. Following the insurrections, the government established a commission of four high-ranking officials to look into the conduct of the party cadre during the crisis. The result was that hundreds of party members were removed from their posts and many arrests were made—especially in the middle Euphrates region where the more serious insurrections took place.

Saddam made a decision to reduce the size of the party, and many members were asked to surrender their party membership. Saddam took the public stand that it was better to revitalize the party by relying on the vanguard that had brought the Ba'ath to power, and on an elitist party organization with more dedicated individuals, rather than see the Ba'ath weakened by the presence of "self-seeking" persons. Saddam put it this way, "let those who wish to leave the Ba'ath party do so, so that the Ba'ath continues as a bright lantern to our people and glorious nation."

In practice, the criteria for selection was the willingness to support Saddam. The Ba'ath was systematically purged in ways that stressed long service and proven loyalty, and this reinforced the generational gap between older leaders who had participated in the struggle for power before 1968, and younger members who were products of an Iraq which the Ba'ath had ruled for more than a quarter of a century. At the same time, the Ba'ath was made into even more of a tool for selecting careerists and obliging technocrats, and providing a parallel bureaucracy to ensure the loyalty of the government and armed forces.

The end result is that the Ba'ath is now almost totally an instrument of state control and is virtually devoid of popular ideological content or appeal. Barzan al-Takriti, Saddam's half-brother, provided an accurate epitaph for the Ba'ath's pan-Arab ideology in 1993, when he stated:[49]

> Now we as a government are unable to persuade the Iraqi citizens to take an interest in any issue except theirs. We have done more than our duty. The Iraqis now need to think about their country. ... The Arabs should not expect anything from Iraq.

Indeed, the participation of Arab states in the destruction of Iraq as a leading Arab power, as well as their near-silence or posturing in the face of the UN sanctions, may make it impossible to revive the Pan-Arab nature of the Ba'ath or create any new political parties which are not focused on Iraq's internal needs. Furthermore, the onset of the Arab-Israeli peace process and the various Israeli-Palestinian agreements also presents problems in reviving the Ba'ath as a political movement. Unyielding hostility to Israel seems to be becoming obsolete as a catalyst for Pan-Arabism and it is unclear that any other catalysts exist which are of serious interest to Iraqis.

Even the regime's efforts to oppose the peace process have been lukewarm and unfocused. Iraqi officials like Tariq Aziz have taken the stand that since Iraq was not a party to the peace process and was not invited, Baghdad can hardly be expected to endorse it while remaining a "prisoner." He expressed Iraq's views starkly in late 1995 when he stated: "Iraq is not party to it (the peace process). Whether it is successful or unsuccessful, right or wrong, Iraq is not concerned, neither legally nor practically."[50]

At the same time, the regime has given the Arab-Israeli peace issue little real emphasis. It has held covert talks with some Israeli officials, and it is unlikely to commit itself to the Palestinian cause in any serious way unless this contributes to Iraq's tactical and political advantage.

The Cabinet and Government Leadership

Iraq has never been stable enough to create a structure of government that has not been the scene of constant struggles for power, and Saddam has long manipulated the cabinet and governmental apparatus to maintain control over the country. He used this power to help restore his authority over Iraq after the Gulf War, although he began this process by cloaking his actions with an image of moderation. As has been discussed earlier, Saddam talked of democratic reform and ethnic autonomy right after the war. On March 23, 1991, he announced that he was making a former Foreign Minister—Sa'dun Hammadi—Prime Minister. Hammadi was a Ba'ath party veteran, but was also a Shi'ite who had advocated a somewhat more liberal, democratic, and less anti-Western form of Ba'athism.

Saddam made several other gestures. Iraq announced its tentative acceptance of Kurdish autonomy on March 24. On May 8, 1991, Iraq announced that the ruling Revolutionary Command Council (RCC) of the Ba'ath would be abolished and replaced with a more democratic government. In March 1991, it declared an amnesty for deserters who were not officers, and expanded the coverage of this amnesty on July 21.

The actions soon proved to be a political smoke screen. Once Saddam and his coterie reconsolidated power in the summer and fall of 1991, they proceeded systematically to purge the military and government, as well as the Ba'ath. They suppressed any real dissent, violated the civil rights of Iraqi citizens, and put additional military pressure on the Kurds and Shi'ites. When the RCC finally did announce the law allowing opposition parties on July 4, 1991, the law had vaguely defined security restrictions that allowed the government to ban virtually any party it wanted and explicitly forbade any ethnic or sectarian parties. By the time the new law was actually passed on September 3, 1991, it effectively prevented any opposition from taking open political form.

The government's total lack of independence was demonstrated when Saddam removed Prime Minister Hammadi from power on September 16, 1991. Saddam Hussein did appoint Hammadi as a Presidential adviser, but the position had little real influence. Saddam's "rehabilitation" of Hammadi seems to have been part of a broader effort to rebuild support from Shi'ites and other leaders in the Ba'ath Party that were not part of Saddam's immediate coterie. While Hammadi was replaced with another Shi'ite—Mohammed Hamza Zubeidi—Zubeidi was little more than a stooge. Even cosmetic efforts at liberalization soon ended, and the Ba'ath elite effectively restored its control over most of Iraq.

The Iraqi government began to take the public stand that it did not face any internal problems and could meet all external threats. On October 12, 1991, at an Iraqi-organized "conference of Arab popular forces," Saddam announced that Iraq could withstand the UN sanctions for "twenty years."

Saddam Hussein also used the government to support his strategy of firing scapegoats. He dismissed the Minister of Health, Abd al-Salam al-Sa'id on December 23, 1991—making him the scapegoat for the deteriorating economic and public health conditions caused by the UN sanctions.[51]

This dismissal set a pattern which Saddam has followed ever since. Saddam constantly finds new officials and businessmen outside his key supporters he can blame for Iraq's problems, while he rotates or "recycles" other supporters to maintain their loyalty while keeping them from emerging as an independent power base. For example, Saddam reorganized the Iraqi cabinet on July 30, 1992. Saddam made his Foreign Minister, Abed Hussein, the Finance Minister and promoted the Deputy Foreign Minister, Mohammed Sa'id Sahhaf, to Foreign Minister. He dismissed the former Finance Minister, Majid Abed Jaafer, and made the head of the Iraqi Atomic Energy Organization, Humam Abd al-Khaliq Abd al-Ghafur, the Minister of Education.

The exact reasons for each of these changes to the cabinet and government are unclear. It is clear, however, that their cumulative effect is to tighten control over domestic affairs and demonstrate Saddam's constant efforts to deal with the faults of others. They also provide Saddam with a way of publicly blaming government officials and cabinets for the fact that Iraq has not been able to make much progress towards genuine reconstruction and the lifting of sanctions.

Saddam has also taken steps to improve his control over the government at lower levels. Throughout 1995, the Iraqi government forcibly transferred hundreds of government workers from one job to another, purportedly to prevent the development of potential opposition in any government institutions. After a failed coup attempt in March and further disturbances in May and June, the Government arrested, removed from their jobs, or otherwise punished numerous Iraqis for their alleged association with these incidents.

Once again, this manipulation of the instruments of state power is certain to present problems for the future. The use of the formal structure of government as a scapegoat makes it more difficult to create an effective administrative structure and to find a substitute for one man rule, or rule by a small elite. At the same time, a number of purges have reached far down into the structure of government, and delayed or undercut the development of modern state institutions. This again makes it difficult for any new regime to change the nature of Iraq's government without massive purges of Saddam's supporters, and without changing the entire way in which the administrative structure of government actually operates.

Financial Resources

Saddam Hussein and his coterie derive further power from their ability to use governmental institutions to exert control over every aspect of Iraq's wealth. They control the state's economy through their ability to allocate oil revenues, regulate all aspects of trade and banking, allocate over foreign exchange, allocate and control the sale of much of Iraq's land and housing, control education and many aspects of salaries and promotions, and more recently through the manipulation of rationing and subsidies.

This centralized control has always been abused, but it did provide some benefits for the Iraqi people during the period before the Iran-Iraq War. The Ba'ath used much of the revenue from Iraq's oil exports to fund economic development. Analysts like Muhammed Al-Zainy, who completed a massive study of Iraq's economy in Arabic in 1995, point out that Iraq had one of the highest economic growth rates in the world in the mid-1970s.[52]

This growth was fueled by the massive rise in oil revenues that followed the 1973 October War. In 1972, Iraqi oil revenues hovered around the $1 billion mark. By 1980, this total was $25 billion. In the space of eight years, this wealth created the opportunity for the regime to engage in economic development, improve the standard of living and diversify the economy. The government embarked on a massive spending spree, and total government expenditure rose from $1.4 billion in current dollars in 1972/73 to $21 billion in 1980.

Even before Iraq invaded Iran, however, many aspects of Iraq's development effort were in serious trouble. Iraq could only absorb a fraction of the wealth pouring into the country and into new industrial production or other forms of productive investment. While Iraq created many elements of a modern infrastructure, it made little progress in diversifying the economy. The crude oil sector contributed 66% of the gross domestic product (GDP) in the mid-1970s, and this only declined to 62% in 1980—reflecting a continuing dependency on primary production and little diversification of the other sectors of the economy. Much of the growth in other areas took place in new service industries whose net effect was to increase Iraq's reliance on imports and foreign labor.

Iraq's efforts in the area of economic planning fell short of their allocated targets between 1950–1980. Iraq had a limited "absorptive capacity" because of poor planning, shortage of skilled labor, and inadequate infrastructure. The state sector remained far too large and inefficient and many barriers remained to private investment and the development of agriculture. Only 58% of Iraq's total financial allocations were spent. Furthermore, the regime experienced serious difficulties in making wise and efficient investment choices in the public sector. It had been cut off from the mainstream of the international capitalist economy for half a decade. It retained stultifying socialist policies and a suspicion of 'Western imperialism' that made it difficult to consult with foreign firms or rely on market incentives. It had few officials experienced in international business. It had no idea of how to draw up specifications, evaluate bids, and award contracts to international firms.

The government's use of its control over Iraq's financial resources had far more negative effects after the start of the Iran-Iraq War. Iraq shifted many of its resources to military spending and arms, spending that totaled 40% to 47% of Iraq's GDP. Arms imports leaped from around 15% of total imports before the war to 60% to 80% of total imports. At the same time, Iraq's GDP per capita in constant 1991 dollars dropped from $3,271 in 1982—when Syria cut off many of Iraq's oil exports—to $2,278 in 1988 at the end of the Iran-Iraq War. It dropped to $1,400 during 1990 because of low oil revenues and a failure to diversify Iraq's exports, and then to $705 in 1991, because of the cut off of all Iraqi exports.[53]

As a result, many of Iraq's current economic problems began long before the UN sanctions were imposed in 1991. They are the cumulative result of vast mismanagement and waste during 1974–1979, and the dramatic accentuation of militarism and military spending that began with the onset of the Iran-Iraq War in 1980, and which lasted until Iraq's defeat in the Gulf War in 1991. Throughout his rule, Saddam has chosen guns over butter, and has used the apparatus of the state to spend massive sums on internal and external security. Military expenditures in constant $1991 dollars increased from $343 million in 1970 to $10,121 million in 1981 (about 30 times) and then attained a wartime peak of $21,360 million in 1984.[54]

Long before the current crisis, Saddam used the state to subsidize and reward his supporters. His internal security strategy has always mixed *targhib* and *tarhib*, the 'stick' with the 'carrot.' Shortly after the 1968 coup Saddam established a separate and independent (i.e., independent of official state control) channel for allocating state funds. He set up large accounts inside and outside Iraq, and used these funds to pay or bribe cronies, potential allies, and large groups of the Iraqi people. For example, Saddam ordered the distribution of thousands of TV sets to the poor following the anti-government riots in the poor Shi'ite suburb of Medinat al-Thawra in Baghdad.

In the 1970s and 1980s, the Iraqi government went on a major land-buying spree by forcing owners to sell land at huge discounts to the state. These lands were then parceled out to supporters of the regime, party officials, the military, and family members. At the same time, the revenues from such sales or transfers went to private accounts. In addition, the government allocated state housing and contracts to supporters, and provided incentives like automobiles, university entry, foreign scholarships, and other consumer goods (or cash payments) to build loyalty. It then expanded these programs to reward the military during the Iran-Iraq War.

The Iran-Iraq War led Saddam to create a new tool of economic power. He set up a massive network of purchasing offices outside Iraq to buy arms, and to put billions into covert accounts to acquire the technology to build weapons of mass destruction. Many of these accounts were held overseas in neutral states, and under blind fronts. They had virtually no government accounting controls or supervision.

There is no way to know how many of these accounts survive, or what funds Saddam has drawn from them since the Gulf War, but they supplement his personal holdings overseas and those of his family, and no Western government has yet reported great success in tracking such accounts. At the same time, Iraq's intelligence and security service maintains surveillance over the foreign accounts of all other Iraqis and the state can control both domestic banking accounts and the allocation of foreign exchange resources.

The UN sanctions have led Saddam and his coterie to add rationing, subsidies, price controls, and foreign exchange controls to this list of instruments of state power. The state cannot control the black market or the private distribution of personal wealth, but it does control the day-to-day economic life of many citizens, significant overseas assets, all banks and most industrial capital transactions, the rationing and allocation process, capital transfers, imports, export revenues, exit permits, and the repatriation of capital.

Money is fungible, and the regime can manipulate the income it receives as a result of agreeing to the terms of UN Security Council Resolution 986 by shifting money that the UN does not control away from food and medicine into other areas, and it has all the tools to find economic scapegoats and seize the private wealth of its opponents. The government may have impoverished the people, but the result is a highly authoritarian poverty where the state still exercises ruthless control.

The Security Structure

Saddam has always relied heavily on Iraq's intelligence services and security structure to maintain his power. The only period in which he made any effort to moderate the public image of these services was after the Gulf War, and this effort virtually ceased by late 1991. On December 23, 1991, the Interior Ministry warned that an amnesty for turning in unlicensed firearms would only last 10 more days. On January 1, 1992, Uday called for the public execution of dissidents in his newspaper, *Babil*. From that time onwards, the security services ruthlessly suppressed any opposition with minimal regard for world opinion.

In 1995, Iraq's security and intelligence forces remained one of the largest single instruments of government power and totaled over 100,000 men. They include massive civil police forces, large intelligence and internal security units, and large military and paramilitary forces like the Republican Guards, Special Republican Guards, and Saddam Hussein's bodyguards or special security force. Saddam's elite security forces alone seem to total up to 15,000 men. There are also state political intelligence and security services that help protect Saddam Hussein and his coterie. These organizations are all headed by officers supposedly loyal to Saddam Hussein—some of whom are related to him, members of his Al Bu Nasser tribe, or the other two branches of the Tikriti tribe.

Iraq's security forces are the subject of constant changes in command, at least some of which involve arrests or executions. The main intelligence and security services include:[55]

- *The Presidential Affairs Department or Special Security Service (Amn al-Khass).* This organization operates within the presidential palace, and was established in the mid-1980s, after an attempt to assassinate Saddam Hussein highlighted gaps or failures in the already extensive cloak of security around the Iraqi leader. Its top leadership is manned by men personally selected by Saddam Hussein. Its overall function is to protect Saddam from assassination attempts emanating from within the Army, his family, or the government at large. Some experts feel it manages Saddam Hussein's secret foreign accounts, intelligence operations involving the purchase of foreign arms and technology, and some aspects of security within Iraq's military industries. It was headed by Major General Fanar Zibin Hassan al-Tikriti during the Gulf War, and is now headed by Saddam's younger son, Qusay. The most important unit within the al-Amn al-Khass is the Quwat al-Himaya whose direct task is to act as bodyguard to the President. The tasks of the Special Security Service are extensive and they include:
  - Guaranteeing the security of the president and providing protection.
  - Ensuring the security of all presidential facilities such as palaces, guest-houses, etc.
  - Supervision of the other security and intelligence services and of government ministries and agencies and maintenance of a close watch on the top brass of the armed forces.
  - Maintain cooperation with (and possibly monitor) a unit of the Republican Guards, the "Special Republican Guard" division formed in 1991/92 which was tasked primarily with regime secu-

rity. The "Special Republican Guard" is not to be confused with the regular Baghdad-based Republican Guard division. The former has three brigades which guard the southern, northern and western arteries into the city.

- *The General Intelligence Service (Al-Mukhabarat al-Amma).*The GIS is the intelligence and security service of the Ba'ath party. It grew directly out of the clandestine Ba'ath party security organization built up by Saddam Hussein in the 1960s and known as the *Jihaz Haneen* (Instrument of Yearning). Not surprisingly, this security-cum-intelligence service has been controlled by trusted and loyal party members. General Intelligence is divided into units or bureaus that are spread throughout the country. Overseas, GI operatives are attached to Iraqi embassies. Its tasks include:
  - Conducting counterespionage and monitoring subversive activities.
  - Supervising of the Ba'ath party and other political organizations.
  - Maintaining a watch over internal minorities such as the Kurds and Assyrians.
  - Suppressing opposition activities emanating from Shi'ites and other minorities.
  - Maintaining a watch over foreigners in Iraq, including those from Arab countries.
  - Conducting sabotage, subversion, and terrorist operations against neighboring countries such as Syria and Iran.
  - Providing financial and military aid, including logistical assistance, to opposition.
  - Targeting groups in countries hostile to Iraq.
- *Military Intelligence (Al-Istikhbarat al-Askariyya).* This organization dates back to the time of the monarchy and is manned largely by army officers. It focuses on foreign military threats, but also is responsible for internal security within the Iraqi military. It has ties to some radical movements and has conducted intelligence operations overseas. During the Gulf War, military intelligence was headed by Major General Sabir Abd al-Aziz Hussein al-Duri—a Sunni Arab from Dur, the hometown of Izzat Ibrahim, the Deputy Chairman of the Revolutionary Command Council. Duri was an old-time Ba'athist with ties to the army and senior party leaders, but was replaced after the Gulf War by Major General Wafiq Jassim Sammara'i. Sammara'i was later arrested and fled to Syria, and was replaced by either Major General Khalid Salih al-Juburi or Major General Abd al-Khadir Salman Khamis (a Tikriti related to Saddam). The head of military intelligence is Mu'tamad Ni'mah al-Takriti who replaced Khalid al-Juburi.[56] Some experts feel that Colonel Abd Hassan al-Majid, Ali Hassan al-Majid's younger

brother, was the true power in military intelligence before his defection. It has the following tasks:
- Ensuring loyalty of the armed forces to the regime.
- Supervision of security and counterintelligence in the armed forces.
- Collection of intelligence and tactical and strategic research on countries deemed hostile or threatening to Iraq.
- Waging of psychological war against enemies.
- Implementation of deception plans during wartime.
- Cooperation with foreign intelligence services.
- Conducting terrorist operations abroad against hostile countries, groups (Kurds), and opponents of Saddam Hussein. During the 1980s military intelligence operatives in the offices of military attaches in Iraqi embassies in Western Europe were involved in such activities. Reportedly agents of the Istikhbarat were responsible for the assassination of Saddam's opponents in Beirut, London, and Paris. Among the victims was Abdul Razzaq al-Nayef, a former senior Ba'athist official in the early days, who was murdered in London in 1978.
- Conducting research and studies on technological issues.
- *General Security or State Internal Security (Al-Amn al-Amm).* Along with Military Intelligence, this organization is the oldest security/ intelligence service in Iraq. Until the Ba'ath came to power in 1968, it was manned by professional policemen and army officers. It was subsequently purged and "Ba'athized" by Saddam's paternal cousin, 'Ali Hasan al-Majid, who ran the service from 1980 to 1987. This organization focuses largely on internal security, but occasionally conducts foreign operations. Major General Abd al-Rahman al-Duri headed this organization before the Gulf War, but Saddam appointed his half brother, Siba'awi Ibrahim, as the head after the Gulf War.

In July 1996 Siba'awi Ibrahim was replaced as director of internal security by General Taha 'Abbas al-Ahbabi. Saddam's relations with his half-brothers, the Ibrahims, have worsened considerably. The Ibrahims no longer trust their half-brother or those closest to him, particularly his two sons, and have reason to fear for their lives. Watban was shot in the leg by Uday and ultimately lost his limb. This was followed by the defection and subsequent murder of Hussein Kamel following his ill-advised return to Baghdad. Then Barzan insulted the pathologically unstable Uday from the relative safety of Geneva, and the latter vowed revenge. When Watban and Siba'awi developed a keen interest in leaving Iraq following the murder of Hussein Kamel and some of his relatives, Saddam responded by putting both Watban and Siba'awi under house arrest in early July 1996.[57]

- *Ba'ath Party Security (Amn al Hizb).* This security office develops intelligence on party members, and has security cells throughout the Ba'ath Party.
- *The Tribal Chief's Bureau (Maktab al-Shuyukh).* This is a new bureau that was created after the Gulf War. This service pays tribal leaders to control their tribes, spy on possible tribal dissidents, and provide arms to loyal tribesmen to suppress any dissidents. It was headed by Major Saddam Kamel, a cousin and son-in-law of Saddam Hussein and Hussein Kamel's younger brother. Saddam Kamel defected with his brother to Jordan.
- *Saddam's Fedayeen.* Saddam's Fedayeen are led by Saddam's eldest son, Uday. They were formed after the defection of Hussein and Saddam Kamel. They are equipped with some heavy weapons, including PT-76 light tanks and BTR-70 armored personnel carriers. They are composed largely of teen age Takritis from the same clan as Saddam, and are trained by the Republican Guard. They dress in black and often keep their faces covered.[58]
- *The Military Bureau of the Ba'ath Party.* The Military Bureau was also strengthened and reorganized after the Gulf War. It is headed by Saddam, and his deputy is his cousin and brother-in-law, Kamel Rashid Yassin. It acts as a commissar system to indoctrinate the armed forces, and check on their political loyalty.
- *The Ministry of Information.* Most Middle Eastern governments control their media and the press, and use it as an intelligence and propaganda service. Iraq's Ministry of Information has served as both a particularly strong and ruthless instrument of control. It tolerates some kinds of criticism—many of which seem to be manipulated to give the image that it is safe to make Saddam Hussein aware of the faults of government or give outsiders the impression of a free press. At the same time, it controls virtually every word written or spoken in the Iraqi media, uses "journalists" to propagandize internally and abroad, and has a long list of "writers," "academics," and "artists" it can use to influence both domestic and foreign opinion. The Ministry also has close links to other intelligence services so that it can control or spy on foreign visitors and journalists, and manipulate crowds and media events in Iraq. For example, it maintains a long list of seemingly private Iraqis who are fluent in foreign languages and who it ensures appear in front of cameras. Some of these Iraqis are allowed to give private interviews that support Iraqi propaganda—even when the spokesperson appears to be somewhat critical. The Ministry of Information also attempts to manipulate foreign scholars and international bodies visiting Iraq. It also has a list of quasi-academic institutions it can use to hold and manipulate meetings and conferences and use to develop contacts between foreigners and seeming "moderates" and "opponents" of the regime.

- *The Foreign Ministry.* This ministry mixes legitimate diplomats with members of the intelligence and security services. Like the Soviet diplomatic service during the Cold War, it is so closely linked to intelligence operations that it is impossible to distinguish between diplomats and the Iraqi equivalents of the KGB.
- *The Iraqi telecommunications services and major academic and research institutions.* All of these institutions have intelligence and security cells designed to improve state control. Many have special sections for military and intelligence efforts, for purchasing equipment to be used for military purposes, and supporting governmental propaganda and outreach efforts in dealing with foreigners.

This Iraqi intelligence and security effort is so large and so permeating that it gives Saddam Hussein far more power than is often apparent. At the same time, its power and ties to virtually every element of the Iraqi government and Iraqi society act as a powerful resistance to political change. The intelligence and security structure may not be loyal to Saddam as a man, but it is almost certainly loyal to its own self-interest, and is likely to prove a lasting barrier to the emergence of any new government or ruling elite which does not make similar use of such instruments of state control.

The Iraqi Armed Forces

The political role of the Iraqi military is a major part of the problem Iraq faces in creating effective forces. Iraq has a formal command structure very similar to that of other regional military forces, with all the required C^4I/BM capabilities and facilities. At the same time, it has highly politicized military forces which have a long history of playing a violent role in Iraqi politics and which have fought repeated civil wars against Iraq's Kurds and Shi'ites. The Iraqi armed forces are as much an instrument of state control as they are a means of national defense and military power. They are a key tool in the ruling elite's efforts to secure means of power, to coerce the Kurds, and to suppress systematically any threat from Iraq's Shi'ites.

The army has intervened in politics many times since the emergence of modern Iraq as a state. The politicization of the Iraqi Army began with the creation of the state in 1920, when King Faisal placed ex-Ottoman Sunni Arab officers at the head of the political, administrative and military posts. The first coup d'etat in the Arab world occurred in Iraq in 1936 under the helm of General Bakr Sidki, an Arabized Kurdish officer from Mosul. There were eight successful—among many other unsuccessful—coups d'etats in Iraqi politics between independence and the return of the Ba'athists in 1968. The first Ba'athist regime was overthrown by the military in 1963. In Syria, the Ba'ath came to be dominated by the military—which remains a source of the bitter ideological disputes between a 'fraternal' Ba'athist Syria and a Ba'athist Iraq.

Iraq's current military forces have been shaped by this history. Saddam and his coterie fully understand both the risks and advantages of using military force as an instrument of state control. Takriti-dominated Ba'athists took over in 1968 with the help of sympathizers within the armed forces, including fellow Takritis in key armored units. Long before that time, however, they had learned ample and painful lessons in what the armed forces could accomplish through a coup d'etat. Saddam understood all too well that cooperation between the military and the Ba'ath could turn to the advantage of the military, which might seek to govern alone or independently of the party's principles and directives.[59]

Since 1968, the Ba'athists and especially Saddam Hussein have had considerable success in their constant efforts to improve their political control over the armed forces.[60] The Ba'ath regime began mass purges and retirement of senior officers immediately after it came to power. By December 1968, the Chief of Staff, Faisal al-Ansari, and eight divisional commanders were purged and replaced by trusted Ba'athists. By the end of 1970, 3,000 new commissions had been announced. These new officers led to the genesis of a political commissar system. Furthermore, the regime ensured that loyal officers held key positions. By the early 1970s the Takriti Ba'athists controlled the Ministry of Defense, the air force, Habbaniyah air base outside Baghdad, Baghdad security and the city's garrison, and the Republican Guards brigade.[61]

Saddam Hussein has steadily consolidated his control over the military, making it a key aspect of his control over the state. Not long after coming to full power in 1979, Saddam stated in an interview with the British journalist David Hirst that the stringent measures of political control being adopted by the Ba'ath would prevent any future group of officers from being able to overthrow a revolutionary government, "Without party methods, there is no chance for anyone who disagrees with us to jump on a couple of tanks and overthrow the government. These methods are gone."[62]

Saddam built on formidable methods of exerting control and surveillance over the armed forces. Iraq already had the equivalent of the former Soviet *zampolit* or party commissars who are attached down to the level of the platoon and who could veto the decisions of professional unit commanders. These commissars, in turn, are controlled by the *Mudiriyat al-tawjih al-siyasi*, the Directorate of Political Guidance which was formed in 1973. The tasks of this directorate include:

- Spreading the ideology of the July 17, 1968, revolution to all military ranks and units.
- Supervising the activities of the officers (i.e., political commissars) attached to the Directorate of Political Guidance.

- Overseeing the development of military culture on the basis of historic, scientific and technological data so as to keep pace with the wind of change.
- Seeking to achieve maximum degrees of military discipline.
- Expounding Saddam Hussein's party line and the "aspirations of pan-Arabism."[63]

At the same time, informers and spies from the security and intelligence services permeated the military. Further, frequent purges, sudden rotations, retirements, and executions were used as a means to keep the officer corps in line and to discourage them from trying to overthrow the government.

Saddam purged the military again in 1979, and rotated or replaced key commanders to ensure their personal loyalty. He also refined his control during the Iran-Iraq War. From 1982 onwards, the Iraqi Army had severe morale problems. Many officers resented the excessive political constraints imposed by political officers, and felt the Iraqi leadership's interference in operational matters was a cause of Iraq's defeats.

These developments led Saddam to loosen some of his day-to-day operational controls over the military, but he made sure that the army never forgot who was commander-in-chief. He regularly rotated commanders, down-played the role of senior commanders in winning victories, gave loyalists in the Republican Guards the credit for victories, and used the media to turn leading officers into virtual non-persons. For example, Saddam took careful steps to ensure that militarily successful generals like Maher Abdul Rashid, who was known as the "Iraqi Rommel" for his outspokenness on political-strategic matters and his military successes, would not pose a political threat in the aftermath of the war. Saddam also used his control over the media and political education process to try to persuade the lower ranks and the Iraqi people that Iraq owed its victories to his 'military genius,' and that he was responsible for providing the military forces with all their needs.

After the Iran-Iraq War, Saddam rotated or dismissed many officers whose reputation or success made them seem like potential rivals. While some reports of executions and purges seem to be exaggerated, he altered the military command structure at every level. He rapidly expanded the Republican Guard—at the cost of sharply reducing the average quality of its forces—and reasserted the role of security services and party "commissars" in supervising the military. At the same time, he continued to offer "carrots" to other officers in the form of promotions, housing and land, cash benefits, civil jobs, and a wide range of other benefits.

The Gulf War ended so quickly and disastrously that there was no time for any organized challenge to emerge from within the Iraqi military as a whole, although some of the forces sent to the Kuwaiti theater of operations participated in the uprisings that followed. At the same time, the fighting failed to cripple the Republican Guard and key elements of the regular army because they were either never deployed forward, or escaped north during the final day of the land battle. As a result, the uprisings right after the war had the effect of spotlighting potentially disloyal forces without depriving Saddam of the power to reassert control. Moreover, the links between the military elements that did participate in the uprisings and various Shi'ite and Kurdish leaders made many in the Iraqi military see such units as traitors.

In the months that followed, Saddam rapidly consolidated Iraq's remaining forces in ways that further emphasized the power of loyalists in the Republican Guards and loyal regular army units. He used the "rebuilding" of the armed forces as a political as well as military tool. He conducted a series of major shake-ups of his military command structure—four of which were completed before June 1991. For example, Saddam replaced his Minister of Defense Lt. General Sa'di Tu'ma 'Abbas al-Juburi—a professional solider and hero of the Iran-Iraq War—with his paternal cousin and son-in-law, Hussein Kamel al-Majid, on April 6, 1991. Saddam Hussein replaced the Shi'ite Lt. General Hussein Rashid Muhammad al-Tikriti as Chief of Staff with Lt. General Iyad Futayyih Khalifa al-Rawi, the commander of the Republican Guard in June 1991. Rashid, who had been chief-of-staff since November 1990, was a respected combat commander, and a former commander of the Guard who had overseen its expansion during the Iran-Iraq War.

Some experts feel that Saddam tried to use the fact that al-Juburi was a Shi'ite, and Rashid was Kurd, to signal that part of the blame for Iraq's defeat could be ascribed to these ethnic groups. Yet, al-Juburi was retained as a senior military advisor and Rashid was later made supervisor of the Republican Guard—a position that ranks above the Guard's operational commander. Accordingly, the shifts may have been part of a long series of rotations designed to prevent any center of power from threatening Saddam's authority.

It is difficult to confirm many of the details of Saddam's other actions in asserting his control over the military. Unconfirmed reports surfaced in late 1991 that Saddam had executed or imprisoned 18 generals for an assassination plot between June and August 1991. These reports seem uncertain, but it is clear that Saddam continued his policy of shifting and rotating commanders to ensure that no group of military or internal security forces would become loyal to a potential rival. For example, he removed Major General Wafiq Jasim Samarrai as head of military intelligence, purged this command, and put in more loyal officers. General Hussein Rashid was brought back to power as supervisor of the Republican Guards in June 1992. Lt. General Iyad Futayyih Khalifa al-Rawi—another hero of the Iran-Iraq War and a key Saddam Hussein loyalist—was made chief-of-staff.

At the same time, Saddam moved more members of his family to senior positions. For example, Kamal Yassin, a member of the Ba'ath ruling council and Saddam's brother-in-law and cousin, was made deputy head of the Ba'ath military bureau. His brother, Arshad Yassin, remained head of Saddam's personal security force—a position he has occupied since 1986.

These actions, however, did not solve Saddam's problems in using the military as an instrument of state control. New reports surfaced in late June 1992, that Saddam had blocked a coup attempt within the military. Initial reports claimed that a mechanized brigade of the Republican Guard under the command of Brigadier Sabri Mahmoud—which was located in Taji, an industrial area northwest of Baghdad—was preparing an assault on Saddam Hussein's headquarters in Baghdad, when the coup attempt was detected and halted by Iraqi security forces. Other reports mentioned fighting between the military and security forces. There were reports of clashes between elements of Saddam's personal security force, the Special Republican Guards, and the regular Republican Guards in Baghdad and Kirkuk during June 30 to July 2.

On the other hand, there has been no confirmation of these details, and a few US experts feel that the coup reports were inspired by a series of command upheavals that followed a new large-scale purge of military officers, possibly totaling up to 135 officers. According to these reports, Saddam called a large meeting of his loyal officers together, charged the US and Jordan with supporting a military coup against him, and used this as a rationale for his purge. While Jordan denied any complicity in a plot against Saddam, Jordan did begin to enforce sanctions on transshipments of goods and oil to Iraq, although it refused to allow UN inspectors in Aqaba.[64]

There have been reports of similar coup attempts, arrests, and executions from late 1992 to the present—some of which involve the Juburi clan. For example, reports appeared in mid-September 1992 that Saddam Hussein had executed a total of 26–30 more officers, including General Abed Mutleq Juburi.[65] In October, he was accused of executing 19 more officers, including Brigadier Anwar Ismael Hentoosh and Brigadier Amir Rashid Hasson, two officers blamed for being insufficiently ruthless in putting down the Shi'ite rebellion in the south.[66]

Unconfirmed reports appeared of the execution or arrest of former Interior Minister Samir Abd al-Wahab al-Shaykhali in April 1993, and another series of arrests and executions of military officers and civilians took place during August through September 1993. These arrests and executions seem to have begun on August 20, 1993, and to have eventually involved a mixture of military officers and civilians associated with the Juburi clan, Ubayd clan, and Saddam Hussein's home town of Tikrit. Up to 100–150 men were involved, evidently including Jassim Mawlud Mukhlis and Saqr Mukhlis. Saqr was the son of the Mawlud Mukhlis who was the Tikriti landlord and the original patron who had opened up the officer corps to Tikritis under the monarchy. Another well known Iraqi executed was Brigadier General Raqhib Tikriti, a military physician who was head of the Iraqi Physician's Association.

While only uncertain reports of fighting or troop movements indicate a major coup attempt took place, there are unconfirmed reports that the arrests followed an effort to obtain Western support for a coup. These reports indicate that the plotters asked for Western air support over Baghdad and assurances that the Kurds would not seize Kirkuk and that Iran would not intervene in the south.[67] A number of US and British experts feel that these arrests were the result of a serious assassination attempt. Yet Saddam Hussein and the Ba'ath elite may have been reacting to threats that had not yet been transformed into plans. Saddam made little effort to lower his visibility, and continued to indulge in media events that seemed designed to show his wealth in spite of Iraq's growing economic problems.[68]

There is little prospect that Saddam can fully secure his control over the military, or that he can ever eliminate the risk that an assassination or coup attempt will finally succeed. He no longer can rely on his key Sunni clans and family. There are growing reports of large-scale desertions from within the regular military, breakdowns in morale, and problems in retaining junior officers. A new series of defections seem to have occurred in late 1995, and there are reports of bombings and fighting within military barracks.

Yet another senior officer, General Nizar al-Khazraji, a former chief of staff, fled to Jordan in late March 1996 where in early April he announced that he would join the ranks of the opposition to Saddam Hussein by seeking membership in the Iraqi National Accord (*Al Withaq al-Iraqi*), the first Iraqi opposition group to be allowed to open an office in the Jordanian capital of Amman. While in Amman the Iraqi General gave an extensive interview to *Al-Hayat* in which he highlights a number of aspects of the modus operandi of Saddam Hussein, particularly as it pertains to his relationship with the armed forces.[69] Khazraji was apparently eased out of his position as Chief of Staff in late 1990 after pointing out the military and strategic dangers to Iraq because of its invasion of Kuwait. His reward was to be "kicked upstairs" as a presidential advisor. Moreover, Khazraji stated that the invasion of Kuwait bypassed the Ministry of Defense and the General Staff and was undertaken by the Republican Guards on the direct orders of Saddam Hussein. There is no reason to doubt a disgruntled Iraqi officer with an ax to grind. In Khazraji's opinion:[70]

> What is left of the Army commanders consists of those who are either grudgingly satisfied or who are weak elements ... He orders and they obey because he has gotten rid of the elements who may have had an opinion or were capable of making decisions.

Further, Saddam took the unusual step of making a regular army officer the commander of the Republican Guard, and of appointing a native of Mosul as his office chief-of-staff. This latter appointee was Awwad al-Bandar, the former head of Iraq's Revolutionary Court, and he seems to have been appointed to counterbalance the internal political impact of Saddam's earlier execution of several officers from Mosul.[71]

In late June–early July 1996 reports indicated that Saddam Hussein survived yet another serious coup attempt by the military, which included a plan to assassinate the Iraqi leader. While it is difficult to sort fact from fiction, it seems that elements of the elite Republican Guards were involved, as well as officers from several other army corps. Operating under the name of a hitherto unknown group called "The Popular Uprising Movement" (*harakat al-intifadhah al-sha'abiyah*), a number of senior army officers decided to rid Iraq of Saddam and accused many external opposition groups of impotence and subservience to foreign powers.

The coup and assassination attempt failed. Scores of officers were detained: some reports indicated that upwards of 160 officers, of whom 12 were from the Republican Guards and 3 from the special or Presidential Guards were arrested. Three senior officers who were also provincial governors were arrested as well. They included: Lieutenant General Iyad Khalil Zaki, governor of Al-Muthanna in southwest Iraq, Lieutenant General Mohammed 'Abd al-Qadir 'Abd al-Rahman, governor of Nineveh (Mosul), and Major General Mahmud Shukr Shahin, governor of Al-Wasit in central Iraq.

By late July a large number of Sunni Arab officers, of mainly junior and middle ranks, were executed. These seem to include the following senior officers:

- Staff Brigadier General Ja'afar al-Tayyar, director of training at the Defense Ministry
- Brigadier General Amjad Tariq 'Aziz, commander of the Administrative Affairs School
- Staff Colonel Khamis Hadi Ni'mah, commander of the 6th Presidential Guards Brigade
- Staff Lieutenant Colonel Ahmad al-Nu'aymi, 6th Brigade staff officer
- Lieutenant Colonel 'Abdallah Sharif al-Rubay'i, 6th Brigade Administrative officer.

Two other senior officers escaped with their lives. Staff Lieutenant General Tali' Ruhayyim al-Duri, a hero of the Iran-Iraq War, fled to nothern Iraq and then Turkey. The alleged participation of this senior officer who held senior commands during the Iran-Iraq War and who is related to Revolutionary Command Council member Izzat Ibrahim al-Duri would seem to indicate serious discontent within the top echelon of the Sunni Arab officer corps which has constituted the key element of Sunni Arab domination of Iraq.[72] Former Air Force General Hamid Sha'ban, who commanded the Iraqi Air Force for part of the Iran-Iraq War, was initially suspected of involvement in the coup attempt because the dissident officers had planned to make him titular head of state in the event they succeeded in getting rid of Saddam but was let go when it transpired he knew nothing about the affair.[73]

These coup and assassination attempts were followed by the Ba'ath regime's customary large-scale purges and dismissals of officers from clans or tribes suspected of dissident behavior. Once again, much of the regime's wrath fell upon officers from the Dulaim and al-Duri tribes of Al-Anbar province. Moreover, Saddam Hussein began to admit large number of officers from the Al-Sa'dun Sunni Arab tribe from Al-Basrah province into the Revolutionary Guards.

At the same time, Saddam retains a massive apparatus to protect himself from the military, and continues to demonstrate that he can use the military as an instrument of state control. The Iraqi military continues to deploy nearly 14 of its 23–24 divisions along the border of the area under Kurdish control, and to deploy several divisions that conduct military operations against Shi'ite rebels in the marshes in the south.[74] Saddam has repeatedly demonstrated that he can deploy the Republican Guard for internal security missions, and that he can ruthlessly purge potential power centers within the military. Moreover, the kind of opposition to Saddam that has surfaced within the military shows little sign of being "democratic." It is the product of clan-oriented struggles for power or a desire to preserve power by getting rid of a man that is perceived as the reason that sanctions continue. The military may be more "pragmatic" than Saddam, but it will only be as moderate as it has to be. The military will also inevitably use any increase in its political power to favor its own interests.

Any "centrist" approach to finding new sources of power in Iraq must accept this reality. The military may prove to be a better power base than Saddam and his coterie, the Ba'ath, or the security services, but it is scarcely a good option. For more than fifteen years, the Iraqi military has been systematically conditioned and structured to be an authoritarian tool and to support Iraqi nationalism and regional ambitions. It will see any civil political movement as a rival and any civil movement that is Shi'ite or Kurdish dominated as a group of "traitors." Similarly, any "peripheral" strategy must recognize that a Sunni-dominated military is likely to both fight and win a civil war against any combination of Kurdish and Shi'ite groups that attempts to seize power and which does not have large-scale foreign military support.

The "Old Boy" Network and the Interaction
Between Informal and Formal Instruments of Power

It is important to note that there is no clear separation between Saddam's use of the informal instruments of power discussed in the previous chapter and his use of these instruments of state control. Saddam reinforces his control over the instruments of state power by using a complex network of trusted associates, aides, and personal supporters within the government, Ba'ath Party, the military, and security services. Many of these supporters have been with him for decades—since the struggle for power before 1968—and share his conspiratorial political mentality and experiences.

The following examples illustrate the kind of men who make up this coterie within the government and Ba'ath Party, and who provide Saddam with an important alternative to his immediate family. They also illustrate the fact that while the ruling elite may be largely Sunni Arab, Saddam has chosen senior members that come from other ethnic groups:

- Izzat Ibrahim al-Duri is a veteran Ba'ath party plotter and is Vice-Chairman of the Revolutionary Command Council. Izzat Ibrahim's daughter is married to Saddam's eldest son, Uday. For his resolve and leadership during the March 1991 insurrections, Saddam bestowed upon Izzat Ibrahim the title of Lieutenant-General. However, Izzat Ibrahim has never been more than a ceremonial leader and is reported to be in poor health.
- Taha Yasin Ramadan al-Jazrawi is a Kurd born in Mosul in 1938 and a senior member of the Revolutionary Command Council. A one time bank clerk, he is considered to be one of the toughest and among the most ruthless members of the regime. He has headed a revolutionary court which handed down hundreds of death sentences in the early years of the regime. He became minister of industry in 1972 and reportedly threatened slackers and the inefficient with execution. He is also reputed to have taken a harsh attitude towards Islamic fundamentalists over the years.
- Mikhail Yuhanna or "Tariq Aziz" is the one senior Christian member of the regime. He has been associated with Saddam for many years, but is unlikely to ever be accepted as a leader of a Muslim country. Nonetheless, he is noteworthy for many reasons. In recent years, he has been the Iraqi Ba'ath party's chief ideologue. In this capacity, he has interpreted the writings of Michel 'Aflaq, the founder of Ba'athism, to fit the Iraqi context. Furthermore, he has written about the torturous twists and turns of Iraq's Ba'athist experience, especially in foreign policy matters. Indeed, in his capacity as Foreign Minister during the 1980s, Tariq Aziz helped lead Iraq's foreign pol-

icy into a pragmatic phase and presented Iraq's view to the outside world in its war with Iran. Since Desert Storm, Tariq Aziz has served as both foreign minister and deputy Prime Minister, and has played a significant role in formulating the Iraqi diplomatic strategy designed to deal with the outside world and with the lifting of sanctions. He is often reported to have taken a soft-line view which urges complete Iraqi compliance with the UN Security Council resolutions pertaining to Iraqi cease-fire obligations.

Implications for Western and Southern Gulf Strategy

At this point in time there are only limited signs that Saddam and his coterie are losing control over the range of tools that help them remain in power, in spite of Iraq's military defeat in the Gulf War and the steadily deteriorating Iraqi economy. There are no signs that independent centers of power are emerging within the formal instruments of state power, or that the regime is losing control over any given instrument or part of the country.

Saddam may be experiencing growing problems with Sunni public opinion, the Sunni elite, key clans, and his immediate family, but there does not seem to be a weakness in Iraqi governmental or political institutions that the West and the Southern Gulf can easily exploit to drive him from power. If there is a "fault line" in Saddam's security, it lies in the fact that he lives in a state whose institutions are vulnerable to "one bullet elections." No matter how often the security services and military forces are purged, Saddam seems to face new opponents within these institutions. This creates a constant risk of an assassination or a catalytic coup attempt.

This kind of risk makes any strategy for dealing with Iraq's formal instruments of state control very uncertain. It must ultimately be dependent on finding a small element within Iraq's institutions that will deal with outside powers, and that is discrete and effective enough to have a reasonable chance of gaining power. The only other option is to wait and hope that that such a group will succeed without outside support.

Such a search presents a number of practical problems. Any group that acquires enough visibility to be noticed outside Iraq, or which tries to contact outside powers, is likely to be detected and destroyed before it can succeed in killing Saddam and his supporters. Most such oppositions groups are also likely to replace Saddam's power elite with one that is very similar in attitudes and conduct. The West and Southern Gulf states might well have to accept a "gentler and kinder" version of Saddam, which is unlikely to sacrifice authoritarian control over Iraq's institutions, and which is likely to have bitter memories of Iraq's defeat in the Gulf War and the impact of UN sanctions—regardless of the political rhetoric used in coming to power.

5

The "Periphery": Opposition Movements and Ethnic and Sectarian Issues

The alternative to a "centrist" strategy is a "peripheral" strategy based on seeking a new regime formed out of Iraq's opposition parties, its Kurds, or its Shi'ites. Such a "peripheral" strategy, however, presents problems and risks that are roughly equal to those inherent in a centrist strategy. Iraq's opposition political parties are very weak, and consist largely of exile groups with a negligible power base. Iraq's Kurds present the risk of separatism or creating a regime that may degenerate into civil war, and Iraq's Shi'ites present the risk of backing an Islamic regime—possibly one sympathetic to Iran.

These risks are not a reason for policy paralysis. There are many Kurds who would accept a federation that recognized Kurdish rights to a separate culture and a fair share of Iraq's oil revenues. Many Iraqi Shi'ites are secular in character, as well as being nationalists and Arabs. In spite of the government's actions, many Iraqi Shi'ites would also welcome a national government that included Sunnis and one focused on economic development. As is the case with a "centrist" strategy, the fact there are no alternatives to the regime of Saddam Hussein that offer any near-term prospect of a high degree of stability, or of creating an ideal regime, does not mean that there are not many possibilities better than Saddam.

An "Artificial" State

Iraq has never had the kind of leadership that has allowed it to overcome the "artificiality" of its origins. The British, who drew Iraq's political boundaries in 1920, created the nation by merging three disparate vilayets—or provinces—of the Ottoman Empire. In the process, they created a country that was a mosaic of competing and mutually antagonistic ethnic, religious and tribal groups. Hanna Batatu provided the following description of the origins of the Iraqi state:[75]

> At the turn of the century the Iraqis were not one people or one political community. This is not meant to refer simply to the presence of numerous racial and religious minorities in Iraq: Kurds, Turkomans, Persians, Assyrians, Armenians, Chaldeans, Jews, Yazidis, Sabeans, and others. The majority of the inhabitants of Iraq, the Arabs, though sharing common characteristics, were themselves in large measure a congeries of distinct, discordant, self-involved societies.

Batatu argues that Islam has proved to be more of a force for divisiveness than for integration. He says of Arab Sunnis and Arab Shi'ites: "socially they seldom mixed, and as a rule did not intermarry. In mixed cities, they lived in separate quarters and led their own separate lives."[76] This Sunni-Shi'ite cleavage was reinforced by the fact that it usually coincided with the social division between classes.

He also argues that the ethnic cleavage between Arab and Kurd was even more acute. The Kurds saw themselves as a separate people with their own culture and language and the rights to their own state. They perceived the Arabs as "occupiers" and interlopers who later "stole" the oil resources and revenues of north Iraq. At the same time, the Arabs saw the Kurds as rebels and as primitives that needed to be made part of a more modern and sophisticated culture.

Finally, the British chose to create a monarchy led by a foreign Arab Sunni family, the Hashemites. This monarchy initially had the support of many Iraqis—including both Sunni and Shi'ite Arabs—but it gradually came to be seen as a pro-Western tool of Britain. It only established uncertain control over the Iraqi military, did little to unify the country, and became the natural target of every opposition group from liberal reformer to extreme Arab nationalist.[77]

The Politics of Conspiracy and Violence

Iraq changed in many ways between its creation in 1921 and the fall of the monarchy in 1958. It became more cosmopolitan, communications improved, oil revenues created some elements of a modern economy, political parties formed that cut across ethnic and sectarian lines, and the army emerged as a major political force.[78] Yet, Iraq was still a politically 'primitive' state when the monarchy fell in 1958—a fact which was reflected in the bloody execution of the king, crown prince, and several senior Iraqi officials. An unstable, left-leaning republic was formed under General Abd al-Karim Qassem.

Iraqi politics remained the politics of conspiracy and violence—with strong elements of inter-tribal and family feuding and divisions between Sunni, Kurd, and Shi'ite. During the 1960s, a myriad number of political groups and parties jockeyed for power or for a way to influence the structure of power in Baghdad. These groups included the Kurds, the Iraqi Communist Party, the largest and best organized in the Arab world, pro-Nasserist pan-Arab nationalists, civilian technocrats without an identifiable party affiliation, the militantly pan-Arab nationalist Ba'ath party, and of course, the armed forces.

A decade of violent struggle between these various groups did little to encourage the rise of moderate political movements or resolve any of the sectarian and ethnic differences that affected Iraq at the time of its founding. If anything, Arab nationalism became less tolerant of the Kurds, and the secularism of the military and Ba'ath helped reinforce the difference between the Sunnis and more religious Shi'ites.[79]

In July 1968, the Ba'ath Party seized lasting power. The power elite that led the Ba'ath was determined not to repeat the ideological extremism and other follies of the short-lived first Ba'ath government of February–November 1963. It concentrated on development and created the infrastructure and communications necessary to integrate Iraq. At the same time, the new regime took steps to reduce the power of the opposition, and Saddam Hussein took further steps to weaken the opposition once he edged out President Hasan al-Bakr in 1979, and "elected" himself to the presidency.[80]

These actions by the Ba'ath elite led to a steady decline in Iraqi political opposition movements. Much of this decline was due to the Ba'ath's ruthless use of the security forces. At the same time, there were other reasons opposition parties lost support:

- Most opposition parties had a long history of extremism, squabbling, and internal divisions. Aside from the Iraqi Communist Party, they were seen as marginal, as offering little by way of solution to Iraq's problems, and as a poor alternative to the Ba'ath. The Communist Party, in turn, was seen as partly under foreign control, and was a natural target for the security services.
- Iraq evolved into both a well-policed and a "self-policing" society, in which the populace internalized "correct" patterns of conformity and norms of behavior. The slightest sign of discontent was dealt with ruthlessly and effectively.
- The regime created a welfare state which seemed to justify its character and actions. This welfare state functioned quite effectively even during the Iran-Iraq War, and provided free education and extensive social and health services. Even when living standards

declined during the Iran-Iraq War, the regime seemed to offer a better economic future than most of its opposition.

- Many Iraqis thought it was unpatriotic of overseas-based opposition groups to take advantage of Iraq's difficulties during the Iran-Iraq War. The opposition to Saddam exhibited severe weaknesses and divisions. Many of the so-called parties were loose groups of exiles centered around individuals with a "party program" that consisted of no more than a call for the overthrow of Saddam. The opposition groups were fragmented and disunited with most groups highly suspicious of the others' political programs. For example, the Supreme Assembly for the Islamic Revolution in Iraq (SAIRI) would never deal with the Iraqi Communist Party (ICP).
- There were a wide range of disparate party programs. There was no easy way to reconcile secular and Islamist groups or Shi'ite aspirations for a greater role in Iraqi political and social life with pan-Arab nationalists who implicitly believed in the political supremacy of the Sunni Arabs.
- Many of the opposition groups claimed to be national, but were structured along ethno-sectarian lines and thus subscribed to particularistic party programs which catered solely to the interests of their respective communities, and
- The opposition to Saddam was bereft of regional and international support. The two groups which did have outside support and which also constituted the most effective internal source of dissent, the Kurds and Shi'ite elements sympathetic to the Islamic Republic of Iran, were skillfully portrayed by the Iraqi regime as unpatriotic traitors at a time when Iraq was struggling for its national existence. In short, during the war years, the regime managed to identify opposition with treason.[81]

In contrast, the divisions between the "center," the Kurds, and Shi'ites steadily widened after the late 1960s. The Ba'ath failed to find an answer to the political problems raised by the Kurds, and became involved in a bloody civil war with separatist Kurds during the early and mid-1970s. From the mid-1970s onwards, the secular policies of the Ba'ath also led to a state of political ferment and religious revivalism in much of the Shi'ite south.

The Iran-Iraq War added a new dimension to the central government's problems with the Kurds and the Shi'ites. Although several Kurdish factions fought Iran on the side of Iraq when Iraq appeared to be winning, the powerful Barzani and Talabani factions turned against Iraq once it began to suffer serious defeats in 1982. As a result, the Iraqi military forces fought six more years of civil war against the Kurds in the midst of the Iran-Iraq War.

Iran's proselytizing efforts failed to gain the support of large numbers of religious Shi'ites, but the Iran-Iraq War created a constant uncertainty as to the loyalty of Shi'ites in the south and over whether they might support Iran during one of its offensives. While Iraq's Shi'ites did little to justify the regime's fears, this did not prevent the regime from exiling more Shi'ites and reinforcing its repressive security arrangements in Southern Iraq. Disloyalty to Saddam Hussein became the equivalent of treason during the Iran-Iraq War, further suppressing the development of any peaceful or legitimate political opposition.

Today, Iraq is almost as divided as it was at the time of its formation as a modern state. There is no meaningful overt political opposition within Iraq and only weak opposition within it. Iraq's Kurds and Shi'ites represent a majority of the population. Recent CIA estimates indicate that 63–68% of Iraq's population is non-Sunni (60–65% Shi'ite) and that 20–25% is non-Arab (15–20% Kurdish).[82] A number of experts believe these figures understate the number of Kurds, but there is little argument over the fact that Iraq is now ruled by a largely Sunni Arab elite that comprises well under 30% of its total population and which has done little since 1980 to maintain national cohesion or unite the country.

Opposition Parties

Saddam Hussein and the Ba'ath are opposed by a number of opposition groups, many based outside of the country. These groups span the political spectrum, and include Islamic fundamentalists, Kurdish autonomists, pan-Arab nationalists, dissident Ba'athists, communists, and liberals. These parties, however, are a weak foundation for a "peripheral" strategy. Some are led by Shi'ite or Kurdish figures that are still tied politically to their sectarian and ethnic origins, and generally lack strong influence even within their own ethnic faction in Iraq. Others have little public support within Iraq, vague or radical ideologies, and no practical experience in governing.

The mobilization of world opinion against Saddam Hussein following the invasion of Kuwait led many of Iraq's fractured opposition groups to try to establish a common anti-Saddam platform, and to begin to court the members of the UN coalition. In December 1990, most of the Iraqi opposition movements held a conference in Damascus. They established a steering group, called the Joint Action Committee, which condemned the dictatorship of Saddam and agreed on the following objectives: toppling the Ba'athist regime, formation of a provisional government which would lay the basis for a constitutional system of government that would dismantle the vast repressive apparatus of the Iraqi state, restoration of political liberties, abolition of ethnic and sectarian discrimination, and the holding of free elections to form a constituent assembly.[83]

It is a sign of their isolation from the political dynamics within their country, however, that the exiled Iraqi opposition groups were as surprised by the outbreak of full-scale rebellions in the Shi'ite south and the Kurdish north following the end of the Gulf War as were outside observers. The opposition groups in exile then underestimated Saddam's staying power, and were stunned by the effectiveness with which the regime crushed the insurrections of March 1991. Since that time, they have only been marginally successful in making themselves seem a valid alternative to Saddam Hussein, despite their attempts to coordinate their activities and present a united front.

The first serious post–Gulf War meeting of Iraqi opposition movements took place in Beirut on March 11–13, 1991. This meeting was held under the protection of the Syrians and organized by two ad hoc committees of Iraqi opposition forces based in London and Damascus. This conference brought together 350 delegates from about 20 distinct groups, organizations, and parties, as well as many independent personalities without any discernible party structure or ideology. The parties to the conference— which took place at the height of the Kurdish and Shi'ite insurrections— concluded that:[84]

- They must unify and organize themselves as a credible alternative to the Ba'athist regime of Saddam Hussein,
- External opposition groups must provide direct support for the insurrections, and
- The various opposition movements must seek foreign backing and sympathy.

The participants did not present any ideas on how to unify and coordinate their disparate party platforms and ideological principles. Further, much of the impact of the Beirut meeting was nullified by the decision of the Kurdish parties to begin negotiations with Saddam Hussein following the defeat of their insurrection in late March.

These negotiations collapsed in the fall of 1991, and seemed to offer a new opportunity for unified action, but their continued lack of cooperation and suspicion of one another ensured that a meeting of opposition groups in Riyadh, Saudi Arabia, in February 1992 produced no meaningful results. Further, most of the key Kurdish leaders avoided meeting.[85]

The Iraqi National Congress

The Iraqi opposition's two greatest weaknesses—their lack of cohesion and coordination—seemed equally evident when the London-based groups decided to call a conference in Vienna, to which they invited all the opposition to participate. The conference met in June 1992, and resulted in the creation of an umbrella group—the Iraq National Council (INC). The conference attendees put forth ambitious plans for the INC. The conference rapporteur declared that the INC did not wish to be seen as yet another coalition of opposition force, and that its goal was to emerge as a "shadow" or alternative government. The communiqué also stated that Rebel-controlled territory in Kurdistan would become the base from which the INC could pursue the conflict against Baghdad and draw adherents to the cause.

Yet, the Vienna conference failed to unite the principal Iraqi groups. The sponsors were the two main Kurdish parties, the KDP and PUK, plus a small group of Western-based and backed Iraqi Arab exiles. Many Islamist, Arab nationalist, liberal, and leftist groups stayed away. These latter groups accused the sponsors of failing to coordinate or consult with them prior to the calling of the conference, and of unfair power-sharing arrangements. Further, many of those groups which did not attend the Vienna meeting reacted by treating the INC as a creature of the West, and as a front which the West supported only because it suited Western designs for Iraq.

These divisions led to another opposition meeting in November 1992, which was held in Salahedin on "liberated" Iraqi in territory in Kurdistan. All Iraqi opposition groups were invited to participate, and the meeting was intended to address the schisms and conflicts within the Iraqi opposition, and to find a way to achieve a truly united anti-Saddam platform. More of the opposition decided to attend, including some groups which had stayed away from the Vienna conference. Some 260 delegates turned up, but the number of groups that stayed away was still significant.

Those who failed to attend included such groups as the:[86]

- Supreme Assembly of the Islamic Revolution in Iraq (SAIRI), which denounced the conference as "confessional" and tribal.
- Democratic Assembly of Salah Dejla.
- Assembly for National Reconciliation of Tahsin Mualla, a former Ba'athist group.
- Islamic Group of Mahdi al Khalisi.
- Tribal Council of Iraq.
- National Democratic Assembly of Ahmad Haboubi, based in Cairo.
- The pro-Syrian Ba'athist splinter group of Fadel al-Amari and Wael al-Hilali.
- Iraqi Socialist Party of Mubder Louays, a Damascus University Professor and ex-officer in the Iraqi military.
- Assembly of National Democratic Alliance of Salah Omar al-Ali. This group denounced the Salahedin conference, adding that the

participants sought to transform Iraq into a "new Lebanon," because they wanted to rely on foreign parties to get rid of the Ba'athist regime.

- A cluster of independent political personalities, among whom there is a large number of officers who have defected from the regime in the past or fled in the aftermath of the Gulf War. These include the following generals: Abdel Amir Oubais, Abdel Wahab al-Amin, Ibrahim Abdel Rahman al-Daud, and Col. Abdel Moneim al-Kattan. These independent personalities shared a preference for a centrist strategy to overthrow Saddam, rather than the emerging peripheral strategy of the Kurdistan-based INC.

In spite of this lack of united support, the conference led to the formation of a presidential council headed by a triumvirate drawn from the three main Iraqi communities and a 27-member Executive Council headed by a leading London-based figure, Dr. Ahmad Chalabi. Chalabi expressed his hope that the institutionalization of the opposition forces on Iraqi territory in the north would result in the steady erosion of support for and legitimacy of the regime as people deserted it to join the INC as follows:[87]

> We hope to develop further and further our links with the Iraqi armed forces and government, to win them over. We do not want the process of change to be bloody and to entail civil war, we want it to be as peaceful as possible and we renounce the idea of collective punishment.

It seemed for a while that the Salahedin meeting had strengthened the INC in spite of the fact that it proved unable to unify the various opposition parties. During 1993 and 1994, however, the INC began to experience growing difficulties.

First, the INC alliance with the Kurds resulted in growing tensions. While the Kurds were pleased to host many of the Iraqi opposition forces, they had no desire to have the territory under their control become the springboard for armed confrontation with Baghdad. This risked re-igniting an armed conflict with superior government forces. Furthermore, the Salahedin conference took place at a time when Kurdistan had achieved some measure of democratic freedom and peace, and before the onset of fratricidal conflict between the KDP and PUK which led to a state of quasi-anarchy. This seemed to offer the hope of Kurdish separatism, and KDP and PUK were aware that many non-Kurdish opposition groups expressed their unhappiness during the conference with the idea of a federal solution to the perennial Kurdish conflicts with the central authorities in a post-Saddam Iraq. On the other hand, from 1994 onwards, the

INC found itself caught up in trying to mediate a growing conflict between the PUK and KDP.

Second, the parties and organizations that were members of the INC became increasingly vocal in their criticism of the allegedly autocratic leadership style of Ahmad Chalabi.[88] By mid-1995, the INC seemed to be in organizational disarray. Of the 19 parties listed as members of the INC in 1993, seven had suspended or withdrawn their membership by 1995, having accused Ahmad Chalabi of turning the INC into the "Ahmad Chalabi party."[89] There were also attempts either to oust Chalabi or to bring about changes in the INC.[90]

Third, the INC did not emerge as a provisional government with its members united on common issues. It remained a broad-based coalition of opposition groups with sharp differences. In addition to quarrels over the leadership, these differences involved the issue of sanctions—with some groups arguing they should be maintained until Saddam is overthrown, while others increasingly became uneasy over their impact on the Iraqi people. The members of the INC also quarreled over the possibility of dialogue with Saddam Hussein. This presented further problems with the Kurds, because Masoud Barzani, the head of the KDP, was perceived as one of the opposition leaders most willing to negotiate with Saddam Hussein.

Fourth, externally-based opposition groups like the INC faced a credibility problem with Iraqis inside the country. These Iraqis often did not believe that outside opposition forces had any credible plans to bring about change in Iraq, a tangible agenda on how to avoid a collapse of central authority once Saddam was overthrown, or meaningful plans to reconstruct Iraq in the post-Saddam era. Furthermore, the exiles' integrity and political judgment were questioned by many Iraqis. Many exile groups were seen as paid agents of Western or Arab intelligence services and governments, or as tainted by having strong ties with an Iran that is seen as the historical enemy. Iraqi officials like Barzan al-Takriti encouraged such feelings by denouncing the opposition for "prostituting" themselves to foreign governments:[91]

> Strangely enough, the Iraqi opposition has broken all moral and psychological barriers and gone about knocking on the doors of foreign ministries and intelligence services in the West to argue their case for rapid action to bring down the system of government in Iraq so they can take over. This kind of conduct is virtually the coup de grace that disqualifies them as patriots.

These weaknesses did not, however, prevent the INC from functioning or from attracting defectors from the regime in Baghdad. In August 1993, two high-ranking ambassadors, Hisham Ibrahim al-Shawi and Hamid Alwan al-Jibouri, defected in London, and declared themselves for the INC. In December 1994, Major-General Wafiq al-Samara'i, the former chief of Military Intelligence joined the INC. Along with other defections, these actions helped the INC retain a sense of optimism that there was a slow and steady erosion in the power of Saddam Hussein and fed it with a steady stream of important intelligence about the situation inside Iraq until Saddam Hussein's alliance with the KPP in September 1996 allowed him to drive the INC and other opposition elements out of Northern Iraq.

Hussein Kamel and the Higher Iraqi Salvation Council

The defection of Hussein Kamel proved to be a different story. The ill-fated defection of one of the leading "henchmen" of the regime exposed serious differences in Takriti support for Saddam Hussein, but the outside opposition had good reasons not to adopt Hussein Kamel as one of their own.[92] First, many opposition groups knew he had been involved in the regime's crimes against the Iraqi people. Rehabilitating Hussein Kamel was like rehabilitating Saddam Hussein himself to many opposition leaders. Second, no one wanted Hussein Kamel to be seen as a possible successor to Saddam.

This helps explain why Kamel's call upon opposition groups to unite and establish a government in exile failed to attract much support. Nonetheless, Kamel set up his own Higher Iraqi Salvation Council at the end of 1995 in an effort to attract opposition forces. Kamel stated that his motive in setting up this opposition group was his belief that the chances of foreign interference in Iraqi domestic affairs would increase if no decisive and organized action was taken to bring about a "change" in the Iraqi political scene soon.

Hussein Kamel set forth the following program for reshaping Iraq's internal, external, and security situation in a post-Saddam Iraq:[93]

- Saddam Hussein must be overthrown, but Iraqis must not rely on the help of outsiders to get rid of him,
- There will be no revenge on and witch-hunts in the shape of trials and executions conducted against officials of the current regime once it is overthrown,
- Opposition groups based on "parochial" tendencies, sectarianism and ethnicity constitute a danger to the integrity of Iraq,
- The Council opposes the idea of a federal solution to Iraq's ethno-sectarian divisions. Iraq must not be divided into "cantons,"
- Iraqis are entitled to democracy, pluralism, and free elections,
- The Kurdish problem is an internal Iraqi matter, and the Kurds are Iraqis who must be granted their national rights within a unified Iraq,

- Iraq will enter into a dialogue with the US in order to explore the possibility of establishing a "strategic relationship" with Washington,
- The Council supports justice, equality among peoples, and economic alliances in the Middle East,
- Iraq will respect the choices made by the Palestinians and the confrontation states bordering Israel. Iraq can no longer "uphold the slogan of liberation" (i.e, calling for armed conflict) with respect to the Arab-Israeli conflict, and the
- Iraqi Army will be rebuilt but the Council is "opposed to wars, aggression, and the acquisition of weapons of mass destruction."

It is clear from this manifesto that Kamel presented a "centrist" program for change that was at odds with the INC's "peripheral" strategy. Whereas the INC hoped to draw the "center" away from Saddam and join it, Kamel hoped that potential opposition groups within the "center" like the army officers with whom he claimed to be in touch would take matters into their own hands. Not surprisingly, Kamel tailored his program to appeal to those in the center, even though he watered down or eliminated some ideological positions that would traditionally appeal to the Arab nationalist Sunni elite in the center, such as the importance of military power and an active role in the Arab-Israeli conflict.

The Jordanian Card

Ironically, a new form of "foreign interference" emerged as the result of Hussein Kamel's defection. King Hussein put forward his own preferred solution to Iraq's problems, and offered to hold a conference of Iraqi opposition parties to discuss the future of the country. At the same time, the Jordanian monarch proposed a "federal solution" with few specifics, but which called for Iraq's major ethno-sectarian groups to live in peace and accept the fact that none would dominate the country. King Hussein said he felt compelled to act because he did not feel that Hussein Kamel presented a viable alternative to Saddam Hussein. Kamel, in turn, expressed his displeasure with the fact that the proposed conference included invitations to "Iranians" or those with Iranian connections—presumably meaning SAIRI and al-Da'awa party.

King Hussein indicated that he felt that the continuation of the status-quo (i.e., continuation of Saddam Hussein in power) in Iraq was aggravating the socioeconomic condition of the Iraqi people and could lead to the breakup of Iraq. He also indicated that he felt that the Iraqi opposition had failed to present an effective united front without his support.

In November 1995, King Hussein contacted the opposition to sound out their views on the proposals to extend his patronage to the opposition by hosting a major opposition conference and the more ambitious call to implement a federal option for Iraq. He sent two advisers—Mustafa al-Qaisi, director of the Jordanian General Intelligence Directorate and one of his deputies, Abdul Illah al-Kurdi—to visit the London-based INC to discuss the new Jordanian strategy. The King himself called the four key players in the Iraqi opposition, namely Ahmad Chalabi as head of the INC, Mohammed Baqir al-Hakim head of the Supreme Assembly for the Islamic Revolution in Iraq (SAIRI), Mas'ud Barzani head of the Kurdish Democratic party (KDP) and Jalal Talibani head of the Patriotic Union of Kurdistan the PUK.

While some Iraqi opposition groups welcomed King Hussein's action, and indicated their support, others showed reservations. Furthermore, some opposition groups were suspicious of Jordan's stance because of the strong relationship that had previously existed between Amman and Baghdad. Others feared King Hussein's ambitions in Iraq, accentuated by the fact that neither the Iraqi opposition nor Jordan's neighbors were accustomed to seeing Jordan take such a leading role in inter-Arab politics.[94]

Jordan scarcely got unified support from other countries. Iran warned opposition leaders like Mohammed Baqir al-Hakim and Mas'ud Barzani against jumping on the Jordanian bandwagon. Most Middle Eastern states and the US gave King Hussein's proposal only a lukewarm endorsement. Egyptian President Hosni Mubarak and his Foreign Minister, Amr Moussa, declared that such a federal solution could lead to the break-up of Iraq. Syria expressed its displeasure with the unexpected foreign policy activism of Jordan, which it sees as an 'insignificant' country, particularly in relation to Iraqi affairs where Syria had tried unsuccessfully to play a role in the summer of 1995. The Saudis, for their part, reacted with their traditional suspicions of Hashemite ambitions, fearing that King Hussein was exploring the option of a Hashemite option for post-Saddam Iraq. King Hussein denied any ambitions to revive the Hashemite monarchy in a speech on August 23, 1995, but this did little to end Saudi suspicions.[95]

Like the INC, King Hussein also suffered a major setback in September 1996. Saddam's alliance with the KDP allowed him to drive Jordanian-sponsored opposition elements out of the Kurdish enclave as well as the INC and the CIA team that had backed such opposition movements. As a result the chances of a unified and effective opposition seemed just as remote at the end of 1996 as they had before the Gulf War, and no group seemed to exist which could act as the nucleus of a credible peripheral strategy.

Iraq's Crisis with the Kurds

Kurdish separatism presents different problems for a "peripheral strategy." Kurdish separatism is the result of a Kurdish search for autonomy or independence with a long and bloody history. Iraq's Kurds have often revolted when the government seemed weak or when they could obtain foreign support. They also have taken advantage of any weakness in the central government, or its preoccupation with other pressing domestic or foreign issues, to pressure Baghdad by bringing demands for autonomy.

Kurdish uprisings occurred long before Iraq's creation in 1920, and occurred sporadically during the monarchy. These uprisings have been influenced by the fact that Iraq was created by the British out of three Ottoman *vilayets* or provinces: Baghdad and Basra which were overwhelmingly Arab, and Mosul which contained a large Kurdish minority.

The Kurds in Mosul province sought their own independent state following the collapse of the Ottoman Empire, only to see their aspirations dashed by the victorious Western powers, namely Britain and France. The League of Nations approved Iraq's possession of Mosul, with the provision that the Kurds be granted substantial political and cultural autonomy. As a result, there were many small Kurdish uprisings, and the Kurds proved politically unruly.

The Kurds proved politically and militarily ineffective, however, because the tribally-factionalized nature of their society—accentuated by poor transportation networks and mountainous terrain—prevented them from forming a united front. This helped defeat the two most serious uprisings before World War II. The British Royal Air Force crushed tribal Kurdish revolts by the Barzani clan, which were headed by Mullah Mustafa Barzani in 1922 and in 1943.

Even so, Barzani emerged as the hero of Kurdish aspirations. In 1946 he recommended the establishment of the Kurdish Democratic Party modeled along the Kurdish Democratic Party of Iranian Kurdistan (now called the KDPI to distinguish it from the Iraqi KDP). When secessionist-minded Kurds within Iran established the short-lived Marxist-dominated Republic of Mahabad in 1945 with its own presidency, Mustafa Barzani crossed the border to offer his services to the new Kurdish Republic. The Iranian government of Mohammed Reza Shah recaptured the town of Mahabad in January 1947 and eliminated the Kurdish leadership with the exception of Mullah Mustafa who fled to the USSR and remained there until 1958.

In 1958, Barzani was invited back to Iraq by the revolutionary and republican regime of General Abdel Karim Qassem to participate in the building of a new and progressive state in Iraq. Iraq was defined for the very first time as a state comprising two major nationalities: Arab and Kurd. Moreover, Qassem saw the Kurds as a powerful countervailing group to his enemies, the Nasserists and pan-Arabists. The Kurds, for their part, were pleased that Qassem's regime did not espouse pan-Arabist or Arab nationalist ideologies, which they saw as working to marginalize the role of the Kurds in Iraqi political life.

It was not long, however, before Barzani and the post-monarchical regime in Baghdad fell out. Qassem became increasingly uneasy over the extent of the concessions the Kurds had wrung from his regime and began to view them as a threat to his rule, while the Kurds thought they had not received enough benefits. Tensions rose following the government's deportation of Kurds from the oil-rich Kirkuk area and the movement of military forces to the north. A full-fledged rebellion headed by Barzani broke out in September 1961.

Even though Qassem fell from power in 1963, the Kurdish insurrection was to last almost uninterrupted from 1963 to 1975, a period of twelve years. The KDP's fighting strength rose from about 1,000 ill-trained *Peshmerga* (literally "those who face death") guerrillas in late 1961 to about 20,000 seasoned guerrillas by late 1963. Throughout the 1960s military-dominated Arab nationalist regimes in Baghdad proved unwilling to grant the Kurds the autonomy they sought and unable to subdue them militarily.

The first Ba'ath regime which seized power in February 1963 made a concerted effort to subdue the Kurds by undertaking a large-scale offensive and by mass deportations of Kurds. This regime did not last more than nine months in office. It was rent by extensive factionalism between the right and left wings of the party and was significantly weakened by the focus on the counter-insurgency war against the Kurds. The new military government, however, pursued very similar policies. Its policy relied on large-scale offensives in the Kurdish areas, shelling and bombing civilians in Kurdish villages, and mass deportations of the Faili Kurds, who live in the mountainous region bordering Iran. Baghdad, however, scarcely had its own way. The Iraqi Army suffered severe reverses at the hands of the Kurds, particularly at Hendrin in mid-1966.

When the Ba'ath seized power again in July 1968, it was determined not to be deflected from its vision of building a modern 'progressive' and socialist Iraq that would play a major role in inter-regional affairs. It recognized that a continuation of the insurgency in the north was bound to lead to increased foreign interference in Iraq's domestic affairs and support for the rebels in a manner detrimental to the regime's determination to widen Iraq's regional role, and the new regime initiated negotiations with the Kurds to discuss autonomy measures.

The result was a March 11, 1970, agreement which stipulated that:

- The ruling Revolutionary Command Council would have Kurdish members;
- One of the Republic's vice-presidents must be a Kurd;
- Kurds should be represented in the armed forces, the security services, the ministries, the state's administrative machinery and bureaucracy in direct proportion to the size of the Kurdish population;

- Kurdistan would become an autonomous region in which the local government officials would be ethnic Kurds, the Kurds would be allowed to set up a legislative assembly, and Kurdish would be the official language in the north.

These terms may still offer a solution to the Kurdish problem in Iraq, but the March 1970 agreement was never implemented. Problems arose over different interpretations of the territorial extent of the autonomous region. Specifically, the Kurds wanted to include oil-rich Kirkuk within the northern autonomous region. Baghdad balked at the idea of losing control of a critically important economic region, and did not give the Kurds any real share of power in the "center." The Kurds who held positions in the central government were powerless. Moreover, the Ba'athists did not cease the practice of "Arabizing" Kurdish areas, nor desist from deportations of Kurds from Kurdistan to the south or of the expulsion of Kurds—deemed to be "Iranians"—to Iran. The Kurds were outraged by Baghdad's suspected involvement in assassination attempts against Kurdish leaders like Mustafa Barzani. In short, trust and goodwill was lacking on both sides.

For its part, Baghdad suspected the Kurds, particularly Barzani, of building links with foreign powers like Iran with which Iraq was on the worst of terms. In December 1973, the government put forward a proposal for the implementation of a watered-down autonomy that made a mockery of its March 1970 agreement with the KDP.

Not surprisingly in this climate of tension and mutual recriminations, relations between Baghdad and the Kurds deteriorated rapidly and a full-scale Kurdish rebellion erupted in March 1974. This stage of the Kurdish conflict lasted a year, and turned out to be the most costly and bloody to date for both the Kurds and Baghdad. Determined that it would not be bogged down in an interminable conflict, Baghdad committed the bulk of its armed forces—eight divisions or 120,000 men of the regular army, most of its armor, and its entire air force in a massive two pronged offensive in spring and summer of 1974 that succeeded in driving the *Peshmerga* into the inhospitable mountains along the Iraqi borders with Turkey and Iran.

Despite suffering extensive casualties among the government's largely Shi'ite infantry units—which prompted an outcry in the Shi'ite south silenced by the execution of a few clerics—and loss of material, the Iraqi Army performed prodigious feats in seizing the mountainous Kurdish strongholds of Ranya, Qala Diza and Ruwanduz in fall 1974, thereby threatening the Kurds' tenuous lines of communications with Iran whose government was providing the guerrillas with weaponry, supplies and safe haven. The Kurds had the backing of the Shah of Iran, and training and military equipment from the US CIA, and between January–March 1975 fought a long, bloody series of battles that held the Iraqi Army to a standstill in spite of its attacks on Kurdish civilians and "ethnic cleansing."

The Kurdish rebels were only defeated once the Shah traded an end to his support of the Kurds for Iraq's agreement to accept Iran's terms on various border disputes and joint control of the Shatt al-Arab waterway. This agreement was formalized by the Algiers Accord of March 1975. Saddam Hussein was the key negotiator of this accord, and it is scarcely surprising that it left him with a permanent suspicion of the Kurds and of their loyalty to the Iraqi state.

Following the collapse of the Kurdish insurgency, Mustafa Barzani fled with thousands of other Kurds to Iran. Barzani then moved to the USA, where he died in 1979. This left the leadership of the KDP in the hands of his two inexperienced sons, Masu'd and Idris. Meanwhile back in Iraq itself a mixture of ruthless force and occasional incentives kept the Kurds relatively peaceful from 1975 to 1980. Moreover, the Kurdish movement itself was weakened when it fragmented following the formation in 1976 of the Patriotic Union of Kurdistan (PUK) by Jalal Talibani, a left-leaning urban intellectual and long-time ideological antagonist of the more conservative Mustafa Barzani.

Furthermore, Barzani's massive political miscalculation in relying so much on Iran's support had robbed the Barzanis of their aura of invincibility in Kurdish lore and had enabled a more modern and cosmopolitan leader like Talibani to challenge the two Barzani sons for leadership of the Kurdish movement. Following the outbreak of the Iran-Iraq War in 1980, the two major Kurdish groups—the Kurdish Democratic Party (KDP) and the Patriotic Union of Kurdistan (PUK)—fought the Iraqi government on the side of Iran.

The Iraqi government responded by deploying two full corps into the Kurdish region, using napalm and poison gas against suspect or hostile Kurdish towns, and forcing mass relocations. The Kurds were able to keep up their resistance as long as they had Iranian support, but developed only limited military strength and were deeply divided. Many Kurds sided with the government and served in pro-government militias. Both the KDP and the PUK were bitter rivals and sometimes fought each other as well as the government.[96]

Operation Anfal

The Iraqi government's attacks on the Kurds became steadily more violent between early 1987 and the fall of 1988. Iran's defeat in the spring of 1988 allowed the government to concentrate on the Kurdish rebellion and it conducted a brutally effective pacification program in the north. The result was the so-called Anfal ("Spoils") Campaign of 1988, in which tens of thousands of Kurds lost their lives, and which is the most prominent example of the mass political killing of dissidents by the Iraqi regime. A final offensive by over 60,000 veterans of the Iran-Iraq War broke the back of the Kurdish rebellion. During this campaign, thousands of Kurdish civilians were murdered. Government forces also arrested thousands of Kurds, who have never been seen again.

There are no precise figures on how many Kurds died. According to the UN Special Rapporteur, the total figure for disappeared Kurds during Anfal could number in the tens of thousands. Human rights organizations quote much higher figures, although these seem to be exaggerated. Middle East Watch estimates the total losses at between 70,000 and 100,000, and Amnesty International estimates them at more than 100,000. Based on forensic evidence and government documents seized by the Kurds in 1991, Middle East Watch and Physicians for Human Rights estimate that up to 4,000 villages were destroyed. The evidence suggests that government efforts to eliminate Kurdish communities were widespread, systematically planned, and ruthlessly implemented.

UN forensics experts are still examining forensic information obtained from mass grave sites in northern Iraq. These graves contain the remains of hundreds of persons presumed killed in the Anfal Campaign. According to opposition sources, a new mass grave, containing up to 250 bodies, was found in April 1994 near the Al-Sharqat district of Mosul. Sources said that the graves were discovered when heavy rains washed away the covering soil.[97] The UN has also uncovered information regarding the Barzani arrests of 1983, in which security forces detained thousands of relatives and tribesmen of the late Kurdish nationalist hero Mustapha Barzani. None of these detainees were ever seen again. The Special Rapporteur observed in February, 1994 that the regime's treatment of the Barzani tribe might constitute violations of the Genocide Convention.[98]

In a February, 1994 report, the Special Rapporteur concluded that the Iraqi regime's policies against the Kurds—in particular, against the Barzani tribe—"raise issues of crimes against humanity and violations of the 1948 Genocide Convention." He noted "significant similarities" between the Iraqi regime's past policies toward the Kurds and its current policies toward Shi'ite civilians living in the southern marshes. The Special Rapporteur recommended that "further consideration be given to establish the facts and responsibilities associated with atrocities committed against the Kurdish population."[99]

The Special Rapporteur of the UN reported that he held the Iraqi regime responsible for "serious breaches" of the 1925 Geneva Protocol on the Prohibition of the Use in War of Asphyxiating, Poisonous or other

Gases, and of Bacteriological Methods of Warfare. He observed that these breaches may demonstrate the Iraqi regime liable under the 1948 Genocide Convention. According to the Special Rapporteur, the activities of the Iraqi regime during the Anfal Campaign "left virtually no Iraqi Kurd untouched." He concluded that "serious violations of human rights committed against the civilian population of Iraq both in times of war and peace involve crimes against humanity committed under and pursuant to the commands of Saddam Hussein and Ali Hassan al-Majid."[100]

The Special Rapporteur has also reported that the widows, daughters, and mothers of the Kurdish victims of the Anfal Campaign are economically dependent on their relatives or villages, because they may not inherit the property or assets of their missing family members. Other reports suggest that economic destitution has forced many women into prostitution.

The Kurdish Uprising

The success of Operation Anfal led the Kurds to change their strategy between the end of the Iran-Iraq War and Iraq's invasion of Kuwait. Along with a number of smaller Kurdish groups, the PUK and KDP formed the Iraq Kurdistan Front (IKF) to better coordinate their activities and their demands in dealing with Baghdad. The IKF stressed autonomy for Kurdistan within the framework of a democratic Iraq as their goal. The Kurds did this in order to allay the suspicions of other Iraqi opposition groups with whom they were seeking closer relations for the first time.

The IKF moved cautiously once Iraq invaded Kuwait. It was aware that international pressure against Iraq was mounting, but it also realized Saddam would have no qualms about using troops and chemical weapons against any rebellion.[101] This fear declined with time. Iraq had to deploy many of its forces south, leaving only three combat effective divisions in the north and a host of other ill-motivated infantry units. The *parastin*—Kurdish intelligence—became aware that the morale of the remaining units was low and that the number of deserters and of reservists who failed to report for duty was high. By the time the Coalition air assault began, Kurdish sources reported that about half of the Kurdish auxiliaries in the Iraqi Army units based in Kurdistan had deserted with their arms.[102] The IKF also initiated discreet contacts with disgruntled elements of the pro-government Kurdish irregulars, the *Fursan*, but derogatively known as the *jash*, or Saddam's donkeys.[103]

As a result, the IKF took the risk of creating new uprisings after Saddam's shattering defeat in the Gulf War, and these uprisings soon became a mass movement. The Kurds had little military strength, but they were able to take advantage of the paralysis of the Iraqi Army and disorganization within the security services. In fact, the various pro-government tribal militias often persuaded the Iraqi Army forces in Kurdistan to leave virtually without a fight.

As a result, the Kurdish revolt rapidly expanded to cover most of the rural and urban areas with large Kurdish populations. Kurdish civilians, including professionals, intellectuals, and tens of thousands of *Fursan* units deserted the government side and joined the IKF.[104] Neither Barzani or Talibani were fully prepared for the scale and success of this uprising, but they acted quickly to take control of an inchoate rebellious mass and engaged their veteran Peshmerga guerrilla units in attacks on government forces. Within days, the guerrillas took over several major urban centers, including the oil-center of Kirkuk. In the process they defeated ill-motivated troops who surrendered in droves, joined the guerrillas, or fled south. Large quantities of heavy military equipment including several tanks, helicopters, anti-aircraft guns, artillery and mortars, fell to the rebels. By mid-March, the IKF declared that 75% of Kurdistan was in their hands.

This Kurdish success, however, only occurred because of the power vacuum created by the Gulf war. Saddam began to redeploy regular army units into the Kurdish area when he realized the UN would allow Iraqi troops and helicopters to operate against the various uprisings. The UN did try to protect the Kurds by forcing Iraq to observe the terms of the cease-fire and to stop using its combat aircraft against the Kurds. US F-15s shot down one Iraqi Air Force Su-22 on March 20, and then another Su-22 on March 22. By limiting itself to attacks on Iraqi fixed wing fighters, however, the UN allowed Iraqi ground troops to attack the poorly armed and organized Kurds and they met little resistance.

The Kurdish force did not stand a chance against the veterans of the Republican Guards and better regular army units brought up from the south, whose residual combat capabilities in the wake of Desert Storm they had underestimated. As Talibani stated, "we did not realize that the Republican Guards were still in such good shape."[105] There was little military coordination between PUK and KDP forces. Both groups had little time after their victory to organize an effective defense, and the guerrillas suffered from acute command and control problems. Kurdish leaders had a great deal of experience in handling small groups of guerrillas, but not the vastly increased order of battle which they had in March 1991. Army deserters did not have the time to train the guerrillas in the use of captured heavy weaponry. When the guerrillas found themselves in possession of many urban centers, they were overwhelmed by the twin tasks of providing military leadership and emergency civilian administration. They lacked any experience in urban war and fled into the mountains, hoping to spare the urban population. Even in the mountains, they found they could not wage war because large tracts of land had been depopulated with no hiding places or access to food from a sympathetic populace and which had been turned into free-fire zones for the Iraqi military.[106]

Iraqi forces retook Karbala in the south and Kirkuk in the north by March 28.[107] Iraq surrounded cities like Irbil and Kirkuk in the north with army units, and sent brigades to control all key routes and bridges. It used artillery, multiple rocket launchers, and armed helicopters against any pockets of resistance. The Kurdish guerrilla forces had only a negligible capability to resist, and the Kurdish uprising collapsed like a burst bubble. The long history of Iraqi attacks on Kurdish civilians and Iraq's use of chemical weapons against Kurdish civilians led many Kurds to flee as the Iraqi troops advanced, and one million to 1.5 million Kurdish refugees had moved near to, or across the Turkish and Iranian borders.[108]

This flood of refugees and the risk a new Kurdish enclave would be created in Turkey, led the US and UN to intervene to protect the Kurds and prevent the establishment of refugee camps and enclaves along the border areas. On April 5, the UN passed Resolution 688, condemning and demanding an end to Iraqi repression of the Kurds. On April 7, the US had begun air drops of food. On April 8, Secretary of State Baker promised the Kurds food, shelter, and medicine, and President Bush established an airlift called Operation Provide Comfort.

Repeated Iraqi attacks on the Kurds then led the US to declare that Iraq would not be permitted to fly aircraft north of the 36th parallel beginning April 10, 1991. The UN also put heavy pressure on the Iraqi government to halt its attacks, and allow US and allied troops to move into northern Iraq to help set up refugee camps in the border area. As a result, Iraq signed an agreement on April 18, 1991, that effectively created a UN controlled and demilitarized security zone for the Kurds, a much larger Kurdish controlled enclave, and a no-fly zone north of the 36th parallel. The agreement allowed the UN to station 500 security guards to protect relief operations, and was to remain in force until December 31, 1991, with the possibility of renewal.

The UN forces in Iraq reached a peak in early May of about 15,000 men, including French, Dutch, Italian, British, and US elements, but there was no political support for the kind of long-term occupation that would have been needed to secure Kurdish autonomy. UN forces left Dahuk on June 15, and the number of troops in Iraq dropped to around 8,000. The UN force was cut to 5,100 on June 23. The UN withdrew all forces from Iraq on July 15, 1991, although it initially left a small brigade in southern Turkey.

Iraq at first responded by testing the UN's resolve. Some 200 Iraqi policemen attacked Kurds in the town of Zakhu on April 21. Iraqi anti-aircraft artillery fired on a US reconnaissance jet patrolling northern Iraq on May 7. Iraqi troops fired on British troops in Dahuk on May 13, and fired on a US army helicopter on May 14. They clashed with Kurdish demonstrators on June 5, and stole 7 tons of relief supplies for the Kurds on June 6. When it became apparent that these tactics did little more than provoke the UN, Saddam used different tactics. He entered into pro-longed negotiations with the Kurds that allowed him to delay any settle-ment until UN forces had left northern Iraq, and the long standing ten-sions between Turkey and the Kurds had reduced support to the Kurds from the north.

The Kurds were willing to negotiate with Saddam because of the sheer scale of their defeat and their belief that the mass exodus of Kurdistan's population to Turkey and Iran was leading to the depopulation of north-ern Iraq and playing into Saddam's hands. These negotiations between Saddam and the Kurds broke down in the fall of 1991, however, and this led the Kurds to create their own autonomous zone within the area that was still under UN protection. Saddam, in turn, established a military line between the evolving Kurdish autonomous entity, withdrew Iraqi civil and administrative personnel from the region, and instituted a strin-gent economic blockade.

Iraq deployed some 16–18 divisions and 150,000–175,000 troops from its I Corps and V Corps and its Republican Guards. It deployed these forces along the southern edge of the Kurdish controlled zone from Dahuk through Al Kuwayr, Irbil, and Kifri to Khanaqin. Iraqi forces reg-ularly shelled Kurdish positions near the border of the Turkish security zone, and often harassed the UN relief and inspection effort.

The Search for Kurdish Unity

The Kurds in the security zone responded by holding elections in May 1992. They established a 'regional' legislative assembly in Irbil, formed a "cabinet" and began economic reconstruction. Although these elections produced a deadlock between the two main Iraqi Kurdish factions— Patriotic Union of Kurdistan and Kurdish Democratic Party—both par-ties agreed to set up a joint "government" with its capital at Irbil. They agreed to create a 105 man assembly, which met for the first time on July 4, 1992. The assembly had 50 delegates each for the Barzani and Talabani factions, and 5 seats for Kurdish Christians. This agreement effectively allowed the Kurdish enclave an autonomous area, although the Iraqi government called the new Kurdish leadership "illegal" and labeled its fifteen ministers as "bandits."

These Kurdish efforts initially had some success. In the months that followed, the Kurdish government was able to function, in spite of occasional feuding between the PUK and KDP. The Kurds gradually built up an economy based partly on agriculture and smuggling between Turkey and Iraq. They began to repair some of the damage to nearly 2,000 of the 4,000 Kurdish towns and villages that the government had attacked in the region since 1970. They maintained a tenuous relationship with Turkey by agreeing to keep Turkish Kurds on their territory from launching military operations against Turkey, and to provide data on those Turkish Kurds who use their territory as a sanctuary. The Iraqi Kurds even fought several clashes with Turkish Kurds in the PKK.

Much of this progress collapsed in mid-1994, however, when a new power struggle began between the Barzani and Talabani factions. This struggle soon degenerated into a continuing state of civil war punctuated by cease-fires that are never honored for more than a few days or weeks at most. The heads of the two rival Kurdish organizations, the KDP and PUK, were deeply divided over basic policy issues and the goals the Kurdish movement should seek in dealing with the Iraqi government. Masoud Barzani, the leader of the KDP and son of the famous Kurdish leader Mullah Mustafa Barzani (who fought both Iran and Iraq), has often stressed the difficulties in trying to get rid of Saddam Hussein. As he told journalists in early 1992:[109]

> I can tell you one thing. Ousting Saddam will not be an easy task. We have fought him for 20 years in which we lost over 150,000 martyrs, and he did not fall. There is no Iraqi opposition which can topple him. He remained in power after a bitter eight-year war with Iran, and stayed in control in Baghdad after the multinational war that was waged against him. The reality is that he is still in power. The difficulty of removing him lies in the fact that he has a powerful army and party, security and intelligence organizations that have remained effectively intact and under his control.

Given this background, it is not surprising that Barzani never ruled out a resumption of autonomy talks with Baghdad. Barzani's pragmatism was also reflected in his analysis of the Kurdish elections for a local assembly in April 1992. Barzani stressed repeatedly that Iraqi law called for the formation of a Kurdish legislature in accordance with autonomy granted the Kurds, but which was never implemented by Baghdad. Furthermore, he said the elections were aimed at filling the "administrative vacuum" prevailing in the north now that Baghdad was prevented from exercising its authority in the north. In contrast, Jalal Talibani saw Barzani as a rival for leadership of the Kurdish movement, and has called for full autonomy or independence. He also leads Kurds with religious, geographic, and linguistic backgrounds that are often different from the Kurds that follow Barzani.

In November 1994, the two Kurdish parties signed yet another cease-fire but this collapsed amid mutual recriminations of bad faith. The PUK accused the KDP guerrillas of pocketing customs duties levied on trucks crossing the Iraqi-Turkish border instead of giving it to the Kurdish regional administration at Irbil. The KDP in turn accused the PUK of corruption and of exploiting their control of the "finance ministry" and of the "central bank" for their own particularistic ends.

Meanwhile, Iraq continued to probe the Kurdish enclave and to try to find new vulnerabilities. The US Government announced in April 1994 that it had information indicating that the government of Iraq had offered monetary "bounties" to anyone who assassinates United Nations and other international relief workers.[110] Iraq also continued to attack humanitarian relief efforts in northern Iraq. In 1994, two aid workers were killed in an execution-style shooting. Several other international workers involved in the relief effort, including six United Nations guards, were injured in bombing and shooting attacks in March and April. On March 27, 1994, Iraqi security forces permitted a crowd in Mosul to attack and damage a UN helicopter attempting to airlift wounded guards to safety. Two Swedish journalists were injured in Aqrah on March 14 when a bomb exploded under their automobile.[111]

The uncertain protection provided by Coalition forces only existed within the security zone. The Iraqi regime pursued its discriminatory resettlement policies outside the Kurdish security zone, including demolition of villages and forced relocations of Kurds, Turkomans, and other minorities. Middle East Watch reported that the Iraqi regime was continuing to force Kurdish residents of Mosul to move to Kurdish-controlled areas in the north, although the Iraqi regime directed most of its resettlement efforts in 1994 and 1995 at the Shi'ite residents of the southern marshes.

Near Civil War Within the Kurdish Enclave

During 1994–1996, the Barzani and Talabani factions continued to fight a low-level civil war within the enclave in spite of repeated US and other attempts to mediate between the two sides. Amnesty International (AI) reported in 1994 and 1995 that three Kurdish political parties in northern Iraq—the Patriotic Union of Kurdistan, the Kurdish Democratic Party, and the Islamic Party in Iraqi Kurdistan—had committed scores of deliberate and arbitrary killings against each other in 1993. Many press reports indicate that the Kurdish parties continued to commit arbitrary killings against each other in 1994.[112]

Violent fighting resumed over control of Irbil, the Kurdish regional capital, in mid-December 1994 and continued into January 1995. This fighting took place because Barzani's headquarters in Salahaddin overlooks Irbil, and Talabani attempted to put Irbil under PUK control. During the conflict, Talibani's forces made some headway and launched a major attack on the strategic road linking Irbil to the Iranian border, but Barzani and the KDP counterattacked.

It was only after Saddam made an offer of mediation that both sides decided to accept a cease-fire brokered by the Iraqi National Congress (INC) on January 12, 1995, which called for a return to the status-quo ante in Irbil (i.e., cessation of fighting) and a separation of the forces of the two rivals by the INC militia.[113]

A tenuous cease-fire between the KDP and the PUK held until April 1995, although minor clashes between the KDP and PUK took place. This cease-fire broke down, however, when Turkish forces advanced into Iraq. The Turkish attack on the PKK triggered new fighting between the two factions, and this resurgence in intra-Kurdish fighting virtually paralyzed the Kurdish regional Parliament in Irbil, whose mandate was due to expire in early June, 1995. The expiration of the mandate was supposed to be followed by fresh elections which the weary Kurdish population hoped would end the cycle of violence. However, the situation became so bad that the USA made a major effort to persuade the Iraqi Kurds to put an end to their fighting—an effort reinforced by US desire to block an Iranian mediation effort.

The KDP and PUK held talks in Drogheda, Ireland, under the auspices of the United States, from August 9–11, 1995. These talks were aimed at resolving the deep-seated differences between the two leading Kurdish groups. The Iraqi National Congress participated and Turkey sent observers. The two parties then appeared to agree to a cease-fire. They agreed to cease media attacks against one another, to respect the rights of the others followers, and to release detainees captured during hostilities between them.

This agreement had the following terms:

- The KDP and PUK will strive to finalize a permanent peace.
- Irbil, the administrative center of the Kurdish zone which has seen its share of violence during intra-Kurd strife will be demilitarized. Forces of both sides in the environs of the city will be reduced.
- A neutral commission to mediate between the KDP and PUK will be formed under the auspices of the INC.
- No later than 48 hours following the certified demilitarization of Irbil, customs and revenues collected by the parties will be deposited in banks to be used in the name of the regional authority.
- The elected regional parliament will be reconvened within 48 hours of the demilitarization of Irbil.

- Following the restoration of order the regional authority will work with all possible haste to fashion a new broad-based administration for the area.
- All of this will be carried out within the framework of the recognition of the legitimacy of Iraq's territorial integrity and will take into consideration the legitimate security interests of Turkey.

Despite the hopes for this accord, fighting between the KDP and PUK intensified at the end of August 1995. In fact, the Drogheda agreement seems to have unraveled before it was even implemented. Three days of intensive talks between the PUK and KDP failed to resolve their differences. They could not agree on how to demilitarize Irbil nor reach an understanding on how to split the lucrative customs revenues that come from the tolls levied on the transport of goods from Turkey into northern Iraq and which represent an income of up to $150,000 a day. The cease-fire did sharply reduce the number of civilian casualties and the use of torture on those detained or arrested.

The Iraqi government maintained its internal embargo on the three governates in northern Iraq, populated primarily by Kurds and other ethnic minorities. The embargo prevented the entry of food, medicine, and other humanitarian supplies to that area. After 1993, the embargo also included electric power cut-offs in specific areas, causing the disruption of water and sanitation systems and interference with the delivery of food and fuel. The United Nations and donor governments installed temporary generators to alleviate the crisis. In July 1995 the Government restored some electricity and allowed increased fuel trade with the northern governate of Dohuk, but the fuel trade was again severely restricted with the onset of winter. Even now, the entire northern area remains subject to the threat of future cut-offs.

The Kurdish situation also deteriorated steadily in mid-1995 when fierce clashes began to take place between PKK guerrillas and KDP Peshmerga units in the areas of Zakho, Sarsank and Badinan. It is not clear what the PKK intended to achieve by the sudden escalation of guerrilla activity, although the consensus of opinion was that its chief, Abdullah Ocalan, was bent on torpedoing the Drogheda agreement between the KDP and PUK. Reconciliation between these two parties would go a long way towards facilitating their control over northern Iraq, and ultimately control over the movement of the PKK guerrillas.

Indeed, in an August 29, 1995 interview with *Al Hayat*, a leading Arab newspaper, Ocalan admitted that he was trying to sabotage the KDP-PUK truce, and then called upon Iraq's Kurds to "rip up" their agreement with Turkey to keep the PKK out of northern Iraq, adding that "we want to drag them"—meaning the Turkish military—"into northern Iraq in order to destroy them there."[114] Regional press reports also added that Ocalan's strategy was designed to please both Syria and Iran, traditionally supporters of the PKK, who were fearful of increased Turkish and US influence in the disintegrating situation in northern Iraq. Furthermore, both Barzani and Talibani visited Tehran, thus signaling their desire to avoid alarming and alienating the Islamic Republic which has repeatedly made its displeasure with the events in Kurdistan widely known.

The situation continued to deteriorate in late 1995 and early 1996, although the US made repeated efforts to prevent this. The US dispatched in mid-November a delegation headed by the director of Northern Gulf Affairs at the State Department, Robert Deutch, to northern Iraq to pressure the two Kurdish parties to resolve their differences. Unfortunately, the new effort failed and resulted in a de facto division of Kurdistan into two conflicting zones of influence. At the same time, tension grew between Washington and some members of the Iraq National Council over the growing role of Iran in the area and US support of new opposition groups backed by Jordan. The presence of units of the Iranian-supported Badr Brigade in Northern Iraq also displeased the US, as did the growth of Iranian influence in the PUK. At the same time, Syria has encouraged PKK attacks on the KDP, and Iran has negotiated with the PUK.

The Impact of Turkey's War Against the PKK

The Iraqi Kurdish problem had increasingly been complicated by Turkey's problems with its large Kurdish minority, which inhabits south-eastern Anatolia, bordering Iraq and Iran. The Turks are fighting a particularly violent Kurdish separatist organization, the Kurdish Workers Party—known as the PKK—which has been waging a guerrilla campaign since the 1980s. This war intensified after a bloody uprising during Kurdish new year celebrations in March 1992. As a result, thousands of Turkish troops supported by warplanes and helicopter gunships moved into northern Iraq in October, 1992 to attack the camps of the PKK guerrillas.

Ironically, this Turkish move came only two weeks after Ankara persuaded the Iraqi Kurdish guerrillas of the PUK and the KDP to begin attacking PKK sanctuaries in northern Iraq. The Iraqi Kurdish leadership felt it had no choice but to comply because the Turkish government controlled the flow of critical supplies to the Iraqi Kurdish enclave As a result, the Turkish operation had considerable success. The PKK was unprepared and because the two Iraqi Kurdish groups cooperated with the Turks and with one another to push the PKK guerrillas into a Turkish blocking force which routed them.

In 1994 and 1995, many Kurdish civilians near the Turkish border were caught in new raids by Turkish military forces on suspected hideouts of the extremist Kurdistan Workers' Party (PKK). On August 8, 1994, Turkish planes bombed a camp near Zakho containing 10,000 Kurdish refugees from Turkey. Although the refugees suffered no casualties, 10 Iraqi guards were reported killed and 7 wounded. The Turkish Government claimed that PKK terrorists were hiding in the camps. On August 23, 1994, Turkish planes attacking a PKK camp in Zele bombed the nearby village of Bidewan, wounding 7 Iraqi Kurdish civilians. On September 8, Turkish planes again bombed the large concentration of Turkish refugees near Zakho. No injuries were reported, but several tents were destroyed.[115]

The Turkish-PKK conflict worsened during 1995. Early in the year, PKK guerrillas increased the tempo of their attacks against Turkey. Turkey responded with its most massive incursion to date into northern Iraq. It launched Operation Steel, with at least 30,000 troops, in late March, 1995. The Turkish operation, which lasted 8 weeks, resulted in some civilian deaths. There were also several unconfirmed reports of civilian casualties during four smaller Turkish operations into northern Iraq during 1995. However, Turkish Government authorities stressed that the operation sought to avoid civilian casualties.

The new Turkish operation was at best a limited military success. The Turks had telegraphed their intentions for weeks. They had made statements that they were going to deal with the PKK "terrorists," and their build-up for the incursion was visible to all who crossed the border between Iraq and Turkey. As a result, the PKK simply withdrew from its exposed forward positions.[116] The lack of Turkish success was evident in the fact that Turkish forces returned for a week in July with quick-reaction mountain commando forces who moved to engage the PKK along a 70-km front, extending 40 kilometers deep into northern Iraq.

Later in 1995, elements of the PKK increased their activity in northern Iraq and reportedly killed local residents in an effort to control a territorial base. These groups sometimes attacked civilians, foreign relief workers, and journalists. Several kidnappings took place during fighting among Kurdish factions in northern Iraq. In September supporters of the PKK took several Iraqi and foreign relief workers hostage at a Turkish Kurd refugee camp. All were eventually released unharmed. The PKK committed numerous abuses against civilians in northern Iraq. In September the PKK seized eight UN relief workers as hostages at the Atrush refugee camp. The camp has been suspected as a base for

PKK terrorist activities. The relief workers were released unharmed after 3 days, and the UNHCR successfully consolidated the Atrush Refugee Camp facilities in late 1995 to enhance protection for the re- fugees there.

There are still approximately 14,000 Turkish Kurds in Northern Iraq who have fled civil strife in southeastern Turkey. The UNHCR is treat- ing these displaced persons as refugees until it reaches an official determination on their status. However, many support the PKK and there is no way to tell when Turkey will attack again into Northern Iraq, or how long the Iraqi Kurds can obtain Turkish tolerance and sup- port. What is clear is that any Iraqi Kurdish effort to build ties with the PKK would alienate Turkey and quite possibly lead to at least tacit mil- itary cooperation between Turkey and Iraq in suppressing all Kurdish resistance.

The Kurdish Crisis of August–September 1996

The economic and military situation of the Iraqi Kurds became steadily grimmer, and more was involved than the fighting between Kurdish fac- tions. Many foreign relief workers were forced to leave southern Iraq in August, 1992, and Iraq continued to harass relief workers in the north.[117] The Iraqi regime maintained an ongoing internal embargo of the north, which included necessities such as food, medicine, and other humanitar- ian supplies. After August 1993, the embargo also included massive elec- tric power cut-offs in specific areas, causing the spoilage of medicines, breakdowns in local water-purification systems, and the loss of certain hospital services. A disaster was averted only by the prompt action of the United Nations and donor governments, who imported and installed temporary generators to alleviate the crisis. Additional electricity cut-offs were imposed in August 1994. This embargo of the north not only impacted on Kurds, but various other minorities such as Turkomans, who also live in the area.[118]

"Kurdistan" became an economic shambles as a result of civil conflict and the internal embargo imposed by Baghdad which cut off the North from the markets it had depended on in the rest of the country. The region had no viable commercial or financial infrastructure. The only source of revenue came from the import/export customs duties imposed on goods coming from Turkey on their way south to Mosul and the rest of the country or on Iraqi oil smuggled out via KDP-controlled territory. But this revenue was more of a bane than a benefit to Kurdistan, because the KDP and the PUK fought and quarreled over control of the "customs" points and the division of the revenue. Nor have the Kurds used this rev- enue to build up their administrative infrastructure. This helped reinforce the semi-permanent state of militarization on the Kurdish enclave because the largest and best equipped militias belonged to the KDP and PUK and represented the only major source of large-scale employment for young Kurdish men.

In spite of this, the Kurds had little military protection. In early 1996, the KDP claimed to have 25,000 troops, and a militia of 30,000 additional men. These forces were armed with light artillery, multiple rocket launchers, mortars, small arms, and SA-7s. The PUK claimed to have 12,000 troops, plus 6,000 men in support forces. It was armed with some T-54 and T-55 tanks, about 450 mortars, 106 mm recoilless rifles, 200 light anti-aircraft guns, and SA-7s. The Socialist Party of Kurdistan claimed to have another 500 men. These divided KDP and PUK forces, however, were better prepared to fight each other than Iraq. They gave the Kurds some defensive capability, but their training was minimal, and they lacked adequate heavy weapons, significant numbers of modern anti-tank, and light anti-aircraft weapons. They were as vulnerable half a decade after Iraqi forces have driven them into Turkey as they were when efforts at Kurdish unity began.

Virtually all UN ground troops had left the Kurdish security zone when the UN agreement with Turkey that allowed it to station troops on Turkish soil expired on September 30, 1991. The only remaining force was a small military mission which patrols the Kurdish security zone, although the US keeps some military personnel in Turkey, and Turkey still provides basing for British, French, and US aircraft to provide security for the Kurds.

Iraqi ground forces remained deployed in positions around Irbil, Chamchamal, Kifri, and Sulaymaniyah. While the deployments currently seem designed to contain the Kurds, they could be altered to invade Kurdish territory. Iraqi-sponsored political killings and terrorist actions have been frequent, and have been directed against civilians, foreign relief workers, journalists, and opposition leaders. The State Department reports that German journalist Lissy Schmidt and her Kurdish bodyguard, Aziz Kader Faraj, were shot to death on April 3, 1994, in an ambush near Suleymaniya. Kurdish authorities later arrested several suspects who reportedly confessed that the Iraqi regime had paid them to commit the murders.[119]

Kurdish villages along the Iranian border were subjected to recurrent shelling by the Iranian military, as well as to sporadic Iranian military incursions into Iraqi territory. For example, Iranian artillery shelled civilian areas in As-Sulaymaniyah province the night of April 17-18, 1996. Iranian forces were also reportedly involved in fighting between the two main Iraqi Kurdish parties in August and December, 1994, and in 1995.[120] The Iraqi government also maintained its efforts to "Arabize" certain areas, such as the urban centers of Kirkuk and Mosul, through the forced movement of local residents from their homes and villages and their replacement by Arabs from outside the area. Further, land mines continued to kill or maim Kurdish civilians. Many of these mines were laid during the Iraq-Iraq War, but the army failed to clear them. The mines appear to have been haphazardly planted in civilian areas. The Special Rapporteur has repeatedly reminded the Iraqi regime of its obligations under the Land Mines Protocol, to which Iraq is a party, to protect civilians from the effects of mines.[121]

Further, Iran became a major player in northern Iraq during the course of 1996. Iran used its support of Talibani and the PUK to supplant the US—which focused on negotiating between the PUK and KDP—and put pressure on Turkey as well by supporting Kurdish elements which had ties to the PKK. Iran also made periodic claims that it was the only country able to bring peace to northern Iraq, and 2000 Iranian Revolutionary Guards entered Iraq in support of the PUK against Barzani's KDP in August 1996. While the Revolutionary Guards withdrew after helping the PUK win a series of victories against the KDP, there were many reports that the Iranians still maintained intelligence and security personnel within PUK territory. Baghdad saw this Iranian presence as a national security threat, and Saddam issued claims that Iranian troops were deployed 50 kilometers inside Iraq.[122]

At the end of August 1996, Iraq reacted with force. It sent elements of three Republican Guards divisions—variously estimated as a force of 25,000 to 60,000 men with artillery and over 100 heavy armored vehicles—into the Kurdish safe haven. Iraq was able to take advantage of the fact that its forces were already positioned within 15 kilometers of the Kurdish regional capital of Arbil, and it had an extensive intelligence network in the city and throughout the Kurdish region. Further, this time Iraq acted at the invitation of Masu'd Barzani of the KDP and was able to claim it was allied to a main Kurdish faction against Kurdish separatists and Iran.

The firepower provided by the Iraqi Republican Guards divisions allowed the KDP to drive the PUK out of the Kurdish regional capital of Arbil by August 31. This, in turn, allowed Iraqi security forces to sweep into the city and drive out, arrest, or execute hundreds of members of the various opposition elements headquartered in the area. The CIA team aiding these opposition groups also fled, along with most foreign relief workers and many of their Kurdish helpers. Within days, Saddam had shattered all of the opposition groups with a foothold on Iraqi soil.

The KDP then repeatedly outmaneuvered a panicked PUK, and tricked it into defending the wrong strong points. By early September, the KDP had pushed the remnants of the PUK to the Iranian border, raising fears that the Iranians might intervene to prevent a mass exodus of Kurdish refugees into Iran. Instead, Iran sealed its border to most refugees and fired artillery salvoes in the direction of the Iraqi border to discourage the KDP from pursuing the PUK too closely.

By the end of the first week of September, the Baghdad-KDP alliance controlled all of northern Iraq. Saddam Hussein then moved to declare a broad amnesty in Iraqi Kurdistan and lifted the five year embargo. This was done partly to allay Kurdish fears that Saddam would seek indiscriminate revenge. On the other hand, Saddam had good reason to fear a mass Kurdish exodus which would focus world attention on the plight of the Kurds and would invite greater Turkish and Iranian action in order to prevent an influx of Kurdish refugees. He also had good reason to fear that Barzani might turn upon the Iraqis if Baghdad was too harsh.[123]

The Iraqi government had a number of reasons to act. Baghdad had been biding its time in order to re-establish its control over the north. Iraqi officials had made repeatedly clear that the 'abnormal conditions' in the northern part of the homeland (i.e., absence of central government authority) was temporary. As a result, Baghdad was ready to exploit any relatively cost-free opportunity to re-establish central authority in the north, and this situation presented itself in late August when the KDP came under pressure from the PUK and Iran. This opened the door for Baghdad to intervene in favor of the KDP, whose leadership the Iraqi government favored over that of the 'traitorous' PUK.

Baghdad was in a good position to make such a move. The PUK had no air support and heavy land weapons. The "no fly" zone in the north had as little impact on Iraqi ground operations against the wretchedly led PUK militia as the "no fly" zone in the south had on such operations against the Shi'ite. Many of Iraq's land forces remained positioned along the edge of the exclusion zone, and its reorganized Republican Guards risked little in supporting the KDP militia against PUK forces that were poorly trained, led, and equipped.

Baghdad was also able to exploit the fact it had contributed greatly to the decline in the security and stability of Iraqi Kurdistan by implementing an internal embargo against the safe-haven, and by selectively encouraging the rivalry between the KDP and PUK. The Ba'ath regime had always made it clear that it favored Masu'd Barzani and the KDP. Unlike Talibani, it never attacked Barzani as a 'closet separatist.' Baghdad did wage a long and vitriolic propaganda campaign against Talibani as a 'political chameleon,' and as a danger to Iraq because he solicited help from Iraq's main ideological and regional enemies: Syria, Iran, and Israel. At the same time, however, the Ba'ath regime had quietly encouraged Barzani to negotiate—an encouragement that drew a growing response because Barzani's father had been betrayed by Iran and the US, because of Barzani's belief that the Kurds of Iraq would eventually have to reach a deal with Baghdad, and because of his six-year-long experience with the failures of the Iraqi opposition.

As a result, Saddam Hussein gained the opportunity to move into the northern part of Iraq where he could defeat the strongest advocate of Kurdish separatism, force opposition elements like the Iraqi National Congress to leave their one sanctuary in Iraq, and secure the Iraqi-Turkish oil pipeline that runs west of the city of Arbil into Turkey and on to the Turkish port of Ceyhan on the Mediterranean.

Sending Iraqi troops to aid the KDP did mean risking a further delay in the implementation of UN Resolution 986, which allowed Iraq to sell $2 billion worth of oil over a period of six months. At the same time, there were compensating advantages. There was little prospect of a prolonged delay and the intervention meant Saddam would greatly reduce the ability of Kurdish separatists to exploit the Kurdish share of the oil revenues and that Baghdad could try to secure the pipeline which was critical to Iraq's agreement to sell oil for food and which was to carry some 500,000 bpd once the agreement went into operation.[124]

Iraqi officials feared the pipeline would become yet another target of the rivalry between the KDP and PUK. From Baghdad's perspective, there was a serious risk that the PUK would try and sabotage the pipeline with Iranian help. Moreover, the Turkish Kurdish movement, the PKK, could choose to target the oil pipeline in order to deny Turkey transit fees and revenue. This raised the prospect of Turkey moving force into northern Iraq and establishing a secure corridor for the pipeline in Iraqi Kurdistan. While Baghdad wanted the pipeline to be secure, its best option would be to have the KDP guarantee the security of the pipeline discreetly backed up by Iraqi firepower. This, however, meant that a combination of Iraqi and KDP forces had to secure Arbil and push the PUK forces as far away as possible from transportation and oil routes to Turkey.

Iraq also moved its forces into the north as a warning to both Turkey and Iran to cease their interference in northern Iraq. The government newspaper, *Al Jamhouriya*, published an editorial following the victory of the government and KDP forces which stated that, "All countries in the region concerned with the Kurdish issue have to extract correct lessons from the latest events in northern Iraq. The roots of this lesson are that meddling in Iraqi affairs is a dangerous game that will eventually burn the hand of those playing it."[125]

Baghdad had reason for its concern. Both Turkey and Iran had moved to exploit the strategic vacuum in northern Iraq during the past six years. Much to Baghdad's discomfort, Turkish forces had moved into northern Iraq almost every year since 1991: by Baghdad's count the Turks had undertaken "90 military incursions" into Iraq since 1991. As a result, the Iraqi regime's alliance with Barzani offered the prospect of bringing stability to the north and "terminat[ing] the power vacuum" in the north.[126]

Baghdad may also have concluded that it could take advantage of the emergence of Turkey's new Islamic government under Prime Minister Necmettin Erbakan. During the past two years, Turkey had already made it clear that it would like to see Baghdad re-establish central control over the north, and the new government actively sought to establish closer political and economic relations with Baghdad. Moreover, the new government had made its discomfort with Operation Provide Comfort well known. Indeed, Iraq claimed that Turkey had given it assurances that US planes based in Incirlik would not be allowed to strike at Iraqi forces in the north.[127]

The Iraqi assault into the northern "no fly" zone did have a price. Although the Iraqi forces withdrew from the safe haven after helping the KDP gain control of Arbil, the US retaliated against Iraq's so-called act of "aggression" on September 2 and 3 by launching 44 cruise missiles against targets in the southern part of Iraq. These strikes took place against targets in the south, rather than in the north where the Iraqi action was taking place, and against targets like air defense installations and command centers rather than against army ground forces such as armor and artillery units. Even then, the action was largely symbolic. Less than half of the cruise missiles hit close enough to the target and only about 15%–20% appeared to hit close enough to do real damage. The cruise missiles did little damage to hardened Iraqi command centers, and the damage they did to radars and surface-to-air missile sites was easily repairable.

More significantly, the US extended the southern air exclusion or "no fly" zone some 70 miles further north from the 32nd parallel to the 33rd parallel. The 33rd parallel is only 30 miles south of Baghdad, and the new territory in the expanded "no fly" zone included an important air force training area, two major air bases, and three critical military installations which the Iraqis had used as staging points in the past for moving military units south in the direction of Saudi Arabia and Kuwait.[128]

Saddam and the Ba'ath leadership initially responded by calling for confrontation and by defiantly declaring that Iraq would not recognize the air exclusion zone, and he ordered his air defense units to fire at British, French, and American planes patrolling the no-fly zone. Iraq launched several fighters in the area where US forces were flying, fired a few surface-to-air missiles and used its radars to illuminate US fighters, delayed moving its aircraft out of the new "no fly" zone until the last minute, and stepped up its resistance to UNSCOM inspections.

These Iraqi actions might well have led to further and much more devastating US action against Iraq. The US dispatched F-117 Stealth fighters to Kuwait and F-16s to Bahrain, deployed a second carrier battle group to the Gulf, and rushed several thousand troops to Kuwait. It prepared the media and its allies for a far larger series of air and missile strikes.

This time, however, Baghdad backed down from further confrontation and declared that it would not shoot at Coalition planes. It emphasized its charges that the US was violating international law and again taking measures to hurt the Iraqi people. Iraqi forces withdrew from Kurdish areas and Iraq said nothing when Barzani met with Turkish and US leaders and sought outside aid. In fact, Iraq's Deputy Prime Minister Tariq Aziz declared on October 8, 1996, that Baghdad had issued an open invitation to Barzani to conduct talks on Kurdish self rule: "The call for dialogue exists. ... It does not need to be announced. It is known ... Iraq is willing for dialogue."

The US actions were controversial. US President Bill Clinton justified the initial US military action on September 2 and 3 by declaring that "our missiles sent the following message to Saddam Hussein: when you abuse your own people and threaten your neighbors you must pay a price ... our policy is equally clear. When our interest in the security of our friends and allies is threatened, we will act with force if necessary."[129]

The US also declared that it was empowered to act in accordance with UN Resolution 688 which calls upon Saddam Hussein to cease oppressing his own people. According to US State Department spokesman Nicholas Burns: "the US has clear authority (to act) under resolution 688. Certainly considering the understandings we had with Iraq and the international community in the spring of 1991—that set up Operation Provide Comfort—we had clear authority to take the military action that we did. There was never a question about that."[130]

However, Resolution 688 did not provide for any enforcement mechanism, and it was unclear that military action could be taken under Chapter 7 of the UN to prevent Iraq from oppressing its own people. It also was not clear that Iraq was oppressing its people when it moved into the north at the direct request of one of the Kurdish factions. France, in particular, believed the American position to be of doubtful legality. The French Foreign Ministry stated that, "we do not see that the UN resolutions are called into question by the Iraqi intervention, especially since there was a written request by one of the main Kurdish movements. Iraq is acting entirely on its own soil."

The situation became even more complex once it became clear the US was not really retaliating for Saddam Hussein's actions in the north or attempting to protect the Kurds, but was rather using the crisis to expand its control over Iraqi military forces in the south which was the focus of US strategic interests. US Secretary of Defense William Perry made the US position clear on September 4, when he declared that "our vital national interests in Iraq are in the south, not in the north." He added that "our objectives, first of all, are protecting our vital strategic interest, which means protecting our friends and allies in the region—Israel, Jordan, Kuwait, and Saudi Arabia. Secondly, keeping the free flow of oil from the Gulf."[131]

As a result, Saddam was able to exploit this situation by backing away from further confrontation, and could claim a limited victory in terms of domestic and regional politics. Domestically, Saddam showed that he was still in control of his military despite the political turmoil brought on by the attempted assassination and abortive coup in the summer of 1996. He improved his political position by destroying the infrastructure of the Iraqi National Congress opposition in the north. This constituted a grave setback for the Iraqi opposition, many of whose members were captured or executed and whose US-supplied infrastructure and equipment was captured or destroyed. Moreover, Saddam's security forces had already penetrated another opposition group, the Iraqi National Accord and had unraveled its operations inside Iraq. This may be a reason why the coup attempt of July 1996 which was instigated by the INA failed.

Only a few countries backed the US retaliatory strikes against Iraq. Many countries had already re-established diplomatic relations with Iraq, and were eagerly awaiting the re-integration of Iraq into the world economy. Furthermore, Iraq was not committing any act of aggression against a neighbor but was asserting control over its sovereign territory. As a result, many countries thought that Iraq had a sovereign right to reassert control over its own territory. These countries included three powers on the UN Security Council—France, China, and Russia. Most Arab and Arab Gulf powers also defended Iraq's right to act within its own territory. Only a relatively few countries—such as Britain, Denmark, Germany, Japan, Israel, Kuwait, and the Netherlands—supported the US retaliatory strikes against Iraq.

While France did not directly criticize the US military action, neither China nor Russia felt the need for such restraint. Following the second cruise missile attacks on Iraq, the Chinese Foreign Ministry stated that "we feel deep regret and want to express our strong displeasure at the missile attack once again by the US against Iraq ... the all too frequent use of force against a sovereign state has not only seriously violated the relevant norms of international law and worsened the situation and tensions in the region concerned but will also give rise to grave consequences."[132] China's strident protest came in the wake of tensions in Sino-American bilateral relations in the past year over trade issues, Taiwan, and human rights concerns, coupled with a Chinese perception that the US is acting in a too 'hegemonic' and 'bullying' manner in global affairs.

Russia's Foreign Minister, Yevgeni Primakov, who has had long-standing relations with the Iraqi leadership, was similarly scathing in his criticism of the US military action. He accused the Clinton Administration of engaging in a cheap pre-electoral stunt, of playing with fire and contributing to a decline in the stability of the Persian Gulf region, of acting in a hegemonic manner, and of conveniently ignoring the UN Security Council as a forum for solving the crisis.[133]

Except for Israel and Kuwait, no regional power lent its support to the US retaliatory action. The reticence of Turkey and Saudi Arabia, both of which host US military forces, was noteworthy. Turkey did allow the US to enforce the "no fly" zone in the North and to evacuate some Kurds through Turkey. It would not, however, allow US warplanes to use Incirlik to strike at targets in Iraq in support of the US effort to punish Saddam for his thrust into the Kurdish enclave, and never endorsed the US cruise missile attacks. The Turkish Ambassador, Nuzhet Kandemir, urged the US not to escalate further: "We hope that these kinds of punitive strikes, particularly dispro-portionate ones, will not take place."[134] Turkey was loath to see a lingering crisis that would destroy all short-term prospects of Iraqi oil flowing into Turkey allowing Ankara to reap financial rewards after losing $25 billion in trade with Iraq over the past seven years.

Saudi Arabia also distanced itself from the US. It became clear that Saudi Arabia did not support the US attack. Prince Sultan, the Saudi Defense Minister, declared that if the US had asked for permission to use planes from Saudi bases, such a request would not have been looked upon favorably. This Saudi Arabian discomfort was understandable both in for-eign policy terms and in light of events in the Kingdom. Saudi Arabia not only did not sympathize with the Kurds, it strongly opposed any move-ment that might divide an Arab-ruled Iraq and which favored Iran. Saudi strategic interests lay in emphasizing territorial integrity and Arab rule. Domestically, King Fahd was in poor health, Saudi Arabia had growing economic woes, and the government faced increased reformist and fun-damentalist pressures. The Saudi monarchy did not wish to be criticized for allowing the US to strike Iraq when Iraq was acting within its own bor-ders, or for any further action that hurt the Iraqi people without hurting the regime—particularly when the Saudis had no guarantee that any action would lead to Saddam's ouster.

The only areas where Saddam did not gain some advantage from his actions were the extension of the "no fly" zone in the south, the fact that he took minor losses as a result of US cruise missile strikes, and in ensur-ing there would be no further Turkish incursions in Iraq. Shortly after the KDP-Iraqi victory over the PUK, Turkey declared it was setting up a secu-rity cordon up to six miles deep into Iraq along its border with Iraq in order to limit the freedom of movement of the PKK guerrillas and Turkey, then launched another series of raids into northern Iraq.

Turkey's action was widely viewed as its version of the Israeli security cordon in Lebanon, and the US tacit acceptance of Turkey's plan became another cause for alarm in Iraq and Arab countries. It also further divided the US from some of its Arab allies as the Turkish zone was seen as a legit-imizing cover for another non-Arab power to establish semi-permanent control over Arab land. Iraq's angry response came in the shape of a statement by Iraqi presidential adviser Hamed Yousef Hammadi who said in mid-September: "There are new facts in the north of Iraq. That area is no longer free for all."[135]

The Role of the Kurds in a "Centrist" or "Peripheral" Strategy

It is, however, far from clear how events will play out over the coming years. The Iraqi Kurds are a deeply divided people. Barzani and Saddam can turn on each other, Talibani can come back, Iran can raise the stakes, Turkey can intervene, and new Kurdish leaders can come to power. What is clear in the near term is that the KDP and PUK have shown that they are more effective in fighting each other than Saddam's forces, and that they can play little role in any outside strategy for dealing with Iraq. Quite aside from their weakness and feuding, they do not command the support of any other major ethnic group in Iraq, Iran, or Turkey, and Iraq's Arab neighbors all oppose the creation of a Kurdish state or permanent Kurdish enclave.

Kurdish separatists have little support from most Iraqi Sunnis and Shi'ites. What some Kurds see as Kurdish patriotism, many Sunni and Shi'ite Iraqis see as treason. Both the KDP and PUK have often taken money and support from Iran in the past. Elements of both factions fought on Iran's side in the Iran-Iraq War, after taking money from Baghdad to fight against Iran for Iraq. Both factions have occasionally made demands for control of territory and oil resources that other Iraqis feel would divide or weaken the country. The Iraqi government's abuse of the Kurds is also not a one-way street. The KDP and PUK have tortured their opponents, attacked Iraqi civilians, and executed prisoners.

It is also important to note that the KDP, PUK, and other separatist Kurds in the security zone scarcely speak for all Kurds or the Turkomans. In spite of Iraqi atrocities against the Kurds, many Iraqi Kurds remain assimilated into Iraq's economy and political structure and do not support Kurdish separatism. Other Kurdish groups have been alienated by the feuding and tribal primitivism of the KDP and PUK, and groups like the National Turkoman Front now see no reason to ally themselves with the Kurds. They confine their efforts to protecting Turkoman areas.

The West needs to accept the fact that the fighting in September 1996 is yet another demonstration that "Kurds have no friends" in the region—including their fellow Kurds. The other Arab states do not support Kurdish ambitions. Iran sees the Iraqi Kurds only a tool to use against the regime in Baghdad, and Turkey fears them. Turkey has not been able to defeat its own radical Kurds, and is increasingly reluctant to support any version of Operation Provide Comfort that is not under its direct control. The Turkish government has problems with both nationalists and Islamists who oppose the presence of foreign forces on Turkish soil, and Iraq's acceptance of UN Security Council Resolution 986 means that Turkey stands to obtain substantial revenues from pipeline fees and food sales to Iraq.

At the same time, if the West does not seek to negotiate on the Kurds behalf, no one will. Nearly four million Kurds in northern Iraq live without any real security other than the UN, and any Western strategy for dealing with Iraq must seek to offer the Kurds a reasonable degree of protection as a precondition for lifting sanctions and better relations.

Such protection—and even limited autonomy—may still be negotiable with a "centrist" regime in Iraq, provided that it is based on a clear recognition that Baghdad is in ultimate control, and that the Kurds do not make unrealistic demands for control of mixed cities like Mosul or for direct control of Iraq's northern oil fields and the revenues from these fields. The Iraqi people have not been educated or propagandized to see Iraqi Kurds as a whole as enemies or traitors. The Kurdish uprising after the war is understandable to many Iraqi Sunnis within the military, and reasonable terms for autonomy have been negotiated in the past—only to fail because of a combination of Kurdish and Iraqi government extremism.

At the same time, any agreement will be difficult to reach, and could prove to be impossible to negotiate as long the Kurdish factions continue to fight each other and/or as long as Saddam is in power. It may also only be obtainable if it is enforced with the threat of far more serious Western military actions than occurred in September 1996 and control of the $50 million a month in food and medicine that the Kurds will receive as a result of Iraq's agreement to UN Security Council Resolution 986. The Iraqi people may not hate the Kurds, but the Iraqis in the security services and some elements of the armed forces have been taught to deal with the Kurds who support Barzani and Talabani as traitors and criminals for more than a quarter of a century, and recent events have almost certainly reinforced that feeling.

It is all too possible that the current cycle of violence and counter-violence will take years to end, even if the Kurds and the central government do negotiate a serious autonomy agreement and Saddam Hussein should fall. Any authoritarian or "centrist" regime that replaces him will draw on many of the same men who have used extreme violence against the Kurds in the past. This could confront the West with another major civil war between the Iraqi regime and the Kurds under conditions where Turkish and Arab support for any intervention on the Kurds' behalf is likely to decline steadily with time.

The West has already found it is almost impossible to protect the Kurds with Operation Provide Comfort in place. The US is also likely to find it steadily more difficult to act in the future, particularly if Iraq continues to ally itself with a Kurdish faction, acts slowly and incrementally, avoids an overt invasion of the Kurdish enclave, offers some form of autonomy, and keeps claiming provocation. Much will depend on Turkey and whether it feels it can best resolve its problems with its own Kurds by supporting the West or dealing with the Iraqi central government. If the Kurds fail to achieve unity and negotiates with the Iraqi central government on realistic terms, the West may ultimately have to write them off as an unsalvageable strategic liability. Suicidal behavior is suicidal behavior. Iraq's Kurds may well continue to divide among themselves no matter how badly they are treated or how seriously they are threatened. If they do, there is little point in the West pursuing the issue. There is little reason for Western strategic involvement with a people who are determined to be their own worst enemy.

Iraq's Crisis with Its Shi'ites

Any strategy towards Iraq must recognize that Saddam Hussein's regime has equally serious problems with its Shi'ites that are likely to continue to exist as long as Iraq is ruled by a Sunni elite. Iraq's Shi'ites are a majority in a country ruled by a Sunni and clan-oriented minority, and their loyalty to any regime in Baghdad is affected by their political and socioeconomic marginalization. As has been noted earlier, the US Central Intelligence Agency (CIA) estimates that 60% to 65% of Iraq's total population is Shi'ite versus 32% to 37% Sunni.[136] These percentages, however, disguise the fact that some Shi'ites identify themselves primarily in religious terms while many do not. There are also major differences within Iraq's Shi'ites over relations with Iran, loyalty to the central government, and the desire for some form of separatism or separate political identity.

The Historical Background to Current Tensions

Once again, forces affecting a future strategy towards Iraq can only be understood with some historical background. The late 1940s and 1950s were a time of profound socioeconomic and political change and ferment for the Iraqi Shi'ites. Rapid urbanization and the exposure to secular education and thus modern political ideas contributed to a decline in the political power and spiritual influence of the Shi'ite theological schools and of the clergy in forming the values of the community.

Ironically, communism made considerable headway in the Shi'ite south during the 1950s and early 1960s, as people were attracted to its militant calls for socioeconomic and political justice and to its hostility to Sunni-dominated Arab nationalist ideas so prevalent in the "center." The Iraqi Communist Party (ICP) won many adherents in the south, including the children of the local Shi'ite clergy, the ulema. As early as 1953 a leading religious scholar, Ayatollah Kashif al-Gita, expressed his unease at the inroads that Marxism had made among the Shi'ites, while in 1960 two other Ayatollahs, Muhsin al-Hakim and Murtada al-Yasin, issued a *fatwa* or religious ruling condemning membership in the ICP.

In 1959, the Shi'ite ulema took more decisive action. Leading clerics founded the *Jami'yat al al-Ulema al-Din* (Association of Religious Ulema), which later became the *Al-Da'awah al-Islamiyah* (Party of the Islamic Call). In its early years Al-Da'awah remained a very clandestine party but was very active in recruiting from among the ulema of the theological schools, Shi'ite intellectuals in universities, and the Shi'ite petit bourgeoisie in towns such as Diwaniyah, Karbala, and Basra. While not specifically anti-Sunni, Al-Da'awah was against secularism, nationalism, and communism. Al-Da'awah received a boost when the massacre of ICP cadre by the first Ba'ath regime left politically active Shi'ites with no organized political voice.

Relations between the Shi'ite community and the Ba'athists deteriorated further after the second Ba'ath regime seized power in 1968. Many factors lay behind the growing antagonism, which exploded into full fury in the late 1970s. First, there was no senior Shi'ite representation in the new regime. Second, the Ba'ath's militant secularism hit the Shi'ite ulema more than any other group in Iraqi society. Determined to break once and for all the power of the clerics in the Shi'ite community—a task which the ICP had failed in—and fearful of their independence, the regime closed down religious schools, imposed censorship on religious publications, and proceeded to deliberately harass the ulema. From the mid-1970s the regime was jolted into the realization that Shi'ite discontent was a major problem when serious disturbances occurred in 1974 and 1977 between Shi'ites and the security services. The later disturbance was widespread in which Shi'ites were heard calling for the overthrow of the regime. Saddam wrote a tract *Nashra fi al-Din wa al-Turath* (A Glance at Religion and Culture) in which he sternly warned against the mixing of religion and politics in Iraq society.

During the 1970s, Iraq's efforts to manipulate the Iranian Shi'ite opponents of the Shah backfired at a number of different levels. Allowing Iranian opposition leaders like the Ayatollah Khomeini into Iraq ultimately backfired. As unrest against the Shah exploded into a full-fledged revolution, Iraq acceded to an Iranian request to expel Ayatollah Khomeini. Many of Iraq's more religious Shi'ites became even more hostile to the Ba'ath regime, and several leading families formed alliances with Iranian Shi'ite factions.

More militant groups such as Al-Da'awah, the *Munazamat al-Amal al-Islami* (Organization for Islamic Action) founded in 1975 in Karbala, and the *Mujahedin* founded in 1979 emboldened by the Islamic Revolution in Iran, initiated a campaign of terror and assassinations in Iraq between 1970–1980. As a result, the Iraqi regime restricted pilgrimages and religious activities in Iran, imprisoned or exiled many Iraqi Shi'ites, and established a network of overlapping security forces in every major Shi'ite city, town, and shrine.[137]

Iraq's Shi'ites and the Iran-Iraq War

These actions by the Ba'ath government did not mean that Iraq's Shi'ites were pro-Iranian or Iran's natural allies. Despite strident Iranian propaganda during the Iran-Iraq War, which urged the Shi'ites to rise up against the Ba'ath regime, most Shi'ites supported the government or remained quiescent. Most of the government's troops during eight years of war were Shi'ite and they often fought with great courage and dedication. Iraq's Shi'ites supported the regime for several reasons. Many were Iraqi nationalists and Arabs first, and Shi'ites second. Others saw Saddam as the lesser of two evils or benefited from state grants and aid. Still others were deterred by Iraq's effective security and intelligence services.

Iraq's Shi'ites could hardly fail to notice the Islamic Republic's failures: political upheavals, large-scale executions, failure to implement socioeconomic programs, and international isolation. Above all, Iran's fanatical insistence on continuing the war after 1982 alienated Iraqi Shi'ites who saw Iran prolonging an irrational war that was killing Iraqi Shi'ite soldiers and was devastating the south with its artillery.[138]

At the same time, powerful Shi'ite families—like the Hakim family—did oppose the Ba'ath regime during the war with Iran. Some of these families had ties to Iran—at least in terms of obtaining Iranian funds, military training and equipment, and the use of facilities on Iranian soil. There are some important differences in clerical politics and ritual between Iranian and Iraqi Shi'ites, but there are also Iraqi Shi'ite clergy who strongly oppose the secular regime in Baghdad and who have close ties to the Iranian clergy. In November 1982, the head of the Hakim family, Mohammed Baqir al-Hakim announced the formation of *the Majlis al-A'la lil Thawra al-islamiyah fi al-'Iraq* (Supreme Assembly for the Islamic Revolution of Iraq). Describing itself as an umbrella organization of all Muslim peoples opposing the Ba'ath regime in Iraq, it set up military units to fight alongside the Iranians and to take advantage of the turn of the tide of war in favor of Iran that occurred in mid-1982.

Further, Shi'ite loyalty to Iraq during the Iran-Iraq War did not mean loyalty to Saddam Hussein and the Ba'ath elite. Even before the Shi'ite uprisings following the Gulf War, Shi'ite cities and areas often received fewer benefits from the central government, and made more sacrifices during wartime. The Ba'ath acted as a pervasive police state, sometimes flaunting Shi'ite custom in activities like the search of mosques, arrests of clerics, limits on religious celebrations, and escorting foreign visitors into Shi'ite sanctuaries. Educational, military, and political opportunities were somewhat restricted for Shi'ites, although mainly in politically sensitive areas. All of these problems grew much worse after the Gulf War, partly because of Saddam's ruthless response to the Shi'ite uprisings that took place immediately after the war, and partly because Saddam has reacted to UN sanctions in ways that favor the Sunni "center" over the Shi'ite south.

The Shi'ite Uprisings After the Gulf War

The Gulf War triggered a very different response from Iraq's Shi'ites than the Iran-Iraq War. A large-scale Shi'ite uprising against Saddam's regime took place in southern Iraq immediately after the Gulf War. There were several reasons why this *intifada* broke out:

- First, there was a political and military vacuum in the south following the Iraqi defeat in Desert Storm: the transportation and communications networks had been devastated by the coalition bombings, the porous border regions with Iran were unguarded, and the military and security services were in disarray. The vacuum and turmoil were fully exploited by the rebels. In contrast, even during the most desperate years of the Iran-Iraq war at times when it seemed that the southern front might collapse, there was no political or military vacuum in the south. The army retained its cohesion and the regime continued to exercise tight control over the south.
- Second, the "social contract" between the populace and the government, wherein the former had tacitly accepted an authoritarian system in return for economic development and material largesse, had unraveled in the south. The region had suffered most of the devastation during two wars, and the male population which provided the Iraqi Army with the bulk of its regular infantry units had seen a disproportionate number of sons, husbands, fathers, and brothers killed or wounded in two ultimately worthless military enterprises. Well before the August 1990 crisis, the bankrupt Iraqi government no longer had the economic or financial wherewithal to satisfy the material needs of the population.
- Third, because many Shi'ites felt they were marginalized in a political system from which they collectively felt excluded from genuine power sharing with their Sunni compatriots, it is not surprising that there existed a deep-seated sense of grievance.
- Finally, the uprisings initially were anti-regime and had none of the character of "treason" that uprisings would have had at the time of the Iran-Iraq War. A sense of loyalty towards Iraq no longer meant

support of Saddam's regime—despite the governments past efforts to equate loyalty to Iraq with loyalty to the Ba'athist regime.

The uprisings began when defeated and disgruntled infantry soldiers streamed back into Basra from the front, bringing back with them harrowing tales of defeat at the hands of a superior foe and mismanagement of the war by their own government. These troops and sympathetic Shi'ites launched attacks against government installations including security, party and popular army buildings. Ba'ath party cadre and security officials, most of whom were Shi'ite, who did not flee or go into hiding were hunted down and murdered. Within days, the revolt had spread to major cities including the holy cities of Karbala and Najaf, as well as the towns of Diwaniya, Al-Hillah, Al Kut, and Al Amarah and Mahmudiya. There was bitter fighting in the area around Basra and Az Zubayr.

The revolt spread because the government initially failed to react effectively to the Shi'ite uprisings, because it was unsure of the Coalition reaction, because many of its forces were maldeployed or still suffering from the shock of the war, and because it only had to deal with easily manageable Shi'ite disturbances since the mid-1970s. It was stunned by the extent and ferocity of the rebellion, which was explained as the failure of "politically confused and weak people" to rise above their sectarian tendencies and it immediately blamed Iran. In August 1991, the Iraqi Prime Minister stated that the "moving force (behind the uprising in the south) was foreign," meaning Iranian.

The rebellion benefited from two other factors. One was the Coalition presence in southern Iraq. This initially inhibited the regime's use of the Iraqi army, and the Coalition made it clear that Iraqi use of fixed wing aircraft or chemical weapons against the rebels would not be tolerated. Second, despite disclaimers to the contrary, Iran allowed the Supreme Assembly of the Islamic Revolution (SAIRI) to infiltrate elements of the Iraqi Shi'ite forces it had built up in Iran into Iraq to help the rebels. These included elements of the Tawabin and Badr brigades,—a 5,000–7,000 man force of exiled Iraqi Shi'ites under the leadership of Mohammad Bakr al-Hakim.

Nevertheless, the uprisings failed to take root and spread. This was partly because the initial uprisings were an explosion of pent-up rage and revenge, characterized by an orgy of looting and destruction without any sustaining organization or ideological vision. It was also a result of the fact that when the uprisings did begin to take on more organized form, they were led by Shi'ite religious leaders and infiltrators from Iran. They acquired an ideological hue which proved disastrous. Many rebel leaders raised the green banner of Islam, portraits of Ayatollah Khomeini, and Mohammed Bakr al-Hakim, the head of the Tehran-based Shi'ite opposition group, the Supreme Assembly for the Islamic Revolution in Iraq. They also called for an Islamic state in Iraq.

This focus on Shi'ite Islamic extremism alienated secular and nationalist Iraqi Shi'ites, most opposition groups outside Iraq, and the members of the UN coalition. It also produced a viscerally hostile reaction of the regime's elite, the Sunni Arabs, and many members of the Shi'ite middle class. For these secular Iraqis, the idea of an Iranian-supported Islamist regime coming to power was a horrifying vision. Furthermore, the atrocities committed against government officials were seen as a portent of the bloodshed to come if the rebels were to prevail.

The rebels soon paid the price. As in the north, the military vacuum in the south proved temporary. The Iraqi government fought back with its best-trained and most loyal units, the Republican Guards, and made liberal use of helicopter gunships in the towns where the rebels were holed up. A large number of hapless civilians caught up in the crossfire fled into the marshy zone, the coalition-controlled areas, or even into Iran itself. The tide turned in the government's favor when Basra and Karbala were secured on March 12 and 17, 1991.

On March 18, 1991, Baghdad declared the rebellion over and accused a horde of "rancorous traitors" and foreign governments of having instigated it. This announcement was somewhat premature. Between March 20–29, disturbances took in the Shi'ite quarters in Baghdad, including Medinat al-Thawra, Shu'la, and Karrada al-Sharqiyah. These disturbances were dealt with by Iraqi main force divisions, however, and were quickly contained. Iraqi forces fully secured Karbala in the south by March 28.[139]

The limited number of regular Iraqi Army units that went over to the Shi'ite side could not fight as an organized combat force, or sustain themselves in combat. The Badr Brigade took heavy casualties and had to withdraw to Iran. Anti-regime Shi'ites never succeeded in creating a separate enclave. Iraqi forces drove some 70,000 Shi'ites across the border into Iran, killed and imprisoned many others, and trapped still others in the extensive marsh areas in the south.[140] Most of the Shi'ite areas quickly returned to central government control, and the remaining Shi'ite rebels were captured, fled to Iran, or fled into the nearly 6,000 square miles of marshes formed at the mouth of the Tigris-Euphrates and east of Amarah, Nasiriyah, and Basra.[141]

There is no way to know how many Iraqi Shi'ites died during this fighting. The Iraqi regime did not permit international visitors into many areas, and forensics experts have not been able to investigate grave sites. The UN Special Rapporteur did report in 1994, however, that he continued to receive accounts of mass graves in southern Iraq. Observers believe these graves contain the remains of many persons killed following the civil uprising of March 1991.

The UN attempted to provide humanitarian relief for the refugees, but the situation was different from the Kurdish crisis in the north. There was never a separate Shi'ite enclave, and Iraqi troops and security forces, as well as Shi'ites loyal to Saddam, were always mixed with the general Shi'ite population. While the UN did set up a humanitarian relief center in the marsh area in July 1991, the Iraqi government organized protest riots and made effective operation impossible. On July 14, 1991, it told the UN personnel manning the center to leave, and cut the Shi'ites off from any aid.

The Fighting in the Marshes

The plight of the Shi'ites who fled into the marsh areas in Southern Iraq grew steadily worse during the fall and winter of 1991, and the spring of 1992. Once the central government recovered full control over the rest of the populated areas in the south, the Iraqi government began a military campaign to root out the Shi'ites in the marshes. In April 1992, 36,000–40,000 Iraqi troops were sent into the area, and Iraqi forces built new roads and fire bases in the swamps. They began to drain the marshes selectively, and fought their way through an area with thousands of small islets, 10 foot reeds, and date palm thickets.

These Iraqi forces were hunting a maximum of 10,000–20,000 deserters and Shi'ites in the marshes, and these opposition forces were so poorly organized that only 3,000–6,000 could be classified as guerrillas. Even these forces were only equipped with small arms and flat bottom boats, although they had limited Iranian and Iraqi exile support. The rebels that did survive only did so because of the cover provided by the marshes, the difficulty government forces had in locating and containing them, and because of the support of the largely Shi'ite and anti-government Marsh Arabs.

Even this protection began to vanish in June 1992. Iraqi Minister of Defense Major General Hassan al-Majid—the same military leader who supervised the Anfal Campaign—took over direction of the fighting in the marshes. Reports soon appeared that Iraq had moved additional elements of its 3rd and 4th Corps above Basra and east of Amarah. These reports indicated that by August 1992, the Iraqi regime had deployed 5–6 divisions against the Shi'ites, including Republican Guard units, and was using artillery, attack helicopters, and fixed wing fighters. Saddam Hussein's son Qusay and his half brother Wathban al-Ibrahimi were also said to play a role in overseeing the security operations in the south.[142]

Strict security measures were taken. Curfews were enforced in most areas, Shi'ite religious schools and printing houses were closed, and some Shi'ite assemblies were forbidden. Government arrests were reported to have reduced the clergy in the Shi'ite holy city of Najaf from 8,000 before the Iran-Iraq War to less than 800 by the end of 1991, and driven most of the remaining members of key opposition groups like Al Dawa al Islamiya (Islamic Call) and the Supreme Assembly for the Islamic Revolution in Iraq (SAIRI) out of the country.

The government also began a major effort to relocate the Marsh Arabs (Ma'dan) out of the marshes and expand its plans to drain the entire marsh area with a 350-mile network of canals. According to Middle East Watch and US Government researchers, Iraqi government files captured by Kurdish rebels in 1991 contain a military plan for the destruction of the marshes and the people living there. The plan appears to have been approved at the highest levels of the Iraqi regime.[143]

These Iraqi government attacks became so intense that on August 11, 1992, Britain, France, and the US issued a formal warning to Iraq to cease violating Security Council Resolution 688, which called for an end to all internal repression in the country.[144] However, these warnings had little practical effect. The same was true of the establishment of a "no-fly zone" over southern Iraq. This no fly zone deterred aerial attacks on the marsh dwellers, but did not prevent artillery attacks or the military's large-scale burning operations.[145] Iraqi troops continued their sweeps into the marshes, and the government continued to drain the marshes and relocate the Marsh Arabs (Ma'dan) in a ruthless effort to deprive the remaining Shi'ites of cover.

Since 1992, Iraq has had some 7–8 divisions, and 75,000 troops, from its IV Corps, III Corps and Republican Guards deployed in the south. These forces have been spread out through the Shi'ite areas from Karbala and Al Kut in the north to An Nasiriyah and Az Zubayr in the south. In June 1996, there was one infantry division in Karbala and one in Al Kut. There were two infantry divisions west of An Nasiriyah, an armored division near Al Amarah, an infantry division near Qalatsalih, an armored division between Qalatsalish and Al Basrah, and a mechanized division near Al Basrah.[146]

The regime has used these forces to virtually destroy the traditional way of life of the marsh Arab Shi'ites. The Iraqi regime's burning, draining, and water-diversion projects created a continuing process of large-scale environmental destruction in the marshes. The army constructed canals, causeways, and earthen berms to divert water from the wetlands. Hundreds of square kilometers of marsh areas have been burned, imperiling the marshes' ecosystem.[147]

The Iraqi regime claimed that the drainage was part of a land reclamation plan to increase the acreage of arable land, spur agricultural production, and reduce salt pollution in the Tigris and Euphrates. However, the evidence of large-scale humanitarian and ecological destruction appears to belie this claim. Aerial and satellite photography the US Government made public in 1994 depicted the almost total destruction of the marshes. Moreover, the regime's diversion of supplies in the south limited the population's access to food, medicine, drinking water, and transportation.[148]

As the marshes dried, military units launched land-based attacks on villages. On March 4, 1994, the military began the largest search-and-destroy operation in the marshes in 2 years. The offensive included the razing of villages and burning operations concentrated in the triangle bounded by Nasiriyah, Al-Qurnah, and Basrah. The magnitude of this operation caused the inhabitants to flee in several directions: deeper into the marshes, to the outskirts of southern Iraqi cities, and to Iran.

In late June 1994, Iraqi military forces attacked several marsh villages in Nassiriya province. Sources said that army engineers burned the village of Al-Abra, containing about 80 homes, to the ground. After the operation, the army transported the village's inhabitants from the scene. In early July, the security forces stormed the villages of Al-Sajiya and Al-Majawid in Al-Chibaish district, near the main road leading into the marshes. Simultaneously, armor units supported by heavy artillery attacked the village of Al-Kheyout in the district of Al-Madina.[149]

The Iraqi military also conducted large-scale artillery bombardment in the Jindala area of the Al-Amarah marshes. Opposition sources said the bombardment destroyed several homes and injured several individuals. The military also attacked Al-Hashriya, Al-Wasdiya, and Al-Malha, and arrested some of their inhabitants. In September 1994, opposition sources reported that military forces used incendiary bombs and launched an armored attack against the area of Al-Seigel in the Al-Amarah marshes. The army later set fire to the entire area.[150]

The UN Special Rapporteur stated in his February 1994 report that the extent of violations against the marsh inhabitants "places the survival of this indigenous population in jeopardy," and noted the similarity between the Iraqi regime's "genocide-type operations" against the Kurds and its operations in southern Iraq. In August, he dispatched two of his assistants to the Iran-Iraq border to interview refugees fleeing the marshes. He reported in October 1994 that the refugees are generally in poor physical and psychological condition, having suffered extreme deprivation of food and medicine. He reiterated his "concern over the survival" of the marsh inhabitants "as a community."

These military operations caused serious civilian casualties in the marshes in 1994, and led to massive movements of Shi'ites out of the area. More than 10,000 refugees from the marshes fled to Iran, where they joined between 50,000 and 60,000 who had fled in previous years. Iraqi security forces relocated many of the inhabitants of the marshes that they detained during the course of military operations to Iraq's main southern cities. Many were later transferred to detention centers and prisons in central Iraq, primarily in Baghdad. Opposition sources reported in September 1994 that the Iraqi regime had relocated more than 300 families from the marshes to a detention area in Diwaniya province. The Iraqi authorities reportedly returned other families who had taken refuge in Baghdad to the province of Amara.[151]

According to the US State Department, large numbers of Shi'ite refugees from southern Iraq fled to Iran, particularly after the escalation in military activity in March 1994. It was difficult to estimate the number of persons displaced by these operations, due to the lack of international monitors in the area. However, in late 1994 the UN High Commissioner for Refugees (UNHCR) estimated that more than 10,000 refugees from the marshes were in camps in Iran.[152]

The fighting in the marshes continued during 1995, while the Iraqi armed forces conducted deliberate artillery and infantry attacks against civilians in the southern marshes. There was little real resistance, and many of the government attacks were designed to root out army deserters and displaced civilians. Nevertheless, the UN Special Rapporteur stated in November 1995 that he continued to receive reports of widespread disappearances, especially in southern Iraq. The Iraqi government did not reply to any of the more than 15,000 cases conveyed to it in 1994 and 1995 by the UN Working Group on Enforcement on Involuntary Disappearances.

Iraqi armed forces continued to conduct artillery attacks against Shi'ite civilians in the southern marshes in 1995 and early 1996. Throughout 1995, the Government announced that it would undertake several water-diversion and other projects, which continued the process of large-scale environmental destruction. The Government continues to claim that the drainage is part of a land reclamation plan to increase the acreage of arable land, spur agricultural production, and reduce salt pollution in the Tigris and Euphrates rivers. However, credible reports confirm the ongoing destruction of the marshes. The army continues to construct canals, causeways, and earthen berms to divert water from the wetlands. Hundreds of square kilometers have been burned in military operations, and the regime's diversion of supplies in the south has limited the population's access to food, medicine, drinking water, and transportation.

According to the Special Rapporteur, security forces continue to relocate Shi'ite inhabitants of the southern marshes to major southern cities. Many have been transferred to detention centers and prisons in central Iraq, primarily in Baghdad, or even to northern cities like Kirkuk as part of the Government's attempt to "Arabize" traditionally non-Arab areas. Large numbers of other Shi'ite refugees continue to flee from southern Iraq to Iran because of the military operations in southern Iraq. There is insufficient information to estimate the number of persons displaced by these operations, but the UN High Commissioner of Human Rights has estimated that as of September 1995 more than 200,000 of the 250,000 former inhabitants of the marshes had been driven from the area since 1991. In late 1995, the UNHCR estimated that approximately 12,000 refugees from the marshes were in refugee camps in Iran. Amar Appeal, a charitable organization operating several of the camps, placed the number at more than 35,000 refugees.

Broader Actions Against Iraq's Shi'ites

The regime's attacks on the Shi'ites in the marsh areas are only part of the story. The Iraqi authorities have arrested many other Shi'ites, and placed them in detention centers in central Iraq. Many witnesses who survived such detention have reported that some of their comrades were executed. The UN Special Rapporteur on Human Rights noted in his 1994 report that the Iraqi regime had expelled several "Faili," or Shi'ite, and Kurdish families in 1993. He reported in 1994 that the Iraqi regime may have expelled a total of more than one million persons in recent years suspected of being "Persian sympathizers." According to the Special Rapporteur, about 500,000 of these displaced persons went to live in Iran.

In 1995 and 1996, Iraqi security forces were still reported to be encamped in the shrine of Imam Ali at Al-Najaf, one of Shi'ite Islam's holiest sites, and using parts of it as an interrogation center. The former Shi'ite theological school in Al-Najaf, which the Iraqi regime closed following the 1991 uprising, was reported to be used as a public market. The Iraqi security forces continued to expel foreign Muslim clerics from Al-Najaf, under the pretext that the clerics' visas had expired.

The government kept up a ban on the Muslim call to prayer in certain cities; a ban on the broadcast of Shi'ite programs on government radio or television; a ban on the publication of Shi'ite books, including prayer books; a ban on funeral processions; and the prohibition of certain processions and public meetings commemorating Shi'ite holy days.

The UN Special Rapporteur and opposition sources reported that the regime continued to target the Shi'ite Muslim clergy and their supporters for arbitrary arrest and other abuses. The Government reportedly forced some Shi'ites of southern Iraq to move to northern areas near Kirkuk, purportedly to "Arabize" that historically Kurdish area. The Government also continued to detain Iraqi writers who criticized or questioned these government policies. In 1995, security forces detained Aziz Said Jasim, a political theorist, and Dhargham Hashim, a journalist who published an article on the marsh Arabs of southern Iraq.

According to the US State Department, the Iraqi regime continued to arrest, detain, torture, and kill Shi'ites who had nothing to do with the military resistance in the marsh area. In 1991 the Iraqi regime arrested the late Grand Ayatollah Abdul Qasim Al-Khoei, formerly the highest ranking Iraqi Shi'ite clergyman, and 108 of his associates. The Ayatollah died while under house arrest in Al-Najaf in 1992, and only two of the persons arrested with him can be accounted for. Moreover, the regime has continued to insist that its own appointee replace the late Grand Ayatollah Abul Qasim Al-Khoei although the Shi'ite religious establishment refuses to accept the Government's choice. The regime has continued to harass and threaten members of the late Ayatollah Al-Khoei's family.

The authorities have continued to subject the Shi'ite religious clergy, Shi'ite inhabitants of the southern marshes, and various ethnic minorities to searches without warrants. The regime routinely ignores the constitutional provisions safeguarding the confidentiality of mail, telegraph correspondence and telephone conversations.[153]

Like the government's relations with the Kurds, the regime's control over the Shi'ites depends on the continuing presence of massive military forces and ruthless repression by Iraq's security forces. The fighting from 1991 to 1995 has alienated many Shi'ites who were previously loyal to the regime. At the same time, it has helped to worsen relations between Iran and Iraq, and to create more tension and hatred between Sunnis and Shi'ites. The central government must now be more oppressive and authoritarian in dealing with the Shi'ites, and the armed forces are more likely to see any Shi'ite resistance as treason, pro-Iranian, anti-Arab, and pro-Western. Authoritarianism and xenophobia are likely to feed upon each other, and grow.

The Impact of the Shi'ites on Iraq's Future

This historical background has mixed implications for both a "peripheral" and a "centrist" strategy. It indicates that a significant number of Shi'ites want Saddam removed from power, and have good reason to want a more representative or Shi'ite-dominated regime. It indicates that many Shi'ites will not turn to Iran if they have any valid alternative.

At the same time, any "centrist" strategy towards Iraq must recognize that it is not the Shi'ites who are a minority, and that any strategy that ends in allowing a narrow Sunni elite to perpetuate power may lead Iraq's Shi'ites to align themselves with Iran. Tyranny has its price, and Saddam's method of treating the Shi'ites since 1991 has almost certainly alienated many Shi'ites that might otherwise have supported or tolerated a Sunni-dominated regime.

Iraq's Sunnis may pay the price tag for such repression in the future, even if they are unlikely to challenge Saddam or an immediate Sunni successor directly, and so may Western and Southern Gulf states that support them. The fact that a small group of Sunni clans and families now control virtually all the instruments of state power does not mean that the Sunnis can retain power indefinitely. Any Western or regional policy towards Iraq must account for the fact that the Sunni repression of Iraq's Shi'ites creates a second threat of civil conflict and a continuing potential for an Iraqi Shi'ite alliance with Iran.

At the same time, any efforts to execute a "peripheral strategy" must recognize that Iraq's Shi'ites have had little recent reason to admire or trust the West. Many seem to blame the West for failing to support them or protect them, and for a sanctions policy that has done them considerably more harm than Iraq's Sunnis. Iraq's Shi'ites may not admire Iran, but Saddam's repression may also have driven them to take more risks in accepting Iranian aid and supporting an Iranian regime. The odds seem to be against it, but there is a definite risk that any outside strategy that attempted to exploit Iraq's Shi'ites could backfire and end in strengthening Iran.

More generally, it is far from clear how any outside "peripheral strategy" that attempted to use the discontent among Iraq's Shi'ites could work in the near term. The Iraqi government now has virtually total control over the South, and has powerful security and military forces in every Shi'ite population center. It can control the flow of food, water, and utilities and virtually all lines of communication. The only outside access to the Shi'ite enclave is through the heavily defended borders of Iran and Kuwait. The more secular Shi'ite opposition groups outside Iraq have little real influence and power, and the Shi'ite religious opposition groups are largely pro-Iranian.

Implications for Western and Southern Gulf Strategy

This brief historical summary can give little flavor for the violence and hatred that has affected many aspects of the recent history of the sectarian and ethnic divisions in Iraq. There also is no way to supplement this analysis with any polls or other measures of how many Kurds and Shi'ites have been alienated by the regime's violence in putting down the Kurdish and Shi'ite revolts after the Gulf War and actions since 1991, and how many Kurds and Shi'ites feel they are part of the "center," rather than owe their primary loyalty to their ethnic and sectarian faction. There are deep divisions within Iraq's Kurds and Shi'ite Arabs, just as there are within its Sunni Arabs.

What is clear is that Iraq lacks strong secular opposition political movements that have any hope of uniting the country, and that its political movements are deeply divided along ethnic and religious lines. Any "centrist" strategy is likely to mean backing movements that will produce a Sunni dominated elite that can only rule through the further oppression of the Kurds and Shi'ites.

At the same time, there are both opportunities and risks in a "peripheral" strategy. The opportunity lies in the disaffection of a large part of Iraq's population with the "center." The risk lies in the fact that most of this opposition is Shi'ite or Kurdish, and is unlikely to acquire power peacefully in the face of opposition by a Sunni-dominated ruling elite, military, and security forces. In spite of the rhetoric of groups like the INC, there is no unity in the opposition movements, there is no opposition outside the "center" that can command nation-wide support, and a "peripheral" strategy threatens to create a civil war between Kurd, Shi'ite Arab, and Sunni Arab and possibly to divide the country.

This risk of division may be more important than the risk of violence. It would take an extraordinary combination of events for Iraq to avoid further civil violence, and Iraq is unlikely to resolve its sectarian and ethnic divisions peacefully—regardless of Western and Gulf policies. The choice is essentially one between continued repression by a Sunni elitist regime and broad civil violence within Iraq, and much depends on whether it will be possible to encourage forms of violence that will be both limited and progressive.

There are no good answers to this question. A strategy that considers relying on Iraq's Kurds must take account of the fact that the Kurds have no unity, few prospects of creating a stable separate identity or federal relationship with the "center," and a long history of seeking independence whenever they feel they have the opportunity. Saddam has made it all too clear that he can exploit the divisions between Kurdish factions. Even if the Kurds were unified, such a strategy would create a significant risk of civil war, and could easily spill over into other nations. There are Kurdish separatist factions in many of Iraq's neighbors. Kurds make up 9% of the population of Iran, 3% of the population of Syria, and 20% of the population of Turkey, and the "Kurdish issue" has led to low-level civil wars in Iran and Turkey.[154] Any movement towards Kurdish separatism in Iraq could trigger new fighting in Iran and more intense conflict in Turkey, and the Kurds already are political pawns in the regional feuds between Turkey, Syria, Iran, and Iraq.

The risk of Iraqi Shi'ites seeking a separate regional identity in a civil conflict seems less serious, although it cannot be disregarded. Iraq's Shi'ites may well want autonomy or a dominant role in a new Iraqi government, and many want a more religious regime, but there have been few signs that Iraq's Shi'ite Arabs want unity with Iran's Shi'ite Persians. There were many opportunities for Iraqi Shi'ite uprisings during the Iranian victories from 1982 to 1987, yet virtually no uprisings took place. Similarly, the Iraqi Shi'ite uprisings after the Gulf War were highly nationalistic in character, and showed little interest in unity with Iran. Nevertheless, any Iraqi Shi'ite dominated government or separate enclave might align itself with Iran to try to influence oil quotas and prices or establish a strategic position in the Gulf—creating the risk of at least a loose coalition between all or part of Iraq and Iran.

6

The "Periphery": Political Alienation and Abuses of Human Rights

It is tempting to focus on Iraq's strategic position and to ignore the violent and repressive nature of Iraq's present regime. The previous analysis has shown, however, that Iraqi authoritarianism is not typical of Third World states and does have an important impact on Western and Southern Gulf strategy. Saddam Hussein's regime enforces its ruthless control over Iraq's population through the systematic abuse of human rights, and the scale of these abuses has important implications for both a "centrist" and "peripheral" strategy. They raise the risks inherent in any strategy that attempts to accommodate Saddam or any other centrist regime that uses similar techniques to stay in power. At the same time, they increase the risks the country will divide, or plunge into civil war, as the result of a peripheral strategy.

The best available sources on Iraq's abuses of human rights seem to be the annual US State Department reports on Human Rights and the work of the UN Special Rapporteur on Human Rights. Both indicate that the Iraqi regime has a long history of executing its opponents, and nothing has changed since the Gulf War. There have been many credible reports since 1992 that the regime has executed persons involved in plotting against Saddam Hussein, including some members of Saddam's family and tribe. It is such reports that led the UN Special Rapporteur to state that the Iraqi regime's "aim of killing is a political one, with the objective of silencing dissent and suppressing opposition" in his October 1994 report to the UN General Assembly.

Killings and Torture

Many of the regime's abuses have already been described, but it is important to stress the systematic nature of its political violence. For example,

111

the UN Special Rapporteur lists several cases of politically-motivated killings during 1993 in his February 1994 report. These include mass executions of Shi'ite Arabs at the Al-Radwaniyah and Abu Ghraib prisons in central Iraq. According to the Special Rapporteur, some of those killed had been involved in the uprising against the Iraqi regime in the spring of 1991. In November 1993, the Special Rapporteur reported that the Iraqi regime had executed several Turkomans whose bodies were mutilated before being returned to their families. The Special Rapporteur also noted the frequent use of the death penalty for such political offenses as "insulting" the President or the Ba'ath Party. His February 1994 report summarizes several RCC decrees that stipulate the death penalty for political and civil offenses.

The killings of high-ranking civilian, military, and tribal leaders have already been described, but Iraq also regularly assassinates opposition leaders outside Iraq. On April 12, an opposition figure, Talib Suhayl Al-Tamimi, was assassinated in Beirut, Lebanon. Lebanese security officials arrested two Iraqi diplomats assigned to Beirut and charged them with the murder. The suspects admitted their guilt, but at the end of 1995, there was no movement toward a trial.[155]

The Iraqi regime arranges many "accidents" and "disappearances." For example, the State Department reports that in July 1994, Taki Al-Khoei (a prominent opponent to Saddam Hussein), and two other members of his family and their driver were killed under suspicious circumstances in an automobile crash in southern Iraq, near Al Najaf. It indicates that strong circumstantial evidence pointed to the regime's involvement. The regime had long targeted the Al-Khoei family for harassment and abuse, as the family is also renowned in Shi'ite circles for its religious leadership and outspoken condemnation of the regime's human rights record.[156]

In February 1994, the UN Special Rapporteur reported that he continued to receive "reports on the widespread phenomenon of disappearance." He stated that the UN Working Group on Enforcement on Involuntary Disappearances had conveyed to the Iraqi regime 10,570 names of disappeared persons and planned to convey another 5,000. The United Nations has documented 16,000 cases of missing persons.

The Iraqi regime has failed to return, or account for, a large number of Kuwaiti citizens and third-country nationals detained during the Iraqi occupation of Kuwait. It denies having any knowledge of the missing persons. UN Security Council Resolution 687 requires the Iraqi regime to "facilitate" the search for and the repatriation of those still missing. In his October report, the Special Rapporteur noted that the Iraqi regime's failure to account for the missing persons violates provisions of the various Geneva Conventions, to which Iraq is a party. Middle East Watch estimates that, apart from the tens of thousands of persons who have disappeared and are presumed dead, another 10,000 to 12,000 persons were being held without charge in prisons and detention centers.

Every Iraqi government has made use of torture, but such abuses became much more systematic following the fall of the monarchy and have grown even worse since Saddam Hussein's rise to power. Although the Iraqi regime is a party to international conventions against torture, and the Iraqi Constitution prohibits the practice, the US State Department reports that the security services routinely torture detainees. The UN Special Rapporteur continues to note the Iraqi regime's "systematic" use of physical and psychological torture. According to former detainees, torture techniques include electric shocks administered to the genitals and other sensitive areas, beatings, burnings with hot irons, suspension from ceiling fans, dripping acid on the skin, rape, breaking of limbs, denial of food and water, and threats to rape or otherwise harm relatives. The tormentors kill many torture victims and mutilate their bodies before delivering them to the victims' families.[157]

The US State Department reports that the Iraqi authorities introduced new forms of torture in September 1994, including the amputation of ears and the branding of foreheads for certain economic crimes and for desertion from the military. Large numbers of persons reportedly bled to death from such punishments. Opposition media reported that the regime's use of ear amputations sparked a large anti-regime demonstration in Mosul on September 8. Opposition media also reported that the authorities executed several doctors who had refused to carry out the amputations.[158]

The Iraqi regime also introduced the traditional Islamic law punishment for thievery—amputation of the right hand. It subsequently stipulated branding of the forehead as the punishment for thieves whose hands already had been amputated and the death penalty for certain categories of thievery. An official newspaper reported on September 9, 1994, that the authorities amputated the right hand and branded the forehead of a person convicted of stealing a television set.[159]

In his October 1994 report, the UN Special Rapporteur condemned the amputations and brandings. He stated that the practices constitute "flagrant and determined violations of Iraq's international human rights obligations insofar as they prescribe cruel and unusual punishments and insofar as implementation of the decrees compounds these violations by the conduct of torture." The relevant obligation in this regard is Article 7 of the International Covenant on Civil and Political Rights, to which Iraq is a party. The UN General Assembly likewise condemned what it termed "mutilations" in a December resolution.

This situation did not improve during 1995, despite reports of Saddam's efforts to liberalize Iraq's politics. In 1995 the UN Human Rights

Committee, the UN Subcommission on Prevention of Discrimination and Protection of Minorities, and the UN General Assembly all adopted resolutions condemning the government's human rights violations. For the third consecutive year, the UNHCR called on the UN Secretary General to send human rights monitors to "help in the independent verification of reports on the human rights situation in Iraq." The UN Subcommission on Prevention of Discrimination and Protection of Minorities adopted a resolution reiterating the UNHCR request for the deployment of monitors. In December the UN General Assembly once again endorsed the request of the Human Rights Commission for monitors for Iraq. The Iraqi government continued to defy these calls for the entry of monitors.

The UN Special Rapporteur, the US State Department, Amnesty International, and Middle East Watch reported a number of trends and incidents during 1995 and 1996 that confirm the fact that there is little chance that Saddam or the Ba'ath elite will ever change their character:

- The UN Special Rapporteur, the international media, and other groups reported an increased number of summary executions in 1995. In his February report to the UN Human Rights Commission, the Special Rapporteur stated that the Government's "aim of killing is a political one, with the objective of silencing dissent and suppressing opposition."
- There were many reports that the Ba'ath regime executed persons involved in plotting against Saddam, including high-ranking civilian, military, and tribal leaders, as well as members of his family and clan. One unconfirmed eyewitness report charged that 200 prisoners were executed in February at the Abu Ghurayb prison.
- Other executions occurred after several anti-regime disturbances. The most serious incidents included an uprising in March led by former Gen. Wafiq al-Samara'i; an uprising in May led by Gen. Turki Ismail Dulaimi and other members of the Dulaimi clan; and the August defections of Hussein and Saddam Kamel, Saddam's sons-in-law who held high-ranking government positions. An undetermined number of people are believed to have been executed extrajudicially after each of these events.
- The Special Rapporteur noted continued reports of the frequent use of the death penalty for such offenses as "insulting" the President or the Ba'ath Party. In reports submitted to the UN Human Rights Commission in September and November 1995, the Special Rapporteur cited several government decrees stipulating the death penalty for certain political and civil offenses. Numerous mid-level officials and local leaders who fled government-controlled areas cited the fear of extrajudicial killing as a reason for their flight.

- The Special Rapporteur, Human Rights Watch (HRW), and other human rights groups reported that the Government executed several doctors who refused to perform amputations imposed on persons convicted of certain crimes, or who performed corrective surgery on such amputees.
- Government forces reportedly executed numerous Shi'ite inhabitants of the south marshes, but there was no independent means to verify these reports.
- Indications persist that the Government continued to offer "bounties" to anyone who assassinates United Nations or other international relief workers in northern Iraq.
- The Special Rapporteur stated in November, 1995 that he continued to receive reports on widespread disappearances, especially in southern Iraq. The Iraqi government did not respond to any of the more than 15,000 cases conveyed to it in 1994 and 1995 by the UN Working Group on Enforcement on Involuntary Disappearances.
- Iraq continued to fail to return, or account for, a large number of Kuwaiti citizens and third-country nationals detained during the Iraqi occupation of Kuwait. Regime officials, including military leaders known to have been among the last to see the disappeared during the occupation continued to refuse to respond to the hundreds of outstanding inquiries about the missing. The regime denied having any knowledge of them and claims that relevant records were lost in the aftermath of the Gulf War.
- The regime continued to practice amputation of ears and hands, as well as branding, as punishment for crimes ranging from theft to military desertion. Eyewitnesses reported that the Government carried out second amputations and brandings on repeat offenders and on those who sought corrective surgery for earlier disfigurements. In some of these cases, the regime executed the offenders as well as the doctors who either performed corrective surgery or refused to carry out amputations. In his November 1995 report, the Special Rapporteur concluded that the amputations and brandings are "gross violations of human rights."
- Several government officials cited Islamic law (Shari'a) as a rationale for amputating the right hands of convicted thieves, but none commented on the punishments imposed on repeat offenders or the Government's disregard for rights protected under Islamic law. One senior official claimed that brandings were instituted in order to avoid confusing criminals with war veterans who had lost limbs in battle.
- Certain prisons continue to be notorious for routine mistreatment of prisoners. The Al-Rashidiya Prison, on the Tigris River north of Taji,

reportedly has torture chambers. The Al-Shamma'iya Prison, located in east Baghdad, holds the mentally ill and is reportedly the site of both torture and disappearances. The Al-Radwaniyah Prison is a former prisoner-of-war facility near Baghdad and reportedly the site of torture as well as mass executions. This prison was the principal detention center for persons arrested following the civil uprisings of 1991, and returned to prominence in May 1995, as the site of executions following an uprising led by members of the Dulaimi clan. Many persons taken into custody in connection with this and other civil uprisings have not been seen since. There are estimates that the Al-Radwaniyah Prison holds more than 5,000 detainees, only a few of whom may have been released following a so-called "amnesty" announcement in July 1995.

- According to international human rights groups, numerous foreigners arrested arbitrarily in previous years remain in detention. In March 1995, the regime arrested two Americans who unknowingly crossed the Iraqi border with Kuwait. The regime's efforts to link the fate of the two men to political issues failed, and the two were released in July.

- In July the Government issued two "amnesty" decrees: Decree No. 61, for certain convicted criminals, and Decree No. 64 for those convicted of political offenses. The Special Rapporteur noted that Decree No. 61 stipulates that criminals granted amnesty may be convicted again of the same crimes for which they were sentenced and that Decree No. 64 requires those granted amnesty to report to competent authorities in order to benefit. He also noted that because "there is no effective rule of law in Iraq, there will be little confidence in the reliability of amnesty decrees." Human Rights Watch observed that when some 3,000 residents of southern Iraq came forward for a similar amnesty in 1991, they were placed on trucks and subsequently disappeared. Further, two Iraqis who specifically were granted amnesties before returning from Jordan, where they had earlier defected, were murdered shortly after their return.

- The Special Rapporteur noted in his November 1995 report that numerous laws were used to support the government's policy of oppression, such as a 1994 decree stipulating the death penalty for automobile theft, smuggling, various categories of theft, and solicitation for the purposes of prostitution. In 1995 the Government also announced the death penalty for possession of stolen goods and for the failure of agricultural workers to supply food for government distribution.

- In contrast, the Government continued to protect certain groups from prosecution for alleged crimes. A 1992 decree grants immunity from prosecution to members of the Ba'ath Party and the security forces who kill anyone while in pursuit of army deserters. Unconfirmed but widespread reports indicate that this decree was applied often in 1995 to prevent trials or punishment of such government officials as Uday Saddam Hussein, the President's son. A 1990 decree grants immunity to men who kill their mothers, daughters, and other female family members who have committed "immoral deeds."

- The security services and the Ba'ath Party maintained their pervasive networks of informers to deter dissident activity and instill fear in the public. Voters in the October 1995 "referendum" were required to name relatives on their ballots and, according to some opposition reports, were threatened with punishment against their families if they voted against extending Saddam's rule. In his November report, the UN Special Rapporteur noted that because of the intrusiveness of the security apparatus "virtually no citizen would risk demonstrating any opposition to the Presidency or Government—or would do so at his mortal peril."

- The UN Special Rapporteur and others report that the Government continued to engage in various abuses against the country's 350,000 Assyrian Christians. Most Assyrians traditionally live in the northern governates, and the Government often has suspected them of "collaborating" with Kurds. Military forces destroyed numerous Assyrian churches during the Anfal Campaign and reportedly tortured and executed many Assyrians. According to HRW and Assyrian sources, the Government continued to harass and kill Assyrians throughout the country by forced relocations, terror, and artillery shelling.

- The Government deported hundreds of Turkomans from their northern Iraqi homes, either to areas outside government control or to southern Iraq. It also refused to allow tens of thousands of Kurds and Turkomans to return to their homes in Kirkuk and Mosul. These forced movements amount to a policy of internal exile.

- The Government continued to pursue its discriminatory resettlement policies, including demolition of villages and forced relocation of Kurds, Turkomans, Assyrians, and other minorities. Human rights monitors reported that the Government continues to force Kurdish and Turkoman residents of Mosul and Kirkuk to move to other areas in the north or the south.

- According to the UNHCR, hundreds of thousands of Iraqi refugees remained abroad—mainly in Iran, Saudi Arabia, Kuwait, Syria, Turkey, Pakistan, and Jordan. Apart from those suspected of sympathizing with Iran, most fled after the Government's suppression of the civil uprising of 1991; others are Kurds who fled the Anfal Campaign of 1988.

- In November, the Special Rapporteur reported eyewitness accounts that the children of senior members of the Ba'ath Party were treated to a variety of favors in the educational system, including privileged entrance and advancement throughout the system. These reports confirm others from recent emigrants alleging systemic corruption that prevents fair advancement by deserving children whose parents do not have the requisite political ties.
- The Special Rapporteur also reported in November that "the obvious imbalance between military expenditures and resources allocated to the fields of health care and education clearly illustrates the priorities of the Government." The Special Rapporteur has repeatedly observed that the ongoing bombardment of civilian settlements in the southern marshes has resulted in the deaths of many innocent persons, including women, children, and the elderly.
- Assyrians are an ethnic group as well as a Christian community and a distinct language—Syriac. Public instruction in Syriac, which was to have been allowed under a 1972 decree, has never been implemented. The Special Rapporteur reported continued discrimination against Assyrians throughout 1995. According to opposition reports, many Assyrian families were forced to leave Baghdad after they had fled to that city for safety following the regime's suppression of the northern uprising in 1991.
- Citizens considered to be of Iranian origin must carry special identification and are often precluded from desirable employment. Over the years, the Government has deported hundreds of thousands of citizens of Iranian origin.

Prisons and the Legal System

The Iraqi legal system is more an instrument of state control than a means of ensuring the rule of law. Iraqi prisons regularly mistreat their prisoners. The State Department reports that the Al-Rashidiya Prison, on the Tigris River north of Taji, contains torture chambers in its basement. The Al-Shamma'iya Prison, located in east Baghdad, holds the mentally ill and is reportedly the site of both torture and disappearances. The Al-Radwaniyah Prison is a former prisoner-of-war facility near Baghdad and is reported to be the site of torture and arbitrary killings, including mass execution by firing squad. This prison was the principal detention center for persons arrested following the civil uprisings of 1991. Many persons taken into custody in connection with the uprisings have not been seen since.[160] Middle East Watch estimated in

1994 that the Al-Radwaniyah Prison holds between 5,000 and 10,000 detainees.

The UN Special Rapporteur, Middle East Watch, and Amnesty International have cited the Al-Radwaniyah Prison and the Abu Ghraib Prison, located in Baghdad, as principal sites where torture and disappearances continue to occur. According to opposition reports, authorities at the Abu Ghraib Prison began to amputate the hands of persons convicted of theft in late 1994.

The Iraqi security forces raped captured civilians during the Anfal Campaign and the occupation of Kuwait and the Gulf War. The UN Special Rapporteur noted in his February report that he had interviewed numerous women who continue to suffer severe depression after they were raped in official custody. The Iraqi regime has never acknowledged or taken any action to investigate reports of rape by its officials.[161]

Although the Iraqi constitution and legal code prohibit arbitrary arrest and detention, the authorities routinely engage in these practices. In his February report, the Special Rapporteur described "widespread arbitrary arrest and detention, in violation of Article 9 of the Universal Declaration of Human Rights," primarily in the southern part of the country. He stated that the military and security services, rather than the ordinary police, carried out most cases of arbitrary arrest and detention.[162]

Like many Middle Eastern countries, Iraq has two parallel judicial systems: the regular courts, which try common criminal offenses, and the special security courts, which try cases involving national security. Trials in the regular courts are public, and defendants are entitled to counsel— at government expense in the case of indigents. Defense lawyers have the right to review the charges and evidence brought against their clients, but there is no jury system: panels of three judges try cases. Defendants do have the right to appeal to the Court of Appeal and then to the Court of Cassation, the highest court.

The State Department reports that Iraq's regular courts have been given steadily greater authority to use the death penalty. In 1994, the regime introduced Shari'a punishments for some types of criminal offenses and for military desertion. The Special Rapporteur also reported in 1994 that the regular courts often assign penalties that are "disproportionate" to the offense. Decree 13 of 1992 imposes the death penalty for automobile theft. In 1994 the Iraqi regime announced the death penalty would be invoked for automobile smuggling, various categories of thievery, and solicitation for the purposes of prostitution. As of late 1994, the penalty for possession of stolen goods was life in prison.[163]

The special security courts have jurisdiction in all cases involving espionage and treason, peaceful political dissent, smuggling, currency exchange violations, and drug trafficking. According to the Special Rapporteur, military officers or civil servants with no legal training head these tribunals, which hear cases in secret. Authorities often hold defendants incommunicado and do not permit them to have contact with their lawyers. The courts admit confessions extracted by torture which often serve as the basis for conviction. Although defendants may appeal their sentences to Saddam Hussein, many cases end in summary execution shortly after trial.

Further, "President" Saddam Hussein may override any court decision, and there are no checks on his power. The UN Special Rapporteur noted in his February 1994 report that the executive interferes regularly in "all aspects of normal judicial competence in matters ranging from property and commercial law, to family law and criminal law."

Freedom of Speech and Political Dissent

Freedom of speech and the press do not exist in Iraq, and political dissent is not tolerated. The Iraqi regime and the Ba'ath Party own all print and broadcast media, and operate them as propaganda outlets. They do not report opposition views. The UN Special Rapporteur noted in his February 1994 report that the regime has criminalized most forms of personal expression. A 1986 decree stipulates the death penalty for anyone insulting the President or other high government officials. Section 214 of the Penal Code prohibits "singing a song likely to cause civil strife." Press Act 206 (1968) prohibits the writing of articles on 12 specific subjects, including those detrimental to the President. Various Ba'ath Party and presidential decrees define political dissent as encompassing a wide range of activities. Persons suspected of engaging in dissent are routinely imprisoned without charge or trial or after trials that do not meet minimum standards of fairness.

The Iraqi regime periodically jams news broadcasts, including those of opposition groups, from outside Iraq. Iraqi citizens may not legally assemble or organize for any political purpose other than to express support for the regime and the Iraqi regime controls the formation of parties, regulates their internal affairs and closely monitors their activities. Several parties are outlawed by name, and membership in them is a capital offense. A 1974 law also prescribes the death penalty for anyone "infiltrating" the Ba'ath Party.[164]

The Iraqi regime frequently disregards the constitutional right to privacy, particularly in cases in which national security is alleged to be involved. The law defines security offenses so broadly that authorities are virtually exempt from the legal requirement to obtain search warrants. The security services and the Ba'ath Party maintain pervasive networks of informers to deter dissident activity and instill fear in the public. As the

UN Special Rapporteur noted in his February report, "the fear of informers and subsequent severe reprisals have prevented virtually the entire population from expressing genuinely held opinions which are not consistent with those of the Iraqi regime."

Treatment of Minorities and Foreigners

The Iraqi regime controls movement within the country of citizens and foreigners. Persons who enter sensitive border areas and numerous designated security zones are subject to arrest. Police checkpoints are common on major roads and highways. As has been discussed earlier, the Iraqi regime requires citizens to obtain expensive exit visas for foreign travel. Citizens may not make more than two trips abroad annually, and some citizens are prohibited to travel abroad. Other citizens are required to post collateral with the Iraqi regime before traveling abroad, which is refundable only upon their return to Iraq. There are restrictions on the amount of currency that may be taken out of the country. Students abroad who refuse to return are required to reimburse any expenses paid by the Iraqi regime. Each student wishing to travel abroad must provide a guarantor. The guarantor and the student's parents may be liable if the student fails to return.[165]

Foreign spouses of citizens who have resided in Iraq for 5 years are required to apply for nationality. The requirement is 1 year of residence for the spouses of Iraqi citizens employed in government offices. Many foreigners thus have been obliged to accept citizenship and are subject to official travel restrictions. The penalties for noncompliance include loss of job, a substantial financial penalty, and repayment for any governmental educational expenses. The Iraqi regime prevents many citizens who also hold citizenship in another country—especially the children of Iraqi fathers and foreign-born mothers—from visiting the country of their other nationality.

Potential opponents, Shi'ites, and Kurds are often driven out of the country. Citizens considered to be of Iranian origin must carry special identification and are often precluded from desirable employment. Over the years, the Iraqi regime has deported hundreds of thousands of citizens of Iranian origin.[166] The UN Special Rapporteur also reported in 1994 that the Iraqi regime may have expelled a total of more than one million persons suspected of being "Persian sympathizers" in recent years. According to the Special Rapporteur, about 500,000 of these displaced persons are now believed to live in Iran. According to the Special Rapporteur, hundreds of thousands of Iraqi refugees now remain abroad— mainly in Iran, Saudi Arabia, Kuwait, Syria, Turkey, Pakistan, and Jordan. In addition to those suspected of sympathizing with Iran, many fled after the Government's suppression of the civil uprising of 1991; others include Kurds who fled the Anfal Campaign of 1988. The UNHCR assists many refugees, notably in Kuwait, Syria, and Turkey.

The Special Rapporteur noted in his February report that the Iraqi regime failed to provide for the basic humanitarian needs of its civilian population and that it is obligated to do so as a signatory to the United Nations Charter. The Special Rapporteur reported that in September the Iraqi regime cut food subsidies by one-third. He once again called on the Iraqi regime to implement United Nations Security Council Resolutions 706 and 712, Section 5, which is titled "Discrimination Based on Race, Sex, Religion, Disability."[167] The cultural, religious, and linguistic diversity of society is not reflected in the country's political and economic structure. Sunni Arabs, a small minority of the population, have effectively controlled Iraq since independence in 1932. Shi'ite Arabs, the overwhelming majority of the population, have long been economically, politically, and socially disadvantaged. Like the Sunni Kurds of the north, the Shi'ite Arabs of the south have been targeted for particular discrimination and abuse, ostensibly because of their opposition to the Iraqi regime.

As has been discussed earlier, the Kurds have long suffered political and economic discrimination. There are, however, other ethnic groups who suffer as well, such as the Assyrians. Public instruction in Syriac, which was to have been allowed under a 1972 decree, has never been implemented. In 1994 the Special Rapporteur stated that in late 1993 the Iraqi regime dismissed or expelled hundreds of Assyrian teachers and students from universities and public positions.[168]

The government also uses Iraq's trade unions as an instrument of state control. The Trade Union Organization Law of June 2, 1987, prescribes a monolithic trade union structure for organized labor. Workers in private and mixed enterprises and cooperatives—but not public employees or workers in state enterprises—have the right to join local union committees. The committees are affiliated with individual trade unions, which in turn belong to the Iraqi General Federation of Trade Unions. The General Federation is linked to the Ba'ath Party, which uses it to promote party principles and policies among union members. The General Federation also is affiliated with the International Confederation of Arab Trade Unions and the formerly Soviet-controlled World Federation of Trade Unions. The Labor Law of 1987 restricts the right to strike, and no strike has been reported over the past two decades.[169]

Implications for Western and Southern Gulf Strategy

There is little point is hoping for an Iraqi government that will end all of these abuses, or for trusting in the promises of the various Iraqi factions who have learned to use the rhetoric of human rights as a tool in seeking Western political support. Iraq's divisions and internal politics virtually ensure that change will come slowly, particularly if it does not come as the result of a violent civil war. Further, even if those factions who claim to support human rights do come to power as a result of a civil conflict, many are likely to turn to repression the moment they take control and have to deal with their rivals or Iraq's ethnic and religious divisions.

At the same time, it is difficult to treat Saddam Hussein's regime simply in terms of *realpolitik*, and any strategy that effectively tolerates the current level of human rights abuses in Iraq is likely to have short-term success at best. Iraq's current level of repression is a recipe for civil war. It forces any "centrist" regime to ride a tiger that is likely to turn on the regime at the first sign of weakness. It suppresses Shi'ite aspirations at the cost of a steadily increasing alienation of Iraq's largest single ethnic faction, and of pushing this faction towards Iran. It creates a Kurdish time bomb in northern Iraq that can explode into Turkey and Iran.

Just as human rights advocates need to approach Iraq without illusions about its future, or the sincerity of those Iraqi's who use human rights as a political tool, Western and Southern Gulf political leaders need to approach Iraq with a clear understanding that major improvements in human rights are the price of any mid to long-term Iraqi stability. The issue ultimately is not one of whether the West and the Southern Gulf can live with Saddam or some leader like him. It is rather, the fact that Iraq cannot be stable or peaceful unless its regime is far less repressive than Saddam's regime is today.

7

Sanctions and Economic Instability

The previous analysis has shown that Iraq's politics, state institutions, ethnic and sectarian divisions, and human rights abuses interact in a matrix of conflicting forces that makes it extraordinarily difficult for the West and the Southern Gulf states to develop an effective strategy for dealing with Iraq. Iraq's current economic problems add to these complications, with one important difference. Iraq faces a growing economic crisis that is impoverishing the country, and which threatens the social fabric of the country, while politics and strategy may be able to wait, food cannot.

This crisis is partly the result of decades of mismanagement by the Iraqi government, and partly the result of massive spending and foreign borrowing during the Iran-Iraq War and Gulf War. The Ba'ath government has long indulged in extensive central planning and has exercised heavy control over agriculture, foreign trade, and industrial production—leaving only small industries, shops, and part of the service industry to the private sector. Its eight year war with Iran led the government to waste the liquidity it had built up during the oil boom of the 1970s, and make Iraq a massive borrower. It then grossly over-extended Iraq's credit between 1988 and 1990 in a simultaneous effort to fund wartime recovery, economic expansion, vast public works projects, and a massive military build-up. As Charts One and Two show, the Ba'ath government had effectively crippled Iraq's economy before the Gulf War began and had forced devastating cuts in Iraqi living standards. In fact, Iraq's average per capita income dropped from a peak of $8,161 in 1979 to $2,108 in 1989—a cut of over 70%.[170]

The current crisis is also, however, the result of damage done during the Gulf War and of more than half a decade of UN sanctions. These UN sanctions forbid member states, companies and individuals from undertaking any economic intercourse with the Iraqi government or with private Iraqi firms, except in regard to goods deemed by the UN Sanctions

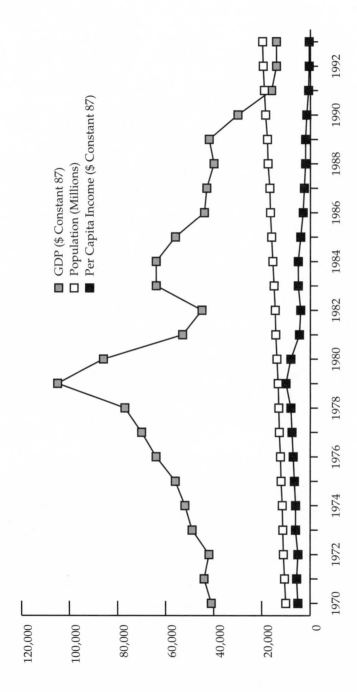

CHART ONE Iraqi GDP, Population Growth in Millions, and Per Capita Income in Constant 1987 US Dollars. *Source:* Adapted by Anthony H. Cordesman from International Energy Agency (IEA), *Middle East Oil and Gas*, Paris, 1995, pp. 247–248.

126

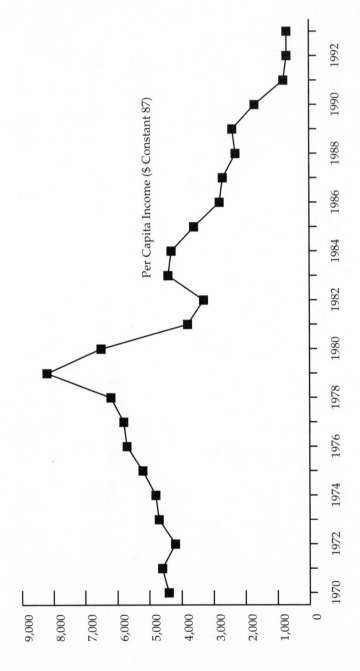

CHART TWO Iraqi Population Growth in Millions and Per Capita Income in Constant 1987 US Dollars. *Source:* Adapted by Anthony H. Cordesman from International Energy Agency (IEA), *Middle East Oil and Gas*, Paris, 1995, pp. 247–248.

Committee to be of a humanitarian nature. While accurate data are not available, Chart One indicates that Iraq's per capita income has dropped from $2,108 in 1989 to well under $1,000 a year in 1992–1995—another cut of well over 50%.[171] Oil exports are at well under 5% of their pre–Gulf War levels, there are shortages of imports and spare parts throughout the economy, and consumer prices have doubled annually since 1993.[172]

Since 1991, Saddam Hussein and the supporters of sanctions have played a game of "chicken" where each side waits to see which side is willing to let the Iraqi people suffer the most. This game has reduced Iraq to an economic and social "basket case" and may limit its economic development for several decades to come. Iraq's per capita income has shrunk from 60% of the OECD average in 1980 to 15% of the OECD average in 1989, and less than 4% of the OECD average in 1993.[173]

The human cost of this game is particularly striking because Iraq had relatively high living standards before the Gulf War and the imposition of sanctions. Before the war, Iraq had achieved a high level of economic and social development which had placed it in the World Bank category of upper middle income countries like Greece, Venezuela, and Czechoslovakia. Further, the caloric intake of Iraqis in the late 1980s was just under 3,000 calories per day—above average for an upper middle income country.[174]

Since the Gulf War, Iraq's per capita income and caloric intake have plunged from the levels of advanced states of the Third World to the levels common to very poor states like Egypt, Yemen, and Sudan, and are approaching the ranks of the "Fourth World" states like Rwanda, Haiti, Zaire, and Somalia. Iraq now has an economy characterized by extreme poverty. There is a huge socioeconomic gap between a tiny, powerful and rich elite and the poor. Further, the middle-class outside the nation's power structure is largely bankrupt, and Iraqi society is characterized by widespread corruption and endemic violence.

The Iraqi Economy Before the Gulf War

Before it invaded Kuwait, Iraq's economy was heavily dependent on oil—which provided 95% of foreign exchange earnings and funded most government operations. While Chart Two shows that Iraq's oil income was sharply affected by world oil prices, and by war, Iraq still had enough income to fund both growth and Saddam Hussein's ambitions during the 1970s, and to survive nearly a decade of war during the 1980s. Iraq's export income rose from only $484.7 million in 1970 to $8.3 billion in 1975, and $26.3 billion in 1980. While it dropped to $10.4 billion in the 1981 because of the Iran-Iraq War, Iraq still had $6.9 billion to $10.7 billion worth of export income between 1981 and 1988, and its export income recovered to $12.3 billion in 1989. Oil, NGL, and refined product exports provided over 98% of Iraq's export income during this period.[175]

Industrial Policy Under the Ba'ath

Iraq made little progress in industrialization before the Ba'athists came to power in 1968. Although the industrialization of the country received high priority in the development plans of successive regimes, the effort was badly mismanaged, suffered from an absence of skilled personnel including managers and administrators, and lacked the requisite capital. The end result was little more than waste—the state spent money on over-ambitious and badly conceived projects which did little more than distort the market and Iraq's economy.[176]

When the Ba'athists came to power, they indicated their determination to proceed rapidly with the industrialization of the country. They produced two development plans that spanned the periods and 1970–1975 and 1976–1980. These plans provided a total allocation of Iraqi Dinars (ID) 5,199 billion for the industrial sector. This was over 15 times the allocation for the period 1959–1969.[177]

Very little was achieved between 1968 and 1975, except in the oil sector. The regime's primary goals in those seven years were the achievement of "political" independence (i.e., consolidation of Ba'athist rule and the elimination of foreign-supported "counterrevolutionary" activities), "economic" independence (i.e., nationalization of the oil industry), and investment in the critically important oil industry itself. These goals reflected the kind of economic absurdism that has crippled virtually every Arab economy, and which are the curse of Arab socialism and efforts to use the state sector to support economic development. They had little to do with promoting growth and the government simply lacked the oil income to finance its efforts—a situation which did not change until the oil price increases between October 1973 and January 1974.

This situation changed with the development plan of 1976–1980. The Ba'ath government now had the money to back its commitment to industrialization—particularly heavy industry. It invested ID 4.4 billion ($14.15 billion) over the life of the five-year plan, and established Iraq's current heavy industrial sector—the Basra petrochemicals complex, the Khor al-Zubair iron and steel works, and sulfur, urea, phosphate and fertilizer industries. Most of this industrial infrastructure was concentrated in the south near Basra, and many of the plants were relatively efficient "turn key" plants supplied by the West.[178]

Nevertheless, Ba'athist industrial policy still had severe weaknesses which became far more apparent once the Iran-Iraq War limited the ability of the Ba'ath party to substitute oil wealth for economic efficiency. By

1982, even the Ba'ath Party was forced to admit publicly that these weaknesses included:

- A lack of a consistent sense of priorities among industrial programs;
- Too much of a focus on grandiose and impressive industrial infrastructure with far too large an investment in buildings and services;
- Not enough of an understanding of the absorptive limitations of the economy;
- Undertaking the creation of an industrial infrastructure without taking into consideration the bottlenecks that would be caused by underdeveloped transportation and port infrastructure;
- A pervasive state sector and a bureaucracy which stifled initiative and made state sector officials afraid of assuming authority and responsibility;[179]
- Widespread technical inefficiency and backwardness of the employees in the industrial sector. The 1982 Ba'athist Political Report commented that this sector had "failed to keep abreast of recent technological developments," and its "human base is still below the required standard in both quantity and quality;"[180]
- The paucity of middle-range technical cadre, forcing engineers to do low to mid-level work instead of showing their creativity in the process of design and production;[181]
- A lack of understanding of modern technology and hence an inability to deal with ordinary repair and stoppages in operation of equipment and machinery;[182]
- The involvement of the socialist public sector in industrial concerns such as food and manufacturing which would have best been left to the private sector. This situation wasted capital and the talents of technical and administrative cadre;[183]
- The lack of quality control of products. The result was that Iraqi-produced industrial goods could not compete with foreign goods;[184]
- When the Iran-Iraq War broke out, Iraq tried to maintain the momentum of its industrial development plans. This proved to be a drawback during the Iran-Iraq War. The proximity of the fighting caused damage or forced the government to mothball the factories.[185] While the government tried to take a "business as usual" approach during the first two years of the war. The government's 1981–1985 five-year plan called for further developing import substitution industrialization (ISI) and the creation of an advanced industrial base.[186]

By 1983, the Iran-Iraq War made it painfully apparent that Iraq could not continue with its massive economic development program in the face of massive military expenditures and a drop in oil export revenues. Many projects were put on hold, pending the end of the war, and the government concentrated on industrial projects that (a) contributed directly and immediately to the national war effort which took priority in terms of manpower, raw materials, machinery and spare parts; and (b) would enhance national military capabilities.

In fact, the Iran-Iraq War had the benefit of teaching the Iraqi leadership the necessity of building a strong and efficient industrial base, supporting and being supported by an indigenous science and technology infrastructure, and establishing a national defense industry. Saddam recognized this in 1987, when he embarked on a series of major reforms in the country's political economy which included jettisoning much of the socialist baggage of twenty years:[187]

> We believe that without stepping into industrialization and accepting risk in the early stages of the 1968 revolution, our country would have been kept far away from this vitally important field, and lacking the necessary expertise and know-how . . . the most important aspect is for the country to be scientifically and technologically developed. Therefore, its industrial progress is a must. Failure to do so leaves us in the category of backward countries, without any important influence on our national and international surrounding.

These same patterns seem to have affected Iraq's attempts to develop its military industries. While little was known about Iraq's military industrialization program prior to the Gulf Crisis which has exposed it, it seems that Iraq had established a small arms industry in the mid-1970s. It was only in the mid-1980s, at the height of the Iran-Iraq War, that Iraq sought to expand military industrialization greatly, in the short-term to deal with the combat and engineering requirements of the war—infantry weapons, ammunition, radios, bombs. Iraq's post-war plans were, in retrospect, more ambitious than that.[188]

Iraq's military industrialization projects were initially directed by the Military Industries Commission (MIC) and the Special Organization for Technical Industries (SOTI). These were attached to the Ministry of Industry and Minerals in 1987, which was then given the title the Ministry of Industry and Military Industrialization (MIMI) which was headed by Hussein Kamel.[189] In various speeches in 1987 Saddam Hussein indicated that he would like to see the organizational set-up, efficiency and product quality of the military industries put to the civilian industries, in order to develop stricter performance standards.

Iraq, however, has had little opportunity to demonstrate how much it has learned from its past mistakes. While it emerged from the Iran-Iraq War with ambitious plans for its industrial sector, it never had time to act between the end of the Iran-Iraq War in 1988 and the onset of the Kuwait crisis in 1990. It also lacked the capital to fund more than urgent reconstruction projects and oil-related projects to increase oil exports.

Iraqi Agriculture and Food Imports

Iraq is the only Gulf state with considerable agricultural potential. About 12% of its land is arable, of which 4% is irrigated. Another 9% is suitable for grazing, and 3% is forested. Iraq has about 42.8 cubic kilometers of internal renewable water resources, which is high for a Middle Eastern country. The Tigris and Euphrates provide about 4,575 cubic meters of water per person, more than twice the total used by the average citizen of the US, although population increases are cutting the total water available per capita.[190] This amount of water has dropped from 14,706 cubic meters per year in 1960 to 5,285 cubic meters in 1990, and is projected to drop to 2,000 cubic meters by 2025.[191]

Iraq, however, has not made effective use of its agricultural potential. Under the monarchy Iraq was self-sufficient in wheat and rice, and produced enough barley to export almost 25% of that crop. Nevertheless, agriculture was not efficient. The land tenure patterns inherited from the colonial Ottoman rulers inhibited agricultural productivity. Farm land was in the hands of absentee landowners. By 1953, 1.7% of landowners owned 63% of the land. About two-thirds of the population owned 5% of the land, and over three-fourths of the rural population was made up of landless peasants.[192]

Farming was undertaken by sharecroppers and tenants who received a tiny portion of the crop they farmed. Any income derived from increased productivity went to the landowners. Consequently, tenant farmers were not motivated to produce beyond subsistence level, and thus agricultural productivity remained low throughout much of the period of monarchical rule. These problems were compounded by the reluctance of landowners to invest more than a minimum of resources, financial or otherwise, in their lands.

Agrarian reform was near impossible because of the political power of the landowners and their class alliance with the monarchy. When agrarian reform was undertaken in the early years of republican Iraq, the government's lack of skilled personnel to ensure its implementation, lack of marketing resources and expertise, and inability to provide basic resources such as seed, pumps, and fertilizer hindered the effectiveness of the process.[193] While 70% of the Iraqi population still earned a living in agriculture in 1958, it only produced 30% of the country's income.[194]

Saddam Hussein reportedly used to say that agriculture is "permanent oil" and urged investment in this sector to attain self-sufficiency.

The Ba'ath regime also tried to do more than its predecessors to improve productivity in this sector.[195] Nonetheless, agriculture fared little better under the Ba'athist government. Government expenditures on agriculture dropped from 18% of total government expenditures in 1976 to less than 10% in 1980, and then dropped even further throughout the Iran-Iraq War.[196]

Socialist policies led to inefficiencies in the agricultural sector: overinvestment in large agricultural schemes and cooperatives with poor pay-offs wasted much of the government's investment. Poor pay rates for agricultural workers helped contribute to the heavy rural-to-urban migration and created an acute labor shortage in the agricultural sector which the government tried to deal with by importing workers from labor-rich/intensive countries such as Egypt. Government interference in the dynamics of the market, poor management skills, and lack of technical expertise further contributed to low productivity. A stark indicator of the regimes failure to increase agricultural productivity during the years of Ba'athist rule is the fact that Iraq became a net importer of food, and the agricultural sector accounted for only 11% of the GNP although it employed 30% of the labor force.[197]

This situation grew so bad that the stagnant state of Iraqi agriculture was the subject of intensive self-criticism during the June 1982 Ba'ath Party Ninth Regional (i.e., Iraqi) Congress. While glossing over the inefficiencies introduced by the socialization of the agricultural sector, the report still highlighted the following problems:[198]

- Tradition and backwardness retarded development in the rural areas and in the agricultural sector itself. The quasi-Marxist tone of the assessment does not detract from the truth of the statement concerning the state of affairs in rural Iraq.
- The agricultural sector was heavily mired in bureaucratic red-tape. Further, the state over-regulated the agricultural sector and micromanaged it to the extent that this contributed to lack of growth. Instead, it was recommended that the "state should focus on big production, vital projects and infrastructure projects such as those of irrigation, desalination, rural electrification. . . ."[199]
- The heavy salinity of the soil acted to reduce agricultural productivity considerably.

Iraqi Debt and Foreign Exchange Holdings

The Ba'ath government compensated for much of its inefficiency during the 1970s by pouring vast amounts of the nation's new oil wealth into dealing with every problem. It had more than enough money to do so. Chart Three shows the patterns in Iraq's liquidity, and on the eve of the Iran-Iraq War in 1980 Iraq had $35 billion in foreign currency reserves.

This situation changed rapidly after 1980. The Ba'ath leadership calculated that they would be able to fight and win a quick and limited border war without disruption of their "home front" and of economic development plans when they launched their war against Iran in September. Their calculations proved terribly wrong. The war dragged on for eight years, and Iraq was forced to adopt a capital and technology-intensive war-fighting strategy which provided servicemen and their families with lavish benefit packages on the home-front while it relied on the vast use and expenditure of combat materiel on the battlefield.[200] Until 1983, Iraq also tried to continue with a "guns and butter" policy and to maintain the momentum of its economic development programs. As a result, expenditures on national economic development peaked at about $24 billion in 1981.[201]

Because of the escalating materiel and human costs of the war coupled with a lack of sound judgment concerning economic priorities between 1980–1983, Iraq was rapidly forced to draw on its reserves and to borrow money overseas. As is discussed in detail in the next chapter, war related cuts in Iraqi oil export capacity and a major slump in oil prices in the mid-1980s sharply affected Iraq's economy. This forced Iraq to continue to borrow, even though it shelved its ambitious development plans and concentrated on waging the war and building a war-related infrastructure which played a direct role in the defense of the country.

As Chart Four shows, Iraq emerged from the Iran-Iraq War as a highly indebted nation.[202] At the Iran-Iraq War's end in 1988, various studies indicate that Iraq's debt lay somewhere between $50 billion and $60 billion.[203] In 1989, an OECD study claimed that the Iraqi debt was $15.4 billion. On closer inspection this figure accounts only for debts owed to the West. But it did not include the military debt owed to France nor the $3.5 billion owed to Japanese companies and trading establishments. Neither did it include the debt owed to the USSR and the Eastern Bloc nor the debt owed to the other Arab states of the Gulf.

By mid-1990, reliable analysts had concluded that Iraq's total indebtedness could be estimated at around $80 billion, of which half was owed to the other Arab states of the Gulf even though Iraq still continued to insist that these were grants for services rendered during the Iran-Iraq War (i.e., protecting the weak Arab states from the Iranian threat). It was estimated that between $7–$8 billion was owed to the Soviet Union and the Eastern Bloc. It was thought that Iraq would retire this largely military aid partly through payment in oil.

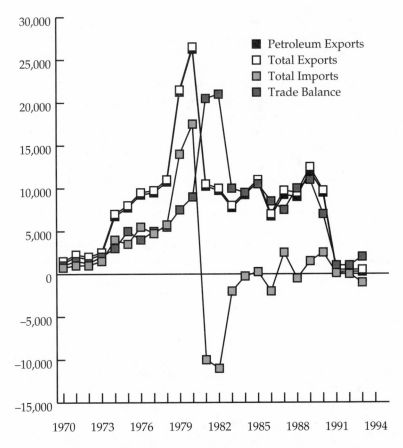

CHART THREE   Iraqi Oil and Total Exports Versus Total Imports in Millions of Current US Dollars. *Source:* Adapted by Anthony H. Cordesman from International Energy Agency (IEA), *Middle East Oil and Gas,* Paris, 1995, pp. 256–257.

However, Baghdad faced a more serious problem in dealing with a short-term—2–4 year loan—debt of $35–$45 billion. Much of this debt had to be paid to Iraq's Western creditors at high interest rates. The principal and interest (P+I) on this debt was anywhere between $7–$8 billion per annum. Many of Iraq's Western creditors tried to convince the Iraqi regime to re-structure its debt burden into medium and long-term debts with lower interest rates, and to undertake multilateral rescheduling of its debt with all its creditors. This would have allowed Iraq to see a rapid improvement of its credit rating and to be able to borrow more capital to refinance its ambitious post–Iran-Iraq War reconstruction.[204]

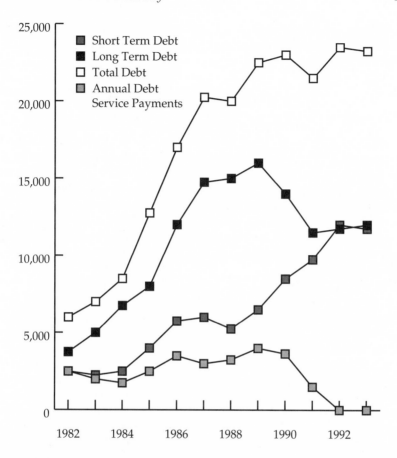

CHART FOUR   Iraqi Debt During 1982–1993 in Millions of Current US Dollars. *Source:* Adapted by Anthony H. Cordesman from International Energy Agency (IEA), *Middle East Oil and Gas,* Paris, 1995, pp. 260–261.

Saddam's regime, however, saw its debt problems in conspiratorial terms. It did not want to get into a close financial relationship with its Western creditors, fearing that they would "gang up on it" and sought instead to pursue its policy of bilateral negotiations with each country. Furthermore, such a relationship would have forced Iraq to make accurate disclosures about the state of its economy and of its finances, including its "real" foreign exchange holdings and its military spending. As a result, Saddam fired his Finance Minister, Hikmet Mukhalif, who was in favor of Iraq publishing economic statistics and indicators in October 1989.[205] Instead of pursuing sound fiscal policies, Saddam decided to fund his ambitious and massive plans for reconstruction, development, and military industrialization by "robbing the bank" to the south.

The Iraqi Economy After the Gulf War

The result of the Gulf War has been the economic disaster summarized at the beginning of this analysis. Instead of rebuilding its wealth, Iraq suffered massive wartime damage and punishing sanctions, and lost virtually all of its capability to export. According to the new Iraqi Oil Minister, Lieutenant General 'Amir Muhammad Rashid, Iraq lost $85 billion in revenue as a result of the ban on the export of its oil between August 6, 1990 and July 1995.[206] At the same time, Saddam Hussein and the ruling elite wasted resources on luxuries for themselves, and dealt with the growing economic crisis through repression and gross incompetence in managing the domestic economy.

It is difficult to determine just how much Iraq has suffered since 1990. Any attempt to reach tangible conclusions about the damage to Iraq's economy as a result of the Gulf War is virtually impossible for a wide variety of reasons.

First, statistics are hard to come by because of the obsessive secrecy of a regime that views statistical and economic data on Iraq as state secrets.[207] This problem has been compounded by the extreme state of uncertainty and abnormality within the Iraqi economy for the past five years under economic sanctions. Even the best figures of the Economist Intelligence Unit, the OECD, the UN or the Bank for International Settlements are "guesstimates." In fact, even as early as 1992 most analyses had given up their attempts to put numbers on industrial and agricultural output, inflation, and wages.

Second, there is no easy way to quantify the relative impact the Gulf War itself has had on Iraq's economy since 1990, as distinguished from the impact of UN sanctions. There is no question that the war and the rebellions caused extensive damage. It may very well be methodologically impossible for anyone to separate the relative cost of each of these calamities visited upon Iraq.[208]

Third, the Iraqi government has fluctuated between exaggerating wartime damage and incredible claims about the speed of its recovery. Further, with the exception of the uncharacteristically detailed presentation of its financial obligations and the costs of reconstruction to the UN in April 1991—which even then, in the view of some, played down the level of Iraqi debts and exaggerated the cost of reconstruction—the Iraqi government has not been forthcoming with more statistics on Iraq's economy between 1990 and early 1996, and may well be unable to provide itself with accurate statistics.

Fourth, while there has been no official US or other Western estimates of the impact of wartime bombing, many independent estimates or immediate post-war assessments have been either exaggerations or impressions which came immediately in the wake of the devastation caused by the war and by the insurrections in March 1991. In this context, the Report of the United Nations Mission, March 10–16, 1991, and headed by Martti Ahtisaari, set a tone for viewing the situation in cataclysmic terms that is typical of the lack of substantive analysis that characterizes many post-war studies of Iraq:[209]

> The recent conflict has wrought near-apocalyptic results upon the economic infrastructure of what had been, until January 1991, a rather highly urbanized and mechanized society. . . . Iraq has, for some time to come, been relegated to a pre-industrial age, but with all the disabilities of post-industrial dependency on an intensive use of energy and technology.

As events have shown, this UN report seriously overestimated the extent of the damage caused by the war and underestimated the ability of the Iraqis to deal with the destruction and rebuild their infrastructure. So have many later reports which have talked about massive medical and nutritional problems years before they actually began to surface. Such exaggerated reports have often done little more than lead outside governments to be indifferent to the very real suffering that now exists because of the cumulative impact of the trade embargo and Saddam's quarter of a century of war-mongering, selfishness, and incompetence.

UN Sanctions and the Policies of the Iraqi Government

Sanctions are scarcely the only problem that the Iraqi economy has faced since 1990, but they are the primary cause of its present crisis. A number of UN Security Council Resolutions affecting Iraq have been issued since August 1990. These resolutions have dealt with a wide range of political-strategic matters, including:

- The condemnation of the Iraqi invasion, calling for withdrawal of Iraqi forces from Kuwait (United Nations Security Council Resolution 660, August 2, 1990)
- Nullification of the Iraqi presence in the emirate (UN Security Council Resolution 662, August 9, 1990)

- Demarcation of Iraq's boundary with Kuwait
- Establishment of the United Nations Iraq-Kuwait Observation Mission (UNIKOM)

The UN Economic Sanctions

It is the resolutions pertaining to economic-strategic matters, however, which are pertinent to the socioeconomic analysis of the impact of the sanctions on Iraq. The UN passed the following resolutions between August 1990 and April 1991:

- *UN Security Council Resolution 661* (August 6, 1990) imposed an economic and trade embargo on Iraq with the exception of the provision of medical supplies and "in humanitarian circumstances, foodstuffs." UN Security Council Resolution 661 also created a Special Sanctions Committee to monitor the embargo.
- *UN Security Council Resolution 665* (August 25, 1990) called upon the implementation of "such measures as may be commensurate to the specific circumstances as may be necessary" to enforce the trade embargo against Iraq.
- *UN Security Council Resolution 666* (September 13, 1990) "Satan's resolution" granted the Special Sanctions Committee the right to investigate whether a humanitarian need had arisen in Iraq and to undertake to distribute food to the Iraqi people in conjunction with the Red Cross and other humanitarian agencies.
- *UN Security Council Resolution 678* (November 29, 1991) granted UN member states the authority "to use all necessary means" to make Iraq withdraw from Kuwait if Iraq had not done so by 15 January. The resolution declared that Iraq was in "flagrant contempt" of the Security Council, and that the deadline was set in order to "allow Iraq one final opportunity" to withdraw from Kuwait.
- *UN Security Council Resolution 687* (April 8, 1991) which came to be described as the "mother of all resolutions" was passed one month following the end of hostilities. Its effect is analyzed in detail in Chapter XV of this study. In brief, the resolution demanded that Iraq eliminate all its weapons of mass destruction, research into weapons of mass destruction, and dismantle any infrastructure associated with those programs in accordance with Section C, paragraphs 7, 8, 9, 10, 11, 12, and 13. Iraq was called upon to undertake these measures subject to monitoring and verification by the UN. The resolution stipulates that in accordance with Section F, paragraph 22 the UN prohibitions against the export of commodities and products originating in Iraq and the

import of goods into Iraq would have no further force or effect once Iraq had eliminated all its weapons of mass destruction and the means to produce them.

These sanctions, and further clarifying sanctions in the years that have followed, have done much more damage to Iraq than the Gulf War. There is no question that the Gulf War did cause serious damage to Iraq's economy and did tens of billions of dollars worth of damage to infrastructure, power generating facilities, telecommunications, and oil and refining facilities. Nonetheless, between 1991 and 1992, using the reconstruction slogan of "To Hell with the Impossible," Iraq was able to rebuild much of this destroyed infrastructure. Its reconstruction efforts have been particularly effective in regional areas which support the government and focused on infrastructure that buttresses the regime.

Most of the reconstruction efforts between 1991 and 1992 concentrated on:[210]

- Strategic industries such as the oil sector addressed in the following chapter,
- Politically important infrastructure such as the security/intelligence agencies and telecommunications ministries,
- Reconstruction projects that the Iraqis characterize as visible symbols of "defiance and steadfastness" ranging from the "wasteful" construction of palaces and guest-houses for the Iraqi leadership to the reconstruction of military-industrial infrastructures and bridges.

Kurdish and Shi'ite areas which are not fully under government control or where the security situation is uncertain generally have not benefited from this reconstruction effort. The wartime damage to industrial infrastructure in the Shi'ite south was also severely compounded by damage from the Iran-Iraq War and the destructive insurrection in March 1991.[211] Even so, the Iraqi Industries Minister at the time, Lieutenant-General, 'Amr Hammoudi al-Sa'adi, claimed in 1992 that 75% of industrial projects destroyed during the Gulf War had been rebuilt.[212]

However, most of Iraq's reconstruction effort of 1991–1992 sputtered out in 1993. Iraq was isolated—without access to spare parts, raw materials, and industrial goods—and had used up available in-house supplies between 1991 and 1992. It had reached the limit of what it could repair and rebuild through sheer determination, improvisation, native ingenuity, and cannibalization. As a result, most industry now continues a slow but steady decline, and the only industrial sectors which have received steady funding are the oil production industry, refineries, and cement factories.[213]

Iraq's industrial sector has been decimated, output having declined by 50% since August 1990.[214] Some economists estimate that Iraq's post-sanctions reconstruction bill for its infrastructure and oil sector will be as much as $50–$100 billion, of which $30 billion must be spent on imported equipment, machinery, and spare parts.[215] Iraq also has not found any way to bypass the sanctions regimes. It has had only limited success in smuggling oil across its borders, and its main illegal export has been dates—exports worth, at most, $10 million a year. Even in the case of dates, Iraq has faced major problems with the Multinational Interception Force (MIF) in the Gulf. The MIF has seized some $9 million worth of Iraqi dates since 1994.[216]

Socioeconomic Impacts of the Sanctions Regime

Iraq's population has been devastated socially, economically, and psychologically.[217] In spite of the near total consumption of savings, the standard of living has been reduced to well below half of its pre-war level. The real gross domestic product has been shrinking steadily almost every year since 1979, and the situation has become much worse since 1991. As has been mentioned earlier, this has sharply affected per capita income which stood at $8,161 in 1979 and had fallen to $609 in 1992 and to about $450–500 in 1995.[218]

This crisis has highlighted Iraqi dependence on food imports and exposed the strategic vulnerability caused by years of neglect and/or inefficient utilization of the agricultural sector. Before the war, Iraq imported 70% of its food needs at an annual cost of $1.1 billion.[219] The sanctions imposed on August 6, 1990, did not immediately have a deleterious effect on food supplies as the country had adequate stocks. When these stocks were run down, Iraqi agriculture proved incapable of rising to the challenge.

While Iraq has made some progress in increasing agricultural output of some crops since 1990, the country has seen uniformly poor harvests for the past five years. In the summer of 1991, the harvest was poor despite a 50% increase in acreage planted, and by 1994 the harvest was a *third* of the level of an already poor harvest in 1993. The harvest of 1995 was the worst yet. The government still continues to interfere by attempting to fix prices and to maintain control of the distribution of many items.

The end result is that Iraq's dependence on imports has not really been diminished and this has been a critical factor in the hardships faced by the Iraqi people. Iraq had a backlog of $4.5 billion in unfunded food imports in 1994, while government subsidized food rations had dropped to about 50%–60% of their previous level. The agricultural infrastructure has not recovered from a lack of fertilizer, animal feed, spare parts for machinery, and war damage to irrigation and drainage.

Iraq is also suffering from severe hyper-inflation.[220] The situation in the country is comparable to the hyper-inflationary situation of Weimar Germany in the 1920s. At the end of 1994 the government estimated that prices *on average* had risen by 5,000% since 1990. More specifically, statistics provided by an outside study indicated that by 1995 wheat prices had risen by 4,531%, powdered milk by 3,661%, bread by 2,857%, and sugar by 2,208%.[221] Rice, a basic staple of the Iraqi diet sold for ID 0.15 in 1990, skyrocketed to ID 14 in early 1993.[222] A combination of rampant inflation and limited agricultural output has made it difficult for the average Iraqi to turn to the open market to find the products now restricted under rationing. Many consumer goods and basic necessities, including medicine, are available on the black market at highly inflated prices.

This hyperinflation has become so serious that Saddam ordered in January, 1996, that the exchange rate must cease to drop below the official rate of ID 1,000 to $1, and described the order in terms of war:

> We are now in a real battle. For no military victory can make up for an economic defeat . . . this year would like to say that the first practical step we can take is to halt the rate of deterioration. That is, we should not allow the exchange rate of the Iraqi Dinar to suffer any further set backs.[223]

The contrast between the government's policy and reality is illustrated by the fact that the black market exchange rate had already shrunk to ID 2,600 to $1 at the time Saddam was speaking. Yet, even a rumor that Iraq might accept the UN offer to allow it to export oil raised the exchange rate to ID 2000 to $1 overnight.[224]

The Iraqi Government's Response to the Sanctions Regime

Furthermore, the regime has been just as incompetent in economic matters in the 1990s as it has been in the past, and has attempted to deal with far too many problems through "economics by fiat" and repression. For example, the government set up a directorate in 1992 to combat economic crimes under Brigadier-General Ibrahim al-Batawi—who reported directly to Watban Ibrahim, the Interior Minster and Saddam's brother. The task of the directorate was to punish merchants and traders guilty of "profiteering." In July 1992, the regime summarily executed 42 merchants in front of their shops in Baghdad's market district.[225] Following Saddam's execution of the 42 merchants and the arrest in March–April 1993 of another 300 merchants, the Iraqi private sector as well as their Jordanian counterparts across the border that had kept the country supplied with necessities were cowed into submission.[226]

Saddam subsequently declared that the role of the private sector was to provide the Iraqi people with goods at cost and that it must not exploit the people: "there is no task above that of serving the people, alleviating their burden and putting an end to their exploitation by middlemen, parasites, and those toying with the wealth of the people and the country."[227] This policy removed the ability of the open market to allocate resources and forced reliance on the black market, while it removed any incentive for legitimate profits and encouraged corruption. Political uncertainties have also aggravated the economic situation. The coalition air raids in January 1993 led to a sharp rise in prices, while Saddam's movement of troops to the Kuwaiti border in October 1994 led to the temporary doubling of food prices.

As might be expected from the drop in per capita income, the purchasing power of the Iraqi people has been dramatically reduced over the years. By 1993 the average income was ID 400, whereas ID 1000 was needed to feed a family adequately.[228] Again, while reliable statistics may not be available, it is safe to say that the cost of basic food items has far outstripped salaries over the past five years: in 1993 as a result of the depreciation of the Dinar, its buying power was 100 times less than in mid-August, whereas salaries had only doubled. The value of the Dinar has also continued to plunge against the dollar. In late 1993, the Dinar traded on the black market at a rate of approximately 100 Dinars to the dollar. In late 1994 the official rate was approximately 500 Dinars to the dollar, while on the black market it traded at 650–750 Dinars to the dollar after Saddam's October 1994, troop movements in the direction of Kuwait.

The government has attempted to deal with these problems by creating a rationing system designed to cushion the poorer elements of the population from the impact of sanctions. This system generally functioned well in meeting basic needs between 1990 and 1993. In early 1993, for example, the rationing system provided Iraqis with 60% of their basic necessities, including 9 kilos of flour, 2.75 kilos of rice, 1.5 kilos of sugar, 500 grams of cooking oil, and small quantities of tea and soap.[229]

Since 1993, however, the government has lost much of its ability to use its available income and savings to fund its rationing system. A UN report at the end of 1995 indicated that the rations only provided 1,000 calories—down from over 3,000 before the Gulf War—while monthly supplies of subsidized items to each individual barely last two weeks. Iraqis must get the rest of their needs from the prohibitively expensive open market.[230]

As a result, the government now controls the stockpile of food and increases or decreases rations as a form of political maneuvering to show the people who is still in control or in order to celebrate an event or "happy" occasion. In the wake of his referendum victory in October 1995, the government announced that ration allotments would "increase," with each Iraqi receiving 15.4 pounds of flour a month instead of 13.2 pounds.[231] Nevertheless, the UN special commission investigating the impact of sanctions on Iraq claimed in January 1996 that "alarm food shortages" had put four million Iraqis "at severe nutritional risk."[232]

Trade with Jordan, Turkey, and Iran

Iraq has also suffered because of its deteriorating relations with Jordan. The UN trade embargo allows Iraq to export a limited amount of oil barrels to Jordan, making Iraq that country's most important oil supplier. The money that comes from the legal sale of this oil has allowed Iraq to pay off part of its debt to Jordan and to cover purchases of food and medicine, and the volume of trade between the two countries increased because Jordanian and Iraqi merchants have used the highway connecting Baghdad to the Jordanian port of Aqaba to move all kinds of goods into Iraq. In late 1995, however, Jordan decided to cut down on the two way trade and smuggling between it and Iraq. Even though Jordan rejected a US request to cut off its trade completely, it decided in early 1996 to cut in half from $400 million to $200 million its trade in food and essential goods with Iraq.[233]

Since the war, trading with Turkey has required transit traffic through unstable northern Iraq in territory controlled by Kurds. In 1992, the volume of this trade was quite significant. The Iraqi Kurds had not yet fallen out among themselves, and the Turkish PKK had not yet established itself in Iraq. As a result, a considerable volume of Iraqi oil was bartered for Turkish goods and products via a free trade zone centered on the Iraqi town of Faydah and which was controlled by the Ministry of Industries and Military Industries. This ministry supplied the oil to Turkish buyers at attractive prices and in return bought goods which it allocated to its own network of distribution centers and government cooperatives throughout the country.[234]

Since that time, however, the volume of trade has been scaled back considerably because of the conflict pitting Kurd against Kurd and Turk against Kurd. By the fall of 1995, merchants on both sides of the border stated that the number of trucks carrying Turkish food and medicine in exchange for Iraqi diesel and gasoline has been cut back from 3,000 trucks a day in 1994 to about 150 a day in late 1995.[235] While Iraq also moves oil east via Iran into the open market with the connivance of the Iranians, this trade has never been of significant importance.[236]

The Social Impact of Sanctions

The deterioration of the Iraqi economy to subsistence levels has contributed to the unraveling of the social fabric of society. There are several aspects to this "decomposition" of the Iraqi society which are noteworthy. There has been a dramatic rise in corruption and bribery in a government which prided itself on being one of the least corrupt in the region and whose leadership once chided its neighbors' governments for these failings. Furthermore, this has been compounded by a seemingly endemic sense of indifference towards or resignation to the state of affairs in the country not only among the population at large but also among government officials, bureaucrats and administrators. Furthermore, thousands of these public sector employees have left their jobs, because apart from the poor, they are the class most affected by the collapse of the Dinar. This has contributed, in turn, to the further deterioration of public services; by November 1994 about 50% of the public sector health employees had left their jobs.[237]

Social ills such as theft, begging, prostitution, and rural thievery that were rare or "efficiently" controlled in this once well-policed authoritarian state have become widespread.[238] Many of these crimes are being committed by the mass of young men who fought in the Iran-Iraq and Gulf Wars. Having spent the better part of their early adulthood in brutalizing war, they have no marketable skills—and no prospects in Iraq's current economy—so they steal and kill to survive.[239] Anecdotal stories seem to indicate that the primary concern of Iraqis is not who rules the country but food, safety from rising crime, and emigration to escape the harsh realities of Iraqi life.[240]

The country's efficient educational institutions have been ravaged with dire implications for the future of the economy, industrial development, and the promotion of a science and technology infrastructure. Between 1991 and 1993 the school dropout rate rose from 2% to 15%. According to the Education Ministry 2000 teachers left the profession in 1994 alone.[241] Another stark statistic claimed that 25% of university professors had made their way to Jordan.[242]

Iraq's health service has sharply deteriorated, gradually approaching near-collapse. Iraq's health system was one of the best in the Third World in 1990. A World Health Organization report issued in 1991 by Prince Saddruddin Agha Khan showed that 96% of the urban population and 78% of the rural population had access to free state health care before the Gulf crisis.[243]

While the government rapidly rebuilt hospitals destroyed during the Gulf War, this has not been enough to prevent the erosion of the quality and quantity of medical service provided by the state. Hospital equipment has deteriorated due to the lack of spare parts, and Iraq has not been able to import new and more sophisticated equipment in the last five years. Water supplies are still polluted in most areas, with the south being worst off. The government does not have the means to repair sanitation facilities and sewage works which are working at 40% of capacity. Iraq has not been able to get chemicals for the manufacture of anesthetics and for the purification of water. Iraq has managed to get only small quantities of vaccines to deal with serious diseases such as diphtheria, TB, meningitis, and polio.

Not surprisingly, mortality in the country has increased.[244] Statistics are not reliable, and Iraqi figures must be treated with some caution. In September 1993, the Health Minister, Umid Midhat Mubarak, claimed that as a result of medical shortages almost 4,000 children under the age of five were dying each month, compared to 700 before the Gulf Crisis, and that 300,000 people had died since 1990 as a direct result of "sanctions-caused shortages in Iraq's health services."[245] In early 1994 Iraqi statistics claimed that 400,000 Iraqis, including 140,000 children under the age of five had died due to severe shortages of food and of medicines.[246]

There is no way to corroborate Iraqi claims, but independent sources and humanitarian agencies have provided strong indications of the dire social conditions in the country.[247] For example, imports of medical supplies, which totaled $500 million per year before the war, dropped to less than $130 million per year by 1994. Hospitals, which now lack not only the basic necessities such as insulin for diabetics and respirators, operate at 30%–50% of capacity. A UNICEF report released in October 1995 concluded that 3.3 million Iraqis, or about 15% of the total population, were at risk of malnutrition and disease, including almost three-quarters of a million children under 5 years of age.[248] The report specifically focused on children, discovering that due to pervasive malnourishment, 12% are "wasted" or underdeveloped and 28% "stunted."[249] By mid-1995, some sources warned that the overall situation throughout the country was catastrophic for the vast majority of the people, irrespective of whether they lived in the north, center, or south.[250]

The normal economic differentiation between social classes has been sharply reduced as Iraq has progressively become a society in which there is a huge gap between the privileged, who are tied to the regime and its security, and the rest of society. On the one hand, the number of destitutes—those with incomes of ID 50 or less has risen to three-quarters of a million in a population that is just under 20 million. This destitution is particularly common among the "urban poor," because the rural poor can grow their own food. At the same time, even those who are unable to grow their own food and without possessions to sell or contacts abroad to help are unlikely to topple the regime."[251]

As for the middle class, they have seen their savings wiped out and most careers become worthless or uneconomical to pursue. Many members of the middle class have been forced to sell their possessions, leave their careers, or take on extra jobs just to provide their families with basic needs.[252] Almost one million Iraqis have emigrated since the Gulf crisis, of whom roughly a quarter of a million reside in Jordan, strategically placed to provide their relatives or friends with basics or money. This exodus of Iraqis means that close to 4 million are now overseas. Most émigrés tend to be members of the middle class simply because they had the money to pay the exorbitant exit fee—the government actually tried to prohibit the emigration of doctors and scientists—and because they had marketable skills.[253]

The political implications of the disintegration of the large, well-educated and secular Iraqi middle class are ominous in the view of some observers:[254]

> The middle class, which had a good level of education and which was liberal and Westernized to a certain extent, is dying out and the West will pay the price for that. Its disappearance will open the way for broad inroads to be made by all the fundamentalist movements, no matter who they are.

On the other hand, a tiny privileged strata made up of the ruling elite exists, comprised of the several thousands of individuals who have become rich by providing the government with basic necessities and goods at highly inflated prices which are trucked over from Jordan, other traders and small-time merchants, farmers, and money-lenders. Parasitic elements of the regime depend on this class of "*nouveaux riches*" for their own profiteering.[255]

One result is a growing gap between the poor who are not allowed to steal and the wealthy who have become a kleptocracy. The seriousness of this socioeconomic situation is illustrated by the growing severity of punishment for economic crimes. Thieves, of which there have been an alarming proliferation in urban centers, are subject to public amputation of a limb. Any hoarding of crops has led the government to withhold seed and fertilizer from farmers who fail to bring their crops to market. Those farmers who fail to cultivate their land altogether have had their land confiscated. Capital punishment has been decreed for those smuggling cars and trucks from the country. Harsh penalties have been levied on currency traders and "profiteers," while merchants have been executed for hoarding and for price fixing.

The Iraqi Government's Refusal
of Relief from UN Sanctions

The human cost of sanction to Iraq's people has scarcely, however, been the fault of the UN. For four years after the imposition of sanctions, Saddam Hussein refused to accept the terms of the United Nations Security Council Resolutions 706 and 712 (1991), which authorized the export of $1.6 billion of Iraqi petroleum during a six-month period. Under the provisions of these resolutions, the proceeds of these sales would have gone to a United Nations escrow account, which would be used to purchase humanitarian supplies for the Iraqi population to be distributed under UN eyes, as well as to fund reparations to Kuwait and other programs mandated by the UN.

The Iraqi regime offered several reasons for refusing the UN offer:

- First, the regime claimed that Iraq only achieved full control of its oil industry from Western oil companies after many years of struggle. To allow the UN (which, in the eyes of the Iraqis is a mere front for the West) to dictate the terms under which Iraq could sell oil, would be unpalatable and unacceptable.[256] One Iraqi technocrat has been quoted as saying: "we are not going to put our main resource, our oil industry, into UN receivership, which is what will happen if we accept their conditions [for the implementation of 706 and 712]."[257]
- Second, the regime claimed that the UN wanted to further infringe on Iraq's sovereignty. It has claimed that these resolutions constitute an attempt by the West to delegitimize the government in the eyes of its own people with the stipulations that the proceeds from the sale would go into an escrow account controlled by the UN and that international observers be placed throughout the country to monitor the distribution of food and medicine. Deputy Prime Minister, Tariq Aziz stated in 1995 that "the UN resolutions on the $1.6 billion oil sale for humanitarian aid would create a parallel government in Iraq."[258]
- Third, the regime ridiculed the revenue from the sale of oil as too small to make much of a difference. According to one source, Iraqi officials had calculated that arrangement would end up providing every Iraqi only $6 worth of food and medicine. In a series of meetings between Iraqi officials and members of the UN Secretariat in Vienna between January and February 1992, Iraq asked for a substantially higher volume of sales and thus revenue than the $1.6 billion allocated over a six-month period. In particular, Usamah al-Hiti, the then Iraqi Oil Minister asked for: a higher volume of exports, a revenue of $2.4 billion over a longer period than the six-month

authorized, and approval for the use of the southern oil terminal at
Mina al-Bakr.[259]

- Fourth, Iraqi oil ministry officials, including the Oil Minister at the
  time, ridiculed the procedures for the distribution and marketing of
  the oil under UN supervision as bizarre and convoluted beyond
  belief. In November 1991 Usamah al-Hitti declared that the oil
  export plan was akin to "a spider's web. . . . The steps which would
  have to be taken, the formalities, the arrangements are so complicated that it would make the sales operations very difficult."[260] The
  following month the Iraqi Oil Minister stated that the UN oil export
  plan was "a totally impractical mess drafted by non-oil people."[261]
  The Iraqis lobbied unsuccessfully to have the government's State
  Organization for the Marketing of Oil (SOMO) remain in charge of
  the sale of oil.[262]

- Fifth, the regime made it clear that it did not want its oil to be
  exported solely or primarily via the pipeline running through
  Turkey. It wanted to be able to export oil to India and Japan from its
  southern off-shore oil terminals which Iraqi engineers and technicians had repaired.

Iraq continued to reject the terms of the UN offer even after the Security Council eased the terms of its initial resolutions and passed Resolution 986. Security Council Resolution 986 was passed in early 1995, as the
successor to Resolution 706.[263] It allowed Iraq to export $1 billion worth
of oil every three months for six months, with the option of renewal. The
resolution also, however, gave the UN authority over the allocation of the
money and required Iraq to accept the following division of revenues:[264]

- 30% to the UN Gulf War Reparations Fund
- 10% to the UN—4% to UN operational costs in Iraq and 6% to fund
  the UNSCOM arms inspection effort.
- 15% for direct humanitarian aid to the three northern Kurdish governates.
- 45% of the remaining funds for food and medicine for the rest of the
  country. The distribution of these basics would be monitored by the
  UN.

These terms gave Saddam's regime roughly $106 million a month for
food, medicine, and humanitarian goods, but they also gave $50 million
to the Kurds, $100 million to compensate victims of the Iraqi invasion,
and $33 million to the UN.[265]

The Iraqi government initially rejected UN Security Council Resolution 986 as an interference with its sovereignty. The regime was also irri-

tated by a stipulation that most of the Iraqi oil must be exported through the northern route via Turkey, and that UN agencies must distribute humanitarian supplies in the three northern (i.e., Kurdish) governates. In November 1995 the new Iraqi Oil Minister, Dr. Amir Abdel Rashid, declared in Vienna that Iraq would not consider UN Security Council Resolution 986 as it stood unless the UN Secretary-General Boutrus Boutrus Ghali would "promise and guarantee that either the resolution is modified to take into consideration the two elements that Iraq rejected. . . ."[266]

Rashid indicated that these two stipulations constituted undue interference in Iraqi sovereignty and domestic affairs, and claimed that the US insisted upon them to force Iraq to reject the resolution. At the same time, he reiterated that Iraq was interested in a complete, rather than partial, lifting of sanctions. Part of the reason for this refusal was that the Iraqi regime evidently hoped that the head of UNSCOM would present a more positive report on the progress of the elimination of Iraqi weapons of mass destruction, thus opening the way for the lifting of sanctions in accordance with paragraph 22 of UN Security Council Resolution 687. Amir Abdel Rashid stated that:[267]

> You can't use your power in a cowboy fashion [here referring to the US penchant to veto anything concerning the rehabilitation of Iraq]. When Mr. Ekeus will report, sooner or later, that Iraq has met its obligations, the French and Russians will table a draft resolution to lift the sanctions. The British, being professional diplomats and legalistic, the least they could do is to abstain. They will not object. The US will find it very hard to stop this process.

It is difficult to ascertain the source of Rashid's optimism. Hussein Kamel's defection had already exposed the fact that the Iraqi government had continued to lie to UNSCOM and that a substantial amount of its equipment and feedstocks for weapons of mass destruction were unaccounted for. There was little prospect that UNSCOM could quickly certify Iraq's compliance with the UN resolutions relating to the destruction of its capacity to build and deliver weapons of mass destruction. UNSCOM had to interpret the nearly half-million pages of new documentation it obtained after the defection of Hussein Kamel. Further, it was confronted with new evidence relating to Iraqi smuggling, concealment of nuclear and missile technology, and lies regarding Iraq's destruction of its biological weapons.[268]

It was hardly likely that Britain would reverse its policy, or respond to pressure from British companies with economic interests in Iraq. Further, even Iraq's "supporters" in the UN Security Council had been embarrassed by the new revelations concerning Iraq's massive biological weapons program.[269] Even states which believed in the broader rehabilitation of Iraq and/or which were deeply concerned by the humanitarian situation in Iraq, urged the Iraqi leadership to accept Resolution 986. France, Russia, and Egypt told Iraq to accept 986 without preconditions, but added that Iraqi views should be taken into account during the implementation of the resolution.[270] In addition, the Iraqi regime had little reason to believe that sanctions could be lifted before the US presidential elections in November 1996 or that any Republican Administration would be more favorable to Iraq than the Clinton Administration.

Accepting UN Security Council Resolution 986

These realities slowly forced the Iraqi regime to change its position during the course of 1996, as did evidence that the decline of Iraq's economy might be reaching the point where it would trigger a political explosion. According to US government estimates, Iraq's per capita income in constant 1994 dollars had dropped from around $3,200 in 1984 to $2,100 in 1989, $1,400 in 1990, and $885 in 1992. By late 1995, it had dropped below $500—less than one-sixth of the level Iraq had achieved during the middle of the Iran-Iraq War and less than 25% of the level in achieved before it invaded Kuwait.[271]

The government had to take increasingly more drastic measures between the fall of 1995 and the winter of 1996. On January 2, 1996, Saddam Hussein announced that there must be an immediate cessation to the printing of money, a situation which had contributed to hyper-inflation. In addition, the government announced belt-tightening measures in the public sector, the further sale of state property including cars, spare parts, factories, machinery and even scrap metal in order to raise revenue.

The Iraqi leader also stated that there would be no salary increases in 1996—in contrast with the past five years—although measures would be taken to protect the living standards of low-income civil servants.[272] Iraqi statistics issued in January 1996 showed the Dinar trading at 3,000 to the US dollar as compared to three Dinars to the dollar in August 1990, and that food prices overall had risen several orders of magnitude since the Kuwait crisis.[273]

The regime tried to accelerate the privatization of public sector enterprises—a process it should have implemented at least twenty years earlier—and which could do little to help in the short term. Further, Saddam indicated that taxes would be raised and that there would be a seven-fold increase in the price of gasoline—although it still cost only about at 14 cents to the gallon and remained a fraction of the world price.[274]

As a result, Iraq began discussions of ways to implement UN Security Council Resolution 986 in February 1996.[275] The Iraqi government issued statements that it was ready to talk, although it indicated that it did not accept the resolution as it stands. The regime also indicated that it was changing its broader strategy for lifting sanctions, and was ready to accept the partial lifting of sanctions as a means to an end, through the slow but steady erosion of the full sanctions regime over a period of time. Saddam's regime then began serious negotiations with the UN.

On January 16, 1996, Deputy Minister Tariq Aziz indicated to UN Secretary-General Boutros-Boutros Ghali that Iraq would enter into talks without "preconditions" concerning limited Iraqi oil sales under the terms of UN Security Council Resolution 986. News reports followed that the government had met with the UN and issued a statement which claimed, "We expect positive results for the dialogue with the United Nations." This announcement had an immediate effect on the Iraqi economy. The Iraqi Dinar, which was valued at 3,000 to the dollars on New Year's eve, suddenly traded at 450 to the dollar. The price of essential food items like sugar, rice, eggs, and flour dropped sharply, and food hoarding was reduced.[276]

At the same time, the Iraqi government continued to raise its concerns relating to the procedures for the export of Iraqi oil and distribution of the humanitarian supplies throughout the country. Nizar Hamdoon, the Iraqi Ambassador to the UN, wrote the Secretary-General on January 17, 1996, that "Iraq will respond to the call to enter into a dialogue on the subject of oil in return for food and medicine on the basis that there should be no conditions imposed on us."[277] Iraq made it clear that it wanted modifications to the resolution to reduce its impact on Iraqi sovereignty and to allow it to accept the operational implementation of the resolution without publicly referring to the fact that Iraq had accepted the UN Resolution. Iraq also sought help from other Arab states, Russia, and France in putting pressure on the UN negotiators to compromise.

Abdul Amir Ambari—the chief Iraqi negotiator—stated that the UN conditions "are not a problem" when he began talks in early February, 1996. However, this statement only set the stage for a first round of intensive "technical deliberations" between UN and Iraqi officials which lasted until February 19. The talks ended with a paper produced by the UN and Iraqi officials which emphasized the technical conditions under which Iraq could sell oil—including the circumstances under which they can make contracts with potential buyers, operating procedures of the escrow account that would receive the proceeds from the sale of oil, and verification mechanisms to keep track of the money and to ensure that it is used to buy food and medicine.[278] However, the two sides did not reach the expected Memorandum of Understanding which would have been the first stage towards the implementation of the resolution.

The second round of talks resolved many *technical* issues but it ended on March 18, 1996, without resolving the remaining *political* issues.[279]

Iraqi opposition to accepting Security Council Resolution 986 now centered around two key elements of resolution:

- Iraq did not want to be limited solely to the use of the oil pipeline to Turkey which ran through Kurdish-controlled territories in northern Iraq. It feared that this export route would provide both Kurds and Turks with too much of bargaining lever vis-à-vis Baghdad. Consequently, the Iraqi government sought to split the limited exports between the Turkish pipeline and Iraq's own export terminals on the Persian Gulf at Mina al-Bakr and Khor al-Amaya.
- UNSCR 986 stipulated that 20% of the proceeds from the sale of oil would go to the autonomous Kurdish region in the north, and that the UN would be responsible for the allocation and distribution of humanitarian supplies to that area. Baghdad saw this as a humiliation and an attempt to legitimize secessionism.[280]

These problems in the talks were accentuated by the Jordanian seizure of spare parts and equipment allegedly for weapons bound for Iraq and by yet another stand-off between Iraqi authorities and members of the United Nations Special Commission. In mid-March Iraq prevented UNSCOM from searching for documents relating to weapons of mass destruction and for missile components, prompting the Security Council to declare on March 19 that Iraqi intransigence constituted "clear violations" of the Gulf War cease-fire.[281]

Iraqi officials made it clear that the deadlocked talks did not mean that Baghdad was no longer interested in reaching a solution amenable to both sides. In particular, the Iraqis managed to maintain a sense of optimism throughout the talks.[282] In mid-March Vice-President Taha Yasin Ramadan stated that, "We are prepared to show flexibility as long as it does not infringe on our sovereignty."[283]

Iraqi Deputy Prime Minister Tariq Aziz reiterated Iraq's concerns in early April, just as a third round of talks were beginning, when he stated, "Important obstacles have been raised. The remaining differences between the two sides are very important. They touch on our country's integrity and sovereignty."[284]

Nevertheless, Iraq accepted the UN's terms—after a compromise on the way in which the Kurd's share of oil revenues would be administered.[285] On May 20, 1996, Iraq and the UN formally concluded a Memorandum of Understanding calling for the complete implementation of UNSCR 986. This compromise followed weeks of heated debates between Iraqi diplomats and UN officials in New York, during which Iraq and other states including members of the Security Council bitterly accused both the US and Great Britain of interfering in the UN-Iraqi negotiations to prevent a resolution of the differences over UNSCR 986.[286]

The memorandum stipulated that Iraq must present the UN Secretary-General with an outline of its plan—which must then be approved by the Secretary-General—for the purchase and distribution of supplies, medicines and food to its people. Furthermore, for each billion dollars worth of oil sold, the UN would act to ensure that $300 million will be allocated to the "victims" of the Gulf War, $30 million would cover the cost of the disarmament of Iraq, and $150 million would be used to cover the costs of a UN-directed effort headed by Japanese diplomat Yasushi Akashi to provide relief for the three northern Kurdish provinces. There would be no Iraqi government presence in the distribution of the supplies in the north.

The Iraqi government was to distribute supplies in the rest of the country on an equitable basis to be supervised by UN observers who would be accorded diplomatic status and allowed freedom of movement throughout the country. Iraq did manage to prevent the establishment of two very separate distribution systems, one in the north and one in the rest of the country by managing to retain the right to buy supplies, food and medicines for the *entire* country from whomever it chose.[287]

The agreement had an immediate impact on Iraq's economy. The exchange rate of the Dinar to the dollar dipped to as few as 450 Dinars to the dollar from the level of 800–1,000 that had existed once it was apparent that talks over sanctions were serious. While the exchange rate climbed back to its original level once the limited nature of the relief from sanctions became apparent, the deal led to popular rejoicing in many areas and the first sign of public confidence in the economy in years. If few Iraqis felt the UN's terms were adequate, or expected the economy to improve to anything like pre-war levels, most seemed to feel that there would be an end to malnutrition and Iraq's worst medical problems.

At present, however, Resolution 986 is still awaiting implementation. Long, painful negotiations took place during May–August 1996 over the details of implementation of the resolution. These negotiations centered around US insistence on detailed UN control of the oil revenues and on the detailed involvement of UN personnel in verifying the ways in which the money was spent. The Kurdish crisis of August–September 1996 then led to a further indefinite suspension of the agreement. It seems likely that the US will lift its objections after the November 1996 election, but nothing is certain.

The Future Political Impact of Sanctions

Sanctions and the decline of the Iraqi economy have unquestionably weakened Saddam's regime, but it is far from clear that sanctions will lead to the Iraqi leader's downfall now that Iraq has accepted UN Resolution 986. In spite of all their suffering, the Iraqi people have been subjected to a massive propaganda campaign blaming the West for sanctions and the war on Western conspiracies and the acts of corrupt Gulf and Arab leaders.

The observations of a Western diplomat in Baghdad in mid-1995 may still be apposite: "There is no direct connection between the sanctions—the suffering of the people—and the future of the regime. The regime could exist under sanctions for another 10 or 20 years."[288] This diplomat in question may or may not have been aware of Saddam's boast three years earlier that Iraq could survive for another 20 years under sanctions, but it is unclear whether accepting Resolution 986 will really affect the regime's credibility or survival.

Saddam's acceptance of Resolution 986 can be interpreted as a sacrifice he makes to protect the Iraqi people in the face of overwhelming force. Such acceptance also does nothing to prevent Saddam Hussein from continuing a line of domestic propaganda line that the blame for sanctions on the West:[289]

> They have imposed sanctions on us under the pretext of demanding our withdrawal from Kuwait. Now that we are out of Kuwait, why should the economic blockade continue? Look how much they hate you. How can man live if he does not eat? . . . There are organizations in the West for the welfare of cats and dogs, to protect them and feed them. . . . They are starving 18 million Iraqi people.

This propaganda had some successes even before the regime accepted the terms of Resolution 986. Western journalists and observers who traveled to Iraq heard many Iraqis express their anger and dismay over what the West had "done to their country." This is not to say that Iraqis did not blame Saddam and the Ba'athist regime for having brought them to this situation. However, it proved easier, safer, and psychologically more reassuring for many Iraqis to pin the blame on outsiders. As a result, many analysts of the Iraqi political and socioeconomic scene, including many Iraqi government officials and intellectuals, felt that sanctions have only had a moderate effect in weakening Saddam Hussein's grip on power.

The Iraqi ruling elite seems to have felt it could ride out the UN sanctions for a surprisingly long time. In spite of the country's situation after 1992, the regime's elite seemed to feel that the system and the leadership could survive. This sentiment was expressed so often by so many Iraqi officials that many may well have believed it. As early as 1992, Tariq Aziz, the Deputy Prime Minister, declared:[290]

> We, as a leadership and a people, are optimistic about the future. This is because sooner or later they will be forced to gradually ease the blockade

restrictions. This blockade ... will disintegrate, not by a Security Council resolution, but rather by the natural course of developments.

Another Iraqi official made a similar statement in an interview with a Western journalist in 1995:[291]

> Is there another country in the world whose government is opposed by every one of its neighbors, and by the only superpower which also funds the main opposition group and by the world media. None. Yet you can see for yourself. There is absolutely no chance of a change. This is not a weak system.

Suffering does not axiomatically lead to revolution and it may end in strengthening revanchism. In spite of the defection of Hussein Kamel, the Iraqi people still have every reason to fear the strength of the regime. There is little opposition that can challenge the regime in any way. The rampant banditry in the country by bands of roving ex-servicemen—particularly in the south—is just that, not acts of political insurrection.[292] Further, the sanctions focus the Iraqi people's attention on sheer survival. Life has become a search for food. This deflects attention and anger away from Saddam Hussein and the manifestly obvious failures and crimes of the regime after a half-decade of privation.

While there is no way to determine Iraqi popular attitudes, it seems likely that many Iraqi see the UN sanctions as a Western-instigated act of collective punishment against all Iraqis, and may actually rally much of the Iraqi people around their government. In the words of one Iraqi professor at the University of Baghdad: "This [the maintenance of sanctions] is part of the strength that this regime has—the outside threat creates a unison [sic] within."[293]

Iraqis have also tended to blame the UN and the West for both the prolongation of sanctions and the terms of Resolution 986, and there has been growing bitterness as the Iraqi people have come to understand how little they would receive. One Iraqi merchant commented that, "We are a petroleum country and this is all we are getting?" Mutafa Tawfeeq al-Mukhtar, an Iraqi economist commented that, "It's a pittance. I don't believe those in the West understand the depth of the problem."[294] As a result, the Iraqi regime can probably easily deal with the political complications of shifting from a total rejection of a compromise with the UN, and will benefit from accepting UN Resolution 986.

At the same time, Saddam Hussein's decision to continue negotiating with the UN over Resolution 986, despite his anger over what he sees as Western attempts to further humiliate Iraq, almost certainly reflects a calcuation by the Iraqi leadership that one dent in the wall of sanctions—

no matter how circumscribed and humiliating—will lead to further cracks. If nothing else, it will allow Iraq to achieve the tactical goal of re-entering the oil market.

Debt and Reparations After the Gulf War

The acceptance of UN Security Council Resolution 986 also highlights the issue of debt and reparations. Iraq must not only deal with its economic crisis, but with the problem of debt and wartime reparations. Iraq has accumulated an immense backlog of payments and potential obligations. Once again, there are no precise figures on the size of these obligations, but it is instructive to consider the financial report the Iraqis submitted to UN Secretary-General Boutrus Boutrus Ghali on April 29, 1991. This is one of the most detailed—if not necessarily accurate—financial statements made public by the Iraqi government:[295]

- *Financial Obligations:* Iraq's total external debt was estimated at $43 billion. Its size constituted 65% of the Gross Domestic Product.
- *Basic Requirements*: The report indicated that Iraq would require financial resources for the reconstitution of the stock of food and of basic commodities, the cost of repairing the damage to the civilian infrastructure, and for the continued implementation of development projects that were under way before the Gulf War. The Iraqis indicated that they would need at least ID 43.5 billion between 1991 and 1995 for imports of basics (food and medicine), other consumer goods and raw materials, spare parts and machinery, reconstitution of strategic reserves of food and medicine (i.e., note that this is not the same as annual imports of food and medicine. Iraq traditionally kept 25% of its imports as a strategic reserve for emergencies), repair of war damage, and continuation of the development plan to restore Iraq to normalcy.
- *Anticipated Revenue:* The Iraqis indicated that if sanctions were to be lifted in 1991, the country would earn an estimated ID 20 billion between 1991 and 1995. The Iraqi report based its figure on the assumption that Iraq would be able to export only 600,000 barrels of crude oil a day at $16 per barrel for a substantial period of time because of the damage sustained by the oil sector.
- *Gap Between Requirements and Anticipated Foreign Currency Revenue:* The Iraqis pointed out that in light of their debt-servicing obligations (P+I) and their various import requirements over a five-year period, Iraq's total foreign currency needs amounted to about ID 67 billion, of which ID 23.5 billion were destined for debt, and ID 43.5 billion were required to meet the needs of the Iraqi economy. Given

the gap between anticipated revenues from the sale of oil and the country's financial requirements, the Iraqi government concluded that the economy would be placed in an "unenviable position in as much as such revenues do not cover its minimum financial obligations or its requirements for food and medicine."

The situation has changed drastically since that time. Sanctions were not lifted in 1991, and Iraq has not been able to export oil at the rate required to deal with its financial obligations and to meet its economic requirements. For the past five years, Iraq's financial obligations have continued to accrue and the cost of rebuilding its economy and infrastructure will require a far greater infusion of capital than in 1991.

Further, UN resolutions stipulate that Iraq will have to compensate those countries, companies and individuals whose interests, financial or otherwise, were damaged or wiped out by the Iraqi invasion of Kuwait. As a result, they call for 30% of Iraq's oil income to be put into a special UN Fund to compensate those with claims against Iraq. Furthermore, Iraq is financially liable for UN operations such as the elimination of its weapons of mass destruction. It is estimated that the cost of these UN programs will require Iraq to divert up to 5% of its oil revenues.

Some estimates place the total cost of debt, and reconstruction, and reparations at approximately $141 billion over the period from 1991–2000.[296] There is no way to know the true amount, but unless debt and reparations are reduced or forgiven, they will be a major hindrance—if not a crippling burden—on Iraq's ability to rebuild its economy regardless of how and when sanctions are lifted.[297]

It seems likely that they will be a lasting source of conflict and revanchism regardless of whether Saddam survives. Even the implementation of UN Security Council Resolution 986 may create such revanchism. Terms where Iraq only gets a maximum of $4 billion a year from oil exports will be unpopular, but Saddam will not be blamed for terms that permit the use of only half of this money to benefit the Iraq people. Few Iraqis are likely to ignore the fact that the roughly $106 million a month they receive for food, medicine, and humanitarian goods will fail to do more than ease a desperate crisis while $50 million will go to the Kurds, $100 million to compensate victims of the Iraqi invasion, $20 million will go to defray the costs of the UN arms inspection effort, and $13 million will go to the UN to administer the oil deal. Such terms may well validate Saddam Hussein's anti-sanctions propaganda in Iraq, as well as win him support in the Arab and developing world.

It is also important to remember that the legacy of impoverishment from the Iran-Iraq War, Gulf War, and sanctions will impact on a nation with a very rapidly growing population and with a steadily growing number of males of military age. Chart Five is based on a conservative World Bank estimate of the trends in Iraq's population. It estimates Iraq's population grew from 18.1 million in 1990 to 21.0 million in 1995, and will grow to 24.5 million by the year 2000, 32.5 million by 2010, and 40.5 million by 2020. The total number of young Iraqi men reaching job age (15–19 years) will rise from 1.2 million in 1995 to 1.4 million in 2000, 1.6 million in 2005, 1.7 million in 2010, 2.0 million in 2015, and 2.2 million in 2020. Unlike many other Gulf countries, Iraq has a large female work force, and the population of young females will also nearly double by 2020.[298]

Implications for Western and Southern Gulf Strategy

There is no easy way out of the current game of "chicken" between Iraq and the nations that support the UN sanctions. Saddam's acceptance the terms of UN Security Council Resolution 986 is only a new move in the game.

The West and the Southern Gulf face a clear dilemma between the strategic benefits of sanctions in limiting the military threat from Iraq and supporting a strategy to remove Saddam from power on the one hand, and the human cost of the sanctions together with the resulting Iraqi popular resentment of the nations supporting sanctions on the other. This dilemma is already dividing the West and the Southern Gulf states, and the US from many nations that support the UN coalition. In fact, this dilemma virtually ensures that the West, other states, and the Southern Gulf will not pursue a united policy. Despite their embarrassment over the revelations of Iraqi lying and cheating about their biological weapons program in fall 1995, major trade partners and creditors of Iraq will always seek a softer line than nations whose primary concern is Gulf security.

Any incremental easing and/or lifting sanctions reduces the pressure on Iraqis in the "center" to remove Saddam, and internal Iraqi support—assuming it exists—for groups based outside. It inevitably increases the risk that Iraq will import new weapons and technologies for weapons of mass destruction. Yet maintaining sanctions inflicts a high cost on the Iraqi people, and makes it progressively less likely that any future regime will not seek revenge, and probably heightens the risk that the internal divisions within Iraq will grow to the point where civil war or fragmentation could occur.

There are no good alternatives to a reliance on sanctions in the sense that such alternatives offer the West and Southern Gulf real hope they can create a stable and friendly Iraq. There may, however, be better options now that Iraq has accepted UN Security Council Resolution 986. These options include:

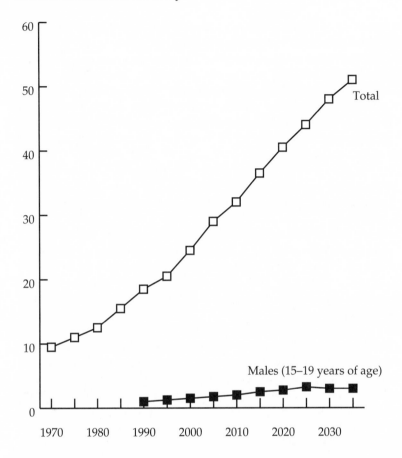

CHART FIVE   Estimated Trends in the Iraqi Population During 1990–2035.
Source: Adapted by Anthony H. Cordesman from World Bank, *World Population Projections, 1994–1995,* Washington, World Bank, 1994, and material provided by the CIA.

- Reaching a clear decision as to whether sanctions really are tied to the survival of Saddam and his coterie, and making the West's position clear to Iraq. The present US, British, Saudi, and Kuwaiti position seems to be to use prolonged sanctions in an effort to remove Saddam, but this policy is all "stick" and no "carrot." It does not make it clear that Iraq would benefit if it gets rid of Saddam, or what kind of new government would be acceptable. It also will fail if Saddam can survive by accepting UN Security Council Resolution 986. The time may well have come to focus on the conduct of the Iraqi regime, rather than its leadership, and to use sanctions to alter Iraq's behavior, rather than its political leadership.

- Setting forth exact conditions for changes in the behavior of the current regime in return for a step by step lifting of sanctions and/or easing of sanctions. Key conditions could be continued UNSCOM operations, full and unconditional recognition of the new border with Kuwait, an autonomy agreement with the Kurds, a halt to military operations in southern Iraq, and an arms import limitation agreement.
- Offering massive increases in shipments of food and humanitarian aid without compensation—effectively limiting what Iraq can import, defusing the human problem, and undercutting Saddam's propaganda.
- Offering stage by stage forgiveness of debt and reparations for any regime whose conduct proves acceptable. This forgiveness recognizes the fact that Iraq almost certainly will never pay all its present debts and reparations, and cannot rebuild its economy if it tries to do so. It instead uses debts and reparations as a "carrot" to create a more stable Iraq.

One thing is clear, any strategy for dealing with Iraq must deal with debt and reparations as well as sanctions. Kuwait and Saudi Arabia need to come fully to grips with the potential political cost of their demands for repayment of debt and reparations. There are disturbing parallels between the present demands on Iraq and the kind of "peace" that Tacitus once warned against—"they created a wasteland and called it peace."

Further, if the UN attempts to enforce all of its current demands on Iraq in terms of sanctions, potential war crimes trials, reparations, and loan repayments, it may end in creating the kind of "peace" the allies forced on Germany after World War I. This was a peace which J. M. Keynes quite correctly warned the victorious powers could only lead to chaos and a second war.

The Iraqi people have already suffered through the Iran-Iraq War and the Gulf War. Not every tragedy has to have a third act. Iraq's rich oil resources should be used to rebuild and rehabilitate the country, and not to pay punitive damages to be shouldered by the next generation. Iraq may have a loathsome, guilty, and incompetent regime, but a Carthaginian peace can only contribute to Iraqi revanchism for years to come.

8

Oil and Iraqi
Export Capabilities

Oil is another critical dimension of any strategy towards Iraq. Iraq has long been a major oil exporting power, and had produced about 22 billion barrels of oil at the time the Gulf War began.[299] Iraq's oil export revenues have allowed it to be a major trading partner, although they have varied sharply according to world oil prices and the impact of Iraq's wars. Iraq had annual exports ranging from $6.8 billion to $26.0 billion during the 1980s, but has not been able to export since it invaded Kuwait in August 1990.[300]

Although Iraqi oil production peaked at slightly under 3.5 MMBD in 1979, Iraq produced only about 600,000 barrels per day (BPD) before it accepted UN Security Council Resolution 986. The acceptance of Resolution 986 adds about 700,000 barrels a day worth of exports to this total at mid-1996 oil prices but scarcely brings Iraqi production back to pre-war levels or meets the production goals set for Iraqi in most Western energy models.

This makes the resumption of Iraqi oil production an important factor in determining world oil prices and in setting OPEC quotas. At the same time, Iraq's oil and gas reserves give it the potential to increase production far beyond its past peak levels, and to become a far more important oil producer than in the past.[301]

Iraq's Strategic Oil and Gas Potential

Iraqi experts and technocrats claim that Iraq has proven reserves of 112 billion barrels, and "probable and possible oil reserves" of up to 214 billion barrels. While this estimate of possible reserves is technically feasible, many outside experts think that Iraq is exaggerating these estimates in order to heighten the interest of foreign companies and convince foreign governments that Iraq must be treated as a critical strategic oil power. Even conservative Western experts agree, however, that Iraq has total oil reserves of at least 100 billion barrels, and proven reserves of at least 85 billion barrels. The US Energy Information Agency (EIA) agrees with Iraq's estimate of total proven reserves of 112 billion barrels, or 13% of the world's reserves.[302] The International Energy Agency (IEA) estimates that Iraq has 100 billion barrels, or 10% of the world's supply of proven reserves. All of these estimates give Iraq the world's second largest oil reserves—surpassed only by Saudi Arabia.[303]

All of Iraq's crude oil production comes from on-shore fields, about two-thirds of which from two large fields: Kirkuk and Ramalia. These fields are in decline, despite water injection, but Iraq has a total of 73 known oil fields and only 15 have been put into production. Six of these fields are considered "super giant" with recoverable reserves of over 6 billion barrels, three are "big giants" with up to 6 billion barrels of reserves, and 20 are "giant" fields with less than 5 billion barrels. Iraq has roughly 1,500 oil wells, of which 820 were actively producing before the Gulf War. Iraq also has a share of the Saudi-Iraqi neutral zone, with another 5 billion barrels of proven reserves.[304] The International Energy Agency (IEA) estimates that Iraq has one of the four lowest production costs per barrel of any country in the world, and the lowest investment cost per barrel of additional oil production. It costs Iraq less than $2 to produce a barrel of oil.

Iraq is certain to be a major future player in world oil and energy production. Industry estimates generally credit Iraq with at least 2.0 million barrels of production per day (MMBD) if UN sanctions and export restrictions are lifted, and estimate that this production will rise by about 0.5 MMBD a year to at least 4.0 MMBD within four years. The IEA estimates that Iraq has the capability to produce 2.5 to 3.0 MMBD, but indicates that it will only be possible to determine Iraq's near-term capability after several months of effort to bring its existing fields on-line. Regardless of which estimate is right, Iraq has enough export capability to make it one of the world's largest sources of spare oil production.[305]

Projections by the US Department of Energy (DOE) estimate that Iraq will produce 4.4 MMBD by the year 2000 (with a range of 4.0–5.1 MMBD), 5.4 MMBD by 2005 (4.6–6.0 MMBD), and 6.4 MMBD by 2010 (5.5–6.6 MMBD). If these estimates are correct, Iraq will be a bigger producer than Kuwait by 2000, and a substantially larger producer than Iran by 2005. This means Iraq will rise from less than 0.3% of total OPEC production in 1995, to 12% in 2000, 13% in 2005, and 14% by 2010. Iraq is projected to provide 18% of all Gulf production by 2010, and 7% of total world production. These projections mean Iraq will rise to the rank of the world's fourth largest oil producer, and will be a major factor in meeting growing world demand and limiting the rise in future oil prices.[306]

Iraq indicated in March 1995 that it would gradually seek to increase oil production to 6 MMBD by 2003, at an investment cost of $25 billion. This cost estimate was said to include the cost of developing new oil fields, increasing the gas processing, storage, pipelines, and export terminals.[307]

The US Department of Energy estimates that Iraq also has 109.5 trillion cubic feet (tcf) of proven gas reserves, or 2.2% of the world supply. The IEA estimates that Iraq's gas reserves total 3.1 trillion cubic meters (tcm), or roughly 2% of the world's supply.[308] Experts estimate that Iraq has another 160 trillion cubic feet of free gas as yet unexplored.[309] Iraq indicated in March 1995 that it is seeking to reduce gas flaring and use gas for power generation, petrochemicals, and possibly for export. It currently estimates its downstream investment costs at $6 billion between 1995 and 2003.[310]

Iraq produced peak levels of 39,000 BPD of natural gas liquids (NGL) in 1987, although production has dropped to 5,000 BPD since the Gulf War. There are no reliable estimates of the size of Iraq's future gas exports, but the International Energy Agency (IEA) estimates that Iraq can export gas to Turkey and Syria, and in LNG form at prices that are lower than, or competitive with, those of the Southern Gulf states. It estimates export prices of $3.55 per million British thermal units (MBTU).[311] Table One and Chart Six show a recent IEA estimate of how Iraq's oil reserves compare to those of other Gulf states.

Iraqi Oil Production Before the Gulf War[312]

Iraq has been an exporter of oil since the early 1930s, but the Iraqi government played no role in Iraq's oil development from the time oil was discovered in Iraq in 1927 until the early 1950s. This resulted in the slow development of Iraq's oil fields. Iraqi oil was left under the control of the Iraq Petroleum Company, a consortium of Western oil companies such as British Petroleum, Esso (now Exxon), and France's Compagnie Francaise de Petrole (CFP). Neither BP nor Esso—giants in the oil business—were interested in quickly developing and expanding Iraq's oil. They had access to cheap and abundant oil supplies elsewhere. CFP struggled to raise Iraqi oil output because it was a smaller partner and had few external reserves, but had only limited impact. As a result, the IPC treated Iraq's oil as a reserve for the future.

Iraq's production began to rise in the 1950s, as Iraq began to gain some control over development decisions. The Iraqi National Oil Company (INOC) was created in 1964, but it was only following Iraq's nationalization of the oil industry in 1972, that a massive increase took place in the output of crude petroleum, and Iraq only liquidated the last traces of foreign control in 1975. It completed the integration of the INOC into the Oil Ministry in 1987.

TABLE ONE   Comparative Oil Reserves and Production Levels of the Gulf States

Comparative Oil Reserves in 1994 in Billions of Barrels

Country	Identified	Undiscovered	Identified and Undiscovered	Proven	% of World Total
Bahrain	—	—	—	.35	
Iran	69.2	19.0	88.2	89.3	8.9
Iraq	90.8	35.0	125.8	100.0	10.0
Kuwait	92.6	3.0	95.6	96.5	9.7
Oman	—	—	—	5.0	NA
Qatar	3.9	0	3.9	3.7	0.4
Saudi Arabia	265.5	51.0	316.5	261.2	26.1
UAE	61.1	4.2	65.3	98.1	9.8
Total	583.0	112.2	695.2	654.1	64.9
Rest of World	—	—	—	345.7	35.1
World	—	—	—	999.8	100.0

(continues)

TABLE ONE (continued)

Comparative Oil Production in Millions of Barrels per Day

Country	1995 OPEC Quota	1995 Actual	DOE/IEA Estimate of Actual Production 1990	1992	2000	2005	2010	Maximum Sustainable 1995	2000	Announced Capacity in 2000
Bahrain	—	—	—	—	—	—	—	—	—	—
Iran	3,600	3,608	3.2	3.6	4.3	5.0	5.4	3.2	4.5	4.5
Iraq	400	600	2.2	0.4	4.4	5.4	6.6	2.5	5.0	5.0
Kuwait	2,000	1,850	1.7	1.1	2.9	3.6	4.2	2.8	3.3	3.3
Oman	—	—	—	—	—	—	—	—	—	—
Qatar	378	449	0.5	0.4	0.6	0.6	0.6	0.5	0.6	0.6
Saudi Arabia	8,000	8,018	8.5	9.6	11.5	12.8	14.1	10.3	11.1	11.1
UAE	2,161	2,193	2.5	2.6	3.1	3.5	4.3	3.0	3.8	3.2
Total										
Gulf	—	—	18.6	17.7	26.8	30.9	35.0	23.5	28.2	28.2
World	—	—	69.6	67.4	78.6	84.2	88.8	—	—	—

Source: Adapted by Anthony H. Cordesman from estimates in IEA, Middle East Oil and Gas, Paris, OED/IEA, 1995, Annex 2 and DOE/EIA, International Energy Outlook, 1995, Washington, DOE/EIA, June, 1995, pp. 26–30, and Middle East Economic Digest, February 23, 1996, p. 3. IEA and DOE do not provide country breakouts for Bahrain and Oman. Reserve data estimated by author based on country data.

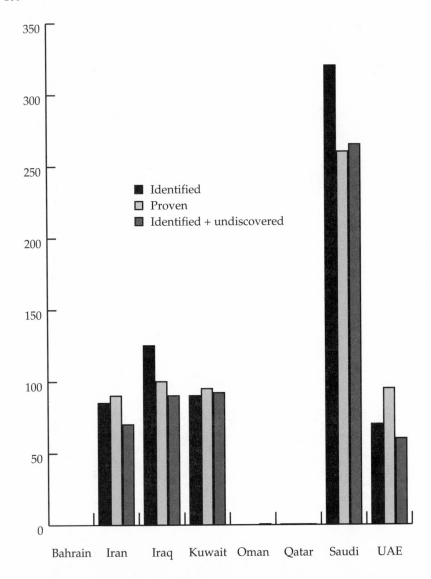

CHART SIX Total Oil Reserves of the Gulf States (in Billions of Barrels).
Source: IEA, *Middle East Oil and Gas,* Paris, OECD, IEA, Annex 2, and data
provided by Bahrain and Oman. Bahrain's reserves are only 350 million barrels
and do not show up on the chart because of scale.

MAP TWO Iraqi Oil Production Before the Gulf War. *Source:* US State Department.

Iraq's exports and oil revenues changed dramatically after 1973. The trends in Iraq's oil exports since the early 1970s are shown in Chart Seven, and the trends in the value of Iraq's oil exports are shown in Chart Eight. These charts show that Iraqi oil production more than doubled between 1971 and 1979, rising from 1.7 MMBD to 3.475 MMBD.

In 1979, the fall of the Shah of Iran led to a sudden cut in Iranian production and Iraq became the world's second largest exporter after Saudi Arabia. Iraqi oil production peaked in 1979 at 3.46 MMBD and annual production totaled 170.6m metric tons, as compared with 83.5 metric tons in 1971, and 47.6 metric tons in 1960. Exports in 1979 and 1980 averaged

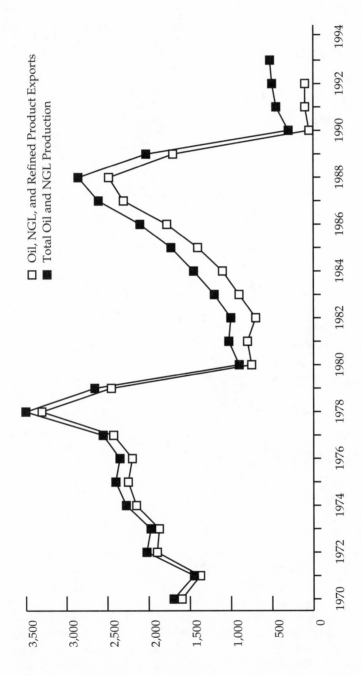

CHART SEVEN Iraqi Oil and Natural Gas Liquids Total Production and Exports (in Thousands of Barrels Per Day).
Source: Adapted by Anthony H. Cordesman from International Energy Agency (IEA), *Middle East Oil and Gas,* Paris, 1995, pp. 252–256.

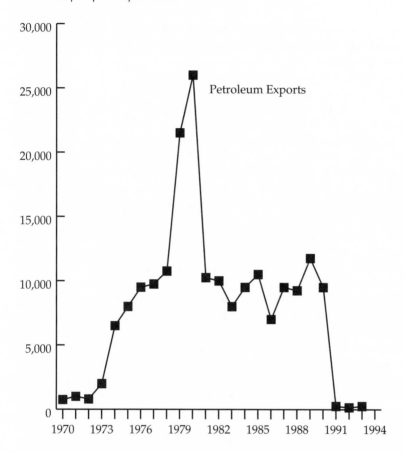

CHART EIGHT   Iraqi Oil Exports in Millions of Current Dollars.
Source: Adapted by Anthony H. Cordesman from International Energy Agency
(IEA), *Middle East Oil and Gas,* Paris, 1995, pp. 256–257.

3.3 million barrels per day, bringing in revenues of $21.3 billion and $26.1
billion respectively. These two years constituted the heyday of Iraqi oil
production.[313]
   The Iran-Iraq War exposed Iraq's vulnerability in terms of oil export
capability. Iraq was dependent on exporting through a narrow and vulnerable coastline only 52 miles long and sandwiched between Kuwait on
the south and Iran on the north-east, and on pipelines carrying Iraqi oil
through neighboring countries. In 1980, these pipelines included a
reversible flow pipeline from Rumalia to Haditha and Kirkuk, linking its
north and south oil fields, a 1,000 kilometer-long pipeline from Kirkuk to
the port of Dortyol on the Mediterranean; a pipeline from Haditha to

Tripoli in Lebanon and Baniyas in Syria; and finally, lines running from the southern oil fields to the off-shore export terminals of Mina al-Bakr and Khor al-Amaya.

Iraqi oil production declined dramatically in early 1981, after Iranian attacks on Iraq's tanker loading terminals at Mina al Bakr and Khor al Amaya in the Gulf. In 1982, the Syrian government closed Iraq's main export pipeline. This Bania pipeline linked the Kirkuk and Rumalia oil fields to terminals on Syria's Mediterranean coast. It had a capacity of 1.4 MMBD and was carrying peak levels of 600,000 BPD. As a result, exports fell to 700,000–800,000 barrels per day in 1981–1983. Iraq then slowly expanded the capacity of its Dortyol pipeline through Turkey to 1.1 MMBD, and exports rose to 911,000 BPD in 1984, and 1.1 MMBD in 1985. This increase in export capacity, however, did little more than compensate for cuts in oil prices. Iraq's crude oil, NGL, and refined product exports were only worth $10.4 billion in 1981, $10.1 billion in 1982, $7.8 billion in 1983, $9.3 billion in 1984, and $10.7 billion in 1985.[314]

Iraq responded by building a parallel pipeline through Turkey which raised the capacity of the Dortyol pipeline to 1.7 MMBD, by exporting through Kuwait, and by building a link to Saudi Arabia's pipeline to the Red Sea. Its average exports slowly rose back to 1.4 MMBD in 1986, but annual revenues only totaled $6.9 billion, due to a collapse of oil prices. The end of the Iran-Iraq War saw a turn for the better in Iraqi oil fortunes. Oil production went from 2.6 MMBD (17.4 million tons) in 1988 to 2.8 MMBD (138.6 million tons) in 1989. This added output and a rise in oil prices earned an increasingly debt-ridden Iraq revenues of $9.4 billion a year in 1988–1989.

By the first half of 1990, Iraqi oil production was averaging about 3.1 MMBD, Iraq had brought enough new facilities on-line to raise its export capacity to 3.5 MMBD, and its total 1990 export earnings were expected to be almost $16 billion. This revenue would have been adequate to meet Iraq's demands if Iraq had not tried to fund both guns and butter, and had not faced the need to pay off a massive war debt while it funded post-war development. Saddam Hussein's ambitions went far beyond such trade-offs, however, and Iraq began to put pressure on its neighbors to reduce their production as a means of raising oil prices. It accused Kuwait and the UAE of driving oil prices down by over-producing, and provoked a crisis with Kuwait that led to the Gulf War.

Oil Production Efforts Since the Gulf War

The UN embargo brought Iraqi oil production to a virtual standstill, while Coalition air attacks during the Gulf War caused extensive damage to Iraq's production and refining capabilities. Iraqi oil exports averaged

1.7 MMBD in 1990, with export revenues of only $9.5 billion. In 1991, Iraqi oil exports averaged only 52,000 BPD, with export revenues of $380 million. Since that time, Iraqi exports to Jordan, Turkey, and Iran have averaged about 110,000 BPD, with annual export revenues of about $400 million.

Iraq has, however, succeeded in rebuilding much of its war-damaged oil industry. Wartime damage to Iraq's oil production facilities was restricted largely to burning wells in the south, although the pumping stations for Iraq's sophisticated pipeline system were extensively damaged. As a result, the Iraqi government announced in its emergency six month reconstruction budget of May 2, 1991, that the restoration of oil production and the rebuilding of refineries and pipelines would be the primary target for reconstruction.

By the early summer of 1991, Iraqi oil production was running at about 270,000 barrels per day, with exports of 20,000–40,000 barrels per day to Jordan. By the end of the summer of 1992, Iraq had a production capacity of about 500,000 barrels per day. Damage assessments by Turkish government sources indicated that the pipeline into Turkey and to the port of Ceyhan was capable of restarting operations almost immediately.

Average oil production—including natural gas—has been limited by Iraq's inability to export legally to any nation other than Jordan, although some production has been trucked into Turkey. Nevertheless it has increased from 235,000 barrels per day in 1991 to 480,000 barrels per day in 1992, and 500,000 barrels per day in 1993. Iraq now produces about 650,000 BPD, with 100,000–150,000 BPD reinjected into reservoirs.

In 1995, the former Iraqi Oil Minister Safa Hadi Jawad claimed that Iraq could export 2 MMBD immediately after sanctions were lifted, and could export up to 3.6 million MMBD within 10–14 months, once it obtained the parts it needs to repair damaged oil export facilities. Iraq's current Oil Minister, Amir Muhammad Rashid, repeated this claim in January 1996.[315] The IEA made a more conservative estimate that Iraq could begin producing 1.5 to 2.5 MMBD within six months of the lifting of sanctions, might regain the capability to produce 2.5 to 3.0 MMBD within a year after it is allowed to resume full production, and could definitely reach or exceed 3 MMBD in two to three years.[316] Iraq only needs about 400,000 BPD for domestic consumption, and such production levels would give Iraq enough export capacity to have a major near-term impact on oil quota and oil prices. Iraq's present OPEC quota is only 400,000 BPD.

Iraq has also laid the groundwork for developing new fields. It began to negotiate with Total and Elf in 1992, and with Russia in 1995. Although no contracts can be signed until the UN sanctions are lifted, Elf seems to have reached an agreement to develop the Majnoon oil field, which has up to 15 billion barrels of reserves and a potential production capacity of 1 MMBD. Total seems to have reached an agreement to develop the Nahr Umr oil field, which has up to 1 billion barrels of reserves. Agip is discussing the development of the Al Halfaya oil field, which also has up to 1 billion barrels of reserves.[317]

Russia has explored development of the West Qurnah oil field, with up to 12 billion barrels of reserves and an initial production goal of 200,000 BPD. The Russian firm of Lukoil seems to have signed a contract for this project in April 1995, which was approved by the Iraqi parliament a month later. Iraq's payment to Lukoil is be made in hard currency and crude oil. Russia also seems to have signed a much larger agreement. Iraq reported in February 1996 that a $10 billion agreement had been reached between Iraq and Russia. This agreement seems to have been signed in April 1995 and was ratified by the Iraqi parliament in November 1995. It allows Iraq to repay its $7 billion debt to Russia with oil exports, and called for cooperative development of the West Qurna and Rumalia oil fields.[318] There may be many similar international investment projects to come. Petronas of Malaysia, Repsol of Spain, and TPAO of Turkey have all held discussions with Iraq. Iraq has 25 appraised fields ready for development, with a potential production capacity of 4.65 MMBD.[319]

If Iraqi exports are to rise much above the 700,000 barrel per day level permitted under the financial terms of Resolution 986, Iraq will have to rebuild much of its pipeline and terminal system, and this could present political and financial problems. Syria has kept the Baniyas line closed since 1982, and Saudi Arabia is unlikely to make its IPSA-1 (500,000 BPD capacity) and IPSA-2 pipelines (1.2 MMBD capacity) available for Iraqi exports in the near future. Iraq has claimed, however, that its engineers have completed the final repairs to its key north-south oil pipeline. The rebuilding of the K-3 oil station in Hadithah, north-west of Baghdad, means that Iraq could transport oil from Kirkuk oil field to the southern oil terminal at Basra. As of mid-1992 this pipeline had a capacity of 800,000 barrels per day. Iraq also claimed that it could export up to 1.6 million barrels a day using its pipeline through Turkey, once it was properly flushed and restored to working condition.

The Turkish pipeline is particularly important because the terms of Resolution 986 ensure this pipeline will carry much of the 700,000 barrels per day that Iraqi can export, and will give Turkey some $50 to $100 million in fees—an issue of considerable importance to a country that had a $14 billion trade deficit in 1995, and which estimates that it lost $2 billion a year after it closed the pipeline in 1990 to comply with UN sanctions.[320]

Iraq and Turkey began to discuss a proposal to drain some 12 million barrels of oil from the Iraq-Turkey pipeline in early 1994. Both Iraq and Turkey claim that unless the oil is flushed from the pipeline, the pipeline will be irreparably damaged by the deteriorating crude. Negotiations have failed to reach a satisfactory agreement, however, and are preventing the flushing and repairs. The delays are due in part to differences concerning the distribution of the humanitarian aid that Iraq would receive as payment for the oil. Iraq has rejected the UN plan that puts 30% of the proceeds into a UN escrow fund for Gulf War victims compensation, while taking control of the distribution of the humanitarian aid away from Iraq. Whether an agreement is made or not, the flushing and needed repairs will have to been done between the spring and late fall, due to the severe weather conditions in the mountains between Iraq and Turkey through which the pipeline passes.

Iraq also has four terminals on the Gulf at Mina al-Bakr, Khor al-Amaya, Umm Qasr, and Khor Al-Zubair, and had the capability to load tankers at Fao before the Iran-Iraq War. Umm Qasr and Khor Al-Zubair are small coastal ports which were incapacitated at the time of the Gulf War, but have since been rebuilt. Mina al-Bakr and Khor al-Amaya are major off-shore loading terminals. Mina al-Bakr had a capacity of 1.6 MMBD from four berths before it was damaged in the Iran-Iraq War. It was restored to 400,000 BPD after that war, damaged in the Gulf War, and then built back to a capacity of 500,000 BPD. Khor al-Amaya had the capability to load three major tankers before it was damaged in the Iran-Iraq War. Rebuilding seems to have begun in 1993, but its present capacity is unknown. The port at Fao has been rebuilt, but its oil export capacity is also unknown.[321]

The IEA estimates that Iraq can now load about 600,000 BPD from all of its coastal facilities without major further work, and has a total export capacity of about 1.7 MMBD—including the capacity of its Turkish pipeline. This is only about 65% to 80% of its near-term export capacity. Iraq has, however, announced an ambitious program to add two 48-inch pipelines and four single buoy moorings to Mina al-Bakr and Khor al-Amaya, and raise their loading capacity to 1.6 MMBD each. The costs of this project would be $1 billion. Iraq also has a fleet of nine tankers which survived the Gulf War, although their present operating status and capacity is not clear.[322]

Iraqi Refining and Petrochemical Capability

Iraq had the capacity to refine 305,500 BPD before the Iran-Iraq War, which was reduced to 215,500 BPD by Iranian attacks on Basra in 1982. Production was rebuilt to 293,500 BPD by 1985, and new projects raised capacity to 550,000 BPD by 1990.[323]

Iraq's refining capability was then sharply reduced by the Gulf War. In a few short weeks of allied bombing, Iraq's refining capacity was reduced from 550,000 barrels per day (b/d) to 60,000 b/d. Much of this production loss, however, was due to attacks on replaceable components rather than massive attacks on entire facilities. By mid-summer 1991, Iraq had carried out major repairs, especially at the two modern refineries of Daura and Baiji—both of which reached full pre-war capacity in June 1991. This allowed Iraq to meet domestic demand. By mid-June 1992, Iraq's oil minister declared that Iraq's repaired refineries could process 580,000 barrels per day or 84 percent of pre-war capacity.

Iraq has fully resumed operations at the three main refineries (Baiji, Basra, and Doura), although Basra has never fully recovered from damage done during the Iran-Iraq War, and has restored additional capacity at several smaller facilities. It now has a total of ten operating refineries with a capacity of 593,000 BPD, and a new 290,000 BPD refinery is under construction near Babylon. This compares with a capacity of 550,000 BPD before the Gulf War. The Iraqi Oil Ministry claims it has no plans to boost capacity further as all domestic consumption needs are being met by the existing facilities.

Iraq has nine petrochemical facilities, with a total potential capacity of 7.68 million tons a year. These plants produce ammonia, ammonium sulfate, benzene, Ethylene, ethylene dichloride, polyethylene, polypropylene, phosphates, sulfuric acid, sulfur, Toluene, and urea. Several suffered damage during the Iran-Iraq and Gulf Wars. They have since had significant repair work completed, but their exact capacity is unclear. Iraq also operates a major phosphate plant at Al-Qaim. This plant was damaged during the Gulf War, but production seems to have largely recovered.

Production and Development Prospects
Once Sanctions Are Lifted or Relaxed

It is difficult to ascertain what Iraq's strategic future for its oil industry will be, given the uncertain political future of the country and the continuation of the sanctions. The UN now permits Iraq to export only 50,000 BPD of crude oil and 25,000 BPD of products to Jordan, with the agreement that half of the crude is delivered free and the other half is subsidized. Some additional oil is delivered to Turkey and Iran by trucks, and sold on the black market, but the amount is limited.

There has been no real progress in resuming large scale exports since Iraq rejected the terms of UN Security Council Resolution 706, which was passed in August 1991 and allowed Iraq to sell $1.6 billion worth of crude oil for humanitarian purposes. Iraq has, however, shown signs of an increasing willingness to accept the UN terms, and the UN eased these terms slightly in 1995. As a result, it is possible that Iraq could suddenly reverse its position on accepting the UN offer with limited warning.

Iraq's longer term plans are more clear and many of its development and production goals are consistent with the strategic plan that Iraq issued following the end of the Iran-Iraq War. In 1988–1989, the Oil Ministry—which was then headed by Issam Abdel Rahim al-Chalabi—announced that Iraq intended to implement the following strategy:

- Widening exploration to make up for the lack of exploration by international companies before nationalization in 1972;
- Increasing production capacity;
- Increasing refining and export capacity; aside from returning the Turkish oil pipeline to Ceyhan to full capacity, Iraq plans to expand export infrastructure significantly. Crude storage facilities will be expanded from 14 million to 21–24 million barrels. Much of this expansion will come as a result of the rebuilding and modernization of the Fao tank farm. The loading capacities of Mina al-Bakr and Khor al-Amaya in the Persian Gulf will be increased to a total of 3.2 million barrels per day;
- Increasing the efficiency of transportation and distribution of oil and gas;
- Building up a strategic reserve of oil and gas for national security reasons;
- Increasing the level of in-house design and construction;
- Enhancing the computerization of the industry.

As has just been discussed, Iraq has since developed these plans into far more detailed objectives since the Gulf War, and has established an oil output target of 6 million b/d by the turn of the century. Iraq appears to be concentrating on the further exploration and development of four giant southern fields: Majnoun, West Qurna, Halfaya, and Nahr-Umar.

Iraq has made it clear that it is planning on the assistance of foreign companies in its future exploration and development efforts. As has been discussed earlier, Iraq is talking with Russian firms about resuming development of the West Qurna field once the UN sanctions are lifted. Original plans for this field, interrupted by the Iraqi invasion of Kuwait, called for production rates of 200,000 b/d in the first stage and 600,000 b/d in the second. Two French companies, Total and Elf, have been negotiating with Iraq as well. Total may develop Nahr-Umar, while Elf is expected to undertake the development of the Majnoun field, by far the largest Iraqi field waiting to be developed. However, no commitments are likely to be made until the uncertain political situation is resolved.

There are good reasons that Baghdad now intends to solicit large-scale foreign investment. Iraq will need about $30 billion in the next eight years for its oil and gas production and export facilities to be revitalized and expanded. Iraq can only get this money by offering unprecedented access to its oil sector—a factor that affects some of the growing opposition to sanctions. Negotiations have been going on with foreign companies for at least four years. Ten fields with a production capacity of 3 million barrels per day have been put forward as suitable for production sharing and service agreements, while 20 other fields with a total capacity of 1.5 million barrels per day are being considered for various cooperative agreements.

Iraq also continues to play a role in oil politics even though it cannot export oil. Iraq continues to attend OPEC meetings. Iraq is a vociferous participant blaming the member states for failing to uphold their own interests as producers. In mid-1993, Tariq Aziz, then Deputy Prime Minister, indicated that Iraq's return to the market would be geared to the country's revenue needs, and that it would make no difference to Baghdad even if the oil price dropped to $5 per barrel, "since now we get nothing." There has been no change in these policies in the years that have followed, and Iraq's return to the oil exporting business may lead to turbulent times for OPEC.

Natural Gas

The size and importance of Iraq's gas reserves is shown in Table Two and Chart Nine, and the trends in Iraqi gas production are shown in Chart Ten. Until the late 1980s, up to 85% of the gas Iraq produced was flared. Iraq's natural gas production was also tied closely to its crude oil production, since all of the gas produced was associated. Most of Iraq's associated gas came from the Ain Zalah, Butma, Kirkuk, Bai Hassan, Rumalia, and Zubair fields. These reserves comprised roughly 750,000 cubic meters of associated gas or on average about 90 cubic meters for each ton of oil. Production from these reserves was used to produce liquefied petroleum gas and dry gas as feedstock for refineries, power stations, and industrial projects.

At the end of the Iran-Iraq War, the government increased its efforts to use gas more widely in the home, industrially, and for export, and began to develop new gas fields. In May 1990, the al-Anfal gas field came online with an initial production rate of 200 million cubic feet per day and estimated reserves of 4.5 trillion cubic feet (tcf), or 127 billion cubic meters (bcm). Al-Anfal was Iraq's first non-associated gas field, and is connected by pipeline to a gas gathering station near Kirkuk, some 30 kilometers away. From there, gas is fed into a regional network that supplies feedstock for the petrochemical industry and fuel to power stations. Iraq has considerable potential to develop other non-associated fields or use associate gas for production and export purposes. Al-Anfal currently produces about 6 million cubic meters (mcm) per day.

TABLE TWO   Gulf and World Gas Reserves and Production

Nation	Reserves in 1995		Percent World Supply	Production in 1993 (BCM)
	TCF	*BCM*		
Bahrain	—	—	—	—
Iran	741.6	21,000	14.9	60.0
Iraq	109.5	3,100	2.2	2.75
Kuwait	52.9	1,498	1.1	5.17
Oman		600–640		
Qatar	250.0	7,070	5.0	18.4
Saudi Arabia	185.9	5,134	4.2	67.3
UAE	208.7	5,779*	4.2	31.63
Gulf	1,548.6	—	31.1	185.25
Rest of World	3,431.7	104,642	68.9	—
World Total	4,980.3	148,223	100.0	—

*Other sources estimate 6,320–7,280 BCM for Abu Dhabi only.
Source: The reserve and production data are adapted by Anthony H. Cordesman from IEA, *Middle East Oil and Gas*, Paris, OECD, IEA, 1995, Annex 2.

Iraq completed a major program to recover associated gas called the Northern Gas Project before the Iran-Iraq War, with an initial handling capacity of 20 mcm a day. It completed another program called the Southern Gas Project during the war, with a capacity of 3 mcm a day. The Southern Gas Project included a pipeline to ship gas to an LPG export terminal at Khor Al-Zubair.

Iraq's gas facilities suffered only limited damage during the Gulf War. Iraq claimed in March 1995 that it had a capacity of 20.5 bcm a year, with 5.6 bcm from the Northern Project and 15.3 bcm from the Southern Project. This is enough output to handle crude oil production of 3.5 MMBD, and it will be expanded in stages as Iraq meets its crude oil production goal of 6 MMBD. Surplus gas will be used for electric power generation, petrochemical, LPG for domestic fuel, fertilizer, and exports. Iraq has a significant near-term need to restore gas-fired electric power, since 11 of Iraq's 20 power plants were destroyed during the Gulf War—including five gas-fired plants—and six more power plants were damaged. However, Iraq plans to give oil exports priority over restoring gas distribution and use.[324]

Implications for Western and Southern Gulf Strategy

The issues relating to Iraqi oil and gas production cannot be separated from the general issue of sanctions discussed in the previous chapter. At

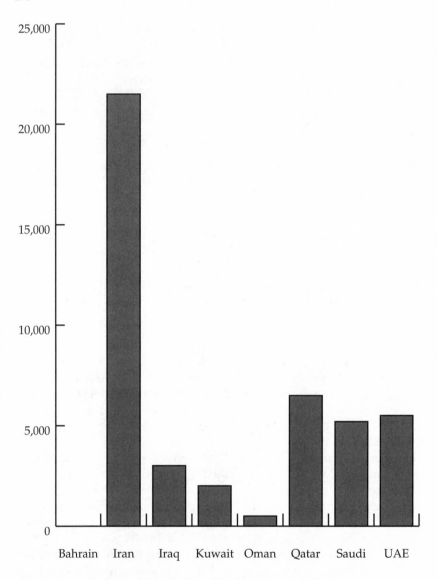

CHART NINE   Total Gas Reserves of the Gulf States (in Billions of Cubic Meters). *Source:* Adapted by Anthony H. Cordesman from IEA, *Middle East Oil and Gas,* Paris, OECD, IEA, 1995, Annex 2, and data provided by Bahrain and Oman. Bahrain's reserves are too small to show on the chart because of scale.

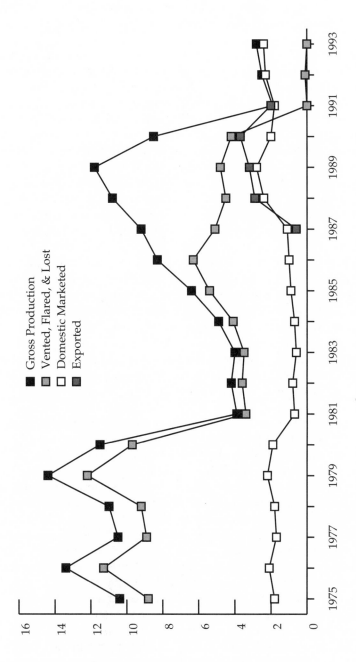

CHART TEN Iraqi Natural Gas Production (in Billions of Cubic Meters). *Source:* Adapted by Anthony H. Cordesman from International Energy Agency (IEA), *Middle East Oil and Gas*, Paris, 1995, pp. 252–256.

the same time, Iraqi oil exports have special implications for Southern Gulf and Western strategy—although somewhat different implications for the Gulf and the West.

On the one hand, Southern Gulf producers have little desire to see Iraq suddenly raise its exports above the level permitted in Resolution 986 exports at a time when oil prices are low and virtually all oil exporters are already violating their quotas. Nations like Saudi Arabia lose over $1 billion for every $1 drop in oil prices, and Iraqi exports in excess of 1 MMBD would almost certainly lead to significant cuts in oil prices. This would sharply reduce the oil export revenues of all the Gulf states, which already have substantial cash flow and budget deficit problems.[325]

The initial impact of Iraq's acceptance of UN Resolution 986 was limited, in part because the market had already anticipated Iraq's acceptance. Some experts believe, however, that even sustained Iraq exports at the limited rate of 700,000 barrels per day permitted under UN Security Council Resolution 986 could cut oil prices by $1–2 a barrel.[326]

On the other hand, Southern Gulf producers have a mid- and long-term interest in a stable world oil market and a stable and predictable flow of oil and oil prices. The resumption of Iraqi production is an essential aspect of creating such a market. Further, Iraqi production is a counterpoint to Iranian production and reduces the risks and uncertainties inherent in any interruption in oil production or exports once Gulf capacity is more fully utilized. Moreover, the Southern Gulf states have to live with Iraq, and Iraq is likely to become progressively more revanchist if it is denied export capability and the ability to develop its oil and gas resources.

The West's short-term interests differ from those of the Southern Gulf states largely in the fact that the West can benefit even in the short-term from any reductions in oil prices that occur once Iraq is allowed to resume its oil exports, and in making use of the opportunity to invest in new Iraqi oil and gas production efforts. Turkey certainly has much to gain from both a resumption of Iraqi oil exports and any expansion of Iraq's oil and gas exports.

The West's long-term strategic interests are clear. All of the major forecasts of world energy supply call for Iraq to be a major exporter by 2000, and a critical exporter by 2010. Iraq cannot instantly resume more than limited production once sanctions are lifted, and the forecasts of future production discussed at the beginning of this chapter already seem dubious. If Iraq was to meet DOE, EIA, IEA, and commercial estimates of its production for 2000, the sanctions on investment in new Iraqi production facilities and the export of the necessary equipment would have needed to have been lifted in 1992. As a result, virtually every world energy projection already assumes total levels of Iraqi oil production in the late 1990s and early 2000s that will not be available.

Iraq's inability to meet such production goals is not a serious near-term problem as long as all other major oil producers are stable, and Saudi Arabia is willing to act as a swing producer. This assumption, however, is an uncertain one given the tensions inside the Gulf and the uncertain future of the FSU. There is no question that the world economy will be more stable if Iraqi production can be brought back on-line and if it increases at the projected levels. The risks involved do not seem serious enough to influence near-term policy regarding sanctions and the regime of Saddam Hussein, but they can scarcely be ignored indefinitely.

9

External Relations

Iraq's external relations and foreign policy are a key reason the West and Southern Gulf states continue to pursue sanctions, and must consider strategies to change the character of Iraq's regime. Twice in the last two decades, Iraq has attacked its neighbors—first Iran and then Kuwait. Iraq has used its military build-up to seek regional hegemony, and has aggressively used its power to try to influence the oil policies of the nations of the Southern Gulf. It has acted to serve the ambitions of Saddam Hussein and one of the most aggressive forms of nationalism in the Middle East.

There are only two ways in which the West and the Southern Gulf states can deal with Iraq's ambitions and approach to external relations. One is through containment. The other is through basic changes in the character of Iraq's regime. Both approaches present the problems discussed earlier, but a passive approach to Iraq's foreign policy—or accommodation and appeasement—would almost certainly trigger new aggression and new conflict.

Iraq's Foreign Policy Since the Gulf War

Ever since the cease-fire in 1991, the primary focus of Iraqi diplomacy has been to find a way to eliminate the sanctions imposed on Iraq by the international community and to allow Iraq to recover the power it had before the Gulf War. Iraq has sought to end the economic sanctions without complying with the terms of the cease-fire, to restore its military capabilities, to rebuild its programs to manufacture and deliver weapons of mass destruction, to renew its pressure on Kuwait, and to exact revenge for its defeat.

Iraq has only been "moderate" to the extent such moderation benefits its own short-term tactical advantage. For example, only three months after October 1994, when Iraq moved troops to its border with Kuwait, Iraq renewed efforts to erode the sanctions by appealing to the international community's moral conscience over the human cost of the sanctions in Iraq. Similarly, Iraq has used its economic potential to try to undermine international support for sanctions wherever possible. An example is its solicitation of bids for the eventual reconstruction of the country in 1994, bids clearly designed to obtain support for lifting sanctions.

Iraqi diplomatic contacts with the outside world have multiplied dramatically since Saddam and the Ba'ath regime defeated the post–Gulf War uprisings. Iraq has focused its diplomatic offensive on states where the sanctions are economically costly, or where Iraq feels it can exploit humanitarian concerns or fears of eventual Iraqi reprisals. While this Iraqi strategy has been undermined by Saddam Hussein's adventures, and by a series of revelations that the regime has continued to lie about its destruction of its weapons of mass destruction, Iraqi diplomacy has continued to try to undermine support for sanctions. As Iraq's Information Minister, Hamad Youssef Hammadi pointed out in early 1995, "We are realistic. The sanctions will be eroded gradually. We know the US administration is adamant because it failed to realize its objectives by military means."[327]

Iraqi diplomats have tried to capitalize on the fact that the international community is becoming increasingly divided over the question of whether sanctions should continue and the Kurdish crisis of September 1996 has shown they are having some success with moderate Arab states and key nations like China, France, and Russia. The Iraqi leadership has sought to build support in the Arab and the broader Islamic worlds from the bottom up by appealing to the masses, intellectuals, students, opposition groups, and nationalists and telling them that what is being done to Iraq is a portent of the future for all in a Western-dominated 'new world order.'

At the same time, the Iraqi leadership clearly realizes that popular sympathy and the support of the masses will not remove the sanctions. The Iraqis, especially veteran diplomats like Tariq Aziz, realize that their diplomatic efforts can only succeed if they influence the real power-brokers within the United Nations and exploit the differences among them. Iraq has aggressively sought to influence Western nations and major trading partners, to exploit humanitarian concerns, and to win over friendly states with economic incentives.

Unfortunately, far more has been involved than diplomatic gamesmanship, humanitarian issues, and economic opportunities. As the previous analysis has shown, Iraq's current regime is highly repressive and has made Iraq a deeply divided and unstable nation. The broad trends in overt Iraqi diplomacy have also concealed a pattern of continuing threats to Kuwait, other nations in the Southern Gulf, and Western strategic interests. These threats are reinforced by Iraq's military capabilities and potential ability to reconstitute its weapons of mass destruction rapidly.

The Continuing Threat to Kuwait

Iraq has no legitimate historical claim to Kuwait. Kuwait's northern border with Iraq had been established as part of the agreement Britain had reached with Turkey in 1913. Iraq accepted this claim when it was given its independence from Turkey, and accepted it again in the "Agreed Minutes between the State of Kuwait and the Republic of Iraq Regarding the Restoration of Friendly Relations, Recognition, and Related Matters" which Iraq and Kuwait signed in 1932. However, Iraqi nationalists began to claim that Kuwait was legitimately part of Iraq as early as the mid-1920s. This laid the ground work for later Iraqi claims and threats to Kuwait.

Iraq only challenged Kuwait's sovereignty once during the time the Iraqi monarchy remained tied to British support and influence—during the reign of King Ghazi in the 1930s. This situation changed dramatically, however, in 1961. The Iraqi monarchy fell in 1958, and Kuwait faced a growing threat from the radical Arab nationalism of Iraq's new regime. This threat was a major factor influencing Kuwait's decision to become fully independent from Britain on June 19, 1961, but this decision led to almost immediate problems with Iraq. Iraq's new regime claimed Kuwait under the pretense that Kuwait had been part of the Ottoman Empire and consequently subject to Iraqi suzerainty.

Only a week after the withdrawal of British forces, Iraqi forces moved to the border and only halted when Britain rushed troops back into Kuwait and when it became clear that the Arab League was prepared to challenge Iraq's claims. Iraq did sign an agreement in 1963 that appeared to recognize Kuwait's sovereignty, and the border demarcation to which Britain and Turkey had agreed in 1913, but Iraq only did so because of a coup that killed the Iraqi dictator that had originally threatened to invade Kuwait.

Iraq threatened Kuwait again in 1965, 1967, and 1972. Iraq occupied Kuwait's border post at Samita on March 20, 1973, in a further effort to put pressure on Kuwait to cede it control of the islands in the Gulf. This led to the deployment of Saudi troops to the border. Iraq withdrew in early April, but only after mediation by Yasser Arafat and a substantial Kuwaiti payment to Iraq. Iraq then attempted to lease Warbah and half of Bubiyan in 1975 for a period of 99 years. According to some reports, Iraq briefly sent troops into Kuwait again in 1976, and only withdrew after another Kuwaiti payment.[328]

Despite these difficulties, Kuwait supported its "Arab brother" during the Iran-Iraq War, and was one of Iraq's most important allies. During 1980–1988, Kuwait supplied Iraq with at least $13.2 billion in grants and loans, and with up to $22 billion in overall assistance.[329] Even so,

Kuwait's problems in its relations with Iraq continued. Iraq again sought to lease Bubiyan and Warbah in 1980 and provoked another border incident in 1983. When Kuwait again refused to lease the two islands, Iraq sent a token force across the border. This Iraqi pressure led to a sudden visit to Baghdad by Kuwait Prime Minister Saad Sabah on November 10–13, 1984. Once again, Iraq was bought off by a substantial payment, although Iraq did establish a Hovercraft base across the river from Warbah.[330]

Control of the two islands had become steadily more important to Iraq during the Iran-Iraq War because it was clear that Iraq was never likely to secure its access to the Gulf through the Shatt al-Arab, which it shared with Iran. Further, the Shatt al-Arab had suffered from 10 years of silting and mining during the Iran-Iraq War. As a result, Iraq steadily expanded the city of Basra to the south; the town of Az-Bayer, just to the southwest of Basra; and its naval base at Umm Qasr. Iraq had moved south into territory that probably belonged to Kuwait near Umm Qasr and the border town of Safwan, and had expanded a canal called the Shatt al-Basra from Umm Qasr to a position midway between Basra and Az Zubayr. This made the Khor Abd Allah, the channel from the Gulf to Umm Qasr to the north of Bubyian and Warbah steadily more important.[331]

Kuwait's support of Iraq during the Iran-Iraq War earned little gratitude. While Iraq emerged as the victor in the Iran-Iraq War, it had borrowed some $37 billion in loans from Kuwait and its other Arab neighbors, as well as massive additional loans from the West and Japan. By late 1989, Iraq desperately needed to reschedule its debts. The required principal and interest on the non-Arab debt alone would have consumed half of Iraq's $13 billion worth of annual oil revenues.[332]

At the same time, repayment costs of this scale scarcely suited Saddam Hussein's growing regional ambitions. Iraq had a military budget of $12.9 billion in 1990, which meant Iraq was spending approximately $700 per citizen, in a country with a per capita income of only $1,950.[333] As a result, Iraq began to demand forgiveness of its Arab loans during 1988 and 1989, and called for new grant aid to be given to Iraq as the sole defender of the Arab cause against Iran. Iraq also made new requests to lease Warbah and parts of Bubiyan island in 1989, and rejected the attempts of Kuwait's Emir to reach a general border settlement when he visited Iraq in September 1989.[334]

By mid-1990, Iraq's cash reserves were only equal to three months of imports and inflation was running at 40%. When Kuwait refused to forgive Iraq's debt, lease the islands, and agree to Iraq's other border claims, Iraq decided on war. Saddam Hussein accused Kuwait of "stabbing Iraq in the back" and Iraqi foreign minister Tariq Aziz claimed that Kuwait had, "implemented a plot to escalate the pace of gradual systematic advances towards Iraqi territory. He claimed that the Kuwaiti government had set up military establishments, police posts, oil installations, and farms on Iraqi territory" that Kuwait and the UAE were conspiring to keep oil prices low and were violating their oil quotas, and that Kuwait was stealing oil from the Rumalia oil field, whose southern tip enters Kuwaiti territory.[335] On August 2, 1990, Iraq invaded a nearly defenseless Kuwait.

Neither the Coalition victory nor the cease-fire agreement, however, ended the threat from Iraq. In August and September of 1992, the confrontation between Iraq and the UN over the elimination of weapons of mass destruction, and Iraq's treatment of its Shi'ites and Kurds, forced the US to transform US Army, Marine Corps, and Navy exercises into a demonstration that the US could protect Kuwait against any military adventures by Iraq. The US rushed Patriot batteries to both Kuwait and Bahrain, and a 1,300 man battalion from the 1st Cavalry Division to Kuwait. It conducted a test pre-positioning exercise called Native Fury 92, and carried out an amphibious reinforcement exercise called Eager Mace 92. By the time these US efforts were over, the US had deployed a total of 1,900 Marines and 2,400 soldiers, including two armored and two mechanized companies.[336]

Kuwait faced continuing Iraqi challenges to its new border with Iraq. As part of the cease-fire terms, the UN set up a special UN Iraq/Kuwait Boundary Demarcation Commission. This commission issued its final report on May 20, 1993, and found that the original border marking points had long vanished, and that Iraqi farmers had steadily expanded their date farms to the south after the border was marked in 1923. As a result, correcting the border to the original line moved it to the north and into territory that Iraq had occupied since before World War II. The Secretary General accepted this final report, and the UN Security Council adopted Resolution 833 on May 27, 1993—reaffirming the Commission's final demarcation of the Iraq-Kuwait border, demanding both states respect that border, and guaranteeing the inviolability of the border.

The new border offered Kuwait considerable advantages at the expense of Iraq. It gave Kuwait greater control over the Ratga and Rumalia oil fields in its northern border area, and reduces Iraqi access to the port facilities at Umm Qasr.[337] At the same time, these advantages created new political problems with Iraq that could prove more costly than the benefits are worth. Only six days after the Secretary General accepted the report, the Speaker of Iraq's National Assembly stated that the new border would keep tensions in the region high. Iraq refused to accept the new demarcation and Iraqi editorials and its media made new claims to Kuwait as Iraq's 19th province.

Iraq created a series of incidents in the border area during the remaining months of 1993 and through most of 1994. Iraq then sent major forces, including two Republican Guards divisions, into the border area in late 1994. These movements forced the US to rush land and air forces into the area, and led to a new crisis between Iraq and the UN.

The continuing threat from Iraq became even more apparent on October 3, 1994, when Iraq began to move its Hammurabi and Al Nida Republican Guards divisions south from the area around Baghdad to positions about 20 kilometers from the border with Kuwait. These units were the two best equipped Republican Guards divisions in the Iraqi Army. They moved by rail and road with full ammunition loads and then deployed in an attack capable formation which had one brigade forward and two in the rear, and a full complement of divisional artillery. These Iraqi movements involved two divisions of 9,000 to 10,000 men each, and movements of FROG, SA-8, and mobile AA units. Iraq also increased the readiness of the Adnan and Baghdad divisions of the Republican Guards in the north in a manner that indicated they might move south, and altered the deployments of the three Iraqi divisions already in the south—the 54th Mechanized Division, which was about 40–50 kilometers from the border, the 2nd Armored Division, and the 4th Republican Guards Infantry Division. Iraq built up a total force of 70,000–80,000 men, which led to significant increases in the major weapons positioned in the area north of Kuwait. Iraqi tank strength increased from about 660 to 1,100, artillery strength from around 400 to 700, and OAFV strength from about 700 to 1,000.[338]

More than any incident since the Gulf War, this Iraqi build-up illustrated the problems that Kuwait and the US face in dealing with a major Iraqi challenge. The Kuwaiti cabinet met in emergency session on October 7, 1994, and decided to send the Kuwait army to the border, and put Kuwait forces on full alert. It took 5–7 days to deploy the Kuwaiti army fully, however, and its effective fighting strength was less than one heavy Iraqi Republican Guards brigade. The US decided to send additional forces to the Gulf on October 9 to supplement the 13,000 US personnel already in the theater. These forces initially included the 18,000 men in the 1st Marine Expeditionary Force, 16,000 troops from the US army 24th Infantry Division, 306 fixed wing aircraft (including A-10s, F-16s, RF-4Cs, F-15Es, F-15Cs, F-111s, EF-111s, F-117s, JSTARS, F/A-18s, B-52s, and E-3As), 58 helicopters (including 54 AH-64s), two batteries of Patriot Missiles, and a carrier battle group. The US subsequently deployed another 73 fixed wing aircraft.

By October 12, the US had a total of 19,241 men in the Gulf area (1,923 Army, 11,171 Navy, 1,977 Marine, 3,844 Air Force, 173 Special Operations, and 153 Joint Task Force Headquarters). It had two carrier task forces with 15 ships (counting one carrier battle group in the Red Sea), and 200 combat aircraft. In contrast, the Gulf Cooperation Council was only able to make a token commitment of the 17,000 man Peninsula Shield force—which lacked the combat capability to play any significant role in defending Kuwait.

Although Iraq backed down, withdrew its forces, and then stated it would recognize the new border with Kuwait, it seems clear that this Iraqi acceptance was little more than a tactic timed to try to put an end to UN sanctions. In fact, there were new indications of Iraqi movements against Kuwait in 1995. On August 8, 1995, two of Saddam Hussein's son-in-laws, two of his daughters, and other members of their family defected to Jordan. This defection was followed by unusual Iraqi movements around Baghdad and in Southern Iraq, and rumors that Iraq may attack Kuwait or make a demonstration near the border.

These indications led Kuwait to create a new security zone near its capital. At the same time, the US responded by deploying naval task forces where they could protect Kuwait as part of "Operation Vigilant Sentinel." On August 10, it alerted the carrier battle group that included the *Roosevelt* (CCG-8), the 8th Carrier Wing, the guided missile cruiser *Mississippi* (CGN), the guided missile cruisers *Hue City* (CG) and *Ticonderoga* (CG), and the guided missile frigate *Nicholas* (FFG). This force was on station near Port Said by August 12, with the capability to launch more than 150 Tomahawk cruise missiles. The US also alerted the 24th Marine Expeditionary Unit (MEU), the carrier battle group in the new US 5th Fleet in the Gulf remained on station, and Kuwait and the US decided to accelerate joint exercises from October to August.

As a result, the US rushed some 28,000 troops to the region by mid-September, including 5,000 in the Eastern Mediterranean. The US deployed 8 prepositioning ships from Diego Garcia to the Gulf, with enough gear to sustain 16,000 Marines in combat for 30 days, and 5,000–7,000 US Army troops. The US deployed four additional prepositioning ships in to the region. It also prepared US Army troops in the US for airlift to "marry up" with the heavy equipment for an armored brigade that is prepositioned at Camp Doha in Kuwait.

New tensions emerged in January 1996, when US intelligence concluded that Iraq had brought five armored divisions to sufficient readiness to deploy to Kuwait with only five hours notice. In response the US deployed 12 prepositioning ships—enough to equip a Marine Division and a US Army Brigade—into the Gulf. The US did not send troops, but this move allowed the US to deploy up to 20,000 troops on short notice. The US also deployed additional combat aircraft to Bahrain and Kuwait, and extended a joint exercise with Kuwait. The US already had some 20,000 troops in the Middle East area, and deployed 35 ships, and 14,000 sailors and US Marines in its Fifth Fleet between the Suez Canal and Indian Ocean. These forces included the *Nimitz* carrier battle group, and a Marine Corps amphibious ready group. It is interesting to note that the US only had 250 naval personnel stationed permanently ashore in Bahrain.[339]

There has, however, been a decline in Iraqi-provoked incidents along the border. Iraqi infiltrations and crossings dropped from several hundred a year between 1992 and 1994 to a few incidents a week in the spring of 1995. However, this decline seems to be a temporary tactic rather than any commitment to a lasting recognition of Kuwait's border. Further, the decline in incidents is partly the result of the deportation of 1,500 Iraqis living in the Umm Qasr area ceded to Kuwait (which occurred after Kuwait paid for new housing), and partly the result of the construction of a nearly 218 kilometer-long security line. This line has a three meter-deep trench, followed by a five meter sand berm, and sensors which can detect the movement of vehicles. It is backed by a patrol road and outposts in the border area.[340]

It seems likely that Iraq will continue to assert its claims in the border area the moment it perceives a political and military opportunity to do so.[341] Kuwait has already had to abandon plans to allow Western oil companies to explore and develop its oil fields near the Iraqi border because of the risk of new clashes and incidents. Iraq, on the other hand, is aggressively attempting to negotiate deals with nations like Russia to exploit the fields on its side of the border once the UN sanctions are lifted. Iraq's ambitions regarding Kuwait are unlikely to vanish, regardless of what Saddam Hussein or any new regime may say to achieve the objective of lifting the sanctions. Iraqi nationalists have claimed that Kuwait is part of Iraq since the 1920s, and while defeat may force Iraqi to accept the inevitable, it is scarcely likely to legitimize Kuwait's independence or new borders in the minds of Iraqi nationalists.

The issue of reparations may poison Iraqi-Kuwait relations for years, and memories of the war and the sanctions that have followed will be slow to die. Iraq's access to the Persian Gulf now consists of a 58 kilometer coastline on relatively shallow Gulf waters. Iraq's only major port on the Gulf is Basra, which can only be reached via the Shattt al-Arab—a river whose waters Iraq shares with Iran. Due to a UN-sponsored border demarcation, Iraq has lost much of its only naval base at Umm Qasr, and even if it builds a new port, it will have to use a channel shared with Kuwait and dominated by the Kuwaiti islands of Warbah and Bubiyan.[342]

Relations with Iran

Iraq's relations with Iran have generally consisted of continuing conflict between the two states. At the same time, the West and the Southern Gulf face the risk of some kind of strategic rapproachment—or "Molotov-

Ribbentrop Pact"—that might create a unified threat in the northern Gulf. However, Iran and Iraq have never reached a full cease-fire or peace settlement after the end of the Iran-Iraq War, and Iran has made claims for up to $100 billion in reparations from Iraq.

Iran has returned some prisoners of war since 1990, but Iraq claims Iran still holds up to 20,000 Iraqis captured during the Iran-Iraq War, and is supporting several thousand Iraqi troops that fled into Iran after the uprisings following the Gulf War. In September 1994, the International Committee of the Red Cross (ICRC) issued a report on "unresolved humanitarian issues" from the Iran-Iraq War. The ICRC noted that the Iranian government violated the Third Geneva Convention by failing to identify combatants killed in action and to exchange information on those killed or missing. According to the report, the fate of almost 19,000 Iraqi prisoners of war (POW's) in Iran "remained unknown." The report criticized the Iranian government for obstructing ICRC efforts to register and repatriate POWs.[343] Iran, in turn, claims that Iraq holds up to 5,000 Iranians, while Iraq claims it has none.[344]

Iran and Iraq have engaged in a low-level conflict in which Iran has backed anti-regime efforts by Iraqi Shi'ites, and Iraq has backed the Iranian People's Mujahideen. During the Gulf War, Iran supported Iraqi Shi'ite military attacks on the People's Mujahideen camps in Iraq. Since that time, the People's Mujahideen has launched attacks on Iran from camps in Iraq, while Iran has attacked the People's Mujahideen camps in Iraq.

Iraqi officials met with Iranian officials before the Gulf War in an effort to persuade Iran not to support the UN Coalition, but this effort failed. Iran supported the UN Coalition during the Gulf War, and seized the Iraqi aircraft that fled to Iran during Desert Storm.[345] On April 5, 1992, Iraq and Iran had their first significant military exchange since the Iran-Iraq War. Iraq had been providing money and arms to the Mujahideen e-Khalq, a radical Marxist Iranian opposition movement which had military camps and forces in Iraq. The Mujahideen launched several small raids on Iran, and Iran sent 12 F-4 and F-5 fighters to attack the Ashraf Camp about 60 miles northeast of Baghdad. The aircraft attacked in six waves, dropping cluster bombs, firing rockets, and strafing. One Iranian F-4 was lost to anti-aircraft fire during the attack. Iraq responded by scrambling ten of its fighters for the first time since the Gulf War, in violation of UN Security Council Resolutions 686 and 687.

Iran claimed—with justification—that these strikes were in retaliation for Mujahideen ground attacks on two Iranian towns near the border on April 5, 1992. Iran also stated that it conducted the raids in response to other People's Mujahideen raids on Iran that had been designed to disrupt its parliamentary elections, sabotage pipelines, and strike at Iranian border posts.

Iran conducted new air raids on Iraq on May 25, 1993, and at least 12 Iranian aircraft struck against two of the People's Mujahideen camps in Iraq. One of these bases was at Jalat, near Sulaymaniyah, about 55 miles from the border. The other was at Ashraf, about 65 miles northeast of Baghdad—a camp reported to have between 1,500 and 5,000 guerrillas. Iran stated that these air raids were in retaliation for Mujahideen attacks in Iran that attempted to disrupt the Presidential elections, and for Mujahideen support of Iranian Kurdish rebels during the previous two weeks.

Iran held maneuvers on the Iraqi border in Khuzestan in May 1993 and deployed an armored brigade, an IRGC force of about 8,000 men, helicopters, and fighters. Iraq retaliated by announcing in June 1993 that it was deploying additional air and land units to the border area, although it is unclear any major redeployments actually took place. On July 23, 1993, Iraq claimed that Iran conducted a major artillery assault on Mujahideen camps in Iraq, including a three hour bombardment by multiple rocket launchers in the area of Sulaymaniyah.[346] Iraqi and Iranian officials met again in October 1993, but the talks produced little result. The only real change in relations between 1991 and 1993 was a growing black market in the border area that traded oil smuggled from Iraq for spare parts and food smuggled in from Iran.[347]

In the late fall of 1994, Iran's attitude towards Baghdad seemed to soften. Javad Larijani, the vice chairman of the Iranian Majlis's Foreign Affair Committee and an advisor to Rafsanjani gave an interview in which he stated that no country was better placed to help Iraq repair its economy than Iran and that "Iran and Iraq will set the course for the major issues of the Persian Gulf." Alik Akbar Nateq-Nouri—the speaker of the Iranian Parliament and a possible candidate from president in 1997—gave another interview which seemed to advocate improving relations with Iraq as a counterbalance to US power.

These initiatives failed for reasons that are not entirely clear, but seemingly are linked to attacks by the People's Mujahideen. In November 1994, Iran announced that it fired four missiles at the Mujahideen camp at Ashraf, and claimed it had inflicted heavy casualties. Iran indicated that attack followed the cancellation of an Iranian diplomatic mission to Baghdad, and Iran strengthened its army deployments in the border area.[348]

The new hard line the US took towards Iran in 1995 did, however, lead Iran to make another attempt to improve its relations with Iraq. Iranian government radio began to call for an end to the UN sanctions on Iraq on February 20, 1995. Iran sent a delegation to Baghdad in May 1995 that was led by Ali Khoram, a senior advisor to Velayati. On May 26, Iran's Deputy Foreign Minister, Hossein Sheikholeslam, announced that arrangements had been made for Velayati to visit Baghdad. There also were news reports that Iran and Iraq had reached an agreement to exchange prisoners of war, and that Iran had asked Iraq to extradite Masoud Rajavi, the leader of the People's Mujahideen, to Iran.[349]

Once again, the talks failed. In early July, Iran seems to have sent gunmen to assassinate three People's Mujahideen leaders in Baghdad. Iran also made statements on July 18, 1995, indicating that it was backing away from its attempts to improve relations with Iraq. Hassan Ruhani, the Secretary of Iran's National Supreme Security Council issued a statement that Foreign Minister Velayati had been invited to Iraq, but had rejected the invitation. Ruhani also stated that Iraq had not complied with many of the provisions in the July 1988 cease-fire and UN Security Council Resolution 598, and that no visit would take place until Iraq did so:[350]

Most of the articles of the resolution have not been implemented yet. The articles dealing with war reparations, reconstruction of war-stricken areas, repatriation of prisoners of war, and some other issues are not resolved. There is strong evidence substantiating that Iraqis are still holding some 5,000 prisoners of war. . . .

The Iranian Armed Forces Command went further on July 30, 1995. It accused Iraq of repeatedly violating the terms of the 1988 cease-fire during the first half of 1995, and of committing 80 violations from January 21 to June 22. It charged Iraq with planting mines and firing artillery shells into Iran, reconnaissance overflights by planes and helicopters, and installing anti-aircraft equipment near the border. It also accused Iraq of provoking clashes with Iranian border guards, and kidnapping Iranian civilians.[351]

Saddam Hussein, in turn, attacked Iran's leaders in a speech on August 8, 1995. He criticized them for keeping Iraqi POWs and Iraqi combat aircraft, and for snubbing Baghdad's peace overtures. Saddam charged that Iran had ignored 245 Iraqi calls for peace since the beginning of the Iran-Iraq War. In reporting Saddam's speech, the Iraqi media referred to 20,000 Iraqi prisoners, 22 IL-76 transports, five Boeing airliners, and over 100 combat aircraft.[352] Iraq and Iran then split again over the Kurds in August and September 1996, with Iran backing the PUK and Iraq backing the KDP.

These developments illustrate how hard it may be to achieve any rapprochement between Iran and Iraq, and give any such rapprochement lasting strategic importance. The history of Iranian-Iraqi relations to date does not make a "devil's bargain" between the two countries seem likely. No one, however, can dismiss an Iranian and Iraqi strategic relationship or "Molotov-Ribbentrop Pact" out of hand. Iraq resumed its calls for dialogue with Iran in January 1996.[353]

Iraqi Support of the People's Mujahideen

It is quite clear that many differences continue to separate Iraq and Iran. Among the most salient of these is Iraq's support for the Mujahedin-e-Khalq opposition group. Iraq has supported the People's Mujahideen in a battle of assassination and counter-assassination against Iranian officials. In late 1992, to the chagrin of Tehran, the Mujahedin-e-Khalq raised its political profile substantially when it held a two-week long conference in Iraq during which it reportedly decided to broaden its social and political base in order to get rid of its undemocratic image and make itself more attractive to Iranians disgruntled with the regime.[354]

Tension between Iraq and Iran increased dramatically in the spring of 1993 primarily because of a rise in Iraqi-sanctioned MKO infiltration of saboteurs into Iran. According to some reports in the first two weeks of May 1993, the MKO launched 14 cross-border operations in which 200 members of the Islamic Revolutionary Guards Corps were killed and seven oil pipelines were blown up. The MKO continued with its cross-border infiltration into Iran in the spring of 1994 attacking more oil pipelines and military installations belonging to the Revolutionary Guards 14th Division and 21st "Imam Reza" brigade.

At the same time, the Mujahedin-e-Khalq is an almost perfect "sacrifice pawn" if Iraq wants to improve its relations with Iran. Saddam's regime has nothing in common with the ill-concealed Marxist Iranian nationalism of the Mujahedin-e-Khalq. The Mujahedin-e-Khalq is little more than an irritant to Iran. It is seen as an organization of traitors by most Iranians, and it has no real chance of seizing power. As a result, Saddam may find the Mujahedin-e-Khalq just as expendable in the future as the Shah found the Iraqi Kurds to be in 1975.

Relations with Syria, Jordan, and Turkey

While much of the focus on Iraq's external relations concentrates on Kuwait and Iran, Iraq also plays an important role in the future of Jordan, Israel, and Syria, and the rest of the Gulf. Further, its oil resources and potential economic wealth make it an attractive target for European and Asian investment and trade—a factor which has already had an important impact on the West's lack of cohesion in dealing with Iraq and the issue of sanctions.

Iraq and Jordan

It is commonly forgotten that Iraq and Jordan were both ruled by different branches of the same Sharifian Hashemite family from the Hijaz.

Both monarchical Iraq and Jordan joined forces to establish the Arab Federation in early 1958 to confront the dynastic hostility of the Al-Sauds of Saudi Arabia and the revolutionary pan-Arabist republicanism of Gamal Abdel Nasser of Egypt. This alliance did not last long. That very year, the Iraqis bloodily overthrew their monarchy and murdered the king. As a result, Iraqi-Jordanian relations remained cool and distant until the late 1970s.

It was the Iran-Iraq War that led to a change in this situation. Iran effectively closed Iraq's ports, and Syria sealed off oil exports and trade across the Syrian border. As a result, the Jordanian port of Aqaba became a major lifeline for the import of goods destined for Iraq. Jordan opposed Iranian religious extremism, had little sympathy for Syria, and needed jobs, hard currency, and arms. As a result, Jordan supplied Iraq with military advice and expertise, while in return Iraq provided Jordan with badly needed captured Western weaponry from the Iranians.

These economic and military ties helped ensure that Jordanian public sentiment was heavily pro-Iraqi during the Gulf crisis. However, many other factors were involved. There was little sympathy for the Kuwaitis and other Gulf Arabs among the Jordanians, particularly among the Palestinian element of the population and the many Jordanians who had worked in the Gulf and felt they were treated as second-class Arabs. Many Jordanians also believed that what they cynically called the "cash-register" coalition was put together by the West to destroy "Arab" and Iraqi power, rather than to liberate Kuwait.[355]

Iraqi-Jordanian relations have, however, deteriorated significantly since the Gulf War. King Hussein has sought to restore his relations with the US, Saudi Arabia and Kuwait. Since 1993, Amman has increasingly expressed its concern over the impact of the sanctions on the Iraqi people. Furthermore, King Hussein is irritated by the reticence with which the Iraqi government dealt with the UN and the international community in general, and the unpredictability of the Baghdad regime.

In October 1994, when Iraq massed two divisions on the border with Kuwait and precipitated an international crisis, King Hussein publicly advised Saddam Hussein not to repeat his "mistakes" of August 1990. Jordan negotiated a peace treaty with Israel and King Hussein used the opportunity provided by Hussein Kamel's defection to improve relations with Saudi Arabia. The Saudis sent their head of intelligence, Prince Faisal al-Turki, on a "secret" visit to Jordan in mid-August to discuss the defection, bilateral Saudi-Jordanian ties, and the political situation in Iraq and prospects for change. Jordanian Foreign Minister Al-Kabariti paid an official visit to Saudi Arabia not long after Turki's cloak and dagger trip, and this seemed to signal the beginnings of a thaw in Jordanian-Saudi relations.

Since that time, King Hussein has been increasingly aggressive in attempting to bring together Iraq's divided opposition movements and support an "external strategy" to overthrow Saddam Hussein. It is also clear from his actions that his goal is to develop a stable neighbor and not to restore Hashemite influence in Iraq. Members of the Jordanian royal family are all too aware of the probable life expectancy of any outside ruler, and of the fact that the days of an Iraqi monarchy are long past.

There are, however, a number of constraints on Jordan's ability to break all relations with Saddam's Iraq. Iraq owes Jordan $1.2 billion and this debt is large enough to threaten Jordan's reserves. Jordan's economy is tied to the Iraqi economy: it gets its oil from Iraq at concessionary rates, and it could cost Jordan nearly $400 to $450 million a year to buy oil at market rates—a cost that would seriously deplete its foreign exchange holdings. Jordanian economic activity and commerce has benefited substantially from ties to Iraq. Jordan now plans to cut exports to Iraq by 50% in 1996 to reduce the growth of Iraq's debt. At the same time Jordan cannot sever all its economic ties without making major sacrifices, and has indicated that it has no intention of doing so. Jordanian popular support for Iraq—and particularly for the Iraqi people who are seen as victims of the West and of the Gulf Arabs—is very strong, especially among Jordanian Palestinians.[356]

Iraq and Syria

Relations between Syria and Iraq had been antagonistic ever since 1969, and relations between the two Ba'athist states reached a new low during the crisis over Kuwait. There are four main factors which shape this Syrian-Iraqi antagonism: personal, ideological, economic, and politico-strategic.

The personal factor is uncertain. There has been an almost inevitable conflict of personality, style, and prestige between Asad and Saddam Hussein, but it is difficult to judge reports that there is a deep mutual loathing between Hafez Asad and Saddam Hussein. Middle Eastern politics are highly personal and it would not be surprising if two men with burning ambitions for their respective countries and who both come from minority sects from within their respective states developed a loathing for one another. It is interesting, however, that Patrick Seale, the biographer of Asad, does not dwell on the personal origins of Syrian-Iraqi differences, but focuses on other factors.

Ideology and Ba'athism have definitely been key causes of the Iraqi-Syrian conflict. Ba'ath ideology—which calls for a sweeping renewal, rebirth and regeneration of the Arab world—does not lend itself to two centers of power any more than Communism did. Baghdad and Damascus, whose rivalry for influence in the Arab world dates back to the Ummayad and Abassid Calpihates, have become just as divided as the Soviet Union and China. They have often attacked each other on ideological grounds, and their conflict has spread to Ba'athist parties in other Arab countries. The Syrians have reacted strongly to Saddam's attempts to use the fact that Iraq had greater resources to establish ideological and geopolitical paramouncy over Syria when both countries sought to establish a union in 1979. Syria has refused to be the junior partner in an Iraqi Ba'athist enterprise, just as it refused to be a junior partner to Nasser.

Syria and Iraq have quarreled over economic and water issues, namely the export of Iraqi oil through Syrian territory to the Mediterranean, and the flow of the Euphrates originates in the mountains of Turkey and passes through Syria into Iraq on its way to the Persian Gulf. In the fall of 1971, Syria demanded higher transit fees from the Iraq Petroleum Company's (IPC) pipeline to the port of Baniyas. The IPC, despite its name was not in the hands of the Iraqi government, and negotiated a 50% increase in fees to Damascus. The pipeline was shut down temporarily in 1979.

Problems over water have led to tensions and resulted in a concentration of troops along the mutual border in mid-1975. The Iraqi leadership, including Saddam, accused Syria of interfering with the free flow of the Euphrates, following their inauguration of the Tabqa Dam, and of causing "social and economic disasters." These problems seem likely to grow in the future since both nations are experiencing a steady drop in renewable water resources per capita. Iraq dropped from 14,706 cubic meters per person per year in 1970 to 5,285 cubic meters in 1990, and is projected to drop to 2,000 cubic meters in 2025. Syria dropped from 1,196 cubic meters per person per year in 1970 to 439 cubic meters in 1990, and is projected to drop to 161 cubic meters in 2025.[357] Such a drop is making the sharing of water a steadily more serious issue for Turkey, Syria, and Iraq.

There has been an enduring strategic rivalry between Syria and Iraq in both inter-Arab affairs and their bilateral relations. The growth in Iraqi power between the mid-1970s and late 1970s alarmed Syria considerably, as did Baghdad's request that Syrian-Iraqi unity discussions in 1979 be conducted on Iraqi terms. Once the Iran-Iraq War broke out, Syria allied itself with Iran in order to cut Iraq down to size. Syria provided substantial help to Iran, and closed down the oil pipeline to Baniyas in April 1982—causing Iraq serious economic damage.

Iraq emerged from the Iran-Iraq War in a vengeful mood towards Syria and tried to isolate Syria in inter-Arab affairs. Further, Iraq sought to increase Syria's difficulties in Lebanon by supporting Damascus's chief nemesis, General Michel Aoun with arms. This helps explains why Syria became a member of the Coalition. Syria could not allow Iraq to succeed in its invasion of Kuwait. Such a victory would have increased Iraq's power and allowed it to dictate the guidelines of inter-Arab politics. At the same time, Syria was concerned by the destruction of Iraq's military power and by the heavy involvement of regional and outside powers in Iraq's domestic affairs.

Asad has sought better relations since the war. Once Asad consolidated his control over Lebanon and no longer felt a strategic threat from a beaten Iraq, he resumed contacts with Iraq. In March 1992, it was revealed by the Lebanese newspaper Al-Nahar that Iraqi technicians and petrochemical engineers had visited Damascus to discuss the reopening of the oil pipeline that runs 650 miles from Kirkuk to the Syrian port of Baniyas and which had remained closed since 1982.

So far, nothing has come from these contacts, although there were unconfirmed reports of meetings between senior Syrian and Iraqi officials in April 1996. There are several reasons why this may be the case. First, it is possible that the pipeline has deteriorated beyond Iraq's or Syria's ability to put it back in operation. Second, Syria was probably reluctant to bring down the wrath of the international community if it were to allow Iraq to resume exports via the Baniyas pipeline. Third, Iraq may have been reluctant to go further in the matter because of potential Syrian "greed," i.e., squeezing as much money as possible from Baghdad in the way of transit fees. Nonetheless, trade resumed between the two countries in December 1991 with an Iraqi shipment of petrochemicals worth $15 million.

During 1995, Saddam Hussein's growing problems in Sunni-dominated central Iraq—Al-Anbar province—positioned Syria to play a more active role in Iraqi politics. The Dulaimi rebellion in the spring of 1995 highlighted the importance of this large tribe that stretches from the outskirts of Baghdad into Syria itself. The location and the nature of the Dulaim revolt led to the crystallization around Syrian patronage of a new Iraqi opposition movement of Sunnis called the "Armed Dulaim Tribes Sons Movement." In mid-June Ahmed Dulaimi, the brother of the executed general fled to Damascus where in conjunction with the Al-Bunimr and Al-Bushammar sub-clans of the Dulaimis, he formed the Iraqi tribes movement called the Supreme Leadership Council of the Union of Iraqi Tribes to bring about a coordinated "united military action plan." It is still not clear whether Syria is playing an active role in Dulaimi affairs or is seeking some sort of rapproachment with Saddam.

It is clear that Syria is in a position to exploit Saddam's troubles in the "center," and can either use this pressure to threaten the Iraqi regime or help force concessions, but there is no guarantee that Syria and Iraq will always be hostile. In mid-1996 there were reports from the Middle East that seemed to indicate that Iraq and Syria were seeking a way out of their decades-old hostility. Rumors that Syrian leader Hafez al-Asad and Saddam met secretly on the Iraq-Syria border early in 1996 cannot be substantiated. However, there were clear-cut reasons why both countries might be seeking a rapprochement. For its part, Iraq had good reasons to exploit any potential crack in the wall of isolation that it has suffered for the past six years. A rapprochement with Syria offered a way either to drive a wedge between Damascus and Tehran or form a channel to improve relations with Tehran.

Syria has its own reasons to seek a rapprochement. From Damascus's perspective, the peace process with Israel had virtually collapsed by the Spring of 1996. The mutual mistrust between Jerusalem and Damascus had been intensified in April 1996 when Israel launched an attack against Hizbollah guerrillas in Lebanon that threatened to escalate into clashes between Israel and Syria.[358]

There were three other reasons for Syria to act. First, in February 1996 details of an Israeli-Turkish military accord emerged, causing consternation and worry among the Arabs and in Iran. This accord between the two most powerful countries in the Middle East called for intelligence cooperation, joint collection of electronic intelligence along Turkey's borders with Syria, Iraq, and Iran, Israeli assistance in the training of Turkish forces stationed in the southeastern borders, and joint air exercises between the Turkish and Israeli Air Forces.[359]

Second, the Jordanian-Israeli peace treaty was followed by King Hussein's strategic decision to undertake a dramatic expansion of relations between Amman and Jerusalem and to distance himself from Iraq. Syria was convinced that it was being encircled from the north by Turkey, from the south by Jordan and Israel, and talk of a Jerusalem-Ankara-Amman axis fueled Syrian alarm.[360] Relations between Amman and Damascus worsened in the summer of 1996 when the former accused the latter of supporting terrorism against it. The Syrian response came in the shape of a statement by Defense Minister Talas' which poured scorn on Jordan's regional pretensions: "Jordan was created to separate Saudi Arabia, the land of the Islamic message, and Syria, the land of Arab conquests. Moreover, this entity was created to protect Israel and be its shield." To Syria's west was a weak vassal state, Lebanon, and to the east was Iraq, now weak but thoroughly hostile and alienated from Damascus. A Syrian opening to Iraq under these circumstances is not inconceivable.

Third, in June Likud leader Benjamin Netanyuhu was elected Prime Minister of Israel and proceeded to state that Israel would never give up the Golan Heights. A war of words erupted between Syria and Israel and Damascus initially acted to reaffirm its strategic understanding with Tehran when Syrian Prime Minister Mahmud Zu'bi visited Tehran in August.[361] At the same time, Syria sought to mobilize a collective Arab response to the rise of hard line government in Israel at the Arab Cairo Summit of June and claimed that the peace process between Israel and the Arabs had ended when clashes took place between Israel and the Palestinians in October 1996.

It is far from clear that leader Hafez al-Asad and Saddam Hussein can ever to any kind of effective working relationship, and any such relationship might force Syria to make a painful choice between Iran and Iraq, but the possibility can never be dismissed.[362]

Iraq and Turkey

Turkey is one of two non-Arab states bordering Iraq, the other being Iran. Iraq's approach towards Turkey has, however, been different from its approach towards Iran. Iraq has been divided from Iran by history, ideology, the struggle over control of the Shatt al-Arab, the Kurdish war of 1969–1975, rivalry for influence in the Gulf, alleged Iranian subversion in Iraq after the fall of the Shah, and the Iran-Iraq War.

In contrast, Turco-Iraqi relations were cordial, even close, from the 1970s until Iraq invaded Kuwait and Turkey joined the UN Coalition. Relations were strengthened by the fact that both countries were secular and highly nationalistic states committed to economic development and progress at a time when Islamism was growing stronger. Both nations avoided interference in each other's domestic affairs, Iraqi exports through Turkish territory to the port of Dortyol steadily expanded, there was a significant increase in Turco-Iraqi trade and commercial ties, and both nations cooperated in curbing Kurdish nationalist activity on both sides of their common border.

This history helps to explain why Iraq began to seek a rapprochement with Turkey almost immediately after the Gulf War. Iraqi officials stressed the need for normalization based on past "ideal" neighborly relations and common political and economic interests. Turkey, suffering from the economic effects of the embargo against Iraq—one of its largest trading partners—called for the lifting of sanctions against Iraq, although it knows that it cannot unilaterally allow the flow of Iraqi oil through the Kirkuk-Dortyol pipeline.

Turkey has so far supported the UN effort to establish a Kurdish security zone, but has never supported Kurdish autonomy and has been deeply unhappy about the absence of Baghdad's authority in the northern part of Iraq. From Turkey's perspective the government in Baghdad was an exemplary security partner in securing their mutual border from the 1970s to the time of the Gulf War. Iraq's fractious Kurds are scarcely a substitute. Turkey also wants command of the UN effort to support "Operation Provide Comfort." It wants either a resumption of Baghdad's control over the Kurds or more Turkish leverage over the Iraqi Kurds, as well as to defuse the criticisms made by Turkish Islamists and nationalists regarding the presence of foreign forces on Turkish soil.

Iraq, in turn, fears Turkey's potential ambitions. These fears were strengthened by the statements of some Turkish analysts and political figures after Turkey joined the UN Coalition in 1990. First, oblique references by some Turks to the 'lost' vilayet of Mosul, which is part of Iraq but which was once a part of the Ottoman Empire, have alarmed the Iraqis. Second, Iraqi fears were aroused by Turkish military incursions into Iraqi Kurdistan after 1992, which were not coordinated closely with Iraq as they had been when similar incursions took place during the Iran-Iraq War. Third, President Suleiman Demirel made a statement in early May 1995 that there should be an adjustment in Turkey's borders with Iraq—just as Turkish forces concluded 'Operation Steel,' its attack into northern Iraq against the separatist PKK:

> The border is wrong. The Mosul Province was within the Ottoman Empire's territory. Had that place been a part of Turkey, none of the problems we are confronted with at the present time (i.e., unstable borders and separatist activities) would have existed.[363]

Demirel retracted his statement following negative reactions from Middle Eastern states, the Iraqi government, and Iraqi opposition forces. However, the Iraqi media began to refer to Turkey as the "sick man," and threatened to "cut off the hands of those who try to harm us." Further, the creation of a Turkish "security zone" in northern Iraq some 10–15 kilometers south of the Turkish border following the Kurdish crisis of September 1996 scarcely reassured Iraq.

Turco-Iraqi relations have also been strained in the past by Iraq's dependence on the oil pipeline through Turkey. In late 1991 when the UN was negotiating the plan for the sale of limited quantities of Iraqi oil via the Dortyol pipeline, Ankara demanded a very substantial increase in transit fees of a one-off lump-sum payment of $264 million regardless of the actual level of Iraqi output. This increase would have drastically reduced the sum of money available to Iraqi purchase of basic necessities. An outraged Baghdad denounced the Turkish demand as "daylight robbery."[364] In any case, the matter became academic as Iraq chose not to exercise the option of selling the limited quantity of oil allowed by the UN. Nonetheless, Iraq has to consider the fact that the Turks may prove recalcitrant in the future when it comes to Iraqi oil exports through Turkey.

Iraq, Egypt, and Other Arab States

Iraq's relations with other Arab states are mixed. A number of Arab states—such as Algeria, Mauritania, and Yemen—provided the UN Coalition with limited or no support during the Gulf War. Since that time many Arab and Islamic states which had opposed or fought Iraq during Desert Storm have become increasingly concerned over the impact of sanctions, and resentful of what they feel are US efforts to use the UN Security Council to impose its own political agenda.

Iraqi officials have tried to exploit these feelings. They have taken to calling the UN Security Council, "the New York branch of the State Department." They have also made every effort to exploit the tragic socioeconomic impact of sanctions, and the issue of sovereignty posed by UN interventions in Iraq. They have tried to generate the perception that the UN's mission is solely to blame for Iraq's plight in spite of the fact that the Iraqi regime has refused the UN's terms to sell oil, and that the UN has been subordinated to the West, which they claim is part of the West's search for a "new world order."

The Iraqi leadership has sought to build support in the Arab and Islamic worlds by appealing to the masses, intellectuals, students, opposition groups, and nationalists. Iraq has appealed to Arab states on the same grounds, sometimes adding threats about the consequences of supporting sanctions that will make Iraq an enduring enemy.

This diplomatic offensive has had some success even in cases like Egypt, whose leader, President Hosni Mubarak was a founder of the UN Coalition. Beginning in early 1993, Mubarak stated that restoration of Egyptian-Iraqi relations was only a "matter of time," and by late 1995 Egypt's position towards Iraq had softened considerably. Cairo was increasingly frustrated by the lack of a move towards inter-Arab reconciliation which would include a reintegration of Iraq into the Arab regional system. Furthermore, Egypt indicated that it felt the absence of Iraq from the regional balance of power was detrimental to the security of the Arab world. Hence, it decided to take the initiative.

In July 1995, Iraqi Foreign Minister, Muhammad Said al-Sahhaf visited Cairo and met with Egyptian Foreign Minister 'Amr Musa. This visit was followed by Mubarak's dismissal of the importance of Hussein Kamel—a position which drew praise from the Iraqi government. Egypt also re-opened its trade center in Baghdad, decided to increase its staff at its embassy and to upgrade diplomatic representation, and to allow Egyptian workers—who once numbered almost 2 million—to return to Iraq.

Iraq and the Gulf States

The Southern Gulf States all supported the UN Coalition, but they have become increasingly divided in their treatment of Iraq. In late 1991, Abdullah Bishara—then the Secretary-General of the Gulf Cooperation Council—declared that the "Iraqi regime is still there and remains a threat, although it is an anachronism. As long as this regime exists, we must stress our regional security." Although Bishara was a Kuwaiti, this statement unquestionably reflected the consensus that existed among the Southern Gulf states at the time.

The Southern Gulf states still collectively and periodically reiterate that Iraq must adhere to all UN Security Council resolutions, especially those pertaining to the dismantling of weapons of mass destruction. However, they no longer have a united approach in dealing with Iraq. Dissension within the Southern Gulf states appeared as early as 1993. Except for Kuwait, the Gulf states expressed their dismay over the periodic Western air attacks on Iraq and at the socioeconomic costs of the sanctions regime on Iraqis. Most of the Southern Gulf states oppose the present rigid policy of economic containment—a position they reiterated during the Kurdish crisis of August–September 1996.

Oman and Qatar began to oppose the indefinite extension of sanctions. Both nations saw Iraq as a potential counterbalance to the growing threat from Iran, and felt that sanctions were creating a revanchist state rather than leading to political change. Qatar took a particularly strong stand. It donated food to Iraq on a number of occasions, and reestablished diplomatic relations with Iraq in October 1992. In February 1995, it called for the rehabilitation of Iraq by the Arab world as a prelude to its return into the international community.[365] Sheik Hamad Bin Khalifa al-Thani, continued to maintain a sympathetic position towards Iraq when he came to power as Emir of Qatar. The Qatari Foreign Minister stated that Qataris sympathize with the Iraqis because of what they were going through and reiterated Qatar's view that Iraq was important to the balance of power in the Gulf.[366] Sheik Hamad Bin Khalifa al-Thani also expressed his concern over the risk of the partitioning of Iraq, and dismissed the defection of Kamel as a dispute within the ruling Takriti family, similar to those that take place within the Qatari ruling family.[367]

The Bahraini position has been more nuanced than policies articulated by Oman and Qatar. Bahrain too may see Iraq as a counterbalance to Iran, but Iraq is more of a direct threat and Bahrain has close relations with Saudi Arabia and Kuwait. In September, Bahraini Foreign Minister, Sheik Muhammad Bin-Mubarak al Khalifa told the Arabic language paper *Al-Hayah*, that "full implementation of the Security Council resolutions is the only way to lift the sanctions and enable Iraq to interact freely with the rest of the world."[368] Bahrain indicated that it was concerned by the socioeconomic situation inside Iraq and their implications for the future stability and integrity of the country. In discussing Hussein Kamel's defection, the Bahraini Foreign Minister reiterated his view that the main problem with Iraq was the issue of the full implementation of the UN resolutions. Bahrain, he added, maintains the position that "what is happening inside Iraq and what the Iraqi opposition does, is an Iraqi matter."[369]

The Saudi and Kuwaiti positions towards Iraq are more hostile. Both Kuwait and Saudi Arabia adhere to positions that are similar to those of the US and Britain: Saddam must go and that there can be no tranquillity and stability in the region until he does. Kuwaiti officials like First Deputy Prime Minister Sheik Sabah al-Ahmad al-Jabir have reiterated the Kuwaiti view that as long as the current regime stayed in power there would be "no stability" in the region.[370] The Kuwaiti Council of Ministers welcomed the decision of the UN Security Council to renew sanctions on Iraq in mid-September 1995 and again in early 1996. Kuwait's Crown Prince, Sheik Saad al-Abdullah al-Sabah also warned in September 1995 that:[371]

> Saddam will never forget how his invading troops were evicted from our land, and he will never forget that one day he called your dear country 'Iraq's 19th province.' I am warning everyone, and in every language that everyone can understand without exception, that this regime in Baghdad will never let Kuwait be.

However, the Saudi position has recently been more sympathetic. Early in 1996, Prince Bandar Bin Sultan—the Saudi Ambassador to Washington—stated that Saudi Arabia supports ending, "the suffering of the Iraqi people." At nearly the same time, however, a top-ranking Saudi official reiterated his country's opposition to any dealings with Saddam Hussein's regime:[372]

> We have the longest border with Iraq, and everyone is aware of our desire for the best of relations with that people. But Saddam is still a risk. No one trusts him. Even George Bush now regrets having allowed Saddam to remain in power in Baghdad.

The UAE has sought conciliation. On October 15, 1995, President Sheik Zayed Bin-Sultan Al Nuhayyan of the UAE called for inter-Arab reconciliation which was to include a rehabilitation of Iraq. Zayed declared that while Saddam Hussein had committed a grave error in invading Kuwait:[373]

> To err is human. The holy Koran teaches us. The important thing is for the mistaken to learn from mistakes. Some people err, and others repeat their errors. . . . Let us take Saddam, as an example. He erred once when he began the war against Iran. . . . Russia, Europe, and America entered confrontations and wars, and then they achieved cooperation and demonstrated solidarity. Why do the Arabs not become like them? Saddam, one person erred. However, who is paying the price now? More than 18 million Iraqis are being exposed to death. . . . Certainly, Saddam learned from his sin, and he will not repeat it. It is time for reconciliation.

The UAE ruler added that the Arabs must take the initiative and rehabilitate Iraq, whether the West likes it or not. The UAE position was endorsed by Oman and Qatar, both of which had previously been at the forefront of the Southern Gulf States calling for reconciliation with Iraq.

Kuwait and Saudi Arabia opposed the UAE's initiative, as they had opposed the policy of Oman and Qatar. Kuwait's Foreign Minister, Sheik Sabah al-Ahmad al-Sabah, declared on October 24, 1995, that "this matter is not on [sic] the hands of Kuwait or any other Arab country or the Arab League. These are international resolutions issued by the UN." They also were able to make their position the official position of the Gulf Cooperation Council. The GCC conference in December 1995, which took place in Muscat amid great dissension, nonetheless censured Iraq severely and called upon the UN Security Council to ensure that Iraq is forced to completely dismantle its weapons of mass of destruction.

Iraq and the International Community

Iraqi diplomacy has also searched for ways to influence the international community to allow Iraq to resume its oil exports, and to free Iraq of the strategic and military constraints of the cease-fire agreement with the UN. The Iraqis realize that neither their propaganda against Western "domination," nor the sympathy of the Arab governments, can remove the sanctions. As a result, Iraqi officials—especially veteran diplomats like Tariq Aziz—have sought to take advantage of differences between the real power-brokers within the United Nations. The Iraqis have tried to exploit humanitarian concerns, and they attempted to obtain the support of their former trading partners by offering incentives like trade, investment, oil, and repayment of past debts.

Deputy Prime Minister Tariq Aziz described this two-tier strategy in an interview with a Russian newspaper. He stated that the UN sanctions regime would end because of:

- *Iraqi 'steadfastness' (sumud) and a principled stance.* Once the West recognizes the fact that "they cannot bring us to our knees," the blockade will end.[374]
- *Iraqi diplomatic activity to make countries understand that their support for the "continuation of the embargo is damaging not only Iraq, but themselves*—particularly Russia, Turkey, Jordan, and France. As well as China, India, and many other states that formerly had mutually beneficial economic and trade contacts in our country."[375]

Aziz reiterated a view that Iraqi officials had advanced since the end of the Gulf War. For example, a former Deputy Prime Minister, Taha Yasin Ramadan described Iraq's strategy of steadfastness in 1991 by referring to history when he said: ". . . we have not conceded our principles. The Arab prophet was victorious in some battles and defeated in others. He did not abandon Islam during the defeats. We have living examples in our history. We Arabs consider the tripartite aggression against the Suez Canal in 1956 a victory, even though it led to the occupation of the canal militarily by the countries that mounted the aggression."[376]

Iraqi officials have focused their efforts to implement this strategy on Russia, France, and the PRC for a wide variety of reasons. First, these three powers were permanent members of UN Security Council. Second, all three resented the perceived Anglo-American domination of the Security Council. Third, all three were important economic, political, and commercial partners of Iraq for the past twenty-five years. Fourth, there was little prospect of persuading the US and Britain to take the lead in lifting sanctions.

The US and Britain

The US and Britain have remained adamant in maintaining the sanctions on Iraq, and have shown every sign that they will continue to do so until Saddam Hussein falls from power. The Bush Administration opted to maintain "excruciating pressure" on Saddam Hussein by the constant threat of renewed military action, continuation of diplomatic and political pressure to keep Iraq isolated internationally, and raising the possibility of covert activities to destabilize the regime in Baghdad.

When President Bush lost the November 1992 elections, Iraq hoped that the new Clinton Administration would "depersonalize" the conflict and move toward better relations. Not only did the new administration fail to do this, it showed an equal ideological hostility towards the entire Ba'athist regime. This was reflected in its policy of "dual containment" directed against both Iraq and Iran. It declared Saddam's regime to be "irredeemable," and a threat to the United States and its allies and friends in the Middle East. It also effectively stipulated that sanctions would be maintained until Saddam fell from power.

The Clinton Administration's policy called for the US to establish strong ties with the Iraqi opposition, especially the INC. Further, the administration insisted that Iraq would have to comply fully with all UN Security Council resolutions, including those relating to missing Kuwaiti persons, return of Kuwaiti property, renunciation of terrorism, ending of repression of the Iraqi population and abuse of human rights, and cooperation with international relief agencies. Last but not least, it demanded that Iraq must convince the world of its "peaceful intentions." These stringent requirements did not mention Saddam by name, but there was little prospect that they could be fulfilled without the regime falling from power.

On January 15, 1996, President Clinton reiterated the US position on Iraq, a day prior to the UN Security Council's decision to carry over sanctions against Iraq for a further two months. Stating that Iraq represented a real threat to peace and stability in the Middle East, Clinton stressed that his "administration will continue to reject any easing of sanctions until Iraq proves its good faith by totally complying with the relevant resolutions." The British government provided strong support for this position, as it had for the previous policy positions of the Bush and Clinton Administrations.[377]

Russia and Iraq

In contrast, France and Russia have substantial commercial and economic interests in Iraq, and have taken a much more pro-Iraqi position. Iraq owes France about $5 billion in military and civilian debts, while it owes Russia about $7–$8 billion. A Russian source claims that Iraq owes Moscow between $10–$16 billion in military and civil debt.[378] The PRC does not have the same economic stake in Iraq as France and Russia do, but has always been ambivalent about imposing sanctions and has little strategic concern over the nature of the Iraqi regime.

Russia began to show its sympathy for Iraq in 1994. On several occasions, Victor Posuvalyuk, President Yeltsin's Special Envoy to the Middle East, expressed Russia's position on the conditions that Iraq needs to fulfill before sanctions are lifted:[379]

> We would like Iraq to come out of this state, but as a matter of principle, provided it abides by the UN Resolution 687 which concerns aspects of disarmament and the termination of its military programs. Baghdad also must recognize the independence and sovereignty of Kuwait and internationally recognized border, and finally, make clear the fate of Kuwaiti citizens taken prisoners or missing during the war with Kuwait.

In March 1995, Russia joined with France and China in circulating a draft resolution in the UN to lift the embargo on Iraqi oil exports. Sergei Lavrov, the Russian ambassador to the UN repeated Russia's well-established position that:[380]

> We act strictly within bounds of the Security Council's resolutions and procedures recorded in them. In its proposals, Russia proceeds from the view that Iraq's recognition of Kuwait's sovereignty and Iraq's fulfilling demands for disarmament under appropriate resolutions of the Security Council have created conditions for reply steps by the world community.

Russia has had several reasons for taking this position. First, Russia wanted to show that it has an independent foreign policy. This search for independence has been accelerated by the replacement of Andrei

Kozyrev by Evgeni Primakov, the head of the Russian intelligence service and a noted Arabist, in January 1996. Russian foreign policy is likely to be even more assertive and independent of the West, and there are likely to be further differences between Moscow and Washington over Iran, Iraq, and China, but not over the Middle East peace process, which Moscow supports.

Second, Russia had extensive commercial interests in Iraq which it wishes to rebuild. The Russian Oil Company, LUKOIL decided to step up its activities in Iraq following a meeting in September 1994 between an Iraqi delegation headed by the Oil Ministry's Chief Engineer, Faysal al-Nasiri, and the LUKOIL president, Vagit Alekperov.

Finally, Russia saw American and British policy as a determination to punish Iraq for keeping President Saddam Hussein in office, rather than as part of an effort to force Iraq to adhere to the conditions of UN Resolution 687. Even a noted "Euro-Atlanticist" such as Andrei Kozyrev, then Russian Foreign Minister stated on July 11, 1995, that "Those sanctions must not become an instrument for punishing peoples or replacing regimes, regardless of whether such regimes are liked or not. . . . (The sanctions) must strictly conform to the goals and reasons for which they have been imposed by the UN Security Council. Otherwise they may have the opposite result. If people do not see any other way out, they will resort to extremism."[381]

France and Iraq Sanctions

France and Iraq had a close political, economic, and military relationship between 1974 and 1990.[382] Ba'athist Iraq admired French independence of the US during the Cold War era and coveted French military and commercial technology in order to lessen Iraq's dependence on the Soviet Union. For its part, France did not see Iraq as a Soviet satellite or puppet state in the 1970s, anymore than it sees Iraq as a "rogue" state in the 1990s. Furthermore, France felt excluded commercially and politically from Imperial Iran—an American domain—and the smaller states of the Gulf which were under British influence despite the withdrawal of British forces from the area in 1971.

Franco-Iraqi relations expanded rapidly during the Iran-Iraq War when it became Iraq's strongest supporter in the West, its second largest supplier of arms after the USSR, providing it with advanced military equipment and advisers. Led by President Francois Mitterrand, the French government viewed Saddam's Iraq as a secular bulwark against the 'religious fanaticism' from Iran which threatened to engulf the Middle East. While France had some qualms at times concerning the wisdom of such strong support for Iraq which were accentuated by the extent of the Iraqi commercial debt to France and fears that Iraq could collapse, the existence of a powerful pro-Iraqi lobby among military, political and industrial figures, continued to ensure France's commitment to Iraq. Following the end of the Iran-Iraq War France believed itself well-positioned to play an important role in the economic and military reconstruction of Iraq, but felt that it had no choice but to condemn Iraq for its aggression against Kuwait and to join the coalition.

This helps explain why France has never made its post–Gulf War policy towards Iraq contingent upon the removal of Saddam Hussein but has consistently demanded that Iraq implement the relevant UN Security Council resolutions requiring dismantling of its weapons of mass destruction and recognition of Kuwait prior to the lifting of sanctions. France's interpretation is completely legalistic; once Iraq implements the resolutions, sanctions must be lifted in accordance with paragraph 22 of Resolution 687. Like Russia, France believes that the goal posts should not be moved to suit American and British wishes.

While analysts continue to ponder the reasons behind Saddam's decision to move troops towards the border with Kuwait in October 1994, the whole affair revealed growing differences between the leading coalition powers, with France in the lead. While Paris did co-sponsor UN Security Council Resolution 949 which demanded that Iraq withdraw the forces it had moved to the border with Kuwait, it declined to support the Anglo-American proposal to create an armor-free zone in southern Iraq. France believed that this constituted a threat to Iraq's territorial integrity.[383]

During the first week of January 1995, Alain Juppe, then France's Foreign Minister, welcomed Tariq Aziz to Paris for discussions on prospects for easing of sanctions. France's action was sharply criticized by both the US and Britain as neither helpful nor constructive.[384] By early spring 1996, even though sanctions still remained and Iraq continued to be caught up negotiating over the 'food for oil' deal in accordance with Resolution 986, Baghdad was clearly pleased by developments in Franco-Iraqi relations. In an interview with a French magazine, Tariq Aziz, when asked whether Iraq was still angry with France for having participated in the Gulf War, replied:[385]

> No. ... Moreover, the government has changed. And we know that Jacques Chirac is one of those leaders who knows Iraq. The Gulf War is a page that has been turned.

Trends in the International Community

To date, the efforts of nations like Russia and France to help Iraq have been set back by the stupidity, lies, and unnecessary belligerence of the regime. Iraq's troop movements to the Kuwaiti border in October 1994 and the lies uncovered concerning its biological weapons program in August 1995 have cost Iraq dearly. Saddam Hussein also lashed out at his neighbors, verbally this time, on the anniversary of Desert Storm, referring to them as "the hyenas, jackals, and crows surrounding Iraq (who) thought that Iraq . . . was going to fall . . . and they proved mistaken."[386]

There is no guarantee, however, that Iraq will be equally clumsy in the future. Its acceptance of UN Resolution 986 is a reflection of the fact that it is becoming more realistic about what it can expect from other states, and international support for the remaining sanctions is likely to decay with time. It also had considerable success in exploiting divisions within the international community after the Kurdish crisis of September 1996. There are limits to how long other nations will be willing to wait for Saddam to fall. The rising human cost of sanctions is gradually providing more support for the Ba'ath regime, and sanctions offer no guarantee of a new or better regime. Saddam can always accept the UN offer to sell oil, and attempt to use this to lift the sanctions in stages.

Implications for Western and Southern Gulf Strategy

Yet again, there is no strategy that can easily resolve the issues involved in Iraqi external relations. Neither the West nor Southern Gulf states can rely on either a "centrist" or "peripheral" strategy to create a new regime. Even those states who are willing to enforce sanctions indefinitely have no assurance that this will bring down Saddam, or that he will not accept UN terms for oil sales in order to remain in power. Further, the extension of sanctions has a very real cost in humanitarian terms, in alienating Arab public opinion and discrediting the use of international sanctions, in increasing Iraqi revanchism, and in limiting Iraq's oil export capability.

However, lifting sanctions with Iraq's current regime in power will not offer Iraq's neighbors any security or ensure that Iraq's oil revenues will be used largely to benefit the Iraqi people. Unless Iraq faces firm military containment by the US and Southern Gulf states—with support from Iran, Syria, and Turkey—appeasement will almost certainly be seen as weakness and accommodation will be exploited. Rather than end Iraqi revanchism, the Southern Gulf states will have to live with an Iraq that is more powerful and better able to act on its ambitions.

This dilemma is another argument for changing the present approach to sanctions, and exploiting the options discussed in Chapter 5. It is also an argument for prolonging military containment, regardless of what happens to the economic sanctions imposed on Iraq. As the following chapters make clear, Iraq is anything but a paper tiger. It retains powerful conventional forces, it has significant capabilities for terrorism, and it will be able to rebuild its capability to deliver weapons of mass destruction once the UNSCOM inspection effort ends.

10

Military Developments

Iran may be the rising military power in the Gulf, but Iraq still presents the most direct threat to the Southern Gulf and the West's supply of oil. Iraq's military forces have been extensively reorganized since the Gulf War, and have regained many of their military capabilities. As Table Three shows, Iraq can still deploy massive land forces against Kuwait and the Eastern Province of Saudi Arabia, and Iraq remains the leading Gulf power in many areas of force strength.

Chart Eleven shows a rough estimate of the trends in Iraqi military manpower, and Charts Twelve and Thirteen show how Iraq's strength compares with that of other Gulf states. Iraq still has an active force structure with over 380,000 men, plus another 650,000 in reserve. It has six corps with 19 regular army divisions, seven Republican Guard divisions, 10 special forces and commando brigades, and a Presidential Guard/special security force. Its equipment holdings include roughly 2,700 tanks, 4,400 other armored vehicles, 1,980 major artillery weapons, 120 attack helicopters, and over 330 combat aircraft. Iraq has also made a major effort to rebuild its military industries and to compensate for its lack of arms imports with domestic production.

Nevertheless, more than half a decade without significant military imports is steadily reducing Iraq's military capabilities. While Iraq was able to rebuild and consolidate its forces after the Gulf War, this period of recovery ended in 1993. Since late 1993, Iraq has been unable to "recapitalize" its forces, and to fund a proper level of training and readiness. Iraq has not been able to obtain the imports necessary to modernize its technology and make up key losses from the Gulf War, or to provide the large deliveries of parts, new equipment, and munitions it needs to make up for the inefficiency of its maintenance and logistics capability. Readiness and morale have declined steadily as a result of Iraq's economic crisis, and desertions have increased. The quality and strength of most units have declined sharply, and even Iraq's elite units have suffered. Iraq has had to cannibalize equipment and take equipment out of some units to maintain the readiness of others.

TABLE THREE   Gulf Military Forces in 1996

	Iran	Iraq	Bahrain	Kuwait	Oman	Qatar	Saudi Arabia*	UAE	Yemen
Manpower									
Total Active	320,000	382,500	10,700	16,600	43,500	11,100	161,500	70,000	39,500
Regular	220,000	382,500	10,700	16,600	37,000	11,100	105,500	70,000	39,500
National Guard & Other	100,000	0	0	0	6,500	0	57,000	0	0
Reserve	350,000	650,000	0	23,700	0	0	0	0	40,000
Paramilitary	135,000	24,800	9,250	5,200	4,400	0	15,500	2,700	30,000
Army and Guard									
Manpower	260,000	350,000	8,500	10,000	31,500	8,500	127,000	65,000	37,000
Regular Army Manpower	180,000	350,000	8,500	10,000	25,000	8,500	70,000	65,000	37,000
Reserve	350,000	450,000	0	0	0	0	20,000	0	40,000
Tanks	1,350	2,700	81	220	85	24	910	133	1,125
AIFV/Recce, Lt. Tanks	515	1,600	46	130	136	50	1,467	515	580
APCs	550	2,200	235	199	7	172	3,670	380	560
Self Propelled Artillery	294	150	13	38	6	28	200	90	30
Towed Artillery	2,000	1,500	36	0	96	12	270	82	483
MRLs	890	120	9	0	0	4	60	48	220
Mortars	3,500	2,000+	18	24	74	39	400	101	800
SSM Launchers	46	12	0	0	0	0	10	6	30
Light SAM Launchers	700	3,000	65	48	62	58	650	36	700
AA Guns	1,700	5,500	0	0	18	12	10	62	372
Air Force Manpower	20,000	15,000	1,500	2,500	4,100	800	18,000	3,500	1,000
Air Defense Manpower	15,000	15,000	0	0	0	0	4,000	0	0

(continues)

TABLE THREE   *(continued)*

	Iran	Iraq	Bahrain	Kuwait	Oman	Qatar	Saudi Arabia*	UAE	Yemen
Total Combat Aircraft	295	353	24	76	46	12	295	97	69
Bombers	0	6	0	0	0	0	0	0	0
Fighter/Attack	150	130	12	40	19	11	112	41	27
Fighter/Interceptor	115	180	12	8	0	1	122	22	30
Recce/FGA Recce	8	0	0	0	12	0	10	8	0
AEW C4I/BM	1	0	0	0	0	5	0	0	0
MR/MPA**	6	0	0	0	7	0	0	0	0
OCU/COIN	0	18	0	11	13	0	36	15	0
Combat Trainers	92	200	0	11	22	0	66	35	12
Transport Aircraft**	68	34	3	4	14	5	49	20	19
Tanker Aircraft	4	2	0	0	0	0	16	0	0
Armed Helicopters**	100	120	10	16	0	20	12	42	8
Other Helicopters**	509	350	8	36	37	7	138	42	21
Major SAM Launchers	204	340	12	24	0	0	128	18	87
Light SAM Launchers	60	200	0	12	28	9	249	34	0
AA Guns	0	0	0	12	0	0	420	0	0
Navy Manpower	38,000	2,500	1,000	1,500	4,200	1,800	17,000	1,500	1,500
Major Surface Combatants									
Missile	5	0	3	0	0	0	8	0	0
Other	2	1	0	0	0	0	0	0	0
Patrol Craft									
Missile	10	1	4	2	4	3	9	10	7

(continues)

TABLE THREE (continued)

	Iran	Iraq	Bahrain	Kuwait	Oman	Qatar	Saudi Arabia*	UAE	Yemen
Other	26	7	5	12	8	6	20	18	3
Submarines	2	0	0	0	0	0	0	0	0
Mine Vessels	3	4	0	0	0	0	5	0	3
Amphibious Ships	8	0	0	0	2	0	0	0	2
Landing Craft	17	3	4	6	4	1	7	4	2

Note: Does not include equipment in storage. Air Force totals include all helicopters, and all heavy surface to air missile launchers.

*60,000 reserves are National Guard Tribal Levies. The total for land forces includes active National Guard equipment. These additions total 262 AIFVs, 1,165 APCs, and 70 towed artillery weapons.

**Includes navy, army, national guard, and royal flights, but not paramilitary.

Source: Adapted by Anthony H. Cordesman from International Institute for Strategic Studies *Military Balance* (IISS, London), in this case, the 1995–1996 edition; *Military Technology, World Defense Almanac, 1994–1995*; and Jaffee Center for Strategic Studies, *The Military Balance in the Middle East, 1993–1994* (JCSS, Tel Aviv, 1994).

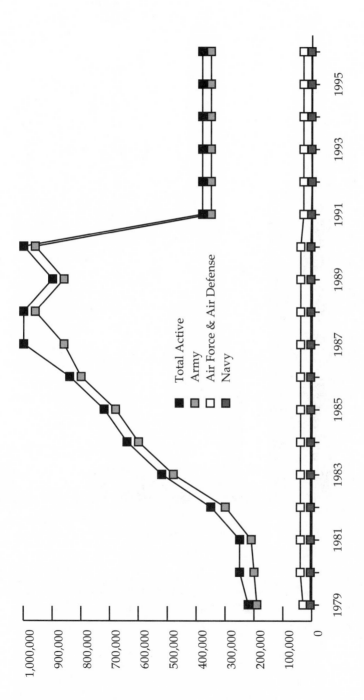

CHART ELEVEN Iraq: Military Manning—1979–1996. *Source:* Adapted by Anthony H. Cordesman from various editions of the IISS, *Military Balance,* the JCSS, *Military Balance in the Middle East,* and material provided by US experts.

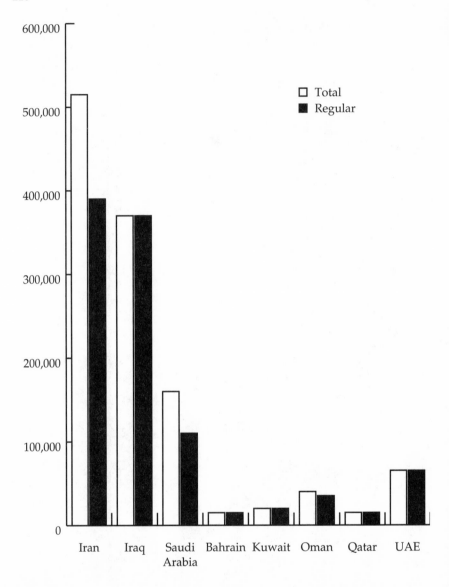

CHART TWELVE   Total Active Military Manpower in All Gulf Forces. *Note:* Iran includes active forces in Revolutionary Guards. Saudi Arabia includes active in National Guard. *Source:* Adapted by Anthony H. Cordesman from the IISS, *Military Balance, 1995–1996.*

Main Battle Tanks in Persian Gulf Forces

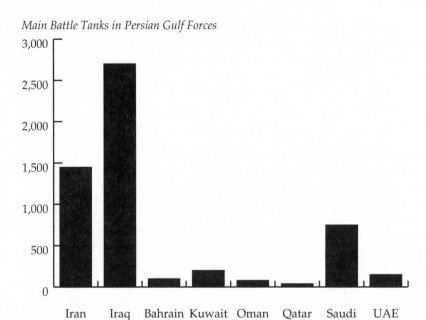

Total Combat Aircraft in Persian Gulf Forces

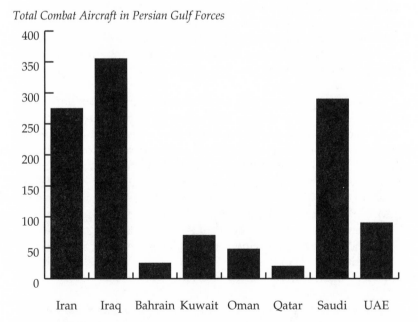

CHART THIRTEEN   Major Measures of Combat Equipment Strength—1996.
Source: Adapted by Anthony H. Cordesman from the IISS, *Military Balance,*
1995–1996.

Iraq can scarcely be called a paper tiger, but it is hardly the military power that won the Iran-Iraq War. In many areas, Iraq's order of battle is becoming a hollow shell. In other areas, military containment is working and is steadily reducing the threat Iraq can pose to Iran, Kuwait, and other states.

Iraqi Military Expenditures

Iraq has been able to remain a major regional military power because of the legacy of Iraq's immense military expenditures and arms transfers before the Gulf War, the heritage of the decades' long arms race with Iran summarized in Table Four, and the fact that the regime has given high priority to the military even at the cost of worsening the plight of Iraq's people. Iraq imported well over one hundred billion dollars worth of conventional arms between 1972 and 1990, and spent nearly $20 billion dollars on the arms and equipment to assemble, manufacture, and deliver weapons of mass destruction. It has been involved in an arms race with Iran since the 1960s. It spent billions fighting the Kurds during the early to mid-1970s, and nearly $200 billion in fighting the Iran-Iraq War.

During much of the Iran-Iraq War, Iraq spent 40% to 75% of its GDP on military expenditures, much of which has been lost in fruitless wars. Iraq's losses of weapons and ammunition expenditures alone total tens of billions of dollars, and it has lost tens of billions more in terms of wartime damage, casualty and death payments, and wasted economic opportunity costs.[387]

Iraq's tragedy is that it has been blessed with immense oil wealth and other natural assets and one of the best educated populations in the Middle East, but cursed with one of the worst governments. Military expenditures and wartime losses have drained Iraq's economy for nearly two decades, and Iraq's oil wealth has not been adequate to pay them. Measured in constant 1988 dollars, Iraq's GNP peaked during 1979 and 1980, with totals of $118 billion and $120 billion respectively. The impact of the Iran-Iraq War rapidly cut Iraq's GDP to $70.4 billion in 1981. A combination of wartime damage, the loss of oil export routes through the Gulf and Syria, and lower oil prices then cut the GNP to levels of $70 billion or less throughout the rest of the 1980s. Iraq's GNP was only $65.8 billion in 1988, the year the Iran-Iraq War ended. This is about half of Iraq's GNP in 1980.

In spite of its growing economic problems, Iraq kept its military expenditures at around 30% of its GNP from 1980 to 1984, the first four years of the Iran-Iraq War. After 1984, when the Iran-Iraq War grew more threatening, military spending rose to 52% of the GNP in 1985, and stayed close

TABLE FOUR   The Iran-Iraq Military Balance: 1967–1995

Country	Manpower (1,000s)**		Tanks	OAVs	Artillery	Combat Aircraft
	Total	Army				
1967 (Time of Arab-Israeli Conflict)						
Iran	221	200	225	278	120	180
Iraq	82	70	400–535	200–250	180–250	215
1973 (Time of October War)						
Iran	212	160	920	1,000	380	159
Iraq	102	90	990	1,330	700	224
1978 (Height of Shah's Military Build-up)						
Iran	413	280–285	1,620–1,775	1,075–1,300	782–1,225	459–470
Iraq	212	180–200	1,800–2,450	1,500–1,600	956–1,160	450–470
1980 (First Major Year of Iran-Iraq War)						
Iran	240	150	1,735	1,075	1,000	445
Iraq	243	200	2,750	2,500	1,240	332
1987 (Last Year of Iranian Military Superiority and Occupation of Part of Iraq)						
Iran	1,030	605–735	1,000	1,060	1,200	60–100
Iraq	1,000	955	4,500	4,700	3,000	500+
1988 (After August Cease-fire and Iranian Defeat in Iran-Iraq War)						
Iran	604	550	500–600	700–800	850–900	60–165*
Iraq	1,100	1,000	5,500	4,750	2,800	500–800*
1990 (Before Iraq Invaded Kuwait)						
Iran	605	555	550–650	760–1,200	800–1,100	121–180
Iraq	1,000–1,200	955–1,100	5,500–7,000	6,000–8,800	3,700–5,600	513–770

(continues)

TABLE FOUR *(continued)*

Country	Manpower (1,000s)**		Tanks	OAVs	Artillery	Combat Aircraft
	Total	Army				
1991 (In Spring, Operational Forces After Iraq's Defeat by UN Coalition)						
Iran	528–600	400–430	680–750	750–850	1,700–1,500	180–210*
Iraq	500–600	300–400	2,900–3,000	4,000–4,400	1,800–2,000	350–375
1993 (In Spring, Estimated Operational Holdings)						
Iran	500–520	500–520	750–850	950–1,050	2,200–2,400	250–280*
Iraq	430–450	390–410	2,900–3,000	4,000–4,400	1,800–2,000	350–375
1995 (In Fall, Estimated Operational Holdings)						
Iran	513	350–450	1,445	1,000–1,200	2,700–2,900	250–300
Iraq	383	330–350	2,200–2,700	4,000–4,400	1,800–2,000	350–375

*Does not count any of 113 Iraqi aircraft that flew to Iran during the Gulf War. Their operational status is unknown as of this writing.

**Includes Revolutionary Guards forces and Popular Army forces omitted from some estimates.

Source: Adapted by the author from interviews and various annual editions of the International Institute for Strategic Studies, *Military Balance*; Arms Control and Disarmament Agency, *World Military Expenditures and Arms Transfers*, and the Jaffee Center for Strategic Studies, *Middle East Military Balance*. These sources are extremely uncertain in many areas. The range of estimates has often been adjusted by the author. As is the case with all numbers shown, there is a high degree of uncertainty. Even data like main battle tank counts differ radically.

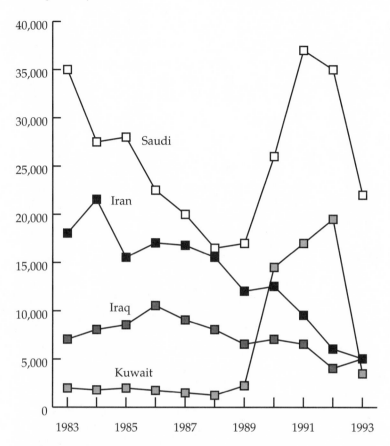

CHART FOURTEEN   Comparative Military Spending of the Major Gulf Powers ($ Millions Constant 1993). *Source:* Adapted by Anthony H. Cordesman from ACDA, *World Military Expenditures and Arms Transfers, 1993–1994*, Table 1.

to 50% for the rest of the 1980s. Iraq could sustain these expenditures only through a combination of massive foreign borrowing and aid from southern Gulf states like Kuwait and Saudi Arabia. Iraq's debt to its Arab neighbors rose to $37 billion.[388]

To put Iraq's military expenditures in perspective, ACDA estimates that Iraq spent $10,010 million in current US dollars on military forces in 1978, $11,350 million in 1979, $19,810 million in 1980, $24,610 million in 1981, $25,070 million in 1982, $13,230 million in 1983, $16,680 million in 1984, $12,670 million in 1985, $14,890 million in 1986, $16,480 million in 1987, $18,400 million in 1988, $13,230 million in 1989, $14,210 million in 1990, and $8,828 million in 1991.[389]

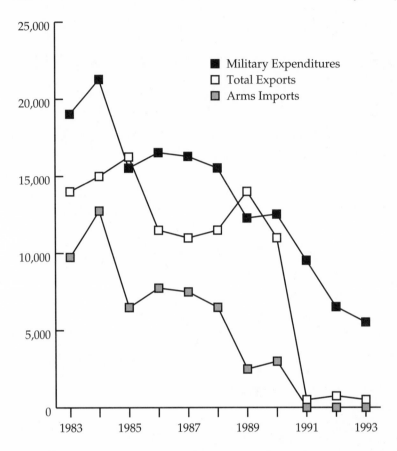

CHART FIFTEEN   Iraqi Military Expenditures, Total Exports, and Arms Import Deliveries: 1983–1993 (Constant $93 Millions). *Source:* Adapted by Anthony H. Cordesman from ACDA, *World Military Expenditures and Arms Transfers, 1993–1994,* ACDA/GPO, Washington, 1995.

The US has not issued official, unclassified estimates of Iraqi military spending for the period since 1991. The IISS estimates that Iraq spent $13,990 million in 1987, $12,870 million in 1988, and $8.61 billion in 1990. It has issued estimates that Iraq spent $2.6 billion in 1992 and 1993, but these estimates seem far too low to include the dollar cost equivalent of the Iraqi effort. Both the ACDA and IISS estimates do not include substantial expenditures on weapons of mass destruction, and massive civil expenditures on preparing and recovering from the Gulf War.[390]

By 1989, the year between the Iran-Iraq War and Iraq's invasion of Kuwait, Iraq's economy was experiencing a serious economic crisis.

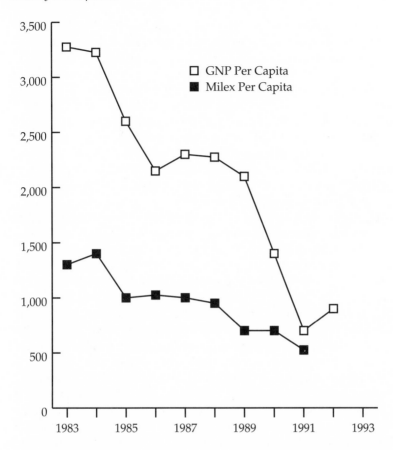

CHART SIXTEEN Iraqi GNP Per Capita Versus Military Expenditures Per Capita (Constant $93). *Source:* Adapted by Anthony H. Cordesman from ACDA, *World Military Expenditures and Arms Transfers, 1993–1994,* Washington ACDA/ GPO, 1995, Table I.

Experts disagree over the economic statistics involved, but not over the seriousness of the crisis. According to the CIA, Iraq's GNP was then $35 billion and its per capita income was only $1,940. This level of per capita income is not unusual by Third World standards, but it was low compared to Iraq's economy in 1979 and to the wealth of a far less developed Saudi Arabia—which had a GNP of $79 billion and a per capita income of $4,800. Iraq also owed $13 billion in annual debt payments to the West, nearly half of its oil revenues in 1989.[391]

While Iraq unquestionably could have funded its economic recovery from the Iran-Iraq War at the cost of further cutbacks in its military expenditures—and done so without risking an attack from Iran or any other neighbor—it chose to try to buy both guns and butter. It was this choice that steadily increased the impact of its debt burden and created the economic crisis which helped lead Iraq to invade Kuwait.[392] Iraq planned an annual military budget of $12.9 billion in 1990, and was spending an average of $721 per citizen on military forces before it invaded Kuwait. Although Iraq had cut its rate of new arms orders, it still took delivery on $1,435 million worth of arms, and ordered $1,125 million more during the first six months of 1990. This level of expenditure raised Iraq's international debt to the West to $40 billion or more. Some experts feel Iraq's total debt was well in excess of $80 billion by early 1990, if one included all of Iraq's debts to Arab states.[393]

There are no reliable estimates of Iraq's military expenditures since the Gulf War, and such estimates are almost impossible to make because Saddam Hussein has used his control over Iraq's economy to shift assets to the military in ways that are not reflected in any Iraqi budget document. It is unlikely, however, that Iraqi expenditures have dropped below $6 billion to $9 billion in terms of their dollar value equivalent. Much of Iraq's armed forces have been constantly involved in civil wars against the Kurds and Shi'ites, and expensive field deployments near the Kurdish security zone in the north, and in the urban and marsh areas in the south.

At the same time, Iraq has poured massive assets into rebuilding its military industry, and trying to maintain its operational readiness. The government has also offered salary increases and other incentives that have become progressively more expensive with time. While no firm data are available, Iraq has probably spent about 33% to 45% of its post–Gulf War GDP on military expenditures in spite of the economic crisis created by the UN sanctions and Saddam Hussein's refusal to sell oil.

Iraqi Arms Imports

Table Five shows an estimate of both Iraq's military expenditures and arms imports over the last decade. Clearly, Iraq's arms imports have placed a major burden on Iraq's economy. During the latter half of the Iran-Iraq War—which covers the period from 1984–1988—Iraq took delivery on $29.7 billion worth of new arms, including $15.4 billion worth of arms from the former Soviet Union, $0.75 billion from Poland, $0.65 billion from Bulgaria, $0.675 billion from Czechoslovakia, and $2.8 billion from the People's Republic of China. Iraq obtained $3.1 billion from France, $0.37 billion from Italy, $0.03 billion from the UK, $0.675 billion from Germany, and $5.2 billion from other countries.[394]

Iraq could not sustain this level of orders immediately following the end of the Iran-Iraq War. During 1989 and 1992—the period from the end of the Iran-Iraq War in August 1988 to the beginning of the embargo on arms shipments to Iraq in August, 1990—Iraq ordered only $1.7 billion worth of arms. Some $200 million were ordered from the Soviet Union, none from the People's Republic of China, $500 million from major West European states, $100 million from other European states, and $900 million from other countries.

This low rate of new arms orders was forced on Iraq by (a) its growing economic crisis, (b) the arms embargo on Iraq after August 1990, and (c) the fact that Iraq was still receiving the backlog from the immense amount of orders Iraq already had placed during the Iran-Iraq War until it invaded Kuwait.[395] While Iraq had consistently ranked among the top 10 arms importers during the Iraq-Iraq War, it dropped off the list after the war. Iran, however, remained on the list with a total of $6.7 billion in new orders during 1989–1992.

The size of the backlog of previous Iraqi arms orders after the Iran-Iraq War is indicated by the fact that Iraq took delivery on $5.0 billion worth of arms during 1989–1990, including $1.5 billion worth of arms from the former Soviet Union, $400 million from the People's Republic of China, $2.1 billion from major West European states, $600 million from other European states, and $400 million from other countries. In spite of the reductions in Iraq's orders and Iraq's massive victory in the Iran-Iraq War, these transfers exceeded those received by Iran. Iran took delivery on $4.5 billion worth of arms and had a much smaller backlog of prior orders.[396]

Since 1990, the Gulf War has cost Iraq both its guns and much of its butter. Iraq's GDP probably would have risen to $40.8 billion in 1990, if it had not invaded Kuwait. Instead, it dropped to around $25 billion. Any estimate of Iraq's GDP after 1990 is speculative, but it seems to have been about $24 billion in 1991, $20 billion in 1992, and substantially less than $20 billion in 1993. Estimates of Iraq's total foreign debt in 1993, including interest, range from $80 billion to $109 billion.[397]

At the same time, Iraq has had no formal arms imports. A military machine that never organized effectively to support and repair its equipment, and which solved its logistic and supply problems by flooding the Iraqi military forces with new imports and replacements, has been virtually cut off from the outside world for five years. This has had a steadily more crippling impact on a military force structure that requires a minimum of $2.5 to $3.0 billion in military imports to sustain its existing readiness, sustainability, and effectiveness. In fact, Iraq has seen the steady collapse of much of its military readiness and effectiveness since 1994, and its efforts to substitute for imports with domestic modifications and production to its major weapons systems have been largely fruitless.

TABLE FIVE   Iraqi Military Expenditures and Arms Transfers by Major
Supplier: 1983–1996 (in Millions of Current US Dollars)

Total Military Expenditures and Arms Sales[a]

	Military Expenditures		Arms Imports	
	$Current	$94 Constant	$Current	$94 Constant
1983	13,230	—	6,900	9,824
1984	16,880	23,360	9,300	12,870
1985	12,670	16,920	4,900	6,544
1986	14,890	19,320	6,000	7,802
1987	16,380	20,770	5,800	7,310
1988	18,400	22,380	5,600	6,797
1989	13,230	15,360	2,400	2,787
1990	14,210	15,820	2,800	3,116
1991	8,828	9,462	20	22
1992	8,000	8,300	18	19
1993	7,000	7,200	24	25
1994	6,500	6,500	34	34
1995	6,000	5,900	26	25
1996	5,800	5,700	26	25

(continues)

Iraqi Efforts to Smuggle
Arms and Parts and Rebuild Its
Iraqi Military Industries Since the Gulf War

Since the cease-fire in the Gulf War, Iraq has attempted to compensate for
its loss of access to arms imports by making use of the extensive purchasing and intelligence network it established overseas during the Iran-
Iraq War. This network includes a mix of firms in Chile, Europe, the US,
China, Japan, Hong Kong, and other Asian countries. Iraq has refused to
provide the UN with a full list of its suppliers, and many of its fronts and
contacts are still operating.[398] Iraq has obtained some supplies by using
covert foreign reserves and funds it obtained by smuggling out petrochemical products, but scarcely enough to meet any of even its most critical military and civilian needs. Iraq did obtain at least two shipments of
tank parts and one artillery shipment, but it has not received any major
shipments of new weapons.

Iraq has attempted to compensate by making a crash effort to restore
and improve its domestic military production capabilities. In the process,
Iraq has been able to build on an investment in the Iraqi Ministry of

TABLE FIVE   (*continued*)

Arms Sales by Source—Grimmett Estimate[b]

Agreements	1983–1986	1986–1989	1990–1993[c]	1988–1993[c]
Soviet Union	11,815	6,100	200	6,300
China	1,760	2,200	0	2,200
United States	0	0	0	0
Major West European	1,005	2,600	400	3,000
All Other European	3,990	3,800	100	3,900
All Others	1,920	1,600	800	2,400
Total	20,490	16,300	1,500	17,800

Deliveries	1983–1986	1986–1989	1990–1993[c]	1988–1993[c]
Soviet Union	12,170	10,900	400	11,300
China	3,180	2,100	200	2,300
United States	0	0	0	0
Major West European	5,225	1,400	2,100	3,500
All Other European	3,615	3,800	100	3,900
All Others	1,920	1,600	100	1,700
Total	26,110	19,800	2,900	22,700

[a]*Source:* Adapted by Anthony H. Cordesman from ACDA, *World Military Expenditures and Arms Transfers, 1994–1995,* Washington, GPO, 1996, Tables I & II. All data from 1992 onwards estimated by Anthony H. Cordesman.[399]

[b]*Source:* Adapted by Anthony H. Cordesman from material provided by the US Government and Richard F. Grimmett, *Conventional Arms Transfers to the Third World, 1983–1990,* Washington, Congressional Research Service, CRS-91-578F, August 2, 1991, *Conventional Arms Transfers to the Third World, 1984–1991,* Washington, Congessional Research Service, CRS-92-577F, July 20, 1991, and *Conventional Arms Transfers to the Third World, 1986–1993,* Washington, Congressional Research Service, CRS-94-612F, July 29, 1994.

[c]These figures effectively apply only to 1990. ACDA indicates that no major transfers took place after the end of August 1990, from ACDA, *World Military Expenditures and Arms Transfers, 1993–1994,* Washington, GPO, 1995, p. 141.

Industry and Defense Industry that totaled $14.2 billion between 1985 and 1989. Many of these plants suffered limited damage during the war, and Iraqi officials have claimed that Iraq has repaired and tooled up 200 factory buildings associated with military production since the end of the Gulf War, and that more than 50 establishments of the former Ministry of Industry and Military Industrialization are now operating—many using machine tools and specialized equipment that were originally exported without proper export licenses.[400]

According to a report by the House Foreign Affairs Subcommittee on International Security, International Organizations, and Human Rights, this equipment and related production facilities include:[401]

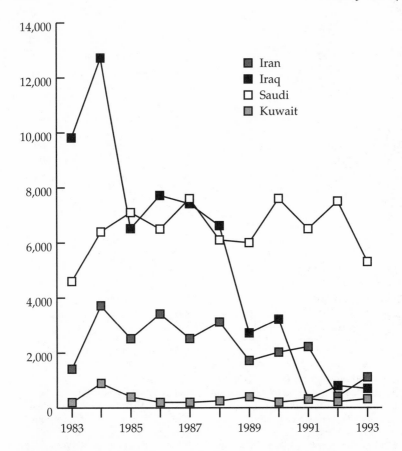

CHART SEVENTEEN   Comparative Arms Import Deliveries of the Major Gulf
Powers: 1983–1993 ($ Millions Constant 1993). *Source:* ACDA, *World Military
Expenditures and Arms Transfers, 1993–1994,* Table II.

- Tank assembly plant operating under Polish and Czech licenses at
  Al-Amen.
- Major armor refitting center at Base West World (Samawa).
- Manufacture of proximity fuses for 155 mm and cluster munitions at
  April 7 (Narawan Fuse) Factory.
- Manufacture of 122 mm howitzers, Ababil rockets, tank optics and
  mortar sights at Sa'ad 5 (Sa'ad Engineering Complex).
- Manufacture of wheeled APCs under East European license, other
  armor, and artillery pieces at Al Taji).

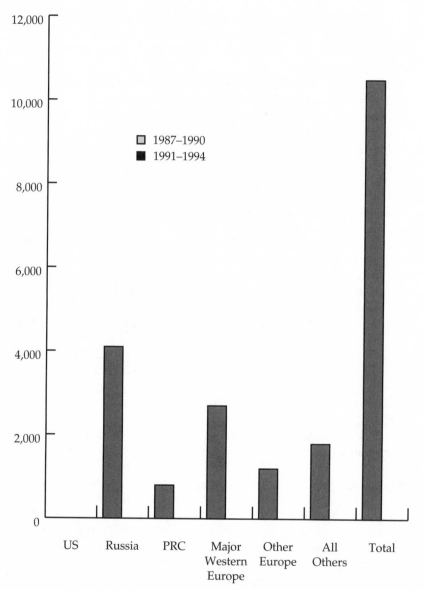

CHART EIGHTEEN   Iraqi Arms Sales Agreements by Supplier Country: 1987–1994 ($Current Millions). *Note:* No arms sales 1991–1994. *Source:* Adapted by Anthony H. Cordesman from work by Richard F. Grimmett in *Conventional Arms Transfers to Developing Nations, 1987–1994,* Congressional Research Service 95-862F, August 4, 1994, pp. 56–57.

- Manufacture and repair of artillery, vehicle parts, and cannon barrels at SEHEE heavy engineering complex (Al Dura).
- Aircraft assembly and manufacturing plant under construction at Sa'ad 38 (Fao).
- Manufacture of aerial bombs, artillery pieces, and tungsten-carbide machine tool bits at Badr (al Yusufiyah).
- Production of explosives, TNT, propellants, and some vehicle production capability at Al Hiteen (Al Iskandariyah).
- Production of cluster bombs and fuel-air explosives at Fao.
- Production of aerial bombs, TNT, and solid rocket propellants at Al Qaqaa.
- Manufacture of small naval boats at Sawary (Basra).
- Production and modification of defense electronics at Mansour (Baghdad).
- Production and modification of defense electronics, radars, and frequency-hopping radios at Sa'ad 13 (Salah al Din-Ad Dawr).
- Digital computer software, assembly of process line controllers for weapons plants, and plastic castings at Diglia (Zaafarniyah).
- Precision machining at Al Rabiyah.
- Manufacture of non-ferrous ammunition cases at Sa'ad 21 (Mosul).
- Liquid nitrogen production at Al Amil.
- Production of ethylene oxide for fuel-air explosives at PCI.
- Production of HMX and RDX explosives at Fallujah chemical plant at Al Muthanna.
- Manufacture of gas masks at Sa'ad 24 (Mosul).

Iraq has also manufactured small arms and artillery ammunition. It has made some artillery weapons like the Ababil multiple launch rocket system, and has reconditioned and assembled some Soviet tanks, including T-72s. It has manufactured and adapted military electronics, and made some small crafts. Iraq has also continued its efforts to try to produce weapons of mass destruction, often seeking to disguise the true purpose of its plants by changing their names or description. For example, an October 1995 report by UNSCOM claimed that Iraq has resumed "its acquisition efforts in support of its missile facilities," adding that it had "placed a number of orders, both directly and indirectly (through middlemen and front companies), for the purchase of equipment, technologies, supplies and material for both missile and non-missile related activities at these facilities."[402] Iraq replied that it was merely expanding its Ababil-100 program to build surface-to-surface missiles of ranges between 100 and 150 km which it is allowed to acquire.

Iraq has, however, had little success in producing and re-manufacturing advanced equipment like tanks and aircraft, and in carrying out many types of major combat repairs. Its efforts have not been able to off-set the steady attrition of Iraq's surviving equipment which has been caused by a lack of spares and specialized support equipment. Further-more, Iraq's problems in maintaining its inventory of operational combat equipment are likely to accelerate with time, in spite of its manufacturing efforts. Cumulative wear and maintenance defaults will produce steadily more serious—and sometimes unrecoverable—problems, as Iraq's re-maining spares are consumed and machines and major subassemblies wear out. Iraq may also exhaust its hidden supplies of hard currency, making it even more difficult to obtain limited supplies of critical spare parts on the world's black-market for arms.

Saddam Hussein's cousin, Hussein Kamel al-Majid, was in charge of the Military Industrialization Commission (MIC), and many aspects of this industrialization effort before his defection in 1995. Senior Jordanian officials who talked to Hussein Kamel found that many of his claims regarding the effectiveness of Iraq's military industry were hollow boasts intended to impress Saddam Hussein, and that most of Iraq's claims to produce major weapons systems never went beyond the pro-totype stage—many of which were unproducable or non-operational showpiece demonstration systems. They report that Hussein Kamel's successor and former deputy—Lt. General Amir Mohammed Rashid—has found that virtually all of Iraq's efforts to carry out major modifica-tions, rebuild and recondition sophisticated equipment, and assemble new advanced weapons from parts have been a failure.[403]

US experts largely agree with this indictment of Iraq's military pro-duction and the assessments of efforts to keep Iraq's major weapons operational. They stress the steady decline of Iraq's equipment readiness and sustainability since late 1993. They note that Hussein Kamel seemed to deceive Saddam deliberately with showpiece projects such as putting an SA-2 surface-to-air missile launcher on a truck and claiming he had created a mobile surface-to-air missile system, falsely reporting the indigenous production of transporter-erector-launchers (TELs) for sur-face-to-surface missiles, and the large scale production of prototype self-propelled artillery systems like the Majnoon and Al Fao.

At the same time, US experts do believe that Iraq has completed much of the rebuilding of plants and facilities necessary to start equipment assembly once sanctions are lifted and that it will aggressively seek to reduce its past dependence on weapons imports once it can obtain access to foreign production equipment. They believe that Iraq can produce indigenous weapons or modifications like long-range missiles when given sufficient priority, and they believe Iraq will begin by seeking assembly facilities with the goal of moving towards indigenous produc-tion and the ability to rebuild and maintain its other equipment for a prolonged period in the face of another cutoff of supplies or embargo. In short, they believe Iraq will seek the capabilities it has been unable to create since the Gulf War.

Implications for Western and Southern Gulf Strategy

The trends in Iraqi military expenditures argue strongly against any policy that lifts sanctions without retaining some controls over how Iraq uses its revenues and without a firm commitment to military containment. They provide overwhelming evidence that Iraq's present regime will divert a large portion of any oil revenues it can to military expenditures, regardless of the cost to the Iraqi people. They also indicate that a major effort will be needed by potential supplier countries to prevent Iraq from importing the equipment it needs to improve its military manufacturing capabilities, and restore its military capabilities.

These trends also raise important issues for a "centrist" strategy, given the risk that any successor regime may well pursue similar policies towards military expenditures, and strengthening Iraq's military industries.

Finally, the trends in Iraqi military expenditures argue for a strong US and Southern Gulf military deterrent to Iraq. Any state that makes this kind of financial commitment to a military build-up cannot be contained purely through diplomatic or military means. Only strong deterrent and defense capabilities can provide security.

11

The Threat from Iraqi Land Forces

In spite of a massive UN Coalition victory in the Gulf War, Iraq maintains an army of 350,000 men. This force has an impressive order of battle and a large inventory of combat equipment. At the same time, the Iraqi Army has scarcely been able to overcome the effects of the Gulf War. It has been cut off from most arms imports. For the last five years, it has not been able to invest even a tenth of the capital that it invested in modernizing and improving its land forces during the five years before the Gulf War. The devastation of the Gulf War, and the five years that have followed, have sharply reduced the composition and capabilities of the Iraqi Army, and this decline has been increasingly precipitous since late 1993.

The Impact of the Gulf War on the Iraqi Army

The Iraqi Army suffered massive losses during the Gulf War, although experts differ sharply on the number of Iraqis who died, on the amount of equipment and munitions destroyed or lost during the air and ground offensive phases of the war, and the number and identity of the Iraqi combat units that lost cohesion or combat effectiveness at any given time.

Just after the war, USCENTCOM estimated that Coalition forces had virtually shattered more than fifteen Iraqi divisions, and only 5–7 of 43 Iraqi divisions were still capable of offensive operations. USCENTCOM estimated that the Coalition had captured 86,000 Iraqi prisoners, 64,000 of which were taken by US forces.[404] The Department of Defense estimated after the war that 10 Iraqi infantry divisions, one armored division, and one mechanized division had been reduced to 0–25% of their combat strength. Six more infantry, two mechanized, and four armored divisions had been reduced to 25–50% of their combat strength. Six infantry, two mechanized, and one armored division had been reduced to 50–75% of their combat strength, and five infantry divisions, one special forces divi-

TABLE SIX   The Impact of Coalition Air and Land Forces on Iraqi Equipment
            Strength in the Kuwaiti Theater of Operations (KTO) at the Time of
            the Cease-Fire

	Tanks	APCs	Artillery
Total in KTO on January 16, 1991, at start of air campaign (Imagery)	3,475	3,080	2,474
Total left at beginning of the land campaign	2,087	2,151	1,322
Total destroyed or abandoned during the land campaign (USCENTCOM estimate)	2,159	521	1,465
Destroyed by air	451	224	353
Destroyed by land or abandoned	1,708	297	1,112
Total destroyed or abandoned during the land campaign (Imagery Based)	1,245	739	1,044
Total destroyed or abandoned during air campaign and land offensive (Imagery Based)	2,633	1,668	2,196
Still in Iraqi control on March 1, 1991 (Imagery)	842	1,412	279

Source: Adapted by Anthony H. Cordesman from work by Eliot Cohen, ed., *Gulf War Air Power Survey, Volume II, Section II,* pp. 259–261, and interviews.

sion, one mechanized, and two armored divisions retained 75–100% of their combat strength.[405]

There are significant differences between the different US Government estimates of Iraqi Army equipment losses, and these estimates have been extensively revised based on after-action analysis of intelligence and damage assessment data. This range of estimates is shown in Table Six, and is based on imagery which are probably most correct. These estimates indicate that the Iraqi forces deployed in the Kuwaiti Theater of Operations (KTO) during the Gulf War lost 76% of their tanks, 54% of their APCs, and 90% of their artillery. Revised US intelligence estimates have also concluded that the Republican Guards units lost roughly 50% of their weapons in these categories in spite of both the air campaign and AirLand battle.[406] These estimates of damage to the Guard are much lower than those the US issued during the Gulf War, and again reflect the difference between battlefield estimates based on the claims of combat units and estimates based on satellite imagery. For example, USCENTCOM's estimate of the Republican Guard's tank losses as of February 23 was 388. The CIA estimates based on imagery indicate the Guard lost 166 tanks.[407]

If one considers the impact of the Gulf War on the entire Iraqi Army, rather than just the Iraqi forces in the KTO, US estimates indicate that the army suffered massive losses in operational capability. The Iraqi Army emerged from the Gulf War with as little as 25–33% of its prewar total national division strength fully operational, with only about 20% of its heavy armored and mechanized brigade strength combat effective, and with only 20–25% of its total manpower under full government control.

Some experts feel that Iraq lost about 50% of its total national operational tank strength, 40% of its other armored vehicles, and 50% of its artillery—although such losses count some equipment that was recovered from Kuwait and northern Iraq after the cease-fire. The Iraqi Army also lost much of its total stocks and infrastructure as the result of coalition air attacks.

This situation worsened immediately after the war. Much of the Iraqi Army was in a state of disruption and political upheaval. Many Iraqi troops were disaffected. Unrest in the Army had triggered the first revolts in the south, and some elements of the armed forces then joined Shi'ite and Kurdish rebels that attempted to seize power. Other commanders and units wavered in their loyalty or hesitated in obeying Saddam Hussein's orders.[408]

However, this disruption of Iraq's forces was relatively short-lived. None of the forces that challenged Saddam were strong enough to confront the Republican Guards and the regular military units that remained loyal. It is also clear in retrospect that Saddam Hussein began to rush Republican Guards forces out of the theater no later than February 27, 1991, to use them to suppress the uprisings in southern Iraq. It is also likely that the Iraqi commanders negotiating the cease-fire at Safwan manipulated his request to Schwarzkopf to ensure that Iraq's helicopters could be used to attack both the uprising in the south and the Kurdish uprising in the north.[409]

Iraq then restructured its army command structure. It purged as many as 1,500 senior officers, and shot others.[410] The Iraqi Army also recovered some of the equipment that it initially abandoned or had fallen into hostile use in Iraq. It conducted a massive scavenging hunt in the Iraqi territory that the Coalition had occupied the moment its forces left. Iraq sent infiltrators into Kuwait in an effort to regain equipment, spare parts, and munitions. In many cases it was able to repair equipment that had been counted as "killed" during the war because the damage was not sufficient to prevent repair or combing of parts from several damaged systems.[411]

By September 1992, Iraq's military forces were able to deploy 500,000 to 650,000 men—including a substantial number of reserves. The Iraqi Army retained 300,000–400,000 actives, or about 40% its prewar strength. Many of the regular army forces were manned by poorly trained and motivated conscripts, which had been drafted after the Gulf War or who had been defeated in that conflict. These lower quality forces were stiffened, however, by reorganized and relatively effective Republican Guards forces, a number of moderate to high-quality regular army units, and reorganized internal security forces.

The Iraqi Army in 1996

There are different estimates of the strength of the Iraqi Army in 1996. A USCENTCOM estimate lists a total strength of 400,000 full time actives, 17 regular army divisions (6 heavy and 11 light), and 6–7 Republican Guards Divisions (4 heavy and 3 light). The Army had a total of three armored divisions deployment in the vicinity of Baghdad—one near Taji, one near Baghdad, and one near As Suwayrah. There were fourteen more divisions in the north, three more divisions in central Iraq, and six divisions south of An Najaf.[412]

Another estimate by US experts indicates that the Iraqi Army had a total of around 350,000 full time actives (including 100,000 recalled reserves), and a total of seven corps, with two Republican Guards corps and five regular army corps. These forces have a total of 22 regular divisions, seven Republican Guard divisions (4 armored/mechanized and 3 infantry), 1 Presidential Guard/Special Security Force, and 15 independent special forces or commando brigades. German, US, and Israeli experts felt that Iraq had up to 400,000 men, five to six corps, and a total of 28–30 divisions with 10 armored and mechanized divisions (four in the Republican Guards and six in the Iraqi regular army), and 18–20 infantry and mountain division equivalents (three in the Republican Guards and 15–17 in the Iraqi regular army), plus a division-sized Special Republican Guards formation.[413]

These Iraqi forces were organized into four major echelons:

- The first echelon was composed of at least one heavy division equivalent of what Iraq called the Special Republican Guards or "Presidential Guards" forces.
- The second echelon included six other divisions, and some independent special forces and support units, in the rest of the Republican Guards. All of the Republican Guards units reported directly to the Presidential Palace, and not to the Chief of Staff or Ministry of Defense.
- The third echelon was composed of a number of Iraqi regular army units under exceptionally loyal commanders. These units had much of the Iraqi regular army's armor, and have an unusually high level of equipment, total personnel, and combat-experienced personnel.
- Finally, a fourth echelon included the rest of the Iraqi regular army. The units in this echelon were under loyal commanders, but were

often seriously understrength. They lacked the manpower and equipment of the other echelons, and could only be used in largely defensive or rear area roles.

In addition, Iraq had 20,000 frontier guards. These frontier guards were deployed along every border—except the "border" along the Kurdish security zone, which was covered by regular Iraqi forces. The frontier guards are little more than a light infantry and surveillance force armed with light weapons and AA guns. Training has generally been poor, but the force does free the army to perform combat missions elsewhere.

The Republican Guards

The Iraqi Republican Guards are still Iraq's most effective land forces and the most effective land forces in the region. The Gulf War forced Iraq to consolidate its Republican Guards forces down from a total of 12 divisions to a current total of seven divisions, and to eliminate a number of smaller formations.

In 1996, the Republican Guards divisions included three armored divisions (the Al Nida division, the Hammurabi division, and the Al Medina al Munawarrah division), one mechanized division (Al Abid), and three to four infantry divisions (the Adnan division, the Nebuchadnezzar division, the Baghdad division, and possibly one unidentified) equivalents. Two special forces brigades seem to have survived from the pre-war special forces division, and up to four independent infantry formations—nominally of brigade strength.[414]

According to US and Israeli experts, the surviving Republican Guards have a total of between 60,000 and 80,000 men, and 26–30 brigade equivalents (6–8 armored, 3–4 mechanized, and the rest infantry). This total manning indicates that Republican Guards have about 65–75% of the total manning needed for their combat units, and about half the total manpower needed to deploy and sustain a force of seven full divisions.[415] This is an indication that Iraq is having some manpower problems with even its most prestigious force, and some US experts note that some of the forces for coup attempts have come from the Guard, that pay and privileges for junior officers and other ranks have declined in real value since late 1993, and that more Shi'ites and non-Takritis are being recruited into the force.

There is also a Special Republican Guards force, under a military command structure reporting directly to Saddam, that acts as a palace guard. This force is deployed in a number of battalions whose mission is to protect Saddam Hussein. It is largely infantry, but has some T-72s, BMPs, D-30s and 122 mm artillery weapons. If the regular Republican Guards act as the "ring" of forces that defends Baghdad and Saddam Hussein, the Special Republican Guards act as Saddam's last line of defense.

The precise equipment holdings of the surviving Republican Guards units are almost impossible to estimate, but they seem to be about 66%–75% of the size their prewar size. A very rough estimate of the total equipment holdings of the Republican Guards would be around 650–800 tanks (at least 550 T-72s), 800–1,100 other armored vehicles (about half BMP 1/2s and 25% MTLBs), and 350–500 artillery weapons. Unlike other Iraqi Army units, these equipment holdings have also been kept largely operational since 1993, largely by consolidating operational equipment out of other combat and support units.

Deployments Against the Kurds

Iraq's land forces are now deployed in the area around Baghdad, near the Iranian border, near the Kurdish security zone, and in the Shi'ite south. The army's key formations include a corps headquartered in Mosul and another corps headquartered in Kirkuk. Another Iraqi corps or large-scale formation is concentrated in the Baghdad area with many of the Republican Guards heavy divisions and the special Republican Guards (or "Presidential guards") formations.[416] Two more corps are deployed in the south, with at least 50,000–75,000 men. These forces seemed to have included 5–10 divisions, with a mix of infantry and heavy divisions, and at least some Republican Guard formations in reserve—although no Republican Guards divisions have been deployed south of the 32nd parallel since October 1994.

Iraq had some 16–18 divisions and 150,000–175,000 troops from its I Corps and V Corps and its Republican Guards deployed near the Kurdish security zone and the north-central part of the Iranian border. These forces were stationed along the southern edge of the Kurdish controlled zone from Dahuk through Al Kuwayr, Irbil, and Kifri to Khanaqin. In June 1966, there were three infantry divisions in the north along the border of Kurdish controlled territory, with one more to the west of Mosul. There were two infantry divisions and two mechanized divisions along the border southwest of Irbil and north of Kirkuk. Three were three infantry divisions along the border with Kurdish controlled territory southeast of Kirkuk, a mechanized division and infantry division east of Tikrit, and an armored division near the Iranian border just south of the Kurdish controlled area.[417] Iraqi forces have regularly shelled Kurdish positions near the border of the Turkish security zone, and often harassed the UN relief and inspection effort. They have, however, done little else and they are basically a "border guard" force of uncertain operational value.

At the same time, the Iraqi Kurds have little capability to defend against these forces. In early 1996, the KDP claimed to have 25,000 troops, and a militia of 30,000 additional men, but these forces were only armed with light artillery, multiple rocket launchers, mortars, small arms, and SA-7s. Similarly, the PUK claimed to have 12,000 troops, plus 6,000 men in support forces, but was armed with some T-54 and T-55 tanks, about 450 mortars, 106 mm recoilless rifles, 200 light anti-aircraft guns, and SA-7. These divisions between the KDP and PUK forces reflected the collapse of efforts to create a unified Kurdish force, with a total of 16 brigades. As a result, the Kurdish forces lacked unity and a meaningful strength of heavy weapons, modern anti-tank, and modern light anti-aircraft weapons.

Deployments Against the Shi'ites

Iraq deploys some 7–8 divisions, and 75,000 troops, from its IV Corps, III Corps and Republican Guards in the south. These forces are spread out near the Iranian border and in the Shi'ite areas from Karbala and Al Kut in the north to An Nasiriyah and Az Zubayr in the south, although most perform occupation duties and are not involved in any military effort. Iraq has used these forces to destroy the traditional way of life of the marsh Arab Shi'ites. In June 1996, there was one infantry division in Karbala and one in Al Kut. There were two infantry divisions west of An Nasiriyah, an armored division near Al Amarah, an infantry division near Qalatsalih, an armored division between Qalatsalih and Al Basrah, and a mechanized division near Al Basrah.[418]

The Iraqi regime's burning, draining, and water-diversion projects created a continuing process of large-scale environmental destruction in the marshes. The army has constructed canals, causeways, and earthen berms to divert water from the wetlands. Hundreds of square kilometers of marsh areas have been burned, imperiling the marshes' ecosystem.[419]

The Iraqi Army has also launched attacks on many villages in the region. On March 4, 1994, the military began its largest search-and-destroy operation in the marshes in two years. The offensive included the razing of villages and burning operations concentrated in the triangle bounded by Nasiriyah, Al-Qurnah, and Basrah. The magnitude of this operation caused the inhabitants to flee in several directions: deeper into the marshes, to the outskirts of southern Iraqi cities, and to Iran. In late June 1994, Iraqi military forces attacked several marsh villages in Nasiriyah province. Sources said that army engineers burned the village of Al-Abra, containing about 80 homes, to the ground. After the operation, the army transported the village's inhabitants from the scene. In early July, the security forces stormed the villages of Al-Sajiya and Al-Majawid in Al-Chibaish district, near the main road leading into the marshes. Simultaneously, armor units supported by heavy artillery attacked the village of Al-Kheyout in the district of Al-Madina.[420]

The Iraqi military also conducted large-scale artillery bombardment in the Jindala area of the Al-Amarah marshes. Opposition sources said the bombardment destroyed several homes and injured several individuals. The military also attacked Al-Hashriya, Al-Wasdiya, and Al-Malha, and arrested some of their inhabitants. In September 1994, opposition sources reported that military forces used incendiary bombs and launched an armored attack against the area of Al-Seigel in the Al-Amarah marshes. The army later set fire to the entire area.[421]

The UN Special Rapporteur stated in his February 1994 report that the extent of violations against the marsh inhabitants "places the survival of this indigenous population in jeopardy," and noted the similarity between the Iraqi regime's "genocide-type operations" against the Kurds and its operations in southern Iraq. In August, he dispatched two of his assistants to the Iran-Iraq border to interview refugees fleeing the marshes. He reported in October 1994 that the refugees are generally in poor physical and psychological condition, having suffered extreme deprivation of food and medicine. He reiterated his "concern over the survival" of the marsh inhabitants "as a community."

These military operations caused serious civilian casualties, and more than 10,000 refugees from the marshes fled to Iran, where they joined between 50,000 and 60,000 who had fled in previous years. According to the US State Department, large numbers of Shi'ites refugees from southern Iraq fled to Iran, particularly after the escalation in military activity in March 1994. In late 1994 the UN High Commissioner for Refugees (UNHCR) estimated that more than 10,000 refugees from the marshes were in camps in Iran. Amar Appeal, a charitable organization operating several of the camps, placed the number at more than 35,000. US Government analysts estimated in September 1994 that more than 200,000 of the 250,000 former inhabitants of the marshes had been driven from the area since 1991.[422]

The fighting in the marshes persisted during 1995, and the Iraqi armed forces continued to conduct deliberate artillery and infantry attacks against civilians in the southern marshes. By 1995, however, there was little real resistance, and many of the government attacks were designed to root out army deserters and displaced civilians.

Land Force Equipment Holdings

Charts Nineteen and Twenty show rough estimates of the trend in the major weapons strength of Iraqi land forces. Charts Twenty-One to Thirty-Four provide summary comparisons of Iraq's strength relative to that of other Gulf forces.

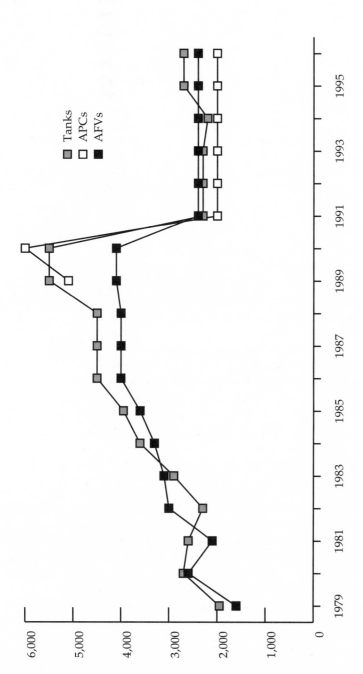

CHART NINETEEN Iraq: Armored Weapons Strength—1979–1996. *Source:* Adapted by Anthony H. Cordesman from various editions of the IISS, *Military Balance*, the JCSS, *Military Balance in the Middle East*, and material provided by US experts.

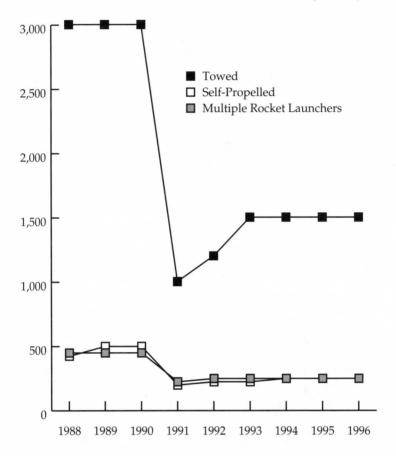

CHART TWENTY   Iraq: Artillery Weapons Strength—1988–1996.
Source: Adapted by Anthony H. Cordesman from various editions of the IISS,
Military Balance, the JCSS, *Military Balance in the Middle East,* and material
provided by US experts.

Estimates of the equipment holdings of Iraqi forces different. USCENT-
COM estimated in mid-1996, that the Iraqi Army had 2,600 tanks, 3,000
APCs and AFVs, 2,100 major artillery weapons and 1,100 other armored
vehicles, include recovery, NBC, command and other vehicles.

A more detailed estimate by other US experts indicates that Iraqi
Army's major equipment holdings to included about 2,700 tanks, less
than half of the 6,700 tanks it had before the war. About half these tanks
were T-54s, T-55s, T-59s, and T-69s. Iraq also has about 600–700 M-48s, M-
60s, AMX-30s, Centurions, and Chieftains captured from Iran or which it

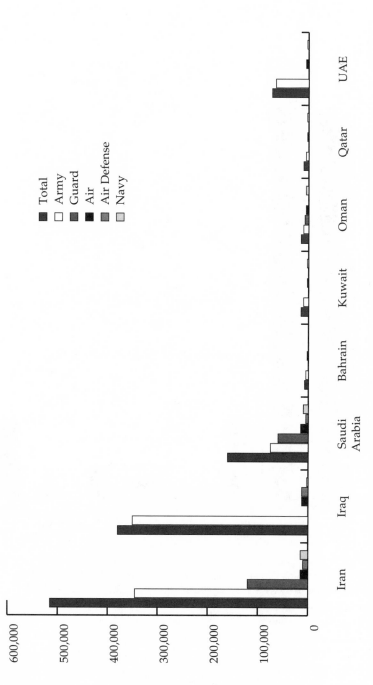

CHART TWENTY-ONE Total Gulf Military Manpower by Service—1996. *Source:* Adapted by Anthony H. Cordesman from the IISS, *Military Balance, 1995–1996.*

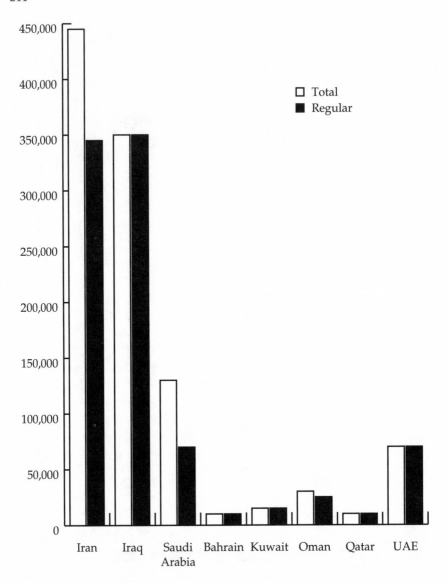

CHART TWENTY-TWO   Total Active Military Manpower in Gulf Armies in 1996. *Note:* Iran includes active forces in Revolutionary Guards. Saudi Arabia includes active in National Guard. *Source:* Adapted by Anthony H. Cordesman from the IISS, *Military Balance, 1995–1996*.

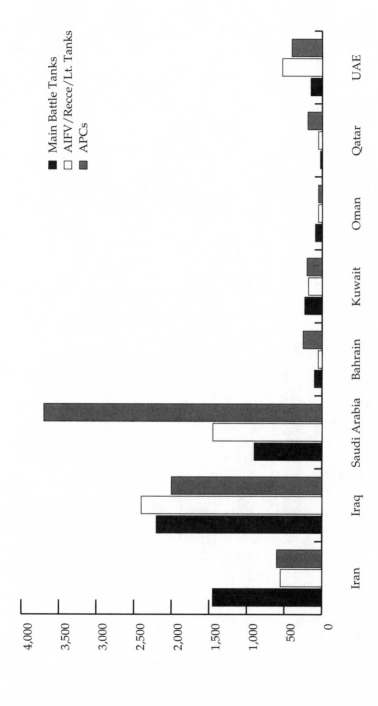

CHART TWENTY-THREE Total Gulf Operational Armored Fighting Vehicles—1996. *Source:* Adapted by Anthony H. Cordesman from the IISS, *Military Balance, 1995–1996.*

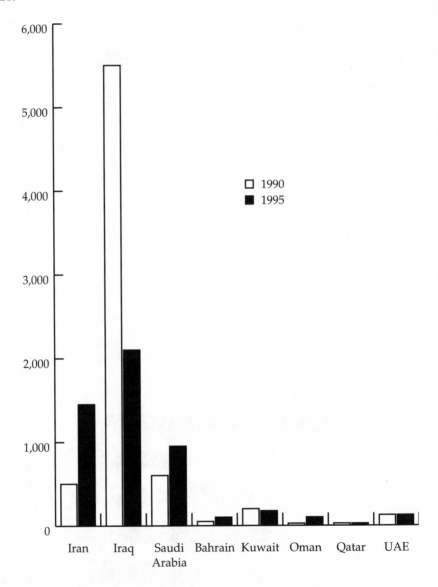

CHART TWENTY-FOUR   Total Operational Tanks in All Gulf Forces, 1990–1995. *Note:* Iran includes active forces in Revolutionary Guards. Saudi Arabia includes active National Guard. *Source:* Adapted by Anthony H. Cordesman from various sources and the IISS, *Military Balance.*

Total Operational Main Battle Tanks

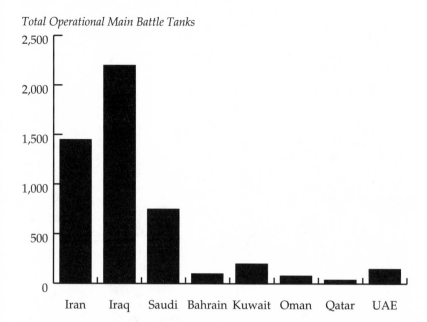

Operational Modern Tanks: T-72, M-84, M-60A2/A3, M-1A1/2, Challenger, Leopard/ OF-40, Le Clerc

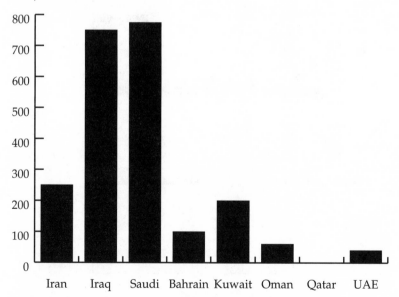

CHART TWENTY-FIVE   Gulf Tanks in 1996. *Source:* Adapted by Anthony H. Cordesman from the IISS, *Military Balance, 1995–1996.*

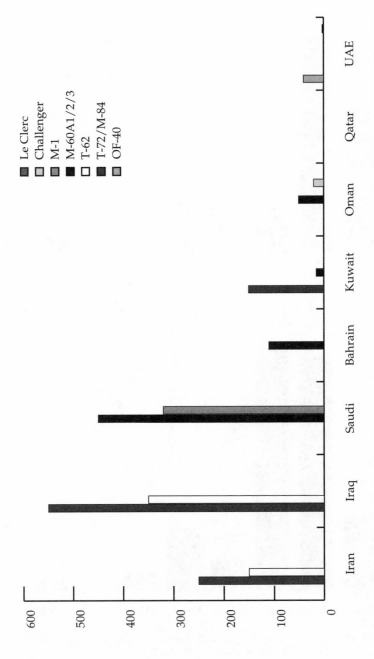

CHART TWENTY-SIX Gulf Modern Tanks in 1996. *Source:* Adapted by Anthony H. Cordesman from the IISS, *Military Balance,* 1995–1996.

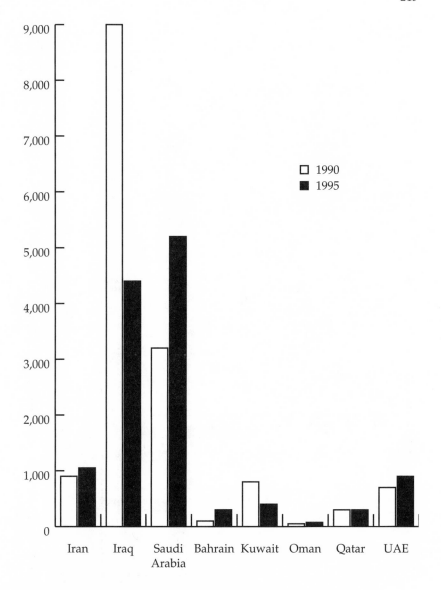

CHART TWENTY-SEVEN   Total Operational Other Armored Vehicles (Lt. Tanks, Scout, AIFVs, APCs, Recce) in Gulf Forces, 1990–1995. *Note:* Iran includes active forces in Revolutionary Guards. Saudi Arabia includes active National Guard. *Source:* Adapted by Anthony H. Cordesman from various sources and the IISS, *Military Balance.*

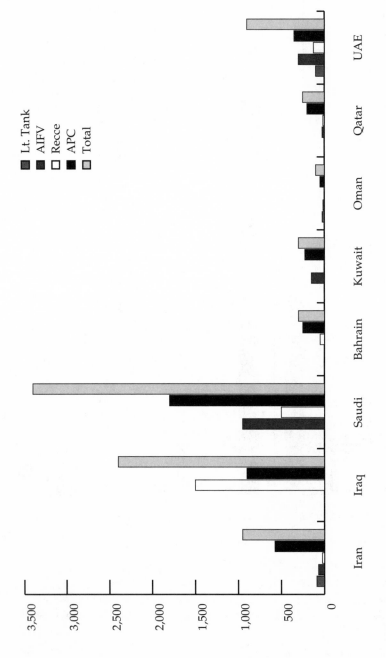

CHART TWENTY-EIGHT Total Gulf Other Armored Fighting Vehicles (OAFVs)—1996. *Source:* Adapted by Anthony H. Cordesman from the IISS, *Military Balance, 1995–1996.*

Total

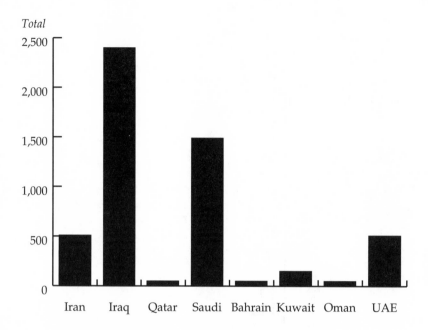

Total Advanced or Modern Types: Scorpion, BMP-1, BMP-2, BMP-3, M-2

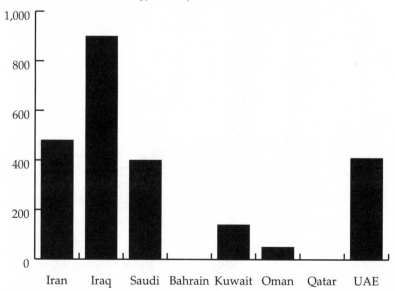

CHART TWENTY-NINE   Gulf Armored Infantry Fighting Vehicles, Reconnaissance Vehicles, Scout Vehicles, and Light Tanks in 1996. *Source:* Adapted by Anthony H. Cordesman from the IISS, *Military Balance, 1995–1996.*

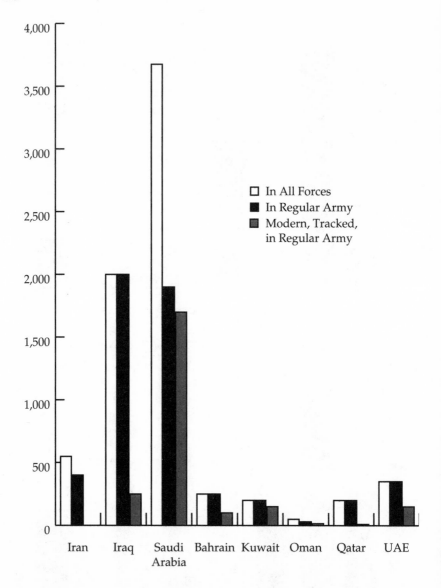

CHART THIRTY   Armored Personnel Carriers (APCs) in Gulf Armies—1996.
Note: Iran includes active forces in Revolutionary Guards. Saudi Arabia includes active National Guard. *Source:* Adapted by Anthony H. Cordesman from the IISS, *Military Balance, 1995–1996.*

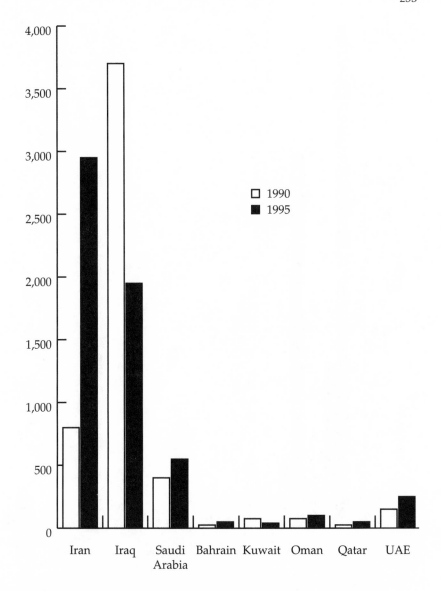

CHART THIRTY-ONE   Total Operational Self-Propelled and Towed Tube
Artillery and Multiple Rocket Launchers in Gulf Forces, 1990–1995. *Note:* Iran
includes active forces in Revolutionary Guards. Saudi Arabia includes active
National Guard. *Source:* Adapted by Anthony H. Cordesman from various
sources and the IISS, *Military Balance, 1995–1996.*

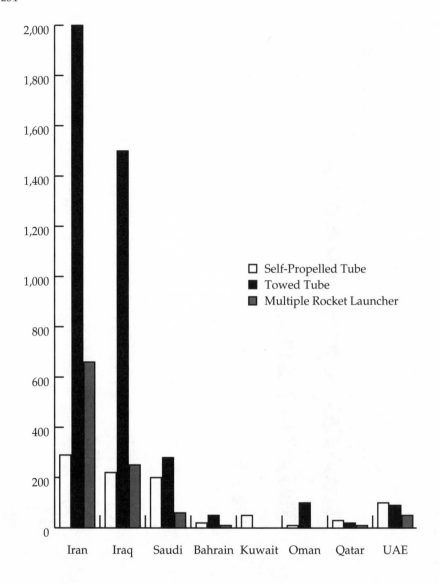

CHART THIRTY-TWO   Total Operational Gulf Artillery Weapons—1996.
Source: Adapted by Anthony H. Cordesman from the IISS, *Military Balance, 1995–1996.*

Total Operational Towed Artillery

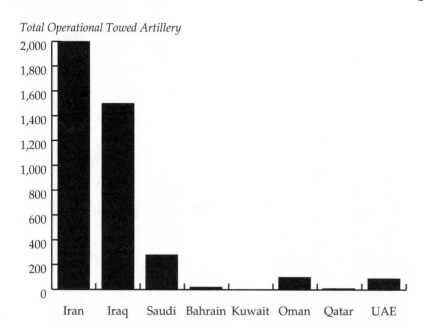

Total Operational Self-Propelled Artillery

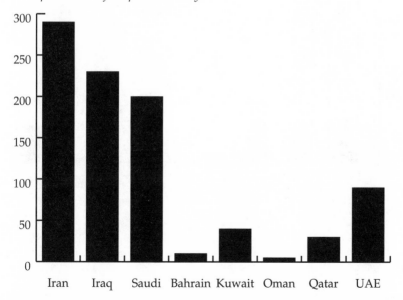

CHART THIRTY-THREE   Gulf Tube Artillery Weapons in 1996. *Source:*
Adapted by Anthony H. Cordesman from the IISS, *Military Balance, 1995–1996.*

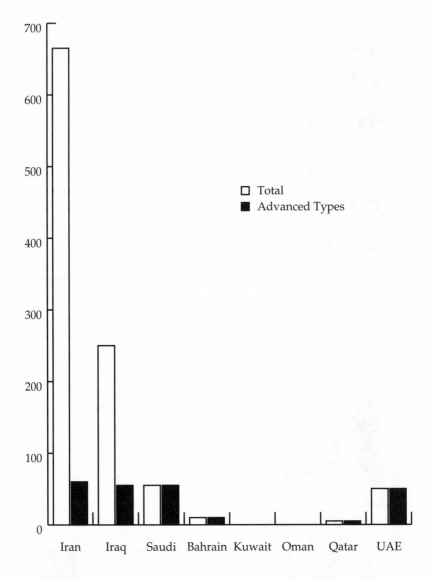

CHART THIRTY-FOUR   Total Operational Gulf Multiple Rocket Launchers—
1996. *Source:* Adapted by Anthony H. Cordesman from the IISS, *Military Balance,
1995–1996.*

obtained in small numbers from other countries. Iraq lost much of its pre-war T-72 strength during the Gulf War. Only about 500–600 T-72s and 200–300 T-62s remained after the war, versus nearly 1,500 T-72s and T-62s before the war. According to some estimates, only about 2,000–2,300 of Iraq's tanks are fully operational. However, Iraq retains over 1,500 tank transporters and heavy vehicle trailers out of the several thousand it bought during the Iran-Iraq War.[423]

These experts estimated that Iraq had some 3,900–4,000 other armored vehicles. Iraq had 1,600 armored reconnaissance and command vehicles (BDRM-2, EE-3, EE-9, AML-60, AML-90, MTLB) versus 2,500 before the war. It had 800–900 armored infantry fighting vehicles (BMP-1, BMP-2, and AMX-10P) versus 2,000 before the war, and 2,300 armored personnel carriers (BTR-50, BTR-60, BTR-152, OT-62, OT-64, MTLB, YW-531, M-113, M-3, EE-11) compared to approximately 7,100 before the war. Regardless of their number, many of these vehicles had only limited operational capability. Iraq did, however, retain large numbers of special purpose armored vehicles like command centers that it had bought during the Iran-Iraq War.[424]

Iraq's surviving artillery included about 1,500 towed artillery weapons (105 mm, 122 mm, 130 mm, and 155 mm). It also includes around 150 self-propelled artillery weapons (2S1 122 mm, 2S3 152 mm, M-109A/1/A2 and GCT AUF-1 155 mm); and 4,000–5,000 (60 mm, 81 mm, 120 mm, 160 mm) mortars. This compares with 3,000–5,000 towed weapons, and 500 self-propelled tube weapons before the war.

The data on multiple rocket launchers are too contradictory to make any estimate of wartime losses possible, although it is clear that many such weapons were destroyed or abandoned in the Kuwaiti Theater of Operations. However, Iraq retains around 120 such weapons (240 mm, 140 mm, Astros I, Astros II, BM-21, 122 mm). Iraq seems to retain many of its pre-war holdings of the FROG surface-to-surface rocket launchers, ·and at least several hundred rockets.[425]

Iraq had over 350 self-propelled mortars mounted on armored vehicles before the Gulf War. These do not seem to have been heavily committed to the Kuwaiti Theater of Operations, and Iraq probably still held several hundred after the conflict. Iraq also retained large numbers of 81 mm and 120 mm Soviet mortars. It has a total of over 2,000 mortars.

The Iraqi Army lost large numbers of its anti-tank weapons during the fighting, many of which were recovered intact by the UN Coalition forces. Nevertheless, Iraq retained substantial anti-tank warfare capability. Its guided weapons include an unknown number of HOTs, AS-11, and AS-12s mounted on PAH-1 and SA-342 helicopters and AT-2s mounted on Mi-8 and Mi-24 helicopters. It had Milan and HOT launchers mounted on VC-TH armored vehicles; Soviet AT-1, AT-3, AT-4 crew-portable anti-tank-guided missiles; and Milan man-portable anti-tank guided missiles. It had several thousand 85 mm and 100 mm anti-tank guns and heavy recoilless rifles.

There are definitional problems in counting Iraq's surviving anti-air-craft guns because some estimates include machine guns, while others only include heavier weapons. Pre-war estimates put the total number of weapons including machine guns at around 7,000, and the number of heavier weapons at 4,000. Iraq lost substantial numbers of self-propelled anti-aircraft guns during the Gulf War, but it seemed to retain 300–500 weapons, including some AMX-30 SAs, Egyptian-made guns and light missile launchers, and 150–200 radar-guided ZSU-23-4s. Iraq retained 4,000–5,000 other anti-aircraft guns—although many may not be opera-tional or may be deployed as anti-infantry weapons. This gives it a total of approximately 5,500 weapons.

Post-war estimates do not provide many details on Iraqi Army surface-to-air missile holdings, although they clearly included thousands of light and medium surface-to-air missiles. These included SA-7, SA-8, SA-9, SA-13, SA-14, and SA-16 vehicle-mounted, crew-served, and man-portable weapons, and perhaps 50–100 surviving Roland fire units on self-pro-pelled armored vehicles. According to most estimates, Iraq retained at least 50–66% of its pre-war anti-aircraft weapons strength, or around 3,000 light surface-to-air missile launchers.

Estimates of Iraqi helicopter strength are equally uncertain. Iraqi Army aviation seemed to possess about 120 armed helicopters out of the 159 it had before the war. These included 20 PAH-1 (Bo-105); attack helicopters with AS-11, AS-12 and HOT missiles, 30 Mi-24s and Mi-25s with AT-2 missiles, 40 SA-342s with AS-12s and HOTs, Allouettes with AS-11s and AS-12s, and 5 SA-321s with Exocet. No reliable estimate exists of the number of surviving heavy, medium, and light transports and utility heli-copters, but it seems likely that Iraq retained 200–300.[426]

Land Force Readiness
and Warfighting Effectiveness

Iraq's land forces still retain significant war fighting capabilities. They can still seize Kuwait in a matter of days or occupy much of Saudi Ara-bia's Eastern Province, *if* they do not face opposition from Western forces. Iraq has the military strength to overrun its Kurds in a matter of weeks if UN forces cease to protect them. The army has already effectively defeated all serious Shi'ite resistance. It can probably defeat any major Iranian attack and should be able to defeat the Iranian army in detail in the border area if given warning about a limited attack. Iraq can pose some threat to Syria, although with some logistical difficulties, and can deploy two to three divisions into an Arab-Israeli conflict if it has Syrian or Jordanian support.

Iraq has refurbished many of its army weapons, vehicles, and equipment to the extent permitted by its industrial base and spare parts. It has created new tailored logistic organizations to try to improve its sustainment in the absence of military resupply. It has slowly improved the reorganization of its army, and in late 1995, it restored competent military professionals to a number of senior military positions.

Nevertheless, the Iraqi Army has severe limitations, and its capabilities are steadily deteriorating. This deterioration is a product of basic weaknesses in the organization and structure of Iraqi Army as well as a result of wartime losses, a loss of imports, and the decline of the Iraqi economy. Iraq's growing readiness, sustainability, and deterioration problems have interacted with these inherent weaknesses to degrade Iraq's ability to conduct effective combined arms and mobile warfare.

Like many other Middle Eastern armies, Iraq has armed with little regard to standardization and ease of supply, training, and maintenance. It has emphasized combat arms over service support, sustainability, and maintenance and never developed an effective cadre of trained NCOs and technicians. Its officers have shown a striking reluctance to become involved in maintenance activity or the kind of close contact and physical effort necessary to lead troops in such functions, initiative was discouraged and they were held responsible for losses and damage that resulted from their actions. Iraq has done little to remedy these problems as a result of the Gulf War. If anything, wartime casualties, morale problems, desertions, and pay problems have made the situation worse. Further, Iraq has consolidated much of its manpower and equipment into its combat arms beginning in 1994—steadily increasing the problems inherent in over-emphasizing combat arms relative to support and sustainability.

Iraq had a relatively efficient logistic system before the Gulf War—particularly at the Corps and division level—by relying on constant resupply and secure rear lines of communication as a substitute for effective maintenance, overhauls, and logistics. However, this system was dependent on continuing imports of a wide mix of equipment supplied by the former Soviet bloc, France, Italy, other European states, and Third World countries. The supply of imports ceased in August 1990, and the UN air offensive did massive damage to the Iraqi Army's facilities and stockpiles. As a result, much of Iraq's equipment is now deadlined—or has limited operational effectiveness. Further, Iraq lost many of its logistic vehicles during the Gulf War, including many specialized vehicles and heavy lifters, and has not been able to replace them. Iraq will find it much harder to sustain operations in the field, particularly in offensive operations, significant distances from its support facilities.

The human element has deteriorated in other ways. Many of Iraq's best armored and mechanized units were shattered in the fighting, including some of its heavy Republican Guards units. Iraq lost many officers and technicians, and the Iraqi forces have since been subject to recurrent purges and upheavals. It has also been seven years since the end of the Iran-Iraq War, and many combat veterans of the war have now left military service. There has been little large-scale unit training since 1991, and much of Iraq's army has either been kept in static deployments or has been involved in low-grade fighting against the poorly armed Shi'ites in the south.

The Republican Guards and best regular army units are relatively well-manned and have had active field training. The Republican Guards have acted largely as a garrison force, and this has given them time to train at least at the battalion level. Even the Republican Guards, however, have had some manpower problems and have had to accept more Shi'ites and promote non-Takritis to more senior positions.

Many other regular army units are now filled in with a mix of inexperienced troops and low-grade conscripts and reservists. Most of Iraq's regular army infantry divisions now have 50–75% of their authorized manning, and the regular army has been ground down by having to act as an occupation force, carry out low-level counter-insurgency operations, and remain in the field. There have been growing problems with desertions, morale, and call-ups, and Iraq has been forced to "exempt" its Kurds and some of its Shi'ites from military service for internal security reasons—depriving it of a substantial part of its manpower base. In spite of steady increases in the fee for exemption, a number of Iraqis also buy their way out of conscription.

Saddam Hussein has taken a number of measures designed to improve the loyalty of the armed forces. He has tried to increase salaries to compensate for inflation and has set up special stores which provide military personnel with better access to food and consumer goods. He has cut the period for conscription from 36 months to 18 for college graduates, and to four months for the holders of advanced degrees. He has revived special privileges for loyal officers like the car loans, land grants, housing benefits, and low-interest loans used to motivate officers during the Iran-Iraq War. He now allows automatic retirement after 25 years of service.[427] These measures, however, have failed to keep pace with inflation and offset the impact of sanctions. Military salaries and living conditions steadily deteriorated since 1993, particularly in the regular army forces.

This combination of problems means at least one-third to one-half of the post–Gulf War Iraqi Army order of battle consists of hollow forces that will take years to rebuild to the level of capability they had before the Gulf War. This situation will continue to worsen until the UN sanctions are lifted. The most critical mid-term limitation affecting the war fighting capability of the Iraqi Army will remain the impact of the UN arms embargo. Iraq can work around some of its equipment problems, but it needs significant imports of spare parts to maintain its army and bring it back to pre–Gulf War readiness. It is also having progressively greater difficulty with "human factors." If the UN embargo continues to be effective, the Iraqi Army will continue to lose force strength and war fighting quality relative to Iran, the Southern Gulf states, and its other neighbors. It is almost impossible to predict the rate at which the army will decline, but it is clear that Iraqi forces have already lost a significant amount of their combat effectiveness and sustainability.

At a minimum, Iraq will require several years to modernize its ground forces in order to react to the lessons of the Gulf War once the UN sanctions and embargo are ended. Iraq not only must rebuild its land forces, but must make major changes in its equipment and technology if it is to compete with the force improvements being made by its neighbors. For example, Iraq needs to upgrade most of its armor, up-gun its older tanks, and use improved tank rounds. Most of its tanks need modern fire control systems, armor, night and thermal vision devices, and need guns and ammunition equal to those in the forces of the US and Saudi Arabia.

If the Iraqi Army is to compete directly with Western or Israeli land forces, however, it must solve its many qualitative defects and convert from the relatively static defensive force that lost the Gulf War to become a force that can match the kind of highly mobile, firepower intensive, maneuver-oriented, 24-hour-a-day force the Coalition deployed during Desert Storm. This is a far more demanding challenge than acquiring spare parts or more modern equipment.

Iraq must greatly improve the long-range sustainability of its forces in maneuver operations and its battlefield recovery and repair capabilities. It must make sweeping improvements in its night and poor weather warfare capabilities, and its ability to rapidly move artillery, mass and shift fires. It must restructure its entire artillery operation to emphasize combined arms and maneuver, precision fire and the ability to shift targets rapidly. Further, it needs to acquire beyond-visual-range and night-targeting systems.

It must restructure its communications, command, control, battle management, and training to support fluid maneuver operations, and a much faster tempo of sustained "24-hour-a-day" operations. This means re-equiping or modifying the fire control, sensors, and communications systems in much of its armor, providing new support and battle management capabilities, retraining the force at the Corps level, and giving

officers far more independence of action. Iraq will have to make fundamental changes in tactics and training, and acquire advanced training
and simulation technology.

The Iraqi Army must stress joint operations as well as combined arms.
It must greatly improve its helicopter operations which have been largely
ineffective, except in small independent operations. Maneuver forces
must train realistically with helicopters and fixed-wing aircraft. Training
must become far more effective above the battalion level, and modern
targeting and reconnaissance capabilities must be integrated into its
corps, division, and brigade level operations. It will need improved
mobile short-range air defenses and man-portable surface-to-air missiles,
tank transporters, secure communications, modern fire control systems,
tracked support equipment, and self-propelled artillery.

The Iraqi Army must also convert from a political to a professional
force. Saddam Hussein and the Ba'ath still interfere constantly with organizational matters, exercises, training, promotions, and equipment and
supply matters down to the battalion (major and lieutenant colonel) level.
Senior commanders still face the constant threat of removal or even execution for the normal failures of war and for petty political reasons.
Domestic political considerations, and ruthless efforts to ensure the loyalty of all officers to the regime often lead to the promotion of the politically loyal over the professionally competent. In many ways, Saddam
Hussein and the Ba'ath elite have been as great a threat to the Iraqi Army
as Iran and the UN Coalition.

Implications for Western
and Southern Gulf Strategy

The trends in Iraqi land forces are a further warning against any policy
that lifts sanctions without retaining some sort of controls over how Iraq
uses its revenues and without a firm commitment to military containment. These trends also argue for efforts to place strong long-term limits
on Iraq's ability to import modern main battle tanks and the equipment
it needs to react to the lessons of the Gulf War. In spite of the deterioration of its land forces, Iraq has no reason to fear a near or mid-term invasion by Iran. In contrast, Kuwait and Saudi Arabia have good reason to
fear that a revitalized Iraqi Army will be used to threaten them, or take
new military action against Kuwait.

12

The Threat from Iraqi Air and Air Defense Forces

In 1996, the Iraqi Air Force had roughly 30,000 men, including some 15,000 air defense personnel. It retained approximately 330 to 370 combat aircraft, although some of the Iraqi aircraft counted in this total were damaged or had limited or no operational combat capability. The Iraqi Air Force not only continued to suffer from its losses during the Gulf War, but also from five years without any significant imports of parts and equipment and foreign technical support.

While Iraq has been able to rebuild many of the shelters and facilities it lost during the war, it has not been able to replace its munitions and the C⁴I/BM equipment it lost. The creation of "no fly" zones in the north and south has severely restricted an already inadequate training program, and the Iraqi Air Force has exhibited few signs of being able to react to the lessons learned during the Gulf War. Further, the participation of some air force officers in coup attempts has led Saddam to limit the resources given to the Iraqi Air Force.

The Cost of the Gulf War to the Iraqi Air Force

As is the case with Iraq's land forces, the Gulf War has shaped the current size and capability of the Iraqi Air Force. While again there are significant differences in official US estimates, Table Seven shows a USAF and US Marine Corps estimate of Iraqi wartime losses. In addition, many Iraqi aircraft that flew to Iran have been seized by the Iranian government. The Iranian government announced in late July 1992 that it would expropriate the Iraqi combat aircraft that had taken refuge in Iran during the war, aircraft worth several billion dollars.[428]

In 1992, Iraqi Prime Minister Muhammed Hamzah al-Zubaydi described this Iranian seizure as part of a plot by Iran that had begun before the Gulf War. He stated, "We realize that all this (Iranian) enthusiasm and readiness to fulfill our demands (before the war)—followed by

TABLE SEVEN   Iraqi Air Strength in Desert Storm/Iraqi Combat Aircraft Losses in Desert Storm

Element of Force Strength	August 1, 1990	January 1, 1991	February 1, 1991	April 1, 1991
Air Force				
Personnel	18,000	18,000	18,000	18,000
Fighters/Fighter Bombers	718	728	699	362
Bombers	15	15	9	7
Reconnaissance	12	12	12	0
Subtotal	745	755	720	369
Combat Capable Trainers	370	400	400	252
Total	1,115	1,155	1,120	621
Helicopters	517	511	511	481
Transports	76	70	70	41
Civil Transports	59	60	60	42
Air Defense Force				
Personnel	17,000	17,000	17,000	17,000
Surface-to-Air Missile				
Batteries	120	120	200	85
Anti-Aircraft Guns	7,500	7,600	7,600	5,850

Iraqi Combat Aircraft Losses in Desert Storm

Aircraft Types	Number on January 12, 1991	Lost in Air Combat	Total Destroyed	Fled to Iran	Remaining on March 1, 1991
Mirage F-1	75	8	10	30	35
Su-24 Fencer	25	0	2	14	9
MiG-29 Fulcrum	41	5	9	7	25
Su-7/17/20/22 Fitter	119	5	14	34	71
MiG-25 Foxbat	33	2	8	0	25
Su-25 Frogfoot	61	2	4	7	50
MiG-23 Flogger	123	8	17	10	96
Mig-21 Fishbed	208	4	16	0	192
Total	685	34	80	102	503

Source: Adapted by the author from Lt. General Walter E. Boomer, "Desert Storm, MARCENT Operations in the Campaign to Liberate Kuwait," US Marine Corps Headquarters, August 31, 1991, and Eliot Cohen, ed., *Gulf War Air Power Survey, Volume V, Part I*, pp. 17–19 and 653–654.

a chapter of treason and treachery by Iranian elements—was part of a prepared plan. Thus, all that plundering, burning, and destruction within the chapter of treason and treachery took place."[429]

There are different estimates of how many aircraft of a given type went to Iran. Iran's Foreign Minister, Ali Akbar Velayati, said in November 1995 that Iran would only give back 22 aircraft once sanctions are lifted— all of which seem to be civilian airliners and transports. The Iraqi government has referred to 115 combat aircraft and 33 airliners, worth some $3 billion.[430] The author's estimate, based on conversations with various experts, is: 24 Mirage F-1s, 22 Su-24s, 40 Su-22s, 4 Su-17/20s, 7 Su-25s, 4 MiG-29s, 7 MiG-23Ls, 4 MiG-23BNs, 1 MiG-23UB, and 1 Adnan. This is a total of 112 combat aircraft.

Iraq's major transport and support aircraft included 2 B-747s, 1 B-707, 1 B-727, 2 B-737s, 14 IL-76s, 2 Dassault Falcon 20s, 3 Dassault Falcon 50s, 1 Lockheed Jetstar, 1 A-300, and 5 A-310s. These aircraft give Iraq a total of 31 major non-combat aircraft—not counting aircraft Iraq had seized from Kuwait.[431]

If Iraq's combat losses are combined with its losses to Iran, the resulting estimates indicate the Iraqi Air Force retained approximately 330 to 370 combat aircraft in combat units. At the same time, about half of the Iraqi aircraft counted in this total were probably damaged or now lack spare parts. This means that about half of the Iraqi Air Force's total inventory of combat aircraft has limited or no operational combat capability.

Current Air Force Equipment Holdings

Chart Thirty-Five shows a rough estimate of the trends in Iraq's air strength, and Charts Thirty-Six to Thirty-Eight and Table Eight show how it compares with the air strength of other Gulf states. Despite its losses, the Iraqi Air Force's total surviving inventory of combat aircraft in 1996 seemed to include 6–7 HD-6, Tu-16, and Tu-22 bombers—although it is not clear that these bombers were still operational. It also included 130 J-6, MiG-23BN, MiG-27, Mirage F-1EQ5, Su-7, Su-20, and Su-25 attack fighters; 180 J-7, MiG-21, MiG-25, Mirage F-1EQ, and MiG-29 air defense fighters; MiG-21 and MiG-25 reconnaissance fighters, 15 old Hawker Hunters, a surviving Il-76 Adnan AEW aircraft, 2 Il-76 tankers, and large numbers of transports and helicopters. Estimates of its total surviving inventory by aircraft type vary by source, but Iraq probably retained about 6 Tu-22, 1–2 Tu-16, 30 Mirage F-1s, 15 MiG-29s, 60 MiG-23s, 15 MiG-25s, 150 MiG-21s, 30 Su-25s, and 60 Su-17s, Su-20s, Su-22s.[432]

Although it is unclear how many air munitions Iraq retained after the Gulf War, some estimates put this figure as low as 50% of the pre-war total. Iraq, however, retains significant numbers of modern air-to-air and

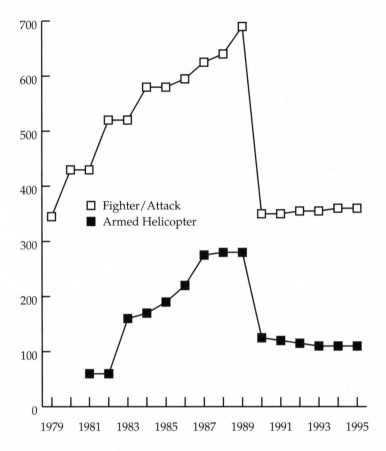

CHART THIRTY-FIVE   Iraq: Fixed Wing and Rotary Wing Combat Air
Strength—1979–1996. *Source:* Adapted by Anthony H. Cordesman from various
editions of the IISS, *Military Balance,* the JCSS, *Military Balance in the Middle
East,* and material provided by US experts.

air-to-ground munitions. These stocks include AA-6, AA-7, AA-8, AA-10,
Matra 530, Matra 550, and Matra Super 530 air-to-air missiles, and AM-39
Exocet, HOT, AS-11, AS-12, AS-6, AS-14, AS-301, AS-37, C-601 Silkworm;
air-to-surface missiles; laser-guided bombs, and Cluster bombs.
     Iraq retained large numbers of combat-capable trainers, transport air-
craft and helicopters, and remotely piloted vehicles. The trainers
included some Mirage F-1BQs, 25 PC-7s, 30 PC-9s, 50–60 Tucanos (EMB-
312s), 40 L-29s and 40 L-39s. Transport assets included a mix of Soviet An-
2, An-12, An-24, An-26, and Il-76 jets and propeller aircraft, and some Il-
76s modified to act as tankers. The remotely piloted vehicles (RPVs)

Total Fixed Wing Combat Aircraft

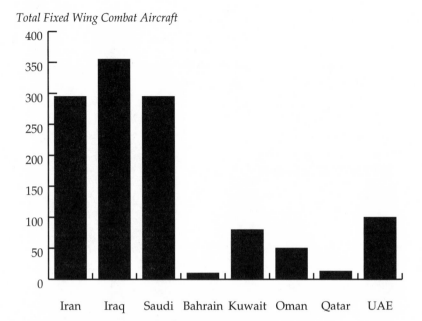

Operational Modern and Advanced Combat Aircraft: MiG-25, MiG-29, F-14, F-15, F-16, F/A-18, Mirage F-1, Mirage 2000

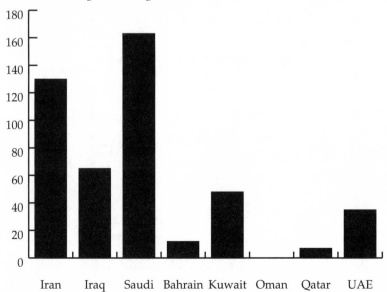

CHART THIRTY-SIX   Gulf Combat Aircraft in 1996. *Source:* Adapted by Anthony H. Cordesman from the IISS, *Military Balance, 1995–1996.*

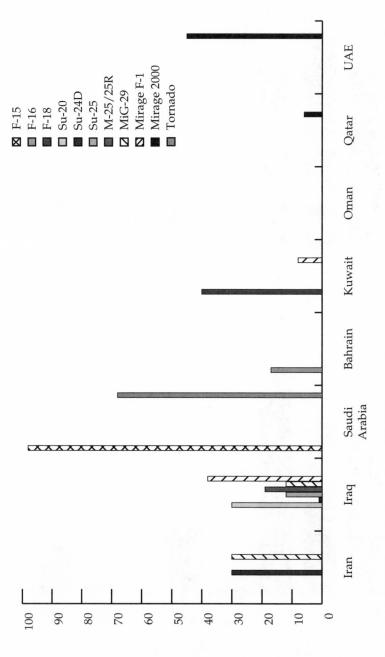

CHART THIRTY-SEVEN   High Quality Gulf Combat Aircraft by Type—1996. *Source:* Adapted by Anthony H. Cordesman from the IISS, *Military Balance, 1995–1996.*

Total Armed Helicopters

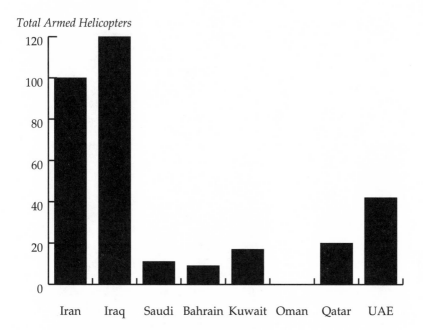

Modern Attack Helicopters: AH-64, Mi-25, Mi-24, SA-330, SA-342, AS-332F

CHART THIRTY-EIGHT   Gulf Attack Helicopters. *Source:* Adapted by Anthony H. Cordesman from the IISS, *Military Balance, 1995–1996.*

TABLE EIGHT   Advanced Combat Aircraft by Type in Gulf Forces

	Number	Type
Bahrain	24	Total Fixed Wing Combat
	16	F-16C/D
Iran	295	Total Fixed Wing Combat
	30	Su-24D
	30	MiG-29
Iraq	353	Total Fixed Wing Combat
	30	Su-20
	1	Su-24D
	12	Su-25
	38	Mirage F-1EQ5/200
	12	MiG-29
	15	MiG-25
	4	MiG-25R
Kuwait	76	Total Fixed Wing Combat
	40	F/A-18C/D
	8	Mirage F-1/CK
Oman	46	Total Fixed Wing Combat
	19	Jaguar (SO) Mark 1, T-2
Qatar	12	Total Fixed Wing Combat
	6	Mirage F-1EDA/DDA
Saudi Arabia	295	Total Fixed Wing Combat
	42	Tornado IDS
	24	Tornado ADV
	98	F-15C/D
	5	E-3A
UAE	97	Total Fixed Wing Combat
	9	Mirage 2000E
	22	Mirage 2000EAD
	6	Mirage 2000DAD
	8	Mirage 2000RAD

Note: Older aircraft with inferior avionics are not included. Supersonic flight performance is not regarded as more than a marginal measure of combat performance.
Source: Adapted by Anthony H. Cordesman from the IISS, Military Balance, 1995–1996.

included some Iraqi-made designs, Italian designs, and Soviet designs. It is unclear how effective Iraq was in using any of these RPV systems, but it did make use of them during the Gulf War.[433]

This equipment gives the Iraqi Air Force considerable combat potential. Furthermore, the Iraqi Air Force flew fighter and attack helicopter sorties against Shi'ites in southern Iraq in June and July 1992, until the UN established no-fly zones north of the 36th parallel and south of the

32nd parallel. These no-fly zones barred any Iraqi use of fighters and helicopters. The northern zone was established shortly after the cease-fire and the southern zone was established on August 26, 1992.

Iraqi fighters initially challenged UN fighters by tracking them or flying into the no-fly zones. At the same time, Iraq moved some of its more expendable land-based air defense systems—like the SA-6—into threatening positions or "surface-to-air missile traps" in or near the no-fly zones. Iraqi fighters also challenged UN forces in December 1992 and January 1993. These actions—coupled with further efforts to bar UN inspections and a challenge of Kuwait's right to secure its new border—provoked a significant clash between UN and Iraqi forces in January 1993. The UN forces shot down at least one Iraqi fighter, and attacked the Iraqi surface-to-air missile traps and any Iraqi radars that illuminated UN aircraft. They also launched two major attacks on Iraqi command and control facilities.

Air Readiness and Warfighting Capabilities

The Iraqi Air Force and air defense forces have since backed down in response to UN challenges, but Iraq has stepped up its air training and has continued to rebuild other aspects of its air defense capabilities. Beginning in late 1992, Iraq started to improve the quality of its air-to-air training, and to reconstitute its surface-to-air missile net. It repaired and modified some of its surface-to-air missile systems in an attempt to improve their resistance to US countermeasures. Meanwhile, Iraq established new missile sites and upgraded its aircraft dispersals.

The Iraqi Air Force, however, is now operating with considerably less than half its pre-war ability to generate and sustain combat sorties, and continues to lose effectiveness with time. Its training and deployment capabilities were also further constrained by the expansion of the "no fly" zone in the south from the 32nd parallel to the 33rd parallel. This brought the northern edge of the zone within easy striking range of Baghdad, deprived Iraq of the use of two main air bases, and meant its aircraft could not fly in joint exercises over several key army training areas.

The Iraqi Air Force has only been able to conduct limited combat aircraft operations since the cease-fire in February 1991 and its training and readiness have deteriorated with time. It has no major repair facilities for many of its Soviet-made fighters—which had previously been overhauled by Soviet technicians or rebuilt in the former Soviet Union. It has growing shortages of spare parts, and has no in-country access to the Soviet and French technical support which it had relied on before the war. The Mirage F-1 is difficult to maintain, and Iraq is likely to have severe problems in keeping this aircraft operational without access to French technical support and new deliveries of parts and equipment.

Iraq cannot rebuild its air force to anything approaching its pre-war strength without massive arms imports and foreign assistance. At some point, Iraq will also need substantial deliveries of more modern French or Russian combat aircraft.

However, imports alone will not suffice. Like most Third World states, Iraq has never organized effectively to fight as an integrated air force—as distinguished from clusters of individual fighting elements. Iraq still seems to confuse having a large order of battle with effectiveness, and puts far too little emphasis on high sortie rates, the effective massing of air power against given types of targets, planning sustained air campaigns, and testing, exercising, and restructuring its mix of air and land-based air defense assets to fight as an effective overall force.

Iraq must reorganize its command structure to provide the same degree of professionalism, and freedom from political interference that is needed in its army. Its jury-rigged airborne sensor aircraft is a poor substitute for a true airborne warning and air control system (AWACS) or integrated airborne sensor and battle management system. Like Iran, Iraq lacks the training and sensors to compete with the West in beyond-visual-range combat, and the advanced training facilities to compete in close or dog-fight combat.

To compete with Western air forces, or that of Saudi Arabia, Iraq must acquire some form of "mini-airborne warning and air control system (AWACS)," a large inventory of modern beyond-visual-range air-to-air missiles, modern remotely piloted vehicles (RPVs), and airborne refueling technology. It will require outside support in repairing and reconditioning its fighters. It must find ways of integrating its fighters into an effective air control and warning system that "nets" them with its ground-based air defense system, and which avoids its past over-dependence on ground-controlled intercepts.

Iraq needs to acquire modern reconnaissance and intelligence aircraft that are capable of real-time transmission of data to effective command centers and terminals in the field. The air force must work with the army to improve the sensors and weapons on its attack helicopters, and to develop an integrated concept for fixed and rotary wing close air support, and armored operations.

Iraqi operations and training have not reflected any significant understanding of modern AirLand Battle techniques. It needs to reorganize its training system to stress far more demanding and realistic offensive training that includes training in combined arms exercises and realistic close support and interdiction missions, and strategic bombing missions. This must include constant training with smart munitions and actual ordnance, and far better training in evading air defenses and stand-off attacks. At present, the Iraqi Air Force has negligible targeting and battle management capabilities for offensive operations, and tends to deliver munitions into the general area of the target, release them, and leave with little or no effect. Outside experts also indicate that it has probably lost most of its capability to operate its Mirage F-1s with Exocet due to a lack of maintenance, training, and outside technical support.

Iraqi air defense has performed dismally, is wretchedly trained, and is poorly organized. The issue is not one of courage; individual Iraqi pilots often pressed home intercepts during the early days of Desert Storm. However, Iraqi air combat tactics were primitive to the point where even the lead pilots of Iraq's MiG-29s often lost their wing man and were forced to seek guidance constantly from ground based sensors and command facilities. Pilot air combat training rarely rose above the initial levels of Soviet combat training even before the Gulf War, and there has been no meaningful training since that time. In fact, every aspect of Iraqi air defense training and organization needs to be completely reorganized. Iraq's air intercept training and tactics fall far short of the aggressive air battle and aggressor squadron techniques used by the Saudi, US, and British air forces, and ground-controlled intercept tactics are virtually unworkable in modern air warfare and are little more than suicidal. Iraq needs modern airborne warning and air control aircraft, beyond-visual-range combat capabilities, and electronic warfare capabilities. It also needs to reorganize its air defense forces completely if its air defense fighters are to operate effectively in the same environment as its attack aircraft, surface-to-air missiles, and helicopters.

Iraq needs to understand that it needs the spares, support organization, and training to greatly improve its sortie rates and sustainability. Like most Arab air forces, Iraq cripples its potential effectiveness by emphasizing aircraft numbers over sustained sortie rates and effective operations. As a result, it could only fly a small fraction of the sortie rates its aircraft strength would have allowed it to fly if the aircraft were operated by a Western air force—roughly 1/10th to 1/20th of the sortie rate of the Israeli Air Force. This situation has grown steadily worse since 1990. As a result, the operational sortie rate of the Iraqi aircraft would probably decline by 75% or more below its initial surge rate in any combat lasting more than a few days.

Iraq's own analyses of the lessons of the Gulf War indicate that it recognizes that it must have effective air defense capabilities to defend its ground forces in any future war. At the same time, Iraq also lacks cohesion as an air force. The mission-oriented weaknesses described earlier are compounded by a lack of effective central air planning and battle management, a clear concept of how to employ large numbers of aircraft, and a lack of any effective concept for joint operations. The Iraqi Air Force fights as individual combat elements, and not as a force.

Even if the present UN embargo and sanctions are lifted, these force improvements will take time and require Iraq to make an investment of several billion dollars. In the interim, the war fighting capabilities of the Iraqi Air Force will remain limited. The Iraqi Air Force can probably dominate the skies over the Iran-Iraq border area until Iran fully absorbs its MiG-29s. It can play a major role in defeating the Kurds, and rapidly defeat the Kuwaiti air force. It probably cannot defeat the Saudi and Turkish air forces in the border areas, but they might need US support to win a quick and decisive victory. The Iraqi Air Force can conduct limited long-range air attacks against its neighbors, retains some refueling capability, and can use some precision-guided weapons, chemical weapons, and possibly biological weapons. Iraq could use these capabilities to mass a few air raids against selected targets in Iran or across the Gulf, and could use its remaining Exocets to attack tanker and other naval targets in the Gulf. Like Iran, however, Iraq is at least half a decade away from rebuilding its air force.

Land-Based Air Defenses

Iraq had a large land-based air defense system before the Gulf War, which had been extensively reorganized after Israel's Osirak raid in 1981. A network of radars, surface-to-air missiles, and anti-aircraft guns surrounded strategic and industrial areas, particularly in the Baghdad area. A French-supplied C^3/BM system called the KARI (Iraq spelled backwards in French) became operational on a country-wide level in 1986–1987, but it was never really tested during the Iran-Iraq War.

The National Air Defense Operations Center (ADOC) in Baghdad controlled Iraq's air defenses. The ADOC maintained the overall air picture and provided Baghdad with information on the course of the air battle. There were five Sector Operations Centers (SOCs) covering the north, west, center-east, south-east and far south which established priorities for air defense engagements. Each was subordinate to the ADOC, and controlled air defense operations in a specific geographic area. The SOCs controlled large numbers of ground-based weapons systems and extensive C^3/BM assets. There were also a large number of Intercept Operations Centers (IOCs) to provide local air defense control. These had headquarters at Ar-Rutbah, H-1, and H-3 in the West; Mosul and Qayyarah in the north, Al-Taqaddum, Salman Pak, Al-Jarrah, An-Najf, and An-Nukhayb in the center-east; and Al-Amrah, As-Salman and Az-Zubayr in the southeast; and Al-Jahrah in the far south.

The Iraqi system, however, was a mix of technologies from different nations with uncertain integration. Although part of Iraq's air defense system was French-supplied, Iraq patterned its overall air defense network and operations on Soviet models. It also concentrated its coverage around Baghdad, Basra, and key military and strategic targets. This left many areas uncovered, particularly in southern Iraq, and along air corridors striking north across the Saudi and Kuwait borders.

Iraq's air defenses were fundamentally flawed because the SOCs could not communicate effectively once the ADOC was destroyed or deactivated. This meant that the Coalition could attack and/or overwhelm each sector in isolation from the others. Moreover, the destruction of a given SOC effectively opened up a corridor that could be used to attack the entire country. While it may not be a general lesson of the war, such design defects and vulnerabilities are common in Third World air defense systems, and almost universal in systems dependent on Soviet or PRC surface-to-air missiles, sensors, and electronics.

There were other problems. Iraq had created a strongly inter-netted, redundant, and layered air defense system that including a wide variety of radars, hardened and buried command- and-control sites, interceptors, surface-to-air missiles, and anti-aircraft artillery. In practice, however, much of the communications, data processing, and software were inferior.[434]

Even so, Iraq's air defense forces were formidable in some respects at the start of the Gulf War. According to one US estimate, Iraq had a total of 16,000 radar-guided and heat seeking surface-to-air missiles, including missiles for the large numbers of lighter army systems described earlier, and smaller numbers of missiles for the heavier SA-2s, SA-3s, and SA-6s. These heavier surface-to-air defense missiles were operated by an air defense force, organized into air defense units that were part of the Iraqi Army, but operationally tied to the Air Force.

At the time of the war, Iraq had approximately 137–154 medium surface-to-air missile sites and complexes in Iraq and 20–21 in Kuwait, and 18 major surface-to-air missile support facilities.[435] These included 20–30 operational SA-2 batteries with 160 launch units, 25–50 SA-3 batteries with 140 launch units, and 36–55 SA-6 batteries with well over 100 fire units. Iraq claimed to have modified the SA-2 missile to use an infra-red terminal seeker, to supplement the SA-2's normal radio command guidance system, but it is unclear that such systems were actually deployed. All of these systems could still be fired on a target of opportunity basis. Iraq's medium surface-to-air defense sites in Iraq were also a threat to a modern air force. They were widely dispersed, often did not require the use of radar, and could be fired on a target of opportunity basis. The missiles on the sites in Iraq included at least 20 SA-8 batteries with 30–40 fire units, 60–100 SA-9 fire units, and some SA-13s, and 50 to 66 Rolands.[436]

To put this level of air defense strength in perspective, Baghdad had more dense air defenses at the start of the Gulf War than any city in Eastern Europe, and had more than seven times the total surface-to-air missile launcher strength deployed in Hanoi during the height of the Vietnam war. The US Department of Defense released a highly detailed post-war estimate of Iraq's land-based air defense at the outset of the Gulf War that credited Iraq with 3,679 major missiles, not including 6,500 SA-7s, 400 SA-9s, 192 SA-13s, and 288 SA-14s. This report indicated that Iraq had 972 anti-aircraft artillery sites, 2,404 fixed anti-aircraft guns, and 6,100 mobile anti-aircraft guns.

Separate US estimates indicate that Iraq had extensive numbers of crew/vehicle deployed SA-9s and SA-13s, and man-portable SA-14s, and SA-16s, dispersed throughout the KTO. These estimates indicate that Iraq had deployed more than 3,700 anti-aircraft guns in the KTO with barrels larger than 14.5 mm, and that these AA guns were supplemented by more than 10,000 12.7 mm guns in the ground forces in the KTO that could be used in some form of anti-aircraft role. While such weapons lacked accuracy, range, and high lethality, they could be deployed to expose aircraft flying under 12,000–15,000 feet to substantial cumulative risk.[437]

Many of the individual surface-to-air missile, anti-aircraft gun, and command and control units in the Iraqi system, however, had low operational readiness and proficiency. System-wide and unit-level electronic warfare capability was good by Third World standards, but was scarcely competitive with that of the US. Iraq's overall sensor/battle management system remained poor. Their training failed to deal with saturation and advanced countermeasure attacks, and was not realistic in dealing with more conventional penetrations by advanced attack aircraft. This was demonstrated all too clearly when Iraqi guns and missiles shot down an Egyptian Alphajet flying to an arms show in Baghdad in April 1989, even though it flew along a pre-announced flight corridor at the scheduled time.[438] Iraq still could not keep its land-based air control and warning and C³/BM systems operational 24 hours a day.

There is no expert consensus on how much of Iraq's land-based air defense assets and air defense system survived the Gulf War, or on Iraq's holdings of surface-to-air missiles in late 1995. Many facilities survived because the Coalition concentrated more on the suppression of air defense activity than the physical destruction of land-based facilities and trying to hunt down and kill individual air defense weapons.

Table Nine shows how Iraq's post-war air defense strength compares with that of other Gulf states. In 1996, Iraq retained 130–180 SA-2 launchers, 100–125 SA-3 launchers, 100–125 SA-6s, 20–35 SA-8s, 30–45 SA-9s, some SA-13s, and around 80 Roland surface-to-air missile units. Some of these systems were operated by the army. In addition, Iraq had large numbers of man-portable SA-7s and SA-14s, and some SA-16s.[439]

Most of these surface-to-air missile units are operational. It is unclear whether Iraq learned enough from the Jordanian officers that assisted it during the war, and during the initial period after the war to operate its Hawks. Iraq may also be avoiding any use of the weapons because it fears the US would attack any captured Hawks that showed signs of becoming operational.[440]

Iraq's ground-based defenses remain concentrated around Baghdad, Basra, and Kirkuk, as they were during the pre-war period. Iraqi territory is too large to attempt territorial defense, and Iraq has always concentrated on defending strategic targets, and deploying air defense zones to cover critical land force deployments. However, Iraq redeployed some missiles during 1992 and 1993 to create surface-to-air missile "traps" near the "no-fly zones" that the Coalition established after the war. These traps were designed to attack aircraft with over lapping missile coverage when they attacked launchers deployed near the no-fly zones. While the Iraqi efforts failed—and led to the destruction of a number of the missile launchers involved—it is not clear what portion survived or what other redeployments Iraq has made in recent years.

Land-Based Air Defense
Readiness and Warfighting Capability

Iraq has made extensive efforts to improve its use of shelters, revetments, dummies, and other passive defenses. It has used such defenses since the beginning of the Iran-Iraq War, and has deployed new decoys after the Gulf War in an effort to reduce its vulnerability. According to most experts, it repaired many of the bases and air facilities that were destroyed or damaged during the Gulf War. It has 16–20 major air bases, with H-3, H-2, and Al Asad in the West; Mosul, Qayarah, and Kirkuk in the north, Al Jarah, Talil, and Shaybah in the South, and 5–7 more bases within a 150 kilometer radius of Baghdad. Many of these bases have surface-to-air missile defenses.

Iraq has been able to restore much of its battle control and management system, reactivate its damaged airfields, and even build one new military airfield in the South.[441] Many of its sheltered air defense and air force

TABLE NINE   Gulf Land-Based Air Defense Systems

Country	Major SAM	Light SAM	AA Guns
Bahrain	None	40+ RBS-70 18 Stinger 7 Crotale	?
Iran	12/150 I Hawk 3/? SA-5 45 HQ-2J (SA-2) ? SA-2	SA-7 HN-5 30 Rapier 15 Tigercat	1,500 Guns ZU-23 ZSU-23-4 ZSU-57-2 KS-19 FM-80 (Ch Crotale)
Iraq	SA-2 SA-3 SA-6	Roland SA-7 SA-8 SA-9 SA-13 SA-14 SA-16	5,500 Guns ZSU-23-4 23 mm M-1939 37 mm ZSU-57-2 SP, 57 mm, 85 mm, 100 mm, 130 mm
Kuwait	4/24 I Hawk	6/12 Aspede	6/2 × 35 mm Oerlikon
Oman	None	Blowpipe 34 SA-7 28 Javelin 28 Rapier	2 VAB/VD 20 mm 4 ZU-23-2 23 mm 12 L-60 40 mm
Qatar	None	Blowpipe 12 Stinger 9 Roland	?
Saudi Arabia	128 I Hawk	Crotale Stinger 500 Redeye 68 Shahine mobile 40 Crotale 73 Shahine static	92 M-163 Vulcan 20 mm 50 AMX-30SA 30 mm 128 35 mm guns 150 L-70 40 mm (in store)
UAE	5 I Hawk Bty.	20+ Blowpipe 10 SA-16 12 Rapier 9 Crotale 13 RBS-70 100 Mistral	48 M-3VDA 20 mm SP 20 GCF-BM2 30 mm

Source: Adapted by Anthony H. Cordesman from the IISS, Military Balance, 1994–1995.

command and control centers remained operational. Iraq's French-supplied KARI air defense communications and data-link system is not particularly effective, but it uses fiber optics and many of the links between its command elements either have survived the bombing or are now repaired.[442] Some radars and limited elements of Iraq's air defense C⁴I system are also operating, including such pre-war systems as the Soviet Spoon Rest, Squat Eye, Flat Face, Tall King, Bar Lock, Cross Slot, and Thin Skin radars. Iraq also has Soviet, Italian, and French jamming and electronic intelligence equipment. There is no way to know how many of Iraq's radars and underground command and personnel shelters survived the Gulf War and the US cruise missile strikes of September 1996. It seems likely that at least 50–66% survived the Coalition bombing campaign or have been rebuilt since the war, and that the more recent US cruise missile strikes in 1996 inflicted no damage on Iraq's command sites and negligible damage on its surface-to-air missile sites and radars. Less than 20% of the 44 US missiles seem to have inflicted significant damage on an Iraqi radar or SAM site, and no command centers seem to have received serious damage.

Nonetheless, Iraq faces major problems in making its air defense forces effective, in modernizing them, and in reacting to the lessons of the Gulf War. Most of Iraq's surface-to-air missile units, radars, automated data processing and transfer system, and central command and communications facilities have only limited operational capability. Iraq must rehabilitate and improve its radar-guided anti-aircraft guns and most of its short-range air defense systems. It needs to either modernize or replace its Rolands. It should replace its surviving patchwork system of radars and command and control equipment, and in the short-term, must find a reliable source of parts for its SA-3s and SA-6s.

Iraq's most serious challenge will be to find replacements for its French and Russian-supplied air defense system, and to create a truly modern and effective air defense system. Iraq has recognized this requirement as a lesson of the Gulf War, but is confronted with the problem that that the only way it can create an effective system is to buy the Patriot, sold by the US, or the SA-10/SA-12, sold by Russia. The C⁴/BM aspects of such a system would have to be tailored to Iraq's needs, integrate its purchase of the Patriot, SA-10 or SA-12 fully into its other air defenses, and provide suitable new sensors and air defense computer technology and software. Such a system could then become operational relatively quickly, but giving full effectiveness by US or Russian standards would require it to be tailored to meet Iraq's specific topographical and operating conditions. This would take a major effort in terms of software, radar deployment and technology, as well as adaptation of US or Russian tactics and siting concepts to make such a system fully combat effective.[443]

Implications for Western
and Southern Gulf Strategy

The trends in Iraqi Air Forces are another warning against any policy that lifts sanctions without retaining any controls over how Iraq uses its revenues and without a firm commitment to military containment. They are a further argument for efforts to create a supplier regime that places strong limits on Iraq's military modernization and provides a particularly strong argument for limits on Iraqi imports of long-range strike aircraft, and advanced, heavy surface-to-air missile defenses.

13

The Threat from Iraqi Naval Forces

Chart Thirty-Nine shows the relative strength of Gulf navies. In 1996, the Iraqi Navy only had a strength of about 1,600–2,000 men, and its surviving forces included only the frigate *Ibn Khaldun*, one Osa-class missile boat, 13 light combat vessels, 5–8 landing craft, the *Agnadeen*, 1 Yugoslav Spasilac-class transport, a floating dry-dock, and possibly one repairable Polnocny-class LST. The IISS and *Jane's* report that Iraq also had three 5,800 ton roll-on roll-off transport ships with helicopter decks, a capability to carry 250 troops and 18 tanks, and the ability to embark small landing craft. These ships may be under commercial flags, and do not have the ability to beach.[444]

This inventory gives Iraq virtually no naval combat capability. The *Agnadeen* and dry-dock are still in Alexandria. The *Ibn Khaldun* is a comparatively large 1,850 ton ship with a maximum speed of 26 knots, but it is designed only for training purposes. Its armament consists of one 57 mm Bofors gun, one 40 mm Bofors anti-aircraft gun, and a four barrel 16/20 mm anti-aircraft gun. The *Ibn Khaldun* can carry a quadruple launcher for Exocet missiles, but this launcher has never been fitted. There are reports that the *Ibn Khaldun* may have been rendered largely inoperable during the fighting in 1991, and even if it was not, it probably has only very limited operational capability because it lacks spares for its Rolls-Royce main engines.

Surviving Combat Ships

Iraq's lighter, surviving combat ships only include a maximum of one Osa-class guided missile patrol boat (doubtful), one or two Soviet-supplied Bogomol-class patrol boats, two Zhuk-class patrol boats, one Poluchat-class patrol craft, six PB-80 coastal patrol craft, some Sawari-class small inshore patrol boats, six SRN-6 Hovercraft, and some small boats. Its surviving five mine craft include two Soviet Yevgenya-class and three Yugoslav Nestin-class boats.

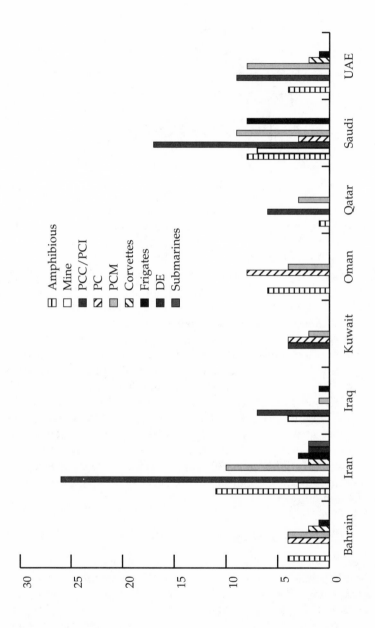

CHART THIRTY-NINE Gulf Naval Ships by Category in 1996. *Source:* Adapted by Anthony H. Cordesman from the IISS, *Military Balance, 1995–1996.*

CHART THIRTY-NINE (continued)

	Bahrain	Iran	Iraq	Kuwait	Oman	Qatar	Saudi	UAE
Submarines	—	2	—	—	—	—	—	—
DE	1	2	1	—	—	—	—	1
Frigates	2	3	1	—	—	—	8	2
Corvettes	4	2	—	2	4	3	—	8
PCM	4	10	1	4	8	—	9	8
PC	—	—	7	4	—	6	3	—
PCC/PCI	—	26	4	—	—	—	17	9
Mine	—	3	—	—	—	—	7	—
Amphibious	4	11	—	—	6	1	8	4

The Bogomal-class patrol boats are the only craft large enough to be taken seriously, and they have limited combat capability. Several may also be damaged. These boats are 245 ton vessels and normally carry only a 76 mm gun, a 30 mm Gatling gun, and one SA-N-5 missile.

Iraq does not have access to any of the larger combat ships it ordered from Italy, and little future prospect of obtaining such access. Italy is holding the *Mussa Ben Nussair* and *Tariq Ibn Ziyad* at La Spezia. Italy has turned the four Lupo-class ships that Iraq ordered before the Iran-Iraq War over to its own navy, and will probably sell the remaining Wadi Mr'agh-class corvettes to some other country. It has sought to sell some ships to Morocco, and two to Malaysia.[445] The *Agnadeen* and Iraq's floating dry-dock are held in Alexandria, Egypt. All three of the roll-on roll-off transports are held in foreign ports. One of the personal yachts that Saddam Hussein ordered before the Iran-Iraq War, the *Al Manuser* was transferred to King Fahd of Saudi Arabia in 1987, and has never even entered Iraqi waters. A second yacht, the *Al Qadissiya*, which Saddam Hussein ordered for use on Iraq's rivers has never been delivered.[446]

Iraq also has even less access to the Gulf than it had when it invaded Kuwait. It has been forced to close its naval base at Umm Qasr. Iraq is forced to use small craft and civilian ships for patrols in coastal areas. Virtually all of the larger ships that are still under its control are now laid up in Khor as Zubair, Basra, and Mina al-Bakr.

Iraq has never been able to implement its plans to acquire a large force of naval helicopters with anti-ship missiles and other specialized helicopters. The Iraqi Air Force does have some Mirage F-1s armed with the Exocet anti-ship missile, but does not seem to retain any remaining capability to operate Soviet bombers with Soviet air-to-ship missiles. The air force lost some armed helicopters during the Gulf War, but may retain six to seven of the 13 Aerospatiale SA-321s, armed with Exocet air-to-surface missiles obtained during the Iran-Iraq War.

The Iraqi Navy ordered five Agusta Bell AB-212s; and 10 Agusta Bell A-103A helicopters from Italy before the war. It was unable to pay for most of this order, however, and it is unclear that it completed training for the few helicopters it did pay for. No armed or special purpose helicopters are currently in service in the Iraqi Navy, and the navy still has no meaningful aviation training or capability. Even if the navy can obtain new deliveries, it will be years before it has operational capability.

The Iraqi Air Force also has not taken delivery on any of the major anti-ship helicopter orders it negotiated with France in 1989. These orders included six French Aerospatiale AB-332F Super Pumas; with Exocets, and six SA-365N/FF Dauphin with AS-15TTM air-to-ship missiles. These aircraft might have given Iraq some added anti-ship capability against the UN, although they scarcely would have altered the outcome of the fighting. The AS-332Fs were to be fitted with Varian search and fire control radars, Agrion chin-mounted radars and four AS-15T air-to-ship missiles each. The AS-15Ts have a range of up to 15 kilometers and are a much cheaper way to attack small ships than the Exocet.[447]

Naval Readiness and Warfighting Capability

Iraq retains some mine warfare capability, and most of its land-based Silkworm missile systems. These Silkworms have ranges of up to 100 kilometers, and Iraq has some experience in using them in combat. On February 25, 1991, Iraq fired two Silkworm missiles against Coalition ships in the Gulf. Both missiles missed. One missile failed and crashed into the sea, the other was destroyed by British Aerospace Sea Darts fired by the *HMS Glocester.*

Iraq can also fire Exocet anti-ship missiles from some of its Mirage F-1 fighters and helicopters. It may also have some Faw 70, Faw 150, and Faw 200 missiles, which it claims are Iraqi-made versions of the Soviet SSC-3 Styx, but these are obsolescent designs at best.[448]

These limitations are so severe that there is no near-term prospect that the Iraqi Navy will acquire more than the most marginal war fighting capability. It can conduct limited raids and fire some anti-ship missiles, but if it attempts to fight Iranian or Western naval and air forces, it is almost certain to be rapidly destroyed.

Implications for Western
and Southern Gulf Strategy

Iraqi naval forces are so weak that they pose only a limited priority for containment. At the same time, careful attention is needed to two kinds of Iraqi imports: Advanced mine laying capabilities and advanced anti-ship missiles. Any supplier regime should focus on such imports as a significant potential risk to the flow of oil and shipping in the Gulf. There are equally good reasons to deny Iraq submarines and modern surface combat ships. Every effort should be made to prevent Iraq from joining Iran as a regional naval threat.

14

Unconventional Warfare
and Terrorism

Iraqi security and paramilitary forces are a key tool in Iraq's efforts to use force to put pressure on its Gulf neighbors and the West. Iraq has long manipulated extremist groups and movements to serve its ambitions and ideological goals. Like other radical Middle Eastern states, Iraq has found such exploitation to be a cheap and effective substitute for overt political and military action. Such activities allow Iraq to partially decouple its actions from public responsibility, and to suddenly shift support from one group to another, and to disavow a given group at will.

Iraqi intelligence maintains a large special operations component which operates directly out of Iraqi embassies, and through independent overseas "fronts" like airline and purchasing offices. While Iraqi intelligence is deeply concerned with suppressing opposition to the Ba'ath regime, Iraqi intelligence has also been deeply involved in buying arms, obtaining the technology for weapons of mass destruction, providing covert support for ethnic and political movements hostile to the enemies of the Iraqi regime, and in attacks on foreign critics, intelligence agents, and political leaders.

Recent Iraqi Terrorist Activity

Iraq has not been able to act as freely in supporting revolutionary and extremist groups since the end of the Gulf War as it has in the past. Many Iraqi agents were expelled from foreign countries during the Gulf War. Nevertheless, Iraq has still been active in terrorism. The US State Department estimates that Iraqi intelligence conducted 39 terrorist attacks between the end of the Gulf War and April 1993. Iraqi agents seem to have trained new hit squads to kill enemies in foreign countries, including an Iraqi scientist who was about to defect in Jordan in December 1992. There have been dozens of attacks on UN relief and aid workers in Iraq, including many bombings. Eight time-bombs were found under

UN trucks in December 1992, and explosives damaged 14 UN trucks a week later.

Iraq continues to host a number of terrorist organizations despite being forbidden to do so by UN Security Council Resolution 687. These groups include the People's Mujahideen of Iran (Mojahedin-e Khalq), which is opposed to the Government of Iran. As has been discussed, the People's Mujahideen has repeatedly launched raids and conducted terrorist attacks in Iran. Iran has retaliated by sponsoring anti-Iraqi forces in Iran, which operate against Iraq and are led by the Hakim family.[449]

Iraq has supported extremist Palestinian groups like the Abu Nidal Organization (ANO), the Arab Liberation Front (ALF), Abu Abbas's Palestinian Liberation Front (PLF), and Abu Ibrahim. Iraq has also assisted the Turkish Kurdistan Workers Party (PKK) and anti-Iranian Kurdish groups in Iran. It supported groups involved in blowing up the Pan Am airliner in 1992. It may have given some support to the group that bombed the World Trade Center, although the available evidence is very weak.[450] The Government continued to provide safe haven and logistical and military support to several terrorist groups and individuals like the People's Mujahideen and ANO. It has also aided Abu Abbas' Palestine Liberation Front (PLF), and the notorious bomb-maker Abu Ibrahim. Both Abbas and Ibrahim enjoyed sanctuary in Iraq.

None of these groups are particularly strong at the moment, or seem to be attracting significant popular support. They are, however, tools which Iraq can use under at least some conditions. Iraq can also use state terrorism, and has tried to do so in the past.

Attempting to Assassinate President Bush

The Iraqi Intelligence Service (IIS) sponsored an assassination attempt on President Bush when he visited Kuwait on April 14–16, 1993. Iraq intelligence agents—including Mohammed Jawad and Abd al-Iman—recruited 11 Iraqis to drive a Toyota Land Cruiser and Chevrolet Suburban across the Kuwait border on April 13. The vehicles contained pistols, hand grenades, timing devices, remote control sensing devices, and a 180 pounds of Semtex plastic explosive. They were also given 12 cases of whiskey to disguise the operation as smuggling. The key device involved in the plot was a car bomb that was intended to be placed along the President's route through Kuwait and kill both him and his entourage. One of the key Iraqis in the plot, Wali Ghazali, was also given a "suicide belt" as a back-up if the car bomb failed.

The US originally suspected that Kuwait might be exaggerating the plot—in part because Iraqi intelligence recruited amateurs and then failed to inform its recruits of changes in President Bush's route. However, later investigations confirmed that Iraqi intelligence was directly involved. While all of the evidence has not been made public, FBI and CIA agents found that a total of 14–17 people were involved in the plot, including 11 Iraqis and three Kuwaitis. Several had clear ties to the Iraqi Intelligence Service, some bomb components were Iraqi, and the bomb design was similar to an Iraqi bomb used in Turkey. Other evidence linked the plot to the highest levels in the Iraqi government.[451]

The United States retaliated on June 26, 1993, by firing 23 Tomahawk cruise missiles against the center of the IIS headquarters in suburban Baghdad. However, the plot on President Bush's life was part of a much broader pattern of challenge and response that Iraq has carried out since the cease-fire in the Gulf War. Iraq continued to challenge UN aircraft in the no-fly zone by tracking them with radar and occasionally subjecting them to anti-aircraft fire. Iraq also continued to attack Shi'ite rebels in the south, to bomb UN aid missions to the Kurds, to keep much of its troop strength on the border of the Kurdish security zone, and to attack Kurdish leaders and villages in the security zone.

In June 1994, the Kuwaiti court found 14 of the individuals accused of participating in the plot to assassinate former President Bush during his April 1993 visit to Kuwait to be guilty. The preceding trial had clearly identified Iraq's complicity in the assassination attempt.

Other Recent Iraqi Acts of Terrorism

The US State Department reports that Iraqi-backed surrogates were probably responsible for two attempts to bomb the Kuwait Airways office in Beirut in 1993, and another attempt to bomb the Kuwaiti Embassy, in Lebanon. The Iraqi regime continued its war of attrition on UN and humanitarian targets in northern Iraq aimed at driving the foreign presence out of the area and depriving the Kurdish population of relief supplies. UN and relief workers were shot at, bombs or grenades were tossed at residences and vehicles, and bombs were placed on UN trucks loaded with relief supplies. In March 1993, a Belgian official of Handicapped International was shot and killed; a local employee of the same organization was killed and six others were injured when an aid station was bombed in December.[452]

On September 26, 1993, a UN truck carrying 12 tons of medical supplies was completely destroyed by a bomb attached to the fuel tank probably by Iraqi agents at an Iraqi checkpoint. The truck driver and 12 civilians were injured by the blast. The incident illustrates Iraqi determination to reduce aid to the Kurds.[453]

In 1992 the Iraqi Government agreed to comply with UN Resolution 687, which requires Iraq to prohibit any terrorist organization from operating within its territory. Nevertheless, Baghdad has maintained contacts with the PKK, which has killed hundreds of people in attacks inside Turkey and mounted two separate terrorist campaigns against Turkish interests in Europe in 1993. The PKK has training camps in Iraq.[454] At the same time, Iraq seems to be supporting rival factions within the Kurdish movement, including the KDP and PUK, to encourage divisions.

During 1994 and 1995, Iraq continued its terrorist attacks against political dissidents, both at home and abroad. It also continued its terrorist war of attrition aimed at driving UN and other foreign aid agencies out of northern Iraq and depriving the Kurdish population of relief supplies. There were at least 17 attacks against UN and international relief personnel. Iraq continued to provide safe haven and training facilities for several terrorist organizations, including Abu Abbas' Palestine Liberation Front (PLF), the ANO, and the Arab Liberation Front (ALF). In April 1994, a prominent Iraqi member of the opposition residing in Beirut was assassinated. The Government of Lebanon stated that it had firm evidence linking the killing to the Government of Iraq. Lebanese authorities subsequently arrested two Iraqi diplomats in connection with the incident, and Lebanon broke diplomatic relations with Iraq.[455]

Implications for Western and Southern Gulf Strategy

The West, and particularly the US, have abused charges of terrorism so often that it is sometimes tempting to ignore such charges when they are legitimate. Iraq is likely to remain a real "terrorist nation" as long as it is under the control of Saddam Hussein, or any similar "centrist" regime. This is not a threat that can be dealt with through sanctions—in fact, Iraq may increase its unconventional warfare and terrorist efforts in reaction to prolonged sanctions. The only answer is strong counterterrorist capabilities and close coordination between the US and its allies in the Southern Gulf.

15

The Threat from Iraqi Weapons of Mass Destruction

It is difficult to estimate the ability of Iraq to recover its delivery capability in regards to weapons of mass destruction. Accurately assessing Iraq's capacity to rebuild its nuclear weapons program is equally problematic. It is clear, however, that Iraq possesses significant potential in these areas and that it is almost certain to apply itself to developing both weapons of mass destruction and a means to deliver them.

The Struggle to Eliminate Iraq's Weapons of Mass Destruction

On April 3, 1991, the UN Security Council passed Resolution 687, which set forth the formal terms for a permanent cease-fire. This resolution required Iraq to renounce and condemn terrorism, repatriate all prisoners, restore all seized and stolen property, establish a fund based on oil revenues as a source for reparations payments to Kuwait, accept a continued arms and economic embargo (except on food, medicine, and essential civilian needs), and accept the eradication of its weapons of mass destruction. Resolution 687 also compelled Iraq to allow the UN to demarcate the Iraqi-Kuwait border, impose a demilitarized zone along that border, and establish an observer force to insure the continued integrity of such a boundary. Saddam later accepted Resolution 687 on April 6, 1991—although he called the resolution "unjust"—and the Resolution was then accepted by the Iraqi National Assembly. The UN Security Council subsequently declared a formal cease-fire to be in effect as of April 11, 1991.

The latter portion of UN Security Council Resolution 687 demanded that Iraq accept the destruction, removal, or dismantling of all biological, chemical and nuclear weapons; all research, development and support facilities associated with these weapons; all stocks of chemical and biological agents; all ballistic missiles with ranges exceeding 150 kilometers;

and all production and repair facilities associated with the manufacturing of such missiles. It linked Iraqi compliance to Iraq's ability to export oil and other materials by stating that once the UN Security Council agreed that Iraq had completed the required actions, the UN prohibitions against the export of commodities and products originating in Iraq would have no further force or effect. To assist in the implementation of Resolution 687 the UN established the UN Special Commission for the purpose of planning the identification and destruction of Iraq's weapons of mass destruction. The UN Special Commission, or UNSCOM, in turn created a force of UN inspectors, while also authorizing the International Atomic Energy Agency (IAEA) to assist UNSCOM in its objective.

From the beginning, Iraq aggressively resisted the UN and IAEA efforts to eliminate its weapons of mass destruction. As early as April 5, 1991, Iraqi forces were detected salvaging equipment for missiles and weapons of mass destruction, as well as cleaning up suspect sites. On April 18, 1991, the Iraqi government lied to the UN in its first declaration regarding its holdings of weapons of mass destruction. Iraq claimed that its post-war stockpile of such weapons consisted of only 52 regular and modified Scud missiles, 10,000 chemical warheads, 1,500 chemical bombs and shells, and 1,000 tons of mustard and nerve gas. The UN later discovered 46,000 surviving chemical weapons, and these discoveries proved Iraq's claims to be grossly inaccurate. Iraq made similar false claims to the International Atomic Energy Agency (IAEA) about its nuclear weapons effort in an April 29, 1991, declaration.

As a result of Resolution 687, a total of 53 UNSCOM and IAEA inspections were completed between June 1991—the date of the first inspection—and March 1993. During this period, the UN made many significant discoveries. The inspections were comprised of 18 nuclear inspections, 15 chemical inspections, 3 biological inspections, 16 ballistic missile inspections, 5 special missions, and one monitoring team visit.[456] Most of these inspections encountered significant Iraqi resistance and lies.

Iraq's continuing attempts at deception resulted in the passage of UN Security Council Resolution 707 on August 15, 1991. Resolution 707 requires Iraq to provide full, final, and complete disclosure of all aspects of its biological, chemical, nuclear, and ballistic missile programs. The Resolution also demands that Iraq allow UN inspectors unconditional and unrestricted access to all areas, facilities, equipment, records, and means which they may wish to inspect. The Resolution further requires that Iraq immediately cease any attempt to conceal, move, or destroy any material or equipment relating to these programs. In addition, Resolution 707 calls on Iraq to halt all nuclear activities of any kind, except for production of isotopes used for agricultural, industrial, or medical purposes.

On October 11, 1991, the UN Security Council also passed Resolution 715, which requires Iraq to meet unconditionally all of its obligations as required in the UN plans for ongoing monitoring of Iraq's compliance with Resolutions 687 and 707.

These resolutions, and UN efforts to implement them, were met with new challenges by the Iraqi government. The Iraqi government sent repeated signals indicating that it intended to regain its capability to deliver weapons of mass destruction. In March 1993, Iraq's continued obfuscation succeeded in prompting Rolf Ekeus, the head of the UN Special Commission, to declare that he was unable to account for 25% of Iraq's known pre-war Scud force.[457] The Iraqi government engineered confrontation after confrontation and backed down only after it had provoked a crisis or the UN Coalition retaliated with force.

When these Iraqi efforts failed, the government changed tactics. On November 26, 1993, Iraq appeared to shift its position and accept the terms of UN Security Council Resolutions 687, 707, and 715. Iraq's Foreign Minister, Mohammed Said Sahaf, sent a letter to the president of the UN Security Council, José Luis Jesus, indicating that Iraq would accept the Security Council requirement that Iraq could only resume its oil exports if it agreed to long-term UN inspection designed to prevent Iraq from resuming its production of weapons of mass destruction. Iraq made this offer only after more than two years of actions demonstrating its intent to cheat on the terms of the cease-fire. Furthermore, Iraq's letter came only days after Iraq had again challenged the demarcation of its border with Kuwait, made new claims to Kuwait, been condemned by the UN for new human rights violations, and attacked the Shi'ites in its southern marshes.[458]

Despite this asserted willingness to accept UN efforts aimed at preventing the resumption of Iraq's weapons of mass destruction program, Iraq continued to try to obfuscate the nature of its efforts and to cheat whenever possible. In May 1995, Deputy Prime Minister Tariq Aziz conditioned further Iraqi cooperation regarding its biological weapons program on certification by UNSCOM that Iraq had complied with the terms of UN resolutions 687 and 715. This ultimatum was rejected by UNSCOM which, in its June 1995 report, declared that, while significant progress had been achieved, Iraq had not yet "met all these terms."[459]

Although UNSCOM refused to certify compliance, Iraq claimed to be pleased with its favorable portrayal in the report, and then responded on July 1 by officially acknowledging an offensive biological weapons program. In its declaration, Iraq admitted to manufacturing a variety of biological agents but denied that any weaponization of these agents occurred. The conciliatory attitude following the June report, however, proved to be short-lived. On July 17, Saddam Hussein himself declared that Iraqi cooperation with UNSCOM would cease pending further progress toward certification. Iraqi Foreign Minister Al-Sahaf subsequently proclaimed August 31 as the deadline for compliance by UNSCOM.[460]

As a result, Rolf Ekeus traveled to Baghdad on August 4, where the Iraqi government presented him with what was termed a "full, final and complete disclosure" of its biological weapons program. During the visit, Deputy Prime Minister Aziz reiterated Iraq's warning that a lack of progress on the lifting of economic sanctions through certification would result in cessation of Iraqi cooperation with UNSCOM. Aziz further urged Mr. Ekeus to inform the Security Council of Iraq's intentions, which he did on August 7. That same day, however, a dramatic development radically altered Iraq's intransigence, while simultaneously undermining confidence in UNSCOM's previous assessments regarding UNSCOM's previous assessments regarding Iraqi capabilities.[461]

On August 7, Lieutenant General Hussein Kamel Majid, who had led part of Iraq's weapons of mass destruction program, defected to Jordan. Baghdad clearly feared that this defection would lead to further disclosures that Iraq was still systematically lying to UNSCOM, and moved quickly to engage in damage control. In an effort to preempt new disclosures and undermine Kamel's credibility, the Iraqi government portrayed him as a rogue officer who had concealed information regarding Iraq's weapons of mass destruction from both UNSCOM and Iraqi officials. They then proceeded to invite Mr. Ekeus to Baghdad to discuss the new information, while simultaneously dropping their August 31 deadline for certification.[462]

Mr. Ekeus arrived in Iraq on August 17 and met with a delegation which included the Deputy Prime Minister and the Foreign Minister. While they revealed that Iraq's efforts in regards to acquiring weapons of mass destruction had been previously understated, no documents were produced for verification. After several complaints by Mr. Ekeus, the Iraqis reported that they had just "discovered" a plethora of documents at the farm of General Kamel. These were subsequently turned over to UNSCOM on August 20. A cursory examination revealed that most of the half-million pages were concerned with Iraq's nuclear program, but that a considerable number also discussed chemical, biological and ballistic missile programs.[463]

These disclosures and past discoveries have revealed the program summarized in Table Ten, along with the similar efforts of Iran and Israel that are locking the region into a pattern of creeping proliferation.[464] There may, however, be many further disclosures to come. In September, 1995, Iraqi officials revealed that other records, whose existence heretofore was denied, did indeed exist. According to UNSCOM, this acknowledgment and the production of the documents was ". . . one of the most significant breakthroughs in the four years of its operations in Iraq."[465] Nevertheless, the new information revealed that Iraq's biological and ballistic missile programs were ". . . larger or more advanced in every dimension than previously declared." Further, in regards to chemical weapons, the UNSCOM report revealed that ". . . Iraq acknowledged a much larger and more advanced program than hitherto admitted for the production and storage of the chemical warfare agent VX."[466]

While these revelations scarcely push UNSCOM back to square one, its October 11, 1995 report to the UN Security Council stated that:[467]

> The revelations cast into doubt the veracity of Iraq's previous declaration in the missile area, including the material balance for proscribed weapons and items. . . . In the chemical weapons area. . . . (whether) Iraq still keeps precursors in storage . . . has not been fully clarified. . . . The Commission must adjust the direction of some of its monitoring activities, especially to prevent Iraq from using its chemical compounds, equipment, and activities for secret acquisition of chemical weapons. Further destruction of some Iraqi chemical assets has to be contemplated.
>
> . . . a hitherto secret offensive biological weapons program in Iraq, comprising large-scale production of biological warfare agents, the filling and deployment of missile warheads and aerial bombs with these agents, as well as biological weapons research and development activities of considerable width and depth. . . . As late as August of this year, Iraq presented to the Commission a formal, but essentially false, declaration on its biological weapons activities. . . . Much remains to be verified with regard to these weapons, in particular the destruction of munitions and bulk agents. . . . The Commission also detected undeclared efforts by Iraq to establish a covert procurement network for activities under monitoring. . . . Questions can still be raised about the intentions of Iraq as regards possible remnants of its proscribed programs.

It has since become clear that Iraq has told new lies—or continued to conceal facts—regarding the destruction of its missile components, radiological weapons, chemical agents, and biological weapons. Iraq has asked UNSCOM to accept its verbal assurances that it destroyed warheads and weapons that include some 500,000 liters of botulism agent and 50,000 liters of anthrax. It has become clear that Iraq set up a clandestine import program following the Gulf War to obtain missile guidance systems and furnaces to make missile components for Scud-type missiles. On November 10, 1995, Jordan intercepted a shipment of Russian-made missile guidance systems, and specialized precision machine tools to Iraq. In December 1995, Jordan also revealed that Iraq had attempted to import 100 sets of advanced missile guidance equipment, including accelerometers and gyroscopes from Russia.[468]

TABLE TEN   Iraqi, Iranian, and Israeli Weapons of Mass Destruction

Iraq
Delivery Systems
- Delivery systems at the time of the Gulf War included:
    - Tu-16 and Tu-22 bombers.
    - MiG-29 fighters.
    - Mirage F-1, MiG-23BM, and Su-22 fighter attack aircraft.
    - A Scud force with a minimum of 819 missiles.
    - Extended range Al-Hussein Scud variants (600 kilometer range) extensively deployed throughout Iraq, and at three fixed sites in northern, western, and southern Iraq.
    - Developing Al-Abbas missiles (900 kilometer range) Al-Abbas which could reach targets in Iran, the Persian Gulf, Israel, Turkey, and Cyprus.
    - Long-range super guns with ranges of up to 600 kilometers.
- Iraq had long-range strike aircraft with refueling capabilities and several hundred regular and improved, longer-range Scud missiles, some with chemical warheads.
- Iraq fired 84 Al-Husayns, 3 Al Husyan-Shorts, and 1 Al-Hijrarah (with a cement warhead) during the Gulf War.
- The Gulf War deprived Iraq of some of its MiG-29s, Mirage F-1s, MiG-23BMs, and Su-22s. Since the end of the war, the UN inspection regime has also destroyed many of Iraq's long-range missiles.
- Iraq, however, maintains a significant delivery capability consisting of:
    - HY-2, SS-N-2, and C-601 cruise missiles, which are unaffected by UN ceasefire terms.
    - FROG-7 rockets with 70 kilometer ranges, also allowed under UN resolutions.
    - Multiple rocket launchers and tube artillery.
    - Several Scud launchers
    - US experts believe Iran may still have components for several dozen extended-range Scud missiles. UN experts believe Iraq is concealing up to 6–7 Scud launchers and 11–24 missile assemblies.
- Iraq has focused its missile programs around the Scud B. During the late 1980s, it began to enlarge the fuel tanks of its Scuds and reduce the weight of its warheads to extend their range beyond the normal 300 kilometer maximum range of the Scud. It also developed a capability to manufacture Scud variants in Iraq, and was working on production facilities for a development of the solid-fueled Argentine Condor missile called the Badr 2000.
- Iraqi missile programs at the time of the Gulf War included:
    - Scud Bs with a maximum range of 300 kilometers.
    - Al Husayns with a 600–650 range.
    - Al Husayn-Shorts (a variant of the Al Husayn) with a 600–650 range
    - Al Hijarahs with a 600–650 range
- Iraqi developmental missile programs at the time of the Gulf War included:

(continues)

TABLE TEN (*continued*)

- Al Fahd. A conversion of the SA-2 with an intended 300 kilometer range. Abandoned in the R&D phase.
- Extended-range Al Fahd. A 500 kilometer range missile abandoned in the development phase after exhibition at the 1989 arms show in Baghdad.
- Al Abbas. A longer version of the Al Husayn with a lighter warhead which was intended to have a 900 kilometer range. Abandoned during R&D.
- Badr 2000. A solid-propellant two-stage missile based on the Condor with a range of 750–1,000 kilometers. Was in R&D when Gulf War began. Facilities were constructed to begin missile production.
- Tammouz 1: a missile based on the Scud with an SA-2 sustainer for a second stage. It had an intended range of 2,000 kilometers but was not carried through to advanced R&D.
- Al Abid: A three-stage space vehicle with a first stage of 5 Al Abbas airframes. Test launch in December, 1989.
- Iraq also engaged in effort to develop a solid-fueled missile with a similar range to the Tammouz.
- Clear evidence that at least one Iraqi long-range missile design was to have a nuclear warhead.
- Iraq attempted to conceal a plant making missile engines from the UN inspectors. It only admitted this plant existed in 1995, raising new questions about how many of its missiles have been destroyed.
- Iraq produced or assembled 80 Scud missiles it its own factories. Some 53 seem to have been unusable, but 10 are still unaccounted for.
- Had design work underway for a nuclear warhead for its long range missiles.
- In addition, Iraq has admitted to:
  - Hiding its capability to manufacture its own Scuds.
  - Iraq claims to have manufactured only 80 missile assemblies, 53 of which were unusable. UNSCOM claims that 10 are unaccounted for.
  - Developing an extended range variant of the FROG-7 called the Laith. The UN claims to have tagged all existing FROG-7s to prevent any extension of their range beyond the UN imposed limit of 150 kilometers for Iraqi missiles.
  - Experimenting with cruise missile technology and ballistic missile designs with ranges up to 3,000 kilometers.
  - Flight testing Al-Hussein missiles with chemical warheads in April 1990.
  - Initiating a research and development program for a nuclear warhead missile delivery system.
  - Successfully developing and testing a warhead separation system.
  - Indigenously developing, testing, and manufacturing advanced rocket engines to include liquid-propellant designs.
  - Conducting research into the development of Remotely Piloted Vehicles (RPVs) for the dissemination of biological agents.
  - Attempting to expand its Ababil-100 program designed to build surface-to-surface missiles with ranges beyond the permitted 100–150 kilometers.

(*continues*)

TABLE TEN (*continued*)

- Starting an indigenous 600mm supergun design effort.
- US and UN officials conclude further that:
- Iraq is concentrating procurement efforts on rebuilding its ballistic missile program using a clandestine network of front companies to obtain the necessary materials and technology from European and Russian firms.
- This equipment is then concealed and stockpiled for assembly concomitant with the end of the UN inspection regime.
- The equipment clandestinely sought by Iraq includes advanced missile guidance components, such as accelerometers and gyroscopes, specialty metals, special machine tools, and a high-tech, French-made, million-dollar furnace designed to fabricate engine parts for missiles.
- Jordan found that Iraq was smuggling missile components through Jordan in early December 1995.
- US satellite photographs reveal that Iraq has rebuilt its Al-Kindi missile research facility.
- Iraq retains the technology it acquired before the war and evidence clearly indicates an ongoing research and development effort, in spite of the UN sanctions regime.
- The fact that UN Security Council Resolution 687 allows Iraq to continue producing and testing short range missiles (less than 150 kilometers range) has meant it can retain significant missile efforts. Iraq's on-going rocket and missile programs include:
  - Luna/Frog-7. A Russian unguided rocket with a 70 kilometer range currently in service and in limited production.
  - Astros II. A Brazilian unguided rocket with a 60 kilometer range currently in service and in limited production.
  - SA-2. A Russian surface-to-air missile which China has demonstrated can be converted into a 300 kilometer range surface-to-surface missile.
  - SA-3. A Russian surface-to-air missile which has some potential for conversion to a surface-to-surface missile.
  - Ababil-50. An Yugoslav-designed Iraqi-produced 50 kilometer range artillery rocket with very limited growth potential.
  - Ababil-100. An Iraqi 100–150 kilometer range system with parallel solid-fuel and liquid-fuel development programs which seems to be used as a "legal" test-bed and foundation for much longerrange missile programs once sanctions are lifted. Many of the liquid-fueled programs are compatible with Scud production.
  - Limited stocks of French- and Chinese-produced land and air launched cruise missiles.

Chemical Weapons
- Produced several thousand tons of chemical weapons from 1984 on. Used chemical weapons extensively against Iran and its own Kurdish population in 1988.

(*continues*)

TABLE TEN   *(continued)*

- Use of Tabun gas against Iranians beginning in 1984 is first confirmed use of nerve agents in war.
- Had roughly 1,000 metric tons of chemical weapons on hand at the time it invaded Kuwait, split equally between blister agents and nerve agents.
- UN destruction efforts at Samara destroyed over 27,000 chemical bombs, rockets, and artillery shells, including 30 Scud missile warheads. About 500 tons of mustard and nerve agents, and thousands of tons of precursor chemicals were burned or chemically neutralized.
- In revelations to the UN, Iraq admitted that, prior to the Gulf War, it:
  - Maintained large stockpiles of mustard gas, and the nerve agents Sarin and Tabun.
  - Produced binary Sarin filled artillery shells, 122mm rockets, and aerial bombs.
  - Manufactured enough precursors to produce 490 tons of the nerve agent VX. These precursors included 65 tons of choline and 200 tons of phosphorous pentasulfide and di-isopropylamine.
  - Tested Ricin, a deadly nerve agent, for use in artillery shells.
  - Had three flight tests of long range Scuds with chemical warheads.
  - Had large VX production effort underway at the time of the Gulf War. The destruction of the related weapons and feedstocks has been claimed by Iraq, but not verified by UNSCOM.
- The majority of Iraq's chemical agents were manufactured at a supposed pesticide plant located at Samara. Various, other production facilities were also used, including those at Salman Pak, Muthanna, and Habbiniyah. Though severely damaged during the war, the physical plant for many of these facilities has been rebuilt.
  - Iraq possessed the technology to produce a variety of other persistent and non-persistent agents.
- The Gulf War and after
  - UN inspection regime may have largely eliminated these stockpiles and reduced production capability.
  - US experts believe Iraq has concealed significant stocks of precursors. It also appears to retain significant amounts of production equipment dispersed before, or during, Desert Storm and not recovered by the UN.
- Iraq has developed basic chemical warhead designs for Scud missiles, rockets, bombs, and shells. Iraq also has spray dispersal systems.
- Iraq maintains extensive stocks of defensive equipment.
- The UN maintains that Iraq is not currently producing chemical agents, but the UN is also concerned that Iraq has offered no evidence that it has destroyed its VX production capability and/or stockpile.
- Further, Iraq retains the technology it acquired before the war and evidence clearly indicates an ongoing research and development effort, in spite of the UN sanctions regime.

(continues)

TABLE TEN   *(continued)*

Biological Weapons
- Systematically lied about biological weapons effort until 1995. First stated that had small defensive efforts, but no offensive effort. In July 1995, admitted it had a major offensive effort. In October 1995, finally admitted major weaponization effort.
- The August 1995 defection of Lieutenant General Hussein Kamel Majid, formerly in charge of Iraq's weapons of mass destruction, led Iraq to reveal the extent of its biological weapons program.
- Iraq reported to the UN in August 1995 that it had produced 90,000 liters of Botulinium toxin, 8,300 liters of Anthrax, and significant quantities of other agents.
- Iraq has, however, continued to lie about its biological weapons effort.
- It has claimed the effort is head by Dr. Taha, a woman who only headed a subordinate effort. It has not admitted to any help by foreign personnel or contractors. It has claimed to have destroyed its weapons, but the one site UNSCOM inspectors visited showed no signs of such destruction and was later said to be the wrong site. It has claimed only 50 people were employed full time, but the scale of the effort would have required several hundred.
- Reports indicate that Iraq tested at least 7 principal biological agents for use against humans.
  - Anthrax, Botulinum, and Aflatoxin known to be weaponized.
  - Looked at viruses, bacteria, and fungi. Examined the possibility of weaponizing Gas Gangrene and Mycotoxins. Some field trials were held of these agents.
  - Examined foot and mouth disease, haemorrhagic conjunctivitis virus, rotavirus, and camel pox virus.
  - Conducted research on a "wheat pathogen" and a Mycotoxin similar to "yellow rain" defoliant.
  - The "wheat smut" was first produced at Al Salman, and then put in major production during 1987–1988 at a plant near Mosul. Iraq claims the program was abandoned.
- The defection of Hussein Kamel prompted Iraq to admit that it:
  - Imported 39 tons of growth media for biological agents obtained from three European firms. According to UNSCOM, 17 tons remains unaccounted for. Each ton can be used to produce 10 tons of bacteriological weapons.
  - Imported type cultures which can be modified to develop biological weapons from the US.
  - Had a laboratory- and industrial-scale capability to manufacture various biological agents including the bacteria which cause anthrax and botulism; Aflatoxin, a naturally occurring carcinogen; clostridium perfringens, a gangrene-causing agent; the protein toxin ricin; tricothecene mycotoxins, such as T-2 and DAS; and an anti-wheat fungus known as wheat cover smut. Iraq also conducted research into the rotavirus, the camel pox virus and the virus which causes haemorrhagic conjunctivitis.

(continues)

TABLE TEN   *(continued)*

- Created at least seven primary production facilities including the Sepp Institute at Muthanna, the Ghazi Research Institute at Amaria, the Daura Foot and Mouth Disease Institute, and facilities at Al-Hakim, Salman Pak Taji, and Fudaliyah. According to UNSCOM, weaponization occurred primarily at Muthanna through May 1987 (largely Botulinum), and then moved to Al Salman. (Anthrax). In March 1988 a plant was open at Al Hakim, and in 1989 an Aflatoxin plant was set up at Fudaliyah.
- Manufactured 6,000 liters of concentrated Botulinum toxin and 8,425 liters of anthrax at Al-Hakim during 1990; 5400 liters of concentrated Botulinum toxin at the Daura Foot and Mouth Disease Institute from November 1990 to January 15, 1991; 400 liters of concentrated Botulinum toxin at Taji; and 150 liters of concentrated anthrax at Salman Pak. Produced 1,850 liters of Aflatoxin in solution at Fudaliyah.
- Produced 340 liters of concentrated clostridium perfringens, a gangrene-causing biological agent, beginning in August 1990.
- Produced 10 liters of concentrated Ricin at Al Salam. Claim to have abandoned work after tests failed.
- Relocated much of its biological weapons effort after Coalition strikes on its facilities at Al Kindi and Salman Pak to Al Hakim and other facilities. This makes tracking the weapons effort extremely difficult.
- Had at least 79 civilian facilities capable of playing some role in biological weapons production still extant in 1995.
- Extensive weaponization program
  - Conducted field trials, weaponization tests, and live firings of 122mm rockets armed with anthrax and Botulinum toxin from March 1988 to May 1990.
  - Total production reached at least 19,000 liters of concentrated Botulinum (10,000 liters filled into munitions); 8,500 liters of concentrated Anthrax (6,500 liters filled into munitions); and 2,500 liters of concentrated Aflatoxin (1,850 liters filled into munitions).
  - Weaponized at least three biological agents for use in the Gulf War. The weaponization consisted of 100 bombs and 15 missile warheads loaded with Botulinum; 50 R-400 air-delivered bombs and 10 missile warheads loaded with anthrax.
  - Also had 16 missile warheads loaded with Aflatoxin, a natural carcinogen. The warheads were designed for operability with the Al-Hussein Scud variant.
  - A total of at least 166 bombs were filled with some biological agent. Iraq produced at least 191 bombs and missile warheads with biological agents.
  - Developed and stored drops tanks ready for use for three aircraft or RPV s with the capability of dispersing 2,000 liters of anthrax. Development took place in December 1990. Claimed later that tests showed were ineffective.
  - Tested ricin, a deadly protein toxin, for use in artillery shells.
- The UN claims that Iraq has offered no evidence to corroborate its claims that it destroyed its stockpile of biological agents after the Gulf War. Further, Iraq

(continues)

TABLE TEN   *(continued)*

retains the technology it acquired before the war and evidence clearly indicates an ongoing research and development effort, in spite of the UN sanctions regime.

- UN currently inspects 79 sites—5 used to make weapons before war; 5 vaccine or pharmaceutical sites; 35 research and university sites; thirteen breweries, distilleries, and dairies with dual-purpose capabilities; eight diagnostic laboratories.
- Retains laboratory capability to manufacture various biological agents including the bacteria which cause anthrax, botulism, tularemia and typhoid.
- Many additional civilian facilities capable of playing some role in biological weapons production.

Nuclear Weapons
- Sought to buy a plutonium production reactor similar to the reactor France used in its nuclear weapons program in early 1970s.
- Contracted with France to build Osirak and Isis reactors in 1976, as part of Tuwaitha complex near Baghdad.
- Osirak raid in June 1981 prevented from acquiring reactors for weapons use. Led Iraq to refocus efforts on producing highly enriched uranium.
- Inspections by UN teams have found evidence of two successful weapons designs, a neutron initiator, explosives and triggering technology needed for production of bombs, plutonium processing technology, centrifuge technology, Calutron enrichment technology, and experiments with chemical separation technology.
  - Iraq used Calutron, centrifuges, plutonium processing, chemical defusion and foreign purchases to create new production capability after Israel destroyed most of Osiraq.
  - Iraq established a centrifuge enrichment system in Rashidya and conducted research into the nuclear fuel cycle to facilitate development of a nuclear device.
- After invading Kuwait, Iraq attempted to accelerate its program to develop a nuclear weapon by using radioactive fuel from French- and Russian-built reactors.
- Made a crash effort beginning in September 1990 to recover enriched fuel from its supposedly safe-guarded French and Russian reactors, with the goal of producing a nuclear weapon by April 1991. The program was only halted after Coalition air raid destroyed key facilities on January 17, 1991.
- Iraq conducted research into the production of a radiological weapon, which disperses lethal radioactive material without initiating a nuclear explosion.
  - Orders were given in 1987 to explore the use of radiological weapons for area denial in the Iran-Iraq War.
  - Three prototype bombs were detonated at test sites—one as a ground level static test and two others dropped from aircraft.
  - Iraq claims the results were disappointing and the project was shelved but has no records or evidence to prove this.

(continues)

TABLE TEN (*continued*)

- UN teams have found and destroyed, or secured, new stockpiles of illegal enriched material, major production and R&D facilities, and equipment—including Calutron enriching equipment.
- UNSCOM believes that Iraq's nuclear program has been largely disabled and remains incapacitated, but warns that Iraq retains substantial technology and established a clandestine purchasing system in 1990 that it has used to import forbidden components since the Gulf War.
- Iraq still retains the technology developed before the Gulf War and US experts believe an ongoing research and development effort continues, in spite of the UN sanctions regime.
- A substantial number of declared nuclear weapons components and research equipment has never been recovered. There is no reason to assume that Iraqi declarations were comprehensive.

Iran
Delivery Systems
- Used regular Scud extensively during Iran-Iraq War. Fired nearly 100 Scud B missiles during 1985–1988. Scud missiles were provided by Libya and North Korea.
- Has 6–12 Scud launchers and up to 200 Scud B (R-17E) missiles with 230–310 km range.
- Has new long range North Korean Scuds with ranges near 500 kilometers.
- Has created shelters and tunnels in its coastal areas to store Scud and other missiles in hardened sites and reduce their vulnerability to air attack.
- Can now assemble missiles using foreign made components.
- Developing an indigineous missile production capability with both solid and liquid fueled missiles. Seems to be seeking capability to produce MRBMs.
- May cooperate with Syria in developing capability to manufacture missiles.
- Probably has ordered North Korean No Dong missile which can carry nuclear and biological missile ranges of up to 900 kilometers. Can reach virtually any target in Gulf, Turkey, and Israel, although CIA now estimates deliveries will only begin in 1997–1999.[469]
- Has recently bought CSS-8 surface-to-surface missiles (converted SA-2s) from China with ranges of 130–150 kilometers.
- May have place order for PRC-made M-9 missile (280–620 kilometers range). More likely that PRC firms are giving assistance in developing indigenous missile R&D and production facilities.
- Has Chinese sea and land-based anti-ship cruise missiles. Iran fired 10 such missiles at Kuwait during Iran-Iraq War, hitting one US-flagged tanker.
- Su-24 long-range strike fighters with range-payloads roughly equivalent to US F-111 and superior to older Soviet medium bombers.
- Iranian made IRAN 130 rocket with 150+ kilometers range.
- Iranian Oghab (Eagle) rocket with 40+ kilometers range.

(*continues*)

TABLE TEN   *(continued)*

- New SSM with 125 mile range may be in production, but could be modified FROG.
- F-4D/E fighter bombers with capability to carry extensive payloads to ranges of 450 miles.
- Can modify HY-2 Silkworm missiles and SA-2 surface-to-air missiles to deliver weapons of mass destruction.
- Large numbers of multiple rocket launchers and tube artillery for short range delivery of chemical weapons.
- Experimenting with cruise missile development.

Chemical Weapons
- At least two major research and production facilities.
- Made limited use of chemical weapons at end of the Iran-Iraq War.
- Began to create stockpiles of cyanide (cyanogen chloride), phosgene, and mustard gas weapons after 1985. Include bombs and artillery.
- Was able to produce blister (mustard) and blood (cyanide) agents by 1987; used them in artillery shells against Iraqi troops.
- Production of nerve gas weapons started no later than 1994.
- Has produced a minimum of several hundred tons of blister, blood, and choking agents. Some are weaponized for support of ground troops. Others are used in chemical bombs.
- Has increased chemical defensive and offensive warfare training since 1993.
- Seeking to buy more advanced chemical defense equipment.
- Has sought to buy specialized equipment on world market to develop indigenous capability to produce advanced feedstocks fo nerve weapons.

Biological Weapons
- Extensive laboratory and research capability.
- Weapons effort documented as early as 1982.
- Bioresearch effort sophisticated enough to produce biological weapons as lethal as small nuclear weapons. Working on toxins and organisms with biological warfare capabilities.
- Has biological support structure capable of producing many different biological weapons. Has evolved from piecemeal acquisition of biological equipment to pursuing complete biological production plants.
- Seems to have the production facilities to make dry storable weapons. This would allow it to develop suitable missile warheads and bombs and covert devices.
- May be involved in active weapons production, but no evidence to date that this is the case.
- Some universities and research centers may be linked to biological weapons program.

Nuclear Weapons
- In 1984, revived nuclear weapons program begun under Shah.

(continues)

TABLE TEN *(continued)*

- Received significant West German and Argentine corporate support in some aspects of nuclear technology during the Iran-Iraq War.
- Limited transfers of centrifuge and other weapons related technology from PRC, possibly Pakistan.
- Stockpiles of uranium and mines in Yazd area.
- Seems to have attempted to buy fissile material from Kazakhstan.
- Has sought heavy water research reactors with no application to peaceful lightwater power reactor development.
- Has sought to obtain uranium enrichment and spent fuel reprocessing technology whose main applications are in weapons programs.
- Russian agreement to build up to four reactors, beginning with a complex at Bushehr—with two 1,000–1,200 megawatt reactors and two 465 megawatt reactors, and provide significant nuclear technology.
- Chinese agreement to provide significant nuclear technology transfer and possible sale of two 300 megawatt pressurized water reactors.
- No way to tell when current efforts will produce a weapon, and unclassified lists of potential facilities have little credibility. We simply do not know where Iran is developing its weapons.
- IAEA has found no indications of weapons effort, but found no efforts in Iraq in spring of 1990. IAEA only formally inspects Iran's small research reactors. Its visits to other Iranian sites are not thorough enough to confirm or deny whether Iran has such activities.
- Timing of weapons acquisition depends heavily on whether Iran can buy fissile material—if so it has the design capability and can produce weapons in 1–2 years—or must develop the capability to process Plutonium or enrich Uranium—in which case, it is likely to be 5–10 years.

Israel
Delivery Systems
- New IRBM/ICBM range high payload booster in development with South Africa. Status unknown.
- Up to 50 "Jericho I" missiles deployed in shelters on mobile launchers with up to 400 miles range with a 2,200 pound payload, and with possible nuclear warhead storage nearby. Unverified claims that up to 100 missiles are deployed west of Jerusalem.
- Jericho II missiles now deployed, and some were brought to readiness for firing during the Gulf War. These missiles seem to include a single stage follow-on to the Jericho I and a multistage longer range missile. The latter missile seems to have a range of up to 900 miles with a 2,200 pound payload, and may be a cooperative development with South Africa. (Extensive reporting of such cooperation in press during October 25 and 26, 1989).
- Jericho II missile production facility at Be'er Yakov.
- A major missile test took place on September 14, 1989. It was either a missile test or failure of Ofeq-2 satellite.

(continues)

TABLE TEN   *(continued)*

- Work on development of TERCOM type smart warheads. Possible cruise missile guidance developments using GPS navigation systems.
- F-15, F-16, F-4E, and Phantom 2000 fighter-bombers capable of long range refueling and of carrying nuclear and chemical bombs.
- Lance missile launchers and 160 Lance missiles with 130 kilometers range.
- MAR-290 rocket with 30 kilometers range believed to be deployed.
- MAR-350 surface-to-surface missile with range of 56 miles and 735 lb. payload believed to have completed development or to be in early deployment.
- Israel seeking super computers for Technion Institute (designing ballistic missile RVs), Hebrew University (may be engaged in hydrogen bomb research), and Israeli Military Industries (maker of "Jericho II" and Shavit booster).

Chemical Weapons
- Mustard and nerve gas production facility established in 1982 in the restricted area in the Sinai near Dimona. May have additional facilities. May have capacity to produce other gases. Probable stocks of bombs, rockets, and artillery.
- Extensive laboratory research into gas warfare and defense.
- Development of defensive systems includes Shalon Chemical Industries protection gear, Elbit Computer gas detectors, and Bezal R&D air crew protection system.
- Extensive field exercises in chemical defense.
- Gas masks stockpiled, and distributed to population with other civil defense instructions during Gulf War.
- Warhead delivery capability for bombs, rockets, and missiles, but none now believed to be equipped with chemical agents.

Biological Weapons
- Extensive research into weapons and defense.
- Ready to quickly produce biological weapons, but no reports of active production effort.

Nuclear Weapons
- Director of CIA indicated in May 1989, that Israel may be seeking to construct a thermonuclear weapon.
- Estimates of numbers and types of weapons differ sharply.
- At least a stockpile of 60–80 plutonium weapons. May have well over 100 nuclear weapons assemblies, with some weapons with yields over 100 Kilotons, and some with possible ER variants or variable yields. Stockpile of up to 200–300 weapons is possible.
- Possible facilities include production of weapons grade Plutonium at Dimona, nuclear weapons design facility at Soreq (south of Tel Aviv), missile test facility at Palmikhim, nuclear armed missile storage facility at Kefar Zekharya, nuclear weapons assembly facility at Yodefat, and tactical nuclear weapons storage facility at Eilabun in eastern Galilee.

(continues)

TABLE TEN   *(continued)*

Missile Defenses
- Patriot missiles with future PAC-3 upgrade to reflect lessons of the Gulf War.
- Arrow 2 two-stage ATBM with slant intercept ranges at altitudes of 8–10 and 50 kilometers speeds of up to Mach 9, plus possible development of the Rafale AB-10 close in defense missile with ranges of 10–20 kilometers and speeds of up to Mach 4.5. Tadiran BM/C4I system and "Music" phased array radar. Israel plans to deploy two batteries of the Arrow to cover Israel, each with four launchers, to protect up to 85% of its population.[470]

Advanced Intelligence Systems
- The Shavit I launched Israel's satellite payload on September 19, 1989. It used a three stage booster system capable of launching a 4,000 pound payload over 1,200 miles or a 2,000 pound payload over 1,800 miles.
- Ofeq 2 launched in April 1990—one day after Saddam Hussein threatens to destroy Israel with chemical weapons if it should attack Baghdad.
- Launched first intelligence satellite on April 5, 1995, covering Syria, Iran, and Iraq in orbit every 90 minutes. The Ofeq 3 satellite is a 495 pound system launched using the Shavit launch rocket, and is believed to carry an imagery system. Its orbit pass over or near Damascus, Tehran, and Baghdad.[471]

Source: Prepared by Anthony H. Cordesman, Co-Director, Middle East Program, CSIS.

The UN has set up an import-export monitoring system to try to deny Iraq the equipment it needs to rebuild its program to deploy weapons of mass destruction. The UN Security Council approved this system in Security Council Resolution 1051 on March 27, 1996, and acted on the basis it was implementing Security Council Resolution 715, which was passed as part of the cease-fire in 1991. The new regime requires exporters to Iraq to notify their governments, the UN, and IEA of exports of dual use items, requires Iraq to declare its intentions in using such items, and empowers UN inspectors to inspect all shipments before they arrive in Iraq. No one, however, has any illusions about the effectiveness of the system. As Rolf Ekeus put it,[472]

> It is clear that prohibited components, as opposed to prohibited components, still exist. (Iraq) retains a weapons option. The issue is not so much what Baghdad now possesses but what it could produce quickly were the decision made to do so.

Iraq's Future Missile Capabilities

Iraq fired a total of 88 long-range missiles during the Gulf War. These included 84 Al-Husayns, 3 Al Husyan-Shorts, and 1 Al-Hijrarah (with a cement warhead). These missiles were the product of a massive development effort that Iraq began during the Iran-Iraq War. During the mid-1980s, Iraq began to enlarge the fuel tanks of its Scuds and reduce the weight of its warheads to extend their range beyond the normal 300 kilometer maximum range of the Scud. It also developed a capability to manufacture Scud variants in Iraq, and attempted to develop production facilities for the development of the solid-fueled Argentine Condor missile called the Badr 2000.

Buy the time of the Gulf War, Iraq had chemical and biological warheads for its missiles, and was attempting to design a nuclear warhead. It had at least 11 missile programs that were deployed or in development:[473]

- Standard Scud B: Russian and Chinese made missile and missile assemblies with a maximum range of 300 kilometers.
- Al Husayn: An extended-range Scud variants with a 600–650 range.
- Al Husayn-Shorts: An extended-range Scud variant of the Al Husayn with a 600–650 range.
- Al Hijarah: An extended-range Scud variants with a 600–650 range.
- Al Fahd: A conversion of the SA-2 with an intended 300 kilometer range. Abandoned in the R&D phase.
- Extended-range Al Fahd: A 500 kilometer range missile abandoned in the development phase after exhibition at the 1989 arms show in Baghdad.
- Al Abbas: A longer version of the Al Husayn with a lighter warhead which was intended to have a 900 kilometer range. Abandoned during R&D.
- Badr 2000: A solid-propellant, two-stage missile based on the Condor with a range of 750–1,000 kilometers. Was in R&D when Gulf War began. Facilities were constructed to begin missile production.
- Tammuz 1: a missile based on the Scud with an SA-2 sustainer for a second stage. It had an intended range of 2,000 kilometers but was not carried through to advanced R&D.
- Al Abid: A three stage space vehicle with a first stage of 5 Al Abbas airframes. Test launched in December 1989.
- A solid fueled missile with a similar range to the Tammuz.

Events since the war have clarified many aspects of Iraq's pre-war missile capability, but Iraq has lied about its efforts at virtually every stage of the UN effort to destroy its capacity to deliver long-range missiles. In its initial report to the UN after the war, Iraq declared that it had 52 ballistic missiles, 38 launchers, 30 chemical-filled warheads, and 23 conventionally armed warheads at five sites.[474]

In the months and years that followed, the UN found the facts were very different. Although Iraq continued to make efforts to hide its missile holdings and production facilities. The UN Special Commission (UNSCOM) identified at least 17 facilities where the Iraqi government had conducted research, production, and testing and repair of ballistic missiles, launchers, and rocket fuel.[475] By February 1992, the UN had destroyed over 80 missiles, 11 missile decoys, dozens of fixed and mobile launchers, 8 missile transporters, and 146 missile storage units.[476]

Iraqi efforts to deceive UNSCOM continued long after these discoveries. They included the deployment of special fuel trucks that were used for launching Scud missiles to areas outside of Baghdad in February 1993 and attempts to deny UN inspectors access to Iraqi missile ranges in June and July 1993.[477] In 1994, UNSCOM's insistence on the destruction of five pieces of manufacturing equipment designed to produce missile engines evoked the Iraqi challenges and delays before Iraq finally complied. At the same time, satellite photographs showed that Iraq had rebuilt its Al-Kindi missile research facility.[478]

In spite of these efforts, the UN team had accounted for over 800 Scud missile assemblies by early 1995, including those Iraq fired during the Iran-Iraq and Gulf wars. A long series of discoveries led UNSCOM to conclude in the spring of 1995 that it would soon be able to certify that it had destroyed Iraq's missile production and delivery capabilities. The UN, however, was relying on import and usage data that UNSCOM had discovered to estimate Iraq's total inventory of Scud variants at 819. It used this figure as a target for its efforts to dismantle or destroy Iraq's Scuds although it was controversial even among members of the UNSCOM team. Many experts believed the UN underestimated the number of Iraqi Scuds. In fact, in testimony before Congress in January 1992, the Director of the CIA estimated that Iraq might still possess "hundreds" of missiles.[479]

Iraq's revelations, following Hussein Kamel's defection, showed that such outside experts were right. The documents Iraq surrendered to UNSCOM in August 1995 revealed a number of previously undisclosed missile projects. These projects included modification and production of missile systems (Project 144), production of missile guidance and control systems (Project Karama), production of liquid-propellant rocket engines (Project 1728), and development of a two-stage solid-propellant missile (Project Badr-2000).[480] Iraq also admitted that it had manufactured some of its own Scuds before the Gulf War and had a previously undisclosed liquid-fuel engine production capability, and that it was developing new long-range missiles with ranges of 900 kilometers, 3,000 kilometers, and 5,000 kilometers, and a nuclear warhead for its Al Hussein missile.[481]

UNSCOM found that Iraq had retained undeclared liquid fuel engine manufacturing facilities for its long-range missiles, and that Iraq had lied about the number of missile warheads it had destroyed before the

UNSCOM destruction effort began. It found that Iraq had built or assembled 80 Scud-type missiles using its own engines, although 53 were unusable. It also found that 10 engines were unaccounted for. In the fall of 1995, UNSCOM also found that Iraq had established a clandestine purchasing network to buy missile components in 1990, and that it had maintained this network following the Gulf War.[482] As a result, UNSCOM reported that the documents Iraq had provided did ". . . not contain the full record of proscribed missile activities," which could have established the extent of Iraqi production.[483]

It also became clear that Iraq had conducted a massive black market smuggling effort after the cease-fire and had created a whole new series of compartmented missile, nuclear, chemical, and biological weapons programs which used new locations and which were not tied to the programs it had created before the Gulf War. In November 1995, Jordan intercepted a major shipment of missile guidance components and manufacturing equipment. This shipment was worth nearly $25 million. It included 115 gyroscopes bound for Iraq, and a total of 10 crates worth of equipment that were air freighted from Moscow to Amman on November 10, 1995. The shipment included entire guidance canisters for Russian ICBMs, although these guidance systems would have required significant reengineering to be used with the much slower reacting missiles Iraq had developed at the time of the Gulf War.

Further, Weaam Gharbiyeh, the Palestinian who had brought the equipment into Jordan as "electrical equipment," was found to have imported significant amounts of additional equipment for chemical weapons. These discoveries proved to be part of a much broader pattern of imports from nations like Russia, Germany, and France, and created further uncertainties about how many missiles and warheads Iraq had produced and needed to be destroyed.

This series of revelations led Ambassador Rolf Ekeus—the head of UNSCOM—to declare that Iraq's missile and biological weapons programs were ". . . larger and more advanced in every dimension than previously declared." UNSCOM's October, 1995, report stated that there was ". . . no firm basis for establishing at this time a reliable accounting of Iraq's proscribed missiles."[484]

Iraq's advanced covert procurement system has become a subject of increasing concern. While the UN has refused to name publicly the countries and firms found to be involved in this effort, UN and US officials have stated privately that France, Germany, Central European and Russian firms were most active. One UN official specifically implicated Ukraine, while a senior US official has expressed concern over recent Russian sales of missile-related equipment to Iraq.[485] UNSCOM recognized the importance of these post-war smuggling efforts in its December

21, 1995, report to the UN Security Council, and Ambassador Ekeus showed the Council a gyroscope that Iraqi engineers had thrown into the Tigris in an effort to conceal it from the UN inspectors.[486]

Iraq's missile program has been closely tied to its efforts to produce weapons of mass destruction. The UN found that Iraq not only possessed the ability to launch missiles with chemical warheads, but had conducted at least three flight tests of Al-Hussein Scud variants with chemical warheads. The UN found the 30 chemical warheads for Iraq's Scud missiles stored in the Dujael area, some 18 miles away from the position Iraq had declared. Sixteen of the warheads carried a unitary nerve agent and fourteen carried binary agents.[487]

The warheads were, however, crudely manufactured and had limited carrying capacity. According to some experts, they possessed inadequate welds and might have tumbled or disintegrated in flight. The warheads also lacked the technology to disseminate chemical agents effectively and reliably. There was little internal structure to the warhead, except for three asymmetrically placed metal bars. The chemical agent was placed in a container within the cone that left substantial empty space between the agent and the cone, and the design did not stabilize the liquid agent. As a result, any sudden acceleration or deceleration during the flight could have caused the warhead to tumble or break up. Even so, it is likely that at least some of these warheads would have penetrated to their targets and released enough agent to make them successful as a terror weapon.[488]

In addition to chemical warheads, Iraq developed a significant stockpile of biological missile warheads. The August 1995 defection of Lieutenant General Hussein Kamel Majid, formerly in charge of Iraq's weapons of mass destruction, prompted a number of revelations by the Iraqi government. Chief among these was a detailed accounting of the number of missiles armed with biological agents and the type of agents employed. Iraq admitted to arming 10 missiles with anthrax-loaded warheads for the Al-Hussein missile, and another 15 missiles with Botulinum-loaded warheads in December 1990 for possible use during the Gulf War.[489]

These discoveries are a grim warning. It appears almost certain that Iraq will recover some of its Scud launch capabilities relatively soon after the end of the UN inspection effort. According to both UN officials and US experts, Iraq has used its clandestine procurement network and front companies to put major resources into rebuilding its ballistic missile program—a level of effort that may be worth several hundred million dollars a year. The equipment involved includes advanced missile guidance components, such as accelerometers and gyroscopes, specialty metals, special machine tools, and a high-tech, French-made furnace designed to fabricate missile engine parts. According to US and UN officials, these imports are promptly concealed and stored once obtained. Furthermore, UNSCOM indicates that Iraq is exploiting the fact that the cease-fire agreement allows it to retain short-range missiles (with ranges of 150 kilometers or less), to test and modify missiles and components to produce much longer-range missiles in the future.

Iraq is known to have six rocket and ballistic missile programs with ranges under 150 kilometers and which are permitted under the terms of UN Security Council Resolution 687:[490]

- Luna/Frog-7. A Russian unguided rocket with a 70 kilometer range currently in service and in limited production.
- Astros II. A Brazilian unguided rocket with a 60 kilometer range currently in service and in limited production.
- SA-2. A Russian surface-to-air missile which China has demonstrated can be converted into a 300 kilometer range surface-to-surface missile.
- SA-3. A Russian surface-to-air missile which has some potential for conversion to a surface-to-surface missile.
- Ababil-50. A Yugoslav-designed, Iraqi-produced 50 kilometer range artillery rocket with very limited growth potential.
- Ababil-100. An Iraqi 100–150 kilometer range system with parallel solid-fuel and liquid fuel development programs which seems to be used as a "legal" test-bed and foundation for much longer range missile programs once sanctions are lifted. Many of the liquid fueled programs are compatible with Scud production.

It is relatively easy to increase the range and payload of a system like the Ababil 100 and to use it to test warhead, guidance, and control systems. The ranges involved also allow this to be done without telemetry. These efforts are another factor that will allow Iraq to rapidly reestablish its missile program once the UN inspections regime is lifted.[491]

US intelligence experts also believe that Iraq is still concealing several Scud launchers and several dozen extended-range Scud missile assemblies, as well as some of the manufacturing equipment, test equipment, and parts purchased before the war. Some US experts also assert that Iraq could be hiding these missiles in underground storage sites built before and after the Gulf War.[492] If so, such missiles are likely to remain operational. An analysis of East German Scuds revealed that such missiles have an unopened shelf-life of up to twenty years.[493] What is more uncertain is whether Iraq could obtain the liquid fuel and oxidizer necessary to launch any covert holdings of Scud missiles without building a new facility. According to one expert, Iraq obtained all of its fuel and oxidizer supplies from the former Soviet Union before the Gulf War and such supplies only have a storage life of 12–18 months.[494]

If Iraq's Scud force does become operational again, it will face new point defenses based on the improved Patriot missile. The US might also be able to preclude large scale Scud assaults by attacking their launch sites with US air power. Currently, however, the US has no way to prevent Iraq from confronting the UN, or some future coalition, with the same "Scud hunt" problems encountered by the US-led coalition during the Gulf War. Now, as then, it would be almost impossible for the US to hunt down and destroy enough of Iraq's missile capabilities to stop all attacks.

Iraq's concealment and import efforts provide strong evidence that it continues to attempt to acquire more lethal chemical and biological warheads for its ballistic missiles. Iraq may even be able to deploy chemical and biological warheads rapidly for its missiles that are superior to those it possessed during the Gulf War. Iraq has had five years to carry out research on such warheads, and they could be produced covertly in laboratories and other non-military facilities.[495]

Iraq may also be changing its missile employment doctrine. Some experts believe Iraq may have concluded that its Scud variants have lost much of their "terror effect" if they are only equipped with conventional warheads. Iraq may also determine that even chemical warheads have a limited terror or deterrent value, prompting it to concentrate on nuclear and biological warheads. While nerve gas warheads might kill several hundred people with a lucky strike and affect some critical targets, Iraq would not be able to launch a large enough volley to achieve critical war-fighting damage until it can access a major source of resupply for its present holdings of missiles and missile parts.

Iraq's capability to develop cruise missiles and UAVs presents a further complication. Cruise missiles and UAVs offer important ways of producing delivery systems while avoiding many of the UN constraints on ballistic missiles, and Iraq experimented with weaponizing UAVs and had much of the technology needed to produce cruise missile weapons before the Gulf War. It was working on modifications of the Chinese Silkworm (HY-2) cruise missile, designed to have ranges of 75, 150, and 200 kilometers, at its Nasr missile factory before the war.[496] It used remotely piloted vehicles (RPVs) during the Gulf War, which led to some initial fears that these RPVs might be equipped with chemical or biological agents. While Iraq has no more capability than Iran to develop and deploy a Tomahawk TLAM-like missile, it may be able to build a missile about half the size of a small fighter aircraft with a payload of about 500 kilograms. Iraq already has the technology needed for fusing and equipping such a system with CBW and cluster war-

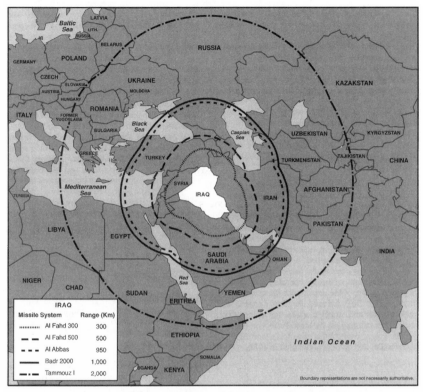

IRAQ	
Missile System	Range (Km)
Al Fahd 300	300
Al Fahd 500	500
Al Abbas	950
Badr 2000	1,000
Tammouz I	2,000

MAP THREE   The Range of Iraq's Missile Developments at the Time of the Gulf War. *Source:* Office of the Secretary of the Defense, *Proliferation: Threat and Reponse,* Washington, Department of Defense, April 1996, p. 19.

heads. Development of navigation systems and jet engines could be a major problem.

Iraq should be able to solve the problem of acquiring a suitable guidance system over time. Iraq's current inertial navigation systems (INS) would introduce errors of at least several kilometers at ranges of 1,000 kilometers, and the risk of total guidance failure could exceed two-thirds of the missiles fired. Iraq, however, has already made a major effort to acquire better guidance through its clandestine procurement network. In December 1995, Jordan revealed that Iraq had attempted to smuggle in at least 100 key guidance components from Russia, including gyroscopes and accelerometers. In spite of Iraq's growing economic crisis, the shipment was worth at least $25 million. Further, UNSCOM revealed that Iraq had already received similar components, and has thrown missile gyroscopes into a canal of the Tigris near Baghdad in an effort to conceal its program.[497]

US studies indicate that a commercial differential global positioning system (GPS), integrated with the inertial navigation system and a radar altimeter, might produce an accuracy as good as 15 meters.[498] Some existing remotely piloted vehicles, such as the South African Skua, already claim such performance. Moreover, commercial technology is becoming available for differential global positioning system guidance with accuracies of two to five meters. Iraq would also have to import cruise missile engines. While there are many suitable, commercially available reciprocating and gas turbine engines, finding a reliable and efficient turbofan engine for such an application might be difficult. It is doubtful that Iraq could design and build such an engine, although it has most of the needed design and manufacture skills.

The ease of building cruise missiles should not be exaggerated. Airframe-engine-warhead integration and testing is challenging and possibly beyond Iraq's manufacturing skills. A cruise missile, however, is inherently easier to integrate than a long-range ballistic missile. It is also less detectable, if using no telemetry or coded telemetry.[499] If Iraq can develop such weapons, they could reach a wide range of targets. A system deployed in border areas with only a 500 kilometer range could cover half of Iran, southeastern Turkey, all of Kuwait, the Persian Gulf coast of Saudi Arabia, Bahrain and most of Qatar, the northern UAE, and northern Oman. A system with a 1,200 kilometer range could reach Israel, the eastern two-thirds of Turkey, most of Saudi Arabia and all of the other Southern Gulf states, including Oman. Such a system could also be programmed to avoid major air defense concentrations at a sacrifice of about 20% of its range.

Iraq's Future Chemical Weapons Capabilities

Iraq has produced thousands of tons of chemical weapons since the early 1980s, many at facilities at Samara and Al Habbinyah. It used many of these weapons against the Iranians and the Kurds in the mid and late 1980s. It first used mustard gas against Iranian troops in 1983, using weapons produced in civil laboratories and facilities at a limited scale. It began to use Tabun nerve gas in 1984, and dropped the first nerve gas bombs in modern warfare. While it initially failed to be able to use chemical weapons in the direct support of ground operations, it developed the skills to do so by 1987, and chemical weapons played a major role in Iraq's victories against Iran in 1987 and 1988. Iraq also used chemical weapons against Kurdish rebels and civilians after the war in late 1988 and in 1989. It has experience in using chemical weapons in artillery shells, rockets, mortar rounds, bombs, and spray tanks.[500]

At the time of the Gulf War, Iraq had an inventory of around 1,000 metric tons of chemical weapons. These were split evenly between blister agents like mustard gas and nerve agents. It was just beginning to weaponize VX, a persistent nerve gas. It was prepared for a massive chemical offensive and has prepared its forces in the Kuwaiti Theater of Operations with chemical defense equipment and extensive written instructions.[501]

Since the Gulf War, Iraq has lied just as systematically about its chemical weapons programs and holdings as it did about it missile capabilities. It has become clear, however, that Iraq's Gulf War stockpile included some 70,000 filled and 79,000 unfilled chemical munitions and 12 types of weapons.[502] The immense scale of this chemical efforts is the result of a production program that started with the production of mustard gas in 1981, and which began the production of nerve agents like Sarin and Tabun in 1984. By 1990, the main Iraqi production plant—the State Enterprise for Pesticide Production at al-Muthanna—occupied a facility with an area of 25 square kilometers. Iraq also had many other research and production facilities.[503]

There is still considerable uncertainty as to why Iraq did not use these weapons during the Gulf War. Iraq did arm and disperse tens of thousands of weapons, and Saddam Hussein seems to have given orders to arm the al-Hussein missiles with chemical warheads and launch them under attack if Baghdad lost its command control capabilities. Iraq did not, however, use such weapons, and—in spite of some reports to the contrary—there is no evidence that Iraq ever deployed chemical weapons forward into Kuwait or the Kuwaiti theater of operations.

Iraq may have been deterred by the threat posed by US possession of nuclear weapons. Iraq may also have feared that such escalation would lead to total war and Coalition occupation of Iraq or destruction of the ruling regime. It may have lost the command and control systems it needed to use such weapons, and it may have kept its weapons stocks so far to the rear that it lost the capability to deploy them forward after the Coalition air attacks on its infrastructure.

Iraq also, however, may have filled its weapons too soon, and found it had severe operational problems in using them. Iraq's mustard agent was the only agent stable enough to be stored at length in bulk or munitions. It was about 80% pure, and UNSCOM found that such munitions remained reliable several years after the war. Mustard gas, however, is of only moderate lethality and is useful largely for attacking static rear areas, suppressing the flanks of an enemy force in a breakthrough, contaminating areas as a defensive barrier, or attacking the rear echelon of an attacking enemy under favorable wind conditions.[504]

Iraq had far more severe problems with its more lethal nerve agents. Its Tabun and Sarin nerve gas agents were only about 60% pure and had very limited shelf-lives. Iraq had not yet developed the technology to purify these agents by distilling them, or the capability to add stabilizing chemicals. It also had crude binary weapons which required the chemical components to be stored separately and to be mixed shortly before use. Its munitions tended to leak in storage and even nerve agents kept at a stable 18° C in al-Muthanna had to be used within weeks of production or they started to break down. As has been discussed earlier, Iraq's missile warheads were crude and largely ineffective, Iraq lost its offensive air capabilities in the first days of the war, and Iraq had not yet begun to produce VX in volume. As a result, Iraq may have been unable to make use of the most effective element of its chemical arsenal.[505]

Most of Iraq's chemical weapons did, however, survive the Gulf War. US reporting on the effectiveness of the bombing effort during the Gulf War proved to be grossly exaggerated, as did the Department of Defense study of the lessons of the war. This study claimed that:

At least 75% of Iraq's CW production capability was destroyed. At Samara, Coalition forces destroyed or severely damaged most known primary CW production, processing, or production support buildings. All three buildings used to fill munitions at Samara were destroyed, although the Iraqis may have moved the equipment from one building before Desert Storm for safe-keeping. All three precursor chemical facilities at Habbaniyah were seriously damaged. Although Iraq previously had produced and distributed many CW agents to storage sites throughout the country, the means for delivering these weapons were badly damaged. Coalition air supremacy made Iraqi Air Force delivery of these weapons unlikely; most artillery (Iraq's preferred method of delivering CW) was disabled.[506]

The Coalition did damage some key Iraqi facilities and chemical weapons, but most of these facilities and virtually all of the weapons survived the bombing. Iraq had time to disperse many of its precursors and key production sub-systems before the Gulf War began and continued to hide and disperse these items after the signing of the cease-fire.[507]

The scale of Iraq's surviving assets is indicated by the size of the stockpiles the UN has been able to locate and destroy. UNSCOM's Chemical Destruction Group (CDG) disposed of 398,046 liters (600 tons) of mustard gas, 21,365 liters (30 tons) of Tabun, 64,133 liters (70 tons) of Sarin. During June 1992 to April 1994 the CDG destroyed 481,044 liters at its main facility at al-Muthanna, including 6,773 122 mm rockets, 12,804 155 mm artillery shells, 8,390 bombs, and 29 al-Hussein missile warheads. It destroyed another 11,829 unfilled chemical munitions, 425 122 mm chemical rockets at other sites, and 1,798,593 liters and 1,040,836 kilograms of precursor chemicals. UNSCOM also verified Iraq's claims to have unilaterally destroyed 24,470 additional chemical munitions during the course of 1991, including 45 ballistic missile warheads.[508]

Impressive as these destruction efforts were, they did not destroy all of Iraq's capabilities. The UN found in the summer of 1995 that Iraq had continued to lie about much of its effort to produce GF and VX nerve gas; had disguised the fact that it had produced large amounts of VX; and was hiding the fact it had been seeking to create an indigenous capability to manufacture cyclohexanol, a precursor of GF, and di-isopropylene, a precursor of VX. Iraq pursued the development of the deadly nerve agent VX from May 1985 to December 1990. As part of this effort, Iraq engaged in the industrial scale production of enough chemical precursors to produce 490 tons of VX. These precursors included 65 tons of choline and 200 tons of phosphorous pentasulfide and di-isopropylamine. Iraq also admitted that it had produced binary Sarin-filled artillery shells, 122 mm rockets, and aerial bombs.[509]

As a result, UNSCOM found that Iraqi declarations as recent as March and May 1995 were false, and a UNSCOM report stated that, "The new information invalidates the material balances provided in the March 1995 (declaration) and subsequent amendments."[510] While UNSCOM's monitoring has failed to reveal any recent chemical production, Ambassador Ekeus has also informed the Security Council that it has no documentary evidence verifying Iraqi destruction of its VX precursors and/or any VX stockpiles. Accordingly, UNSCOM reported that it could ". . . not exclude the potential existence of stocks of VX, its direct precursors and undeclared munitions in Iraq."[511]

Iraqi lies and concealment efforts led Robert Gates, a former Director of Central Intelligence, to testify to Congress in early 1992 that much of Iraq's "hard to get production equipment" for chemical weapons had been dispersed and "hidden" before the allied bombing attacks. He also estimated that ". . . if sanctions are relaxed, we believe Iraq could produce modest quantities of chemical agents almost immediately, but it would take a year or more to recover the chemical weapons capability it previously enjoyed."[512]

More recent information obtained by UNSCOM and intelligence sources has revealed a continuing Iraqi effort to indigenously develop the precursors for chemical agents that appears to support this assessment.[513] It is clear that Iraq has continued to import precursors and chemical weapons manufacturing equipment clandestinely since the Gulf War— disguising some as pharmaceutical supplies and manufacturing equipment which it imported through Jordan.[514]

Many experts do feel that it might take several years and several hundred million dollars worth of imported equipment to develop a major war-fighting capability. They note that Iraq lost much of its feed-stock production capacity during the bombing of Samara, which was very heavily damaged during the war. As a result, it will probably take Iraq three to five years to recover a significant capability to employ enough chemical shells, rockets, bombs and warheads to fight a major land war.[515]

At the same time, the large amounts of chemical agents needed to support a major land offensive are very different from the comparatively limited amounts needed to arm several hundred missile warheads and aircraft bombs. A nation as advanced as Iraq could covertly produce enough chemical agents to arm several hundred weapons, including warheads, at small laboratory facilities, and it would be virtually impossible for any current inspection and control regime to prevent this. Further, Iraq has had half a decade in which to develop ways of producing purer chemical agents, and more effective bombs and warheads.

Table Twelve shows that even limited numbers of chemical weapons can be highly effective in a number of war fighting contingencies. Iraq, therefore, will almost certainly be able to recover a significant capability to threaten enemy population centers and area targets with missile and air strikes within a relatively short time after it is freed from UN controls.[516]

Iraq's Future Biological Weapons Capabilities

It is now clear that Iraq was ready to employ biological weapons against Iran if the Iran-Iraq War had continued and that Iraq had a major biological weapons program ready to use against the UN Coalition at the time of the Gulf War. Iraq had at least 90,000 liters of Botulinum toxin and 8,300 liters of Anthrax, as well as large stocks of an agent that causes cancer. It had loaded both Botulinum and Anthrax on Scud missile warheads and aerial bombs. Iraq was also experimenting with infectious agents and Mycotoxins. These programs were initially centered around Al Kindi and Salman Pak, but were moved to Al Hakam and other facilities before the war, and were extensively dispersed before the fighting began.[517]

Iraqi biological weapons activity did not receive the same attention given to Iraq's other weapons of mass destruction since the end of the Gulf War until new evidence surfaced in September, 1995. This was evident from a comparison of the number of biological weapons inspections UNSCOM conducted relative to the number of inspections devoted to chemical and nuclear weapons, and ballistic missiles.[518]

TABLE ELEVEN   Major Chemical Agents That May Be in Iranian and Iraqi
Forces

NERVE AGENTS: Agents that quickly disrupt the nervous system by binding to enzymes critical to nerve functions, causing convulsions and/or paralysis. Must be ingested, inhaled, and absorbed through the skin. Very low doses cause a running nose, contraction of the pupil of the eye, and difficulty in visual coordination. Moderate doses constrict the bronchi and cause a feeling of pressure in the chest, and weaken the skeletal muscles and cause fibrilation. Large doses cause death by respiratory or heart failure. Can be absorbed through inhalation or skin contact. Reaction normally occurs in 1–2 minutes. Death from lethal doses occurs within minutes, but artificial respiration can help and atropine and the oximes act as less lethal gases. Recovery is normally quick, if it occurs at all, but permanent brain damage can occur:

Tabun (GA)

Sarin (GB)—nearly as volatile as water and delivered by air. A dose of 5 mg/min/m^3 produces casualties, a repiratory dose of 100 mg/min/m^3 is lethal. Lethality lasts 1–2 days.

Soman (GD)

GF

VR-55 (Improved Soman)—a thick oily substance which persists for some time.

VK/VX—a persistent agent roughly as heavy as fuel oil. A dose of 0.5 mg/min/m^3 produces casualties, a repiratory dose of 10 mg/min/m^3 is lethal. Lethality lasts 1–16 weeks.

BLISTER AGENTS: Cell poisons that destroy skin and tissue, cause blindness upon contact with the eyes, and which can result in fatal respiratory damage. Can be colorless or black oily droplets. Can be absorbed through inhalation or skin contact. Serious internal damage if inhaled. Penetrates ordinary clothing. Some have delayed and some have immediate action. Actual blistering normally takes hours to days, but effects on the eyes are much more rapid. Mustard gas is a typical blister agent and exposure to concentrations of a few milligrams per meter over several hours generally at least causes blisters and swollen eyes. When the liquid falls onto the skin or eyes it has the effect of second or third degree burns. It can blind and cause damage to the lungs leading to pneumonia. Severe exposure causes general intoxication similar to radiation sickness. HD and HN persist up to 12 hours. L, HL, and CX persist for 1–2 hours. Short of prevention of exposure, the only treatment is to wash the eyes, decontaminate the skin, and treat the resulting damage like burns:

Sulfur Mustard (H or HD)—a dose of 100 mg/min/m^3 produces casualties, a dose of 1,500 mg/min/m^3 is lethal. Residual lethality lasts up to 2–8 weeks.

Distilled Mustard (DM)

Nitrogen Mustard (HN)

Lewisite (L)

Phosgene Oxime (CX)

Mustard Lewisite (HL)

(continues)

TABLE ELEVEN *(continued)*

CHOKING AGENTS: Agents that cause the blood vessels in the lungs to hemorrhage, and fluid to build up, until the victim chokes or drowns in his or her own fluids (pulmonary edema). Provide quick warning through smell or lung irritation. Can be absorbed through inhalation. Immediate to delayed action. The only treatment is inhalation of oxygen and rest. Symptoms emerge in periods after exposure of seconds up to three hours:
  Phosgene (CG)
  Disphosgene (DP)
  PS Chloropicrin
  Chlorine Gas

BLOOD AGENTS: Kill through inhalation. Provide little warning except for headache, nausea, and vertigo. Interferes with use of oxygen at the cellular level. CK also irritates the lungs and eyes. Rapid action and exposure either kills by inhibiting cell respiration or it does not—casualties will either die within seconds to minutes of exposure or recover in fresh air. Most gas masks have severe problems in providing effective protection against blood agents:
  Hydrogen Cyanide (AC)—a dose of 2,000 mg/min/m^3 produces casualties, a respiratory dose of 5,000 mg/min/m^3 is lethal. Lethality lasts 1–4 hours.
  Cyanogen Chloride (CK)—a dose of 7,000 mg/min/m^3 produces casualties, a respiratory dose of 11,000 mg/min/m^3 is lethal. Lethality lasts 15 minutes to one hour.

TOXINS: Biological poisons causing neuromuscular paralysis after exposure of hours or days. Formed in foo or cultures by the bacterium clostridium Botulimun. Produces highly fatal poisoning characterized by general weakness, headache, dizziness, double vision and dilation of the pupils, paralysis of muscles, and problems in speech. Death is usually by respiratory failure. Antitoxin therapy has limited value, but treatment is mainly supportive:
  Botulin toxin (A)—six distinct types, of which four are known to be fatal to man. An oral dose of 0.001 mg is lethal. A respiratory dose of 0.02 mg/min/m^3 is also lethal.

DEVELOPMENTAL WEAPONS: A new generation of chemical weapons is under development. The only publicized agent is perfluoroisobutene (PFIB), which is an extremely toxic odorless and invisible substance produced when PFIB (Teflon) is subjected to extreme heat under special conditions. It causes pulmonary edema or dry-land drowning when the lungs fill with fluid. Short exposure disables and small concentrations cause delayed death. Activated charcoal and most existing protection equipment offers no defense. Some sources refer to "third" and "fourth" generation nerve gases, but no technical literature seems to be available.

CONTROL AGENTS: Agents which produce temporary irritating or disabling effects which in contact with the eyes or inhaled. They can cause serious illness or death when used in confined spaces. CS is the least toxic gas, followed by CN and DM. Symptoms can be treated by washing of the eyes and/or removal from the area. Exposure to CS, CN, and DM produces immediate symptoms. Staphylococ-

(continues)

TABLE ELEVEN   (continued)

cus produces symptoms in 30 minutes to four hours, and recovery takes 24–48 hours. Treatment of Staphylococcus is largely supportive:
    Tear—cause flow of tears and irritation of upper respiratory tract and skin. Can cause nausea and vomiting:
    Chlororacetophenone (CN)
    O-Chlorobenzyl-malononitrile (CS)
    Vomiting—cause irritation, coughing, severe headache, tightness in chest, nausea, vomiting:
    Adamsite (DM)
    Staphylococcus
INCAPACITATING AGENTS: Agents which normally cause short-term illness, psychoactive effects (delirium and hallucinations). Can be absorbed through inhalation or skin contact. The psychoactive gases and drugs produce unpredictable effects, particularly in the sick, small children, elderly, and individuals who already are mentally ill. In rare cases they kill. In other, they produce a permanent psychotic condition. Many produce dry skin, irregular heart beat, urinary retention, constipation, drowsiness, and a rise in body temperature, plus occassional maniacal behavior. A single dose of 0.1 to 0.2 milligrams of LSD-25 will produce profound mental disturbance within a half hour that lasts 10 hours. The lethal dose is 100 to 200 milligrams:
    BZ
    LSD
    LSD based BZ
    Mescaline
    Psilocybin
    Benzilates

Source: Adapted from Matthew Meselson and Julian Perry Robinson, "Chemical Warfare and Chemical Disarmament," *Scientific American,* Vol. 242, No. 4, April 1980, pp. 38–47; "Chemical Warfare: Extending the Range of Destruction," *Jane's Defense Weekly,* August 25, 1990, p. 267; Dick Palowski, *Changes in Threat Air Combat Doctrine and Force Structure, 24th Edition,* Fort Worth, General Dynamics DWIC-01, February 1992, pp. II-335 to II-339; US Marine Corps, *Individual Guide for NBC Defense,* Field Manual OH-11-1A, August 1990; and unpublished testimony to the Special Investigations Subcommittee of the Government Operations Committee, U.S. Senate, by Mr. David Goldberg, Foreign Science and Technology Center, US Army Intelligence Center on February 9, 1989.

Biological weapons, however, can be as effective as small nuclear weapons. One US study of the Gulf War notes that:

Experimental data indicate Botulinum toxin is about 3 million times more potent than the nerve agent Sarin. A Scud missile warhead filled with Botulinum could contaminate an area of 3,700 square kilometers (based on ideal

TABLE TWELVE   Typical Warfighting Uses of Chemical Weapons

Mission	Quantity
Attack an infantry position: Cover 1.3 square kilometers of territory with a "surprise dosage" attack of Sarin to kill 50% of exposed troops.	216 240 mm rockets (e.g., delivered by 18, 12 tube Soviet BM-24 rocket launchers, each carrying 8 kilograms of agent and totaling 1,728 kilograms of agent.
Prevent launch of enemy mobile missiles: Contaminate a 25 square kilometer missile unit operating area with 0.3 tons of a persistnet nerve gas like VX per square kilometer.	8 MiG-23 or 4 Su-24 fighters, each delivering 0.9 ton of VX (totaling 7.2 tons).
Immobilize an air base: Contaminate a 2 square kilometer air base with 0.3 tons of VX twice a day for 3 days.	1 MiG-23 with six sorties or any similar attack craft.
Defend a broad front against large scale attack: Maintain a 300 meter deep strip of VX contamination in a front of a position defending a 60 kilometer wide area for 3 days.	65 metric tons of agent delivered by approximately 13,000 155-mm artillery rounds.
Terrorize population: Kill approximately 125,000 unprotected civilians in a densely populated (10,000 square kilometer) city.	8 MiG-23 or 4 Su-24 fighters, each delivering 0.9 ton of VX (totaling 7.2 tons) under optimal conditions.

Source: Adapted by Anthony H. Cordesman from Victor A. Utgoff, The Challenge of Chemical Weapons, New York, St. Martin's, 1991, pp. 238–242, and Office of Technology Assessment, Proliferation of Weapons of Mass Destruction: Assessing the Risks, US Congress OTA-ISC-559, Washington, August 1993, pp. 56–57.

weather conditions and an effective dispersal mechanism), or 16 times greater than the same warhead filled with Sarin. By the time symptoms occur, treatment has little chance of success. Rapid field detection methods for biological warfare agents do not exist. Although Botulinum can debilitate in a few hours and kill in as few as 12, and anthrax takes two to four days to kill, anthrax is much more persistent and can contaminate a much larger area using the same delivery means.[519]

The UN is now actively engaged in trying to discover and destroy Iraq's biological weapons capabilities. It has included 79 Iraqi facilities in its biological monitoring and verification regime. Of these, nine are considered Category A, requiring the most intense monitoring, while 15 are Category B, 10 are Category C and 45 are Category D. Many of the Category A sites were damaged during the Gulf War, but one facility at Al-

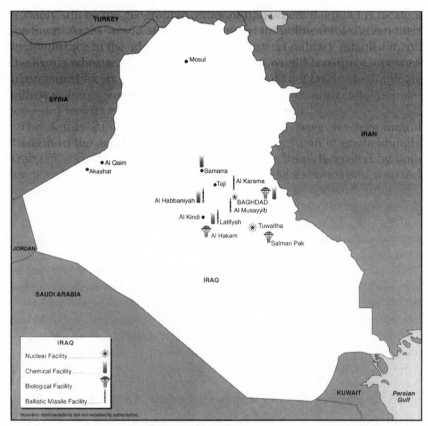

MAP FOUR The Location of Iraq's Largest Nuclear, Chemical, Biological, and
Missile Facilities at the Time of the Gulf War. *Source:* Office of the
Secretary of Defense, *Proliferation: Threat and Response,* Washington,
Department of Defense, April 1996, p. 19.

Hakam was missed entirely by both Coalition intelligence and
bombers.[520] The Iraqi government has admitted that these plants produced large quantities of anthrax, Botulinum, clostridium perfringens,
and other agents prior to the Gulf War.

Iraq's Efforts Before the Gulf War

The conceptual origin of Iraq's biological weapons program dates back to
1974, when the government officially endorsed its development. At that
time, the program was assigned to the Al Hazen Ibn Al Haytham Institute

at Al Salman. By 1978, poor management and incompetence resulted in the termination of activities. The program was revived in 1985, however, in accordance with the recommendation of the Muthanna State Establishment, the primary facility responsible for chemical weapons development and production. By the end of the year, the nascent program had a 150-liter fermenter and a staff of 10 who devoted themselves to investigating the character of the bacterium which produce anthrax and Botulinum.[521]

In May 1987, the program, with its fermenter and eight more staff, was transferred back to Al Salman. Here, Botulinum and anthrax were tested on animals and this was followed by the first initial weapons field trials in early 1988. A second production facility with a 450-liter fermenter was established at Taji to concentrate on the production of Botulinum. The Taji plant produced Botulinum for about six months in 1988, while the Al Salman plant accumulated 1,500 liters of anthrax. The success of these small trial runs convinced the Iraqi government to proceed with full-scale production and weapons tests.[522]

The first of these tests occurred in early March 1988 at al-Muthanna's weapons testing range. Aerial bombs were selected as the weapon of choice for this test and, according to the Iraqis, the results were considered a failure. A second test later the same month, however, proved to be successful. The next weaponization test occurred in November of 1989, when 122 mm rockets were filled with Botulinum, an anthrax simulant and Aflatoxin, a naturally occurring carcinogen. These trials were considered successful as were identical trials held in May 1990. These trials were followed by tests involving R400 aerial bombs filled with the same three agents.[523]

Construction of a main biological weapons facility started at Al Hakam in early 1988 and was completed by the end of the year. To expand production capabilities, the new plant was equipped with two 1,850 liter and seven 1,480 liter fermenters, transferred from the Veterinary Research Laboratories in November 1988. The 450 liter fermenter from Taji was also transferred to Al Hakam in October 1988. By April 1989, production of Botulinum had started, with an anthrax simulant following in May for the purpose of weapons tests. Iraq claims that production of anthrax and Botulinum at Al Hakam during 1990, amounted to 6,000 liters of concentrated Botulinum and 8,425 liters of anthrax.[524]

In addition, research was started at Al Salman on a number of other agents. In April 1988, a gangrene causing agent known as clostridium perfringens was added to the list, followed a month later by Aflatoxin, which was produced by growing the fungus aspergillus. Other agents included a grain destroying fungus known as wheat cover smut, a deadly protein toxin called Ricin, and debilitating tricothecene Mycotoxins, such as T-2 and DAS. Research into clostridium perfringens was transferred to Al Hakam in 1989, while the production of Aflatoxin moved to a plant at

Fudaliyah where, between April/May 1990 and December 1990, where 1,850 liters were produced. Work on the wheat cover smut moved to Mosul, but according to the Iraqis, the infected wheat necessary to propagate the fungus was burned at Fudaliyah in 1990. Ricin appeared the most promising of these agents, and ten liters of concentrate were prepared for weapons trials using artillery shells. According to the Iraqis, these trials were failures and the project was discontinued.[525]

In July 1990, while Al Hakam became the center of toxin production, Al Salman started to conduct research into viruses. It acquired the Foot and Mouth Disease Facility at Daura and subsequently isolated three viruses indigenous to Iraq for possible weapons use. The first was haemorrhagic conjunctivitis, which results in extreme pain and temporary blindness. This was followed by the debilitating rotavirus and the virus which causes camel pox. The initiation of research, however, occurred only months before the eruption of the Gulf War, and the Iraqis have maintained that very little progress was achieved.[526]

After Iraq's invasion of Kuwait, it accelerated its biological weapons program, and placed a strong emphasis on production and weaponization. The Daura Institute was converted from viral research to Botulinum production and subsequently produced 5,400 liters of concentrate between November, 1990, and January 15, 1991. During the same period, Al Hakam's fermenters were converted from Botulinum production to anthrax, while its older 150 liter fermenter was used to manufacture 340 liters of clostridium perfringens concentrate.[527]

In December 1990, three of the biological agents—Botulinum, anthrax, and Aflatoxin—were selected for weaponization. One hundred R400 aerial bombs and 13 Al Hussein Scud warheads were filled with Botulinum, 50 bombs and 10 warheads were filled with anthrax, and 16 bombs and 2 warheads were weaponized with Aflatoxin. These weapons were subsequently dispersed to four different locations, where they remained through the war. In addition to warheads and aerial bombs, the Iraqis attempted to develop a drop tank for either manned aircraft or RPVs that would dispense up to 2,000 liters of anthrax. Trials are said to have been conducted in January 1991, and the Iraqis contend that the tests were a failure. Nevertheless, Iraq maintained three of the drop tanks in a ready-to-use posture until July 1991, when it says they were destroyed.[528]

Iraq admits it had amassed a stockpile of some 19,000 liters of concentrated Botulinum, 8,500 liters of anthrax, 2,220 liters of Aflatoxin, 340 liters of clostridium perfringens, and unknown quantities of various other biological agents by the end of the war. Iraq admits that 10,000 liters of Botulinum were weaponized, as were 6,500 liters of anthrax and 1,580 liters of Aflatoxin. It also admits that it imported some 39 tons of growth media before the Gulf War. Each ton of growth media can be used to produce 10 tons of biological weapons, and 17 tons of this total are unaccounted for.[529]

There is no way to determine whether Iraq retains significant stocks of dry, storage biological agents. As has been discussed earlier, the Iraqi government has admitted that it had at least five primary production facilities for biological weapons at the time of the Gulf War, including the Sepp Institute at Muthanna, the Ghazi Research Institute at Amaria, the Daura Foot and Mouth Disease Institute, and facilities at Al-Hakim, Salman Pak and Taji.

Iraq has so far admitted that it manufactured 6,000 liters of concentrated Botulinum toxin and 8,425 liters of anthrax at Al-Hakim alone during 1990. Iraq has admitted that it has manufactured 400 liters of concentrated Botulinum toxin at Taji; 150 liters of concentrated anthrax at Salman Pak, and 1,850 liters of Aflatoxin in solution at Fudaliyah. Iraq has admitted it manufactured a number of agents it claimed it did not weaponize, although some were extensively tested. It has admitted that it produced 5,400 liters of concentrated Botulinum toxin at the Daura Foot and Mouth Disease Institute from November 1990 to January 15, 1991, and there are some indications that it may have attempted to produce a variant of hoof and mouth disease for military purposes.[530] Yet, these admissions are not supported by records, evidence, or testimony. The details of each of these Iraqi production efforts remain uncertain.

The same uncertainties apply to the disposition of the weapons and munitions that Iraq could fill with biological agents. The Iraqi government's admissions in the fall of 1995 have already provided an indication of the massive scale of Iraq's massive weapons production effort. Iraq's known weaponization programs consist of at least:

- 166 bombs loaded with Botulinum.
- 50 R-400 air-delivered bombs loaded with anthrax.
- 10 anthrax-loaded missile warheads for the Al-Hussein missile.
- 15 Al-Hussein missile warheads loaded with Botulinum.
- 16 missile warheads loaded with Aflatoxin, a natural carcinogen. These warheads were designed for operability with the Al-Hussein Scud variant, and were loaded in December 1990, for possible use during the Gulf War.[531]
- Field trials, weaponization tests, and live firings of 122 mm rockets armed with anthrax and Botulinum toxin (carried out during March 1988 to May 1990).[532]
- Bombs, 122 mm rockets, and artillery shells filled with 10,000 liters of concentrated Botulinum toxin, and at least 1,580 liters of concentrated Aflatoxin.[533]
- Spray tanks prepared for use by helicopters, aircraft, or UAVs. Iraq has provided UNSCOM with information regarding the December 1990.

- Development of a 2,000 liter aircraft or RPV drop tank designed to dispense anthrax. While Iraq claims that its test on the drop tank was a failure, it stored three of them in a ready to use posture during the Gulf War.[534]

The Iraqi government claims that it took all of its biological bombs to an airfield at some point during May–June 1991, in order to use a chemical agent to deactivate them, and then to have explosively destroyed and burnt them. The Iraqi government claims that it did the same with its missile warheads at a different site. The government has said, however, it has no record of the precise date it did this, or even the site. It took UN inspectors to one site that had no evidence of such destruction, and then changed its story and claimed it could no longer find the site. The Iraqi government also claims to have used such procedures to destroy about 8,000 liters of concentrated Botulinum, over 2,000 liters of concentrated Anthrax, 340 liters of concentrated perfingens, and an unspecified amount of Aflatoxin that was stored at Al Hakim.[535]

The Major Uncertainties Regarding Iraq's Efforts

The revelations the Iraqi government made during 1995 have forced the UN to reassess its efforts in regards to seeking out and destroying Iraq's biological warfare program. Until August 1995, UNSCOM was unaware of the advanced state of Iraq's biological warfare program. Rolf Ekeus has stated as much in a August 1995 press interview, "I probably did underestimate the biological program."[536] In an October 1995 report to the UN Security Council, Mr. Ekeus described the advances achieved in Iraq's biological weapons program as "remarkable."[537]

Although the Iraqi government released some 688,000 pages of new documentation after Hussein Kamel defected, it did so under conditions where it claimed the documents had been hidden in a chicken coop and were only found after Hussein Kamel defected. In fact, the documents were spotless and had clearly been moved to the area days before the UNSCOM teams were notified of their existence. These documents are also very general, and Iraq seems to have held back most documentation that would reveal the level of sophistication it has achieved, data on any current suppliers, and data that might reveal the development of its program since 1991.[538]

Iraq has repeatedly asserted that it destroyed all of these agents after the war, but thus far has failed to provide any documentation to verify such an action. The inconsistency of Iraqi assertions regarding the destruction have generated skepticism at UNSCOM, which ". . . does not believe that Iraq has given a full and correct account of its biological weapons program."[539]

Iraq has had ample time to redistribute equipment, personnel, and technology since the Gulf War. Some of Iraq's biological weapons production facilities were damaged during the Gulf War, but much of their equipment may have been dispersed before or during the war, and Coalition intelligence and bombers missed key facilities like the one at Al-Hakim.[540] In fact, Rolf Ekeus warned that UNSCOM inspectors believed that Iraq might still have 16 operational Scud variants with biological warheads that it kept moving around Iraq to evade inspection in testimony to the US Congress on March 20, 1996.[541]

Further, it is now clear that Iraq created the same highly secret and compartmented program to carry on with its biological weapons program after the Gulf War that it created for its missile, chemical warfare, and nuclear programs. This program is particularly trace since all key components are dual use items that can be used for peaceful medical purposes and food processing and include everything from bio-medical equipment and micro-encapsulation equipment for cold tablets to brewery fermenters and dry food storage equipment for infant formula. British, French, German, and Swiss experts are aware of Iraqi imports that can be used for biological weapons, as are US and UNSCOM experts. Further, both research and production efforts can be widely dispersed and can be concealed in relatively small buildings—particularly if a government is willing to take moderate risks of contamination of the kind widely taken by the Soviet Union during the Cold War.

The Iraqi government admits it had imported extensive amounts of equipment and materials suitable for biological weapons production before the war—largely from Europe. These imports have not yet been accounted for in any detail, and there is no way to know how many have been dispersed or have been used since the Gulf War in undeclared facilities. Iraq's imports also included tons of growth media for biological agents, which were obtained from three European firms. According to UNSCOM, 17 tons of these media remain unaccounted for. Further, Iraq imported a wide range of type cultures, which can be modified to develop biological weapons, and some came from the US.[542]

There also is no way of knowing exactly what agents Iraq examined before the war, or has examined since. Outside experts add tularemia and typhoid agents to the list of agents Iraq has examined. Iraq's declarations admit to conducting research on a Mycotoxin similar to "yellow rain" defoliant. Iraq examined a wide range of viruses, bacteria, and fungi. It examined the possibility of weaponizing gas gangrene and other Mycotoxins, and some field trials were held of these agents. It also examined the use of haemorrhagic conjunctivitis virus, rotavirus, and camel pox virus.[543]

This means that UNSCOM may never be able to determine the exact types of biological weapons Iraq did or did not develop, how much it modified them before the Gulf War, how well it weaponized them, or what it has done covertly in the five years since the Gulf War ended. Table Thirteen provides a list of some of the weapons that Iraq may have examined. It is important to stress that all pre-production research, testing, and weaponization for many of these weapons could be conducted in small covert facilities that have been established since the Gulf War.

At this point, only another series of major defections is likely to reveal the full details of Iraq's accomplishments before 1991, or what it has done covertly since that time. At least one of the principal UNSCOM investigators of the Iraqi biological weapons program feels that no effort by UNSCOM can prevent Iraq from retaining a major biological weapons effort and resuming production and deployment within months of the end of the UNSCOM effort.

There is a broad consensus among experts that even if the UN could account for all growth media, cultures, and Iraq's overt biological weapons production facilities at the time of the Gulf War, Iraq can rapidly establish new covert production at university research centers, medical goods and drug manufacturing plants, or virtually any other facility that can maintain a secure biological research and production activity.

Robert Gates, Director of Central Intelligence in the Bush Administration, made this point as early as January 1992. He responded to questions about Iraq's biological weapons effort by stating that ". . . the biological weapons program was also damaged, but critical equipment for it, too, was hidden during the war." He went on to note that Iraq could produce biological agents within "a matter of weeks," once the UN sanctions and constant intrusive UNSCOM challenge inspections ended.[544]

Any such covert stockpile of highly lethal biological weapons would give Iraq considerable potential to deter and intimidate the Southern Gulf states and the West. Iraq could make use of biological weapons in much the same way as chemical weapons. Iraq could also employ such weapons covertly, since they lend themselves to tailored attacks in terms of delay effects and are well suited to unconventional warfare, or "terrorism." Biological weapons are Iraq's only near-term answer to the effectiveness of the UN's inspection and destruction regime of Iraq's far more visible nuclear, chemical and missile capabilities. Given Iraq's history, this makes biological weapons an option that Iraq is likely to choose.

The Warfighting Effectiveness of Iraq's Weapons

Although the effectiveness of Iraq's missiles, bombs, and warheads in disseminating biological agents is uncertain, the potential consequences of even inefficient dissemination are potentially disastrous. The amount of anthrax in those 10 missiles had the theoretical ability to kill some

TABLE THIRTEEN   Key Biological Weapons That May Be in the Middle East

Disease	Infectivity	Transmissibility	Incubation Period	Mortality	Therapy
Viral					
Chikungunya fever	high	none	2–6 days	very low (–1%)	none
Dengue fever	high	none	2–5 days	very low (–1%)	none
Eastern equine encephalitis	high	none	5–10 days	high (+60%)	developmental
Tick borne encephalitis	high	none	1–2 weeks	up to 30%	developmental
Venezuelan equine encephalitis	high	none	2–5 days	low (–1%)	developmental
Hepatitis A	—	—	15–40 days	—	—
Hepatitis B	—	—	40–150 days	—	—
Influenza	high	none	1–3 days	usually low	available
Yellow fever	high	none	3–6 days	up to 40%	available
Smallpox (Variola)	high	high	7–16 days	up to 30%	available
Rickettsial					
Coxiella Burneti (Q-fever)	high	negligible	10–21 days	low (–1%)	antibiotic
Mooseri	—	—	6–14 days	—	—
Prowazeki	—	—	6–15 days	—	—
Psittacosis	high	moderate-high	4–15 days	mod-high	antibiotic
Rickettsi (Rocky mountain spotted fever)	high	none	3–10 days	up to 80%	antibiotic
Tsutsugamushi	—	—	—	—	—
Epidemic typhus	high	none	6–15 days	up to 70%	antibiotic/vaccine
Bacterial					
Anthrax (pulmonary)	mod-high	negligible	1–5 days	usually fatal	antibiotic/vaccine
Brucellosis	high	none	1–3 days	up to 25%	antibiotic
Cholera	low	high	1–5 days	up to 80%	antibiotic/vaccine
Glanders	high	none	1–2 days	usually fatal	poor antibiotic

(continues)

TABLE THIRTEEN (continued)

Disease	Infectivity	Transmissibility	Incubation Period	Mortality	Therapy
Meloidosis	high	none	1–5 days	usually fatal	moderate antibiotic
Plague (pneumonic)	high	high	2–5 days	usually fatal	antibiotic/vaccine
Tularemia	high	negligible	1–10 days	low to 60%	antibiotic/vaccine
Typhoid fever	mod-high	mod-high	7–21 days	up to 10%	antibiotic/vaccine
Dysentery	high	high	1–4 days	low to high	antibiotic/vaccine
Fungal					
Coccidioidomycosis	high	none	1–3 days	low	none
Coccidiodes Immitis	high	none	10–21 days	low	none
Histoplasma Capsulatum	—	—	15–18 days	—	—
Norcardia Asteroides	—	—		—	—
Toxins[a]					
Botulinum toxin	high	none	12–72 hours	high neuromuscular paralysis	vaccine
Mycotoxin	high	none	hours or days	low to high	?
Staphylococcus	moderate	none	24–48 hours	incapacitating	?

[a]Many sources classify as chemical weapons because toxins are chemical poisons.

Source: Adapted by Anthony H. Cordesman from Report of the Secretary General, Department of Political and Security Affairs, *Chemical and Bacteriological (Biological) Weapons and the Effects of Their Possible Use,* New York, United Nations, 1969, pp. 26, 29, 37–52, 116–117; *Jane's NBC Protection Equipment,* 1991–1992; James Smith, "Biological Warfare Developments," *Jane's Intelligence Review,* November 1991, pp. 483–487.

60,000,000 people, while the Botulinum in the remaining 15 missiles could have contaminated an area of over 21,000 square kilometers.[545]

It is doubtful that Iraq's pre-war biological weapons—particularly its missile warheads—would have been highly lethal. While the details of these weapon designs have not been disclosed, Iraq's chemical weapons were relatively unsophisticated and most of Iraq's pre-war designs were rushed into service. The weaponization and deployment of more lethal munitions and warheads involves technical challenges in terms of dry storable agents, microencapsulation, dissemination at critical heights, and predictions of wind and temperature over the target area that may be well beyond Iraq's pre-war capability.

There is no reason to believe, however, that Iraq has not taken advantage of the last five years to tailor more lethal weapons, improve their storability and resistance to heat and light, and improve the design of its bombs and other dissemination devices.

Missile warheads may still be a serious problem. There are some experts that question whether Iraq can meet the challenge of developing a suitable combination of biological weapons and suitable warhead technology, and can develop a missile warhead that would achieve extremely high lethalities. Iraq, however, had a decade to work on this problem before the Gulf War and the UNSCOM effort has not been designed to prevent substantial additional further research and development since the war. Furthermore, it would be much easier for Iraq to weaponize a biological agent for delivery by a relatively slow flying aircraft or cruise missile, than to weaponize it for delivery by a ballistic missile.[546]

Iraq almost certainly can now deliver moderately lethal weapons, and the "terror" effect of even crude and inefficient biological warheads should not be dismissed. UAVs and slow flying civilian aircraft make excellent delivery systems for such weapons, require minimal amounts of advanced technology, do not produce major indications of testing and development, and are inherently difficult to detect and track to a given source and location.

A successful weaponization of highly lethal biological weapons could give Iraq major political and strategic advantages in terms of both war fighting and intimidation. It would give Iraq the potential ability to deploy a force rapidly that could be used covertly in "terrorism," or used offensively, under launch-on-warning and launch-under-attack conditions, and/or in a retaliatory mode. Such weaponization could provide Iraq with the ability to launch strikes whose political impact was out of all proportion to their direct military value. The use of toxins or persistent biological agents, like anthrax, could achieve significant military effects or population damage. Such potential results could prompt Iraq to take the risk of using an agent that was a communicable disease, rather than military agents which require direct exposure to the original payload, or which are tailored to control their infectiousness.

Iraq has also shown that even its pre-war mix of delivery systems and weapons could have allowed the Iraqi government to use biological weapons at both the strategic and tactical level. Iraq dispersed biological weapons to at least four sites in January 1991 for use during the Gulf War. According to Iraqi sources, the commanders at these main storage sites were given authority in January 1991 to use these weapons in the case of a devastating attack on Baghdad, and the collapse of the Iraqi command and control system. This release authority was granted in order to ensure that Iraq had a retaliatory capability. The release authority seems to have applied to massive conventional attack on Baghdad, as well as a nuclear attack, and may have applied to a successful attack on Iraq's leadership.[547]

Iraq's Future Nuclear Capability

None of Iraq's weapons development efforts have been subject to more scrutiny than its nuclear weapons program. UNSCOM and the IAEA have been actively involved in the discovery and destruction of Iraq's massive nuclear weapons program ever since 1991. This program is so large that it is difficult to summarize, but UNSCOM and IAEA reporting indicates that Iraq spent up to $10 billion on its nuclear program before the Gulf War, and simultaneously pursued several different enrichment methods.[548]

Iraq's pre–Gulf War efforts aimed at acquiring traditional nuclear weapons were conducted under the auspices of the Iraqi Atomic Energy Commission, with the code-name Petrochemical-3 or PC-3. The ultimate aim of this program was the production of an implosion-type nuclear device. To accomplish this, PC-3 concentrated on two areas. The first was the production of fissile material through uranium enrichment and the second was the weaponization of an actual nuclear device.[549]

The fissile material production efforts relied primarily on the employment of electromagnetic isotope separation (EMIS) and gas centrifuge enrichment processes. According to reports in *Der Speigel*, Iraq obtained the details of URENCO's TC-11 centrifuge from a German traitor, Karl-Heinz Schaab.[550] Iraq was completing massive electromagnetic isotope separation (EMIS) and gas centrifuge enrichment production facilities at the time of the Gulf War, although these had a number of major technical problems. Iraq also researched chemical and gaseous diffusion processes and succeeded in enriching a small quantity of uranium, prior to the Gulf War, in the hot cells of their small reactors at Tuwaitha. It had at least 16 major sites of facilities involved in nuclear weapons research and production by the time of the Gulf War, and was attempting to rush forward the production of at least one nuclear weapon by April 1991 by cannibalizing the highly enriched material in its reactors.[551]

General Hussein Kamel's defection led to the disclosure of the fact that Iraq began a crash program to extract and further enrich the uranium in its French and Russian safeguarded reactors, including the reactor at Tuwaitha, in September 1990. Iraq intended to use the resulting weapons-grade material to advance its nuclear program to the point where it would have a bomb in April 1991. These plans, however, fell victim to coalition bombs which destroyed the equipment necessary for such an activity. In March 1991, the IAEA accounted for all of the uranium at Tuwaitha. However, the IAEA also found samples of enriched uranium whose origin could not be determined.[552]

In late 1995, UNSCOM and the IAEA also discovered Iraqi efforts aimed at developing a radiological weapon capable of scattering lethal radioactive debris without the necessity of a nuclear explosion, and that Iraq produced the casings for 80 such weapons. The weapons used irradiated zirconium oxide, and were designed to produce an "area denial" weapon for the Iran-Iraq War. Three prototype bombs were detonated at test sites. One as a ground-level static test and two others were dropped from aircraft. Iraq claims the irradiated material did not disperse widely enough from the crater and these tests proved to be a failure, but has no detailed records to prove this or to describe the scale of its program.[553] While UN resolutions do not specifically refer to radiological weapons, Rolf Ekeus, the chief UN weapons inspector, has said that the newly discovered research would be covered by UN Resolution 707, which refers to all Iraqi nuclear programs.

Estimates of how soon Iraq could have developed a nuclear weapon if the Gulf War had not occurred differ. It is clear, however, that Iraq would have developed a nuclear weapon within several years if had not been for the Coalition bombing and UN inspections. The Coalition bombings had only a moderate impact. Coalition intelligence and bombers were not successful in identifying and destroying many of Iraq's facilities. The Coalition only targeted three of Iraq's 25 major facilities for producing weapons of mass destruction before the air campaign began. It attacked only seven of these sites during the war—several largely by accident— and it did not fully destroy many of the facilities attacked.

The UNSCOM and IAEA effort have been more effective. Much of Iraq's nuclear equipment was too big to conceal or disperse, and the UN effort has been successful in destroying Iraq's remaining large nuclear facilities and in developing a continuing monitoring effort.[554] UNSCOM and the IAEA are monitoring 150 different sites to prevent a revival of Iraq's chemical and nuclear program. The monitoring effort consists of

177 remote control cameras and sensors, or "sniffers," linked by microwave signals to a 94 meter tower above the UN base in Baghdad. The UN also uses information provided by satellites, U-2Rs of the USAF 9th Reconnaissance Wing, and 3 helicopters armed with 600 mm cameras, ground penetrating radar, chemical detection systems, and radiation detection systems.[555]

These measures have led Ambassador Ekeus to declare that Iraq currently has ". . . no nuclear program in the sense that there is no centrifuge operating, that there is [not] any production of fissile materials."[556] At the same time, the US has deemed them "inadequate" and has urged that UNSCOM's surveillance capability be "upgraded and adjusted." While admitting the need for minor adjustments, UNSCOM disputes any suggestions of inadequacy relating to its monitoring activities.[557]

There is no way to resolve this debate. No inspection effort can be totally successful, and Iraq's game of nuclear hide and seek between the UN and Iraq is likely to go on for years. Iraq retains all of the nuclear technology it developed before the Gulf War, and a substantial amount of laboratory and test equipment remains unaccounted for. It can carry out much of its nuclear weapons design effort in small, scattered facilities with limited equipment other than dual-use computers and testing equipment. It can aggressively seek enriched or weapons-grade material from the Former Soviet Union or other sources. It can stockpile larger production and test equipment away from areas likely to be subject to inspection. For example, the IAEA announced that critical equipment for the manufacture of centrifuges had somehow "gone astray" in Iraq in late January 1996.[558]

Even if Iraq allows the UN to continue and expand its monitoring of activities—and UNSCOM can continue intrusive inspection and soil and water sampling at suspect sites—Iraq will retain the technological base that it acquired before the Gulf War. Iraq can still go on with a great deal of research and engineering activity with little fear of a challenge from the UN.[559] Iraq has also developed a long list of secret suppliers, and it is clear that it is reestablishing what is referred to in UNSCOM's September 1995 report to the UN Security Council as a ". . . very advanced procurement system."[560]

Implications for Western
and Southern Gulf Strategy

There is no way to be certain how many resources Iraq will allocate to conventional weapons, unconventional warfare and security operations, or weapons of mass destruction in the future. Even if Iraq has formulated detailed plans, which seems doubtful, it must react to outside factors like the duration and intensity of UN sanctions, the level of UNSCOM inspections, future oil revenues, its problems in dealing with its Kurds and Shi'ites, its problems with Iran and Kuwait, and the need to balance domestic demand against military ambition. Much will also depend on how long Saddam Hussein remains in power, although it is easy to overemphasize his importance.

The trends in Iraq's efforts to acquire weapons of mass destruction are, however, a strong argument that any strategy for dealing with Iraq must assume that Iraq will pursue its effort to acquire weapons of mass destruction indefinitely into the future, that it will carry out a major clandestine purchasing effort, that it will maintain clandestine facilities, and that it will systematically lie about its efforts and that nothing the Iraqi government says can be taken seriously without total independent verification. They are also strong arguments for continuing the UNSCOM effort as long as possible, for pushing Iraq into arms control agreements and making every effort to enforce them, and for establishing the tightest possible supplier nation controls on this aspect of Iraq's imports.

It is also dangerous to assume such efforts can be linked to the survival of Saddam Hussein and the Ba'ath elite. Most future Iraqi leaders are likely to have somewhat similar fears and ambitions—at least in the near term. No Iraqi leader will be able to ignore the efforts of Iran or Israel, or the potential challenge posed by the US and its allies in the Southern Gulf. Such leaders are likely to be products of the same Sunni elite as Saddam, and to rely on a high degree of authoritarianism and use of the instruments of state power. Even "pragmatic" or "moderate" replacements for Saddam will not ignore the potential threat posed by Iran and Iran's weapons of mass destruction programs. They are also likely to seek to use weapons of mass destruction as at least covert counters to US power projection capability and ways of intimidating or influencing their Southern Gulf neighbors.

Barring regional arms control agreements with a degree of intrusiveness that now seems impossible to negotiate or implement, they are likely to pursue Iraq's weapons of mass destruction programs at some level. For similar reasons, virtually all near-term Iraqi leaders are likely to see arms control agreements as irritants or products of necessity forced on Iraq from the outside, and see cheating on such agreements while attempting to enforce them on neighboring states as legitimate. Iraqi leaders other than Saddam may use all the right words, but they are almost certain to lie.

Regardless of what Iraqi leader is in power, it seems likely that Iraq's efforts to develop weapons of mass destruction will be pursued on a target of opportunity basis, and to meet broad political ambitions and the personal goals of Iraq's leaders. Iraq is unlikely to take completely reckless steps or ignore basic technological realities, but it is also unlikely to articulate and implement highly structured force development plans or to develop and implement a detailed military doctrine for employing weapons of mass destruction.

Furthermore, any Iraqi leader is likely to improvise his approach to deploying and using such weapons in reaction to a given crisis, and to alter employment doctrine on the basis of events. It is extremely unlikely that Iraq will seek to create a highly structured pattern of deterrence similar to the one that helped shape the Cold War, and will develop detailed targeting doctrines and escalation ladders.

This does not mean such leaders, including Saddam, will be suicidal, fanatical, or take what they regard as irrational risks. It may, however, mean that such leaders identify themselves with the state and with Iraq's future. It may mean they will use weapons of mass destruction against Iraq's neighbors at the tactical level, and/or against Iraq's Shi'ites and Kurds to stay in power or protect their conventional forces. It may mean they will strike preemptively against a key enemy like Iran, or create forces designed to deter the US with a launch-on-warning/launch-under-attack or retaliatory capability. The West and the Southern Gulf cannot ignore the fact that the Iraqi leadership might well feel that a "ride out" strategy would simply reinforce Iraq's weakness and be fundamentally "irrational" in character.

Iraqi war fighting with weapons of mass destruction may follow fundamentally different patterns from those that were institutionalized during the Cold War. Regardless of whether Iraq is led by Saddam, it may:

- Fail to articulate a strategy of deterrence or employment, or only describe one consisting of rhetoric rather than detailed war fighting capabilities
- Develop and produce weapons of mass destruction using massive efforts at concealment, denial, and compartmentation—focusing more on the acquisition and development effort than employment. Targeting plans, test and evaluation, and understanding of lethality will be limited. Joint warfare concepts will rarely be articulated, and doctrine will not be practiced.
- Keep actual delivery units covert or compartmented from other forces, and under the direct control of ruling elites with little real military experience. Actual weapons may often be held separately from delivery systems and by special units chosen more for loyalty than capability.
- Provide separate lines of C⁴I/BM reporting which go directly to the leadership.

- Employ weapons in ways which are crisis driven, and utilization and escalation will be more a product of the attitudes and decisions of a narrow ruling political elite rather than the result of the advice of the military command chain. Risk taking will be leader-specific and based on perceptions of a crisis shaped more by internal political attitudes than an objective understanding of the military situation.
- Show limited restraint in attacking civilian targets or mass employment against armed forces. Regimes may take existential risks in escalating if they feel they are likely to lose power.
- Use proxies and unconventional delivery means where this seems politically desirable, and improvise such employment without warning.
- Pay detailed attention to US counterproliferation and ATBM efforts at the technical level, and the lessons of previous wars. They will seek to steadily improve concealment, denial, and countermeasures.
- See arms control as an extension of conflict and rivalry by other means; not as a valid security option.
- Consider using proxy groups or unconventional delivery of weapons of mass destruction to attack outside the context of a war. Such an attack might be launched against a peace process, US commitment to the defense of a given region, a peace keeping force, an election, a ruling elite, or internal groups hostile to the Iraqi ruling elite.
- Find covert or unconventional delivery of weapons of mass destruction to be preferable to the use of advanced delivery systems. For example, Iraq could use cargo ships, passenger aircraft, commercial vehicles, dhows, or commercial cargo shipments, and route them through multiple destinations. Iraq has a well established series of covert transport and smuggling networks throughout the region, and might use proxy or terrorist groups to manufacture biological weapons in situ.
- Use biological agents for indirect attacks. Iraq might consider the use of such agents to mirror image local diseases or with long gestation times. Persistent nerve agents could be used in subways, large buildings, shopping malls/bazaars, etc. to create both immediate casualties and long term risks.
- Use mixes of different biological and chemical agents to defeat detection and protection gear or vaccines.
- Develop a covert "break out" capability. The development of a capability to manufacture several hundred biological and chemical weapons suddenly, with little or no warning is well within Iraq's state of the art using nothing but commercial supplies and equip-

ment, and much of the effort could be conducted as civil or defensive research.

- See an increasing incentive for the unconventional use of weapons of mass destruction in proportion to Iraq's lack of parity in conventional weapons, and/or or the prospect of catastrophic defeat.

Table Fourteen shows the possible relative strengths and weaknesses Iraq may see in given types of weapons of mass destruction. Table Fifteen shows that Iraq does not need nuclear weapons to achieve nuclear lethalities against its neighbors or US forces—it already has the biological weapons technology to produce far more lethal weapons than the ones shown in Table Thirteen, and these weapons clearly have the lethality of tactical nuclear weapons. The previous analysis of Iraq's biological weapons efforts has also shown that Iraq can rapidly manufacture biological agents by converting civil facilities.

This analysis should be a clear warning to those Southern Gulf states and other countries interested in minimizing the risks inherent in Iraq's future capability to use weapons of mass destruction. It should be an equal warning to those in the West who focus on a counterproliferation strategy that is oriented towards nuclear weapons to the exclusion of other types of weapons of mass destruction or who focus on counterproliferation strategies that assume that an enemy will not strike first or will simply ride out an attack.

TABLE FOURTEEN The Strengths and Weaknesses of Weapons of Mass
Destruction

Chemical Weapons

Destructive Effects: Poisoning skin, lungs, nervous system, or blood. Contaminating areas, equipment, and protective gear for periods of hours to days. Forcing military units to don highly restrictive protection gear or use incapacitating antidotes. False alarms and panic. Misidentification of the agent, or confusion of chemical with biological agents (which may be mixed) leading to failure of defense measures. Military and popular panic and terror effects. Major medical burdens which may lead to mistreatment. Pressure to deploy high-cost air and missile defenses. Paralysis or disruption of civil life and economic activity in threatened or attacked areas.

Typical Military Targets: Infantry concentrations, air bases, ships, ports, staging areas, command centers, munitions depots, cities, key oil and electrical facilities, desalinization plants.

Typical Military Missions: Killing military and civilian populations. Intimidation. Attack on civilian population or targets. Disruption of military operations by requiring protective measures or decontamination. Area or facility denial. Psychological warfare, production of panic, and terror.

Military Limitations: Large amounts of agents are required to achieve high lethality, and military and economic effects are not sufficiently greater than carefully targeted conventional strikes to offer major war fighting advantages. Most agents degrade quickly, and their effect is highly dependent on temperature and weather conditions, height of dissemination, terrain, and the character of built-up areas. Warning devices far more accurate and sensitive than for biological agents. Protective gear and equipment can greatly reduce effects, and sufficiently high numbers of rounds, sorties, and missiles are needed to ease the task of defense. Leaves buildings and equipment reusable by the enemy, although persistent agents may require decontamination. Persistent agents may contaminate the ground the attacker wants to cross or occupy and force use of protective measures or decontamination.

Biological Weapons

Destructive Effects: Infectious disease or biochemical poisoning. Contaminating areas, equipment, and protective gear for periods of hours to weeks. Delayed effects and tailored to produce incapacitation or killing, treatable or non-treatable agents, and be infectious on contact only or transmittable. Forcing military units to don highly restrictive protection gear or use incapacitating vaccines and antidotes. False alarms and panic. High risk of at least initial misidentification of the agent, or confusion of chemical with biological agents (which may be mixed) leading to failure of defense measures. Military and popular panic and terror effects. Major medical burdens which may lead to mistreatment. Pressure to deploy high-cost air and missile defenses. Paralysis or disruption of civil life and economic activity in threatened or attacked areas.

(continues)

TABLE FOURTEEN *(continued)*

Typical Military Targets: Infantry concentrations, air bases, ships, ports, staging areas, command centers, munitions depots, cities, key oil and electrical facilities, desalinization plants. Potentially far more effective against military and civil area targets than chemical weapons.

Typical Military Missions: Killing and incapacitation of military and civilian populations. Intimidation. Attack on civilian poulation or targets. Disruption of military operations by requiring protective measures or decontamination. Area or facility denial. Psychological warfare, production of panic, and terror.

Military Limitations: Most wet agents degrade quickly, although spores, dry encapsulated agent, and some toxins are persistent. Effects usually take some time to develop (although not in the case of some toxins). Effects are unpredictable, and are even more dependent than chemical weapons on temperature and weather conditions, height of dessemination, terrain, and the character of built-up areas. Major risk of contaminating the wrong area. Warning devices uncertain and may misidentify the agent. Protective gear and equipment can reduce effects. Leaves buildings and equipment reusable by the enemy, although persistent agents may require decontamination. Persistent agents may contaminate the ground the attacker wants to cross or occupy and force use of protective measures or decontamination. More likely than chamical agents to cross the threshold where nuclear retaliation seems justified.

Nuclear Weapons

Destructive Effects: Blast, fire, and radiation. Destruction of large areas and porduction of fallout and contamination—depending on character of weapon and height of burst. Contaminating areas, equipment, and protective gear for periods of hours to days. Forcing military units to don highly restrictive protection gear and use massive amounts of decontamination gear. Military and popular panic and terror effects. Massive medical burdens. Pressure to deploy high-cost air and missile defenses. Paralysis or disruption of civil life and economic activity in threatened or attacked areas. High long-term death rates from radiation. Forced dispersal of military forces and evacuation of civilians. Destruction of military and economic centers, and national political leadership and command authority, potentially altering character of attacked nation and creating major recovery problems.

Typical Military Targets: Hardened targets, enemy facilities and weapons of mass destruction, enemy economy, political leadership, and national command authority. Infantry and armored concentrations, air bases, ships, ports, staging areas, command centers, munitions depots, cities, key oil and electrical facilities, desalinization plants.

Typical Military Missions: Forced dispersal of military forces and evacuation of civilians. Destruction of military and economic centers, and national political leadership and command authority, potentially altering character of attacked nation and creating major recovery problems.

(continues)

TABLE FOURTEEN *(continued)*

Military Limitations: High cost. Difficulty of acquiring more than a few weapons. Risk of accidents or failures that hit friendly territory. Crosses threshold to level where nuclear retaliation is likely. Destruction or contamination of territory and facilities attacker wants to cross or occupy. High risk of massive collateral damage to civilians if this is important to attacker.

Source: Adapted by Anthony H. Cordesman from Office of Technology Assessment, *Proliferation of Weapons of Mass Destruction: Assessing the Risks,* US Congress OTA-ISC-559, Washington, August 1993, pp. 56–57.

TABLE FIFTEEN   The Comparative Effects of Biological, Chemical, and Nuclear
Weapons Delivered Against a Typical Urban Target in the
Middle East

Using missile warheads: Assumes one Scud sized warhead with a maximum payload of 1,000 kilograms. The study assumes that the biological agent would not make maximum use of this payload capacity because the country deploying such systems cannot make an efficient warhead. It is unclear if this assumption is realistic.

	Area Covered in Square Kilometers	Deaths Assuming 3,000–10,000 People Per Square Kilometer
Chemical: 300 kilograms of Sarin nerve gas with a density of 70 milligrams per cubic meter	0.22	60–200
Biological: 30 kilograms of Anthrax spores with a density of 0.1 milligram per cubic meter	10	30,000–100,000
Nuclear:		
One 12.5 kilotron nuclear device achieving 5 pounds per cubic inch of over-pressure	7.8	23,000–80,000
One 1 megaton hydrogen bomb	190	570,000–1,900,000

Using one aircraft delivering 1,000 kilograms of Sarin nerve gas or 100 kilograms of anthrax spores: Assumes the aircraft flies in a straight line over the target at optimal altitude, and dispenses the agent as an aerosol. The study assumes that the biological agent would not make maximum use of the weapons weight carrying capacity. It is unclear this assumption is realistic.

	Area Covered in Square Kilometers	Deaths Assuming 3,000–10,000 People Per Square Kilometer
Clear sunny day, light breeze		
Sarin Nerve Gas	0.74	300–700
Anthrax Spores	46.00	130,000–460,000
Overcast day or night, moderate wind		
Sarin Nerve Gas	0.8	400–800
Anthrax Spores	140.00	420,000–1,400,000
Clear calm night		
Sarin Nerve Gas	7.8	3,000–8,000
Anthrax Spores	300.00	1,000,000–3,000,000

Source: Adapted by the author from Office of Technology Assessment, *Proliferation of Weapons of Mass Destruction: Assessing the Risks,* US Congress OTA-ISC-559, Washington, August 1993, pp. 53–54.

16

The Problem of Policy: Beyond Sanctions and "Dual Containment"

Any strategy towards Iraq must recognize the fact that it will remain a revanchist state as long as it is under the control of Saddam Hussein or other members of its present ruling elite. Iraq has already attempted to assassinate former President Bush, has systematically resisted the UN's efforts to destroy its capacity to produce weapons of mass destruction, has backed the People's Mujahideen in attacks on Iran, and has repeatedly infiltrated the Kuwaiti border. Iraqi media have often repeated Iraq's claim to Kuwait, and Iraq long delayed its recognition of the new border the UN demarcated between Iraq and Kuwait.

Iraq continues to fight a low-level war with its Shi'ites. It has challenged the UN no-fly zones. It has sent small intelligence groups into Kuwait, and about 40% of its army is currently positioned to attack into the Kurdish security zone in the north. Senior Iraqi leaders have been clear about their desire for revenge in their discussions with Arab leaders, and Tariq Aziz has stated that it is dishonorable to leave revenge to one's sons. This may seem to be yet another example of rhetoric, but Iraq has already demonstrated that rhetoric can easily slip into reality.[561]

While Iraq has since appeared to recognize Kuwait and the new border, there is little doubt that it has done so as a tactical move. Iraq will continue to try violate the UN sanctions whenever this seems possible and to resume its military build-up the moment that sanctions on dual-use and military imports are ended. Iraq is already fighting a low-level war with its own rebel Shi'ites. It regularly challenges the UN no-fly zones. It has sent a number of small intelligence groups into Kuwait, and it positioned major armored forces near the Kuwaiti border last fall. About 40% of its army is currently positioned to attack across the Kurdish security zone in the north, and at least 60% of the Iraqi Army could redeploy to the Iranian border within a week.

The Case for Continuing Military Containment

Iraq's current military weakness does not deprive it of the ability to fight a number of types of war that do not involve committing major forces against the organized opposition of Western and Southern Gulf forces. It can fight irregular or unconventional forms of war. The use of third party terrorists, extremists, and proxies offers Iraq both a means of revenge and far more security than large-scale military action, so does playing a spoiler role at the political level, and financing political rivals to its enemies in the southern Gulf and rest of the Arab world.

A number of types of military conflict remain possible, and typical scenarios could include:

- Clashes with Turkey or Iran over Iraqi efforts to attack its Kurds, or support of Kurds hostile to Iraq and Iran.
- Mid-intensity conflict with the US over a major Iraqi attack on the Kurds in the Kurdish security zone.
- War with the Kurds in the Kurdish security zone.
- Conflict with Iran over Iraqi treatment of the Shi'ites in southern Iraq, and/or Iranian attacks on the Iraqi front group, the People's Mujahideen.
- Major clashes resulting from refusal to allow UN inspection, over challenges to "no-fly zones," and incursions into Kuwait.
- Military confrontation growing out of US or UN attacks in response to Iraqi support of terrorism or use of unconventional warfare.
- Use of chemical or biological terrorism.
- Use of mines or missiles against tanker traffic to Kuwait.
- Unconventional attacks on facilities and ships in Gulf.
- Confrontation with Syria over a potential Syrian peace agreement with Israel or some other factor.
- Conflicts with Syria or Turkey over water.

This list of possible contingencies shows how difficult it is to try to set bounds on the broad range of unpredictable contingencies that could result from the actions of even one of the radical powers in the Gulf. Further, the Southern Gulf states and the West cannot ignore the need to plan for a worst case scenario: a large-scale Iraqi combined operations attack on Kuwait and/or Eastern Saudi Arabia launched with limited warning. Once again, the Southern Gulf and the West also cannot simply plan for today. They already must plan forces and capabilities for the year 2000 and well beyond. Someday the UN sanctions will end. Someday Iraq will be able to rebuild its forces with new technology based on its interpretation of the lessons of the Gulf War.

Prospects for Future Conflict

Prophecy is a dangerous game at any time and is virtually impossible in the case of Iraq. There is no way to predict how long Saddam Hussein and the Ba'ath regime will last, or whether any successor government will ultimately prove less authoritarian or aggressive. The future unity and resolve of the UN Coalition is uncertain, and there are limits to how long and how thoroughly the current embargo and sanctions can be applied.

In the near-term, Iraq seems likely to limit itself to internal, low-level, and/or unconventional conflicts. There is still a real risk that Kurdish and Shi'ite separatism could provoke some form of Iraqi civil war, but it is a war the Ba'ath regime would quickly win unless the UN intervenes. The risk of new fighting between Iraq and its Kurds is particularly high. In spite of its alliance with Barzani in September 1996, the Ba'ath elite is almost certain to make every effort to undermine the Kurdish enclave, and to use force the moment it feels it is safe to do so. It will probably have the support of most Iraqi military officers. Turkey's confrontation with its own Kurds, and Iran's support of Iraqi Shi'ites, are other major wild cards in the equation. Turkey may well reach the point where it fears Kurdish separatism more than Iraq.

Iraq's Shi'ites are now under tight government control, and many are Iraqi nationalists. A new uprising seems unlikely, but it might still occur. If it does, such an uprising seems far more likely to lead to bloody repression than partition of the country or any lasting alignment between Iraqi Shi'ites and Iran. There seems to be only a very limited possibility that a major uprising might create a significant pro-Iranian Shi'ite resistance in Iraq, might create a pro-Iranian Shi'ite enclave similar to the Kurdish enclave, or even give Iran part of Iraq's territory.

What seems to be a more likely scenario is that the Ba'ath regime will systematically eliminate the last traces of Shi'ite opposition in the marshes, and defeat the Kurds by a mixture of political and economic action, low-level military action, and military intimidation. Such an Iraqi victory over the Kurds, and final elimination of the Shi'ite resistance, could increase tension with Iran and Turkey, and seriously undermine the credibility of Western military capabilities.

Such a victory would also allow Iraq to shift from a focus on internal issues to revenge and efforts at intimidation. Iraq's current regime is almost certain to see reparations, the threat of war crimes trials, and competition for oil quotas and revenues as issues that merit at least the tacit threat of the use of military force. Iraq may be deterred from attacking Kuwait, but it certainly retains the capability to seize Kuwait if Kuwait does not have US support. Iraq could also pose a threat to Saudi Arabia, although it would have to reorganize its logistic and support capabilities to carry out a major invasion of the Eastern Province.

Active Iraqi efforts at revenge and intimidation are possible—perhaps likely. At least some border incidents with Iran, Saudi Arabia, and Kuwait are likely, and so is the use of terrorism and unconventional warfare against leaders or elites which Saddam Hussein and the Ba'ath see as responsible for Iraq's defeat, continued sanctions or reparation, or as placing limits on the reassertion of Iraqi power in the region.

Even if Iraq does not force another military confrontation with the UN, Iraq will remain a major threat to regional peace. Iraq not only retains a significant capability to build weapons of mass destruction, its overall mix of conventional forces is still formidable by regional standards. Iraq's forces are still large enough to pose a major threat to Kuwait and Saudi Arabia if the two do not obtain American aid. Iraq has enough conventional forces to enable it to defend against any attack by Iran, and its forces should be fully capable of dealing with any of the various Kurdish or Shi'ite militias that are internal threats to Saddam Hussein's power.

Iraq has less ability to attack its neighbors. It has lost much of its prewar offensive capability. It cannot use its present forces in a sustained conflict without major resupply of munitions and spare parts, and its forces will continue to deteriorate with time. Iraq not only is currently limited in military power, the UN embargo on arms and military technology ensures that it will slowly and steadily decline to a limited defensive capability. This decline in Iraq's military forces, however, will not make it vulnerable to Iran unless Iran receives major additional arms and reorganizes and retrains its forces to the point where they can gain a decisive qualitative edge over Iraq. Such an improvement in Iranian forces now seems highly unlikely.

The mid- and long-term prospects for conflict also depend heavily on Iraq's regime and access to new supplies of conventional weapons and the technology to make weapons of mass destruction. It seems likely that Iraq will be a revanchist state as long as it is either under its present Ba'athist regime or under the control of another authoritarian leader or hard-line military officer. The issue is not really whether Saddam survives, but the future character of the state. If any hard-line regime does survive, and Iraq can obtain significant flows of arms and technology, it is likely to be exceedingly dangerous. It is certain to make growing use of the politics of intimidation and may reach the point of risk taking and significant conflict.

The Value of Military Containment

These trends and risks form a strong argument for separating the issue of military containment from other aspects of any strategy for dealing with Iraq. There is every reason to continue to enforce the UN Security Council Resolutions that deny Iraq arms imports and deny it imports of dual-use technology it can use for weapons of mass destruction.

Iraq has played the role of an aggressor or destabilizing state for much of its history since the fall of the monarchy. It retains enough military capability, in spite of the Gulf War, to threaten its southern neighbors if they do not receive outside support, and the technical skills and at least some of the equipment to manufacture and deliver weapons of mass destruction. Unless Iran becomes far stronger than it is today, no case can be made for arms transfers unless a more democratic, stable, and ethnically balanced government comes to power in the future. Until a fundamental change takes place in Iraq's government, there is a clear case for military containment, and for taking every possible step to limit Iraq's military build-up and its efforts to rebuild its capacity to deliver weapons of mass destruction.

Every step that strengthens Iraq's military capabilities increases the risk of more military adventures like its invasion of Iran and Kuwait. A military build-up in Iraq not only threatens the region, it threatens Iraq's people, and means an Iraqi regime will allocate resources to military expenditures that do not benefit Iraq's people in any way. It provides an authoritarian regime with the tools necessary to oppress Iraq's Kurds and Shi'ites, and to maintain control over its Sunnis. It also means the continued diversion of vast resources from recovery and development to useless expenditures on force. To put this in perspective, the US estimates that Iraq spent over $180 billion (in constant $1995) on military expenditures in the decade before the Gulf War, and over $80 billion on arms imports plus another $10 billion on weapons of mass destruction.[562]

Additional Measures to Limit Iraqi Military Capabilities

At the same time, a realistic policy must recognize that the success of military containment will always be relative. Iraq retains a major military-industrial complex. There are many dual-use technologies that are not practical to ban because they are "civil" in character, but that can aid Iraq in improving its military forces, in strengthening its military industries, and in rebuilding its program to build and deliver weapons of mass destruction.

The UN resolutions and cease-fire accords resulting from the Gulf War cannot provide a lasting basis for preventing all military exports to Iraq, and neither can arms control agreements on supplier regimes. Present international accords allow the sale and transfer of significant amounts of biological, chemical, and nuclear technology to Iraq, once it "complies" with the key sanctions now affecting it. Some nations or individual companies will always be willing to deal with Iraq on a covert or overt basis. There is no clear difference between "guns" and "butter," and any easing of "civil" economic sanctions will inevitably give Iraq some aid in strengthening its military capabilities.

Given these uncertainties, it is clear that the US and its Southern Gulf allies must take every possible action to limit Iraq's present and future war fighting options. This involves four sets of interrelated measures: arms control, supplier regimes and limits on the transfer of technology and equipment, strengthening the deterrent and defensive capabilities of Southern Gulf forces, and building up Western power projection capabilities.

These measures should be taken in concert. Focusing on one measure—such as arms control or efforts to strengthen Southern Gulf forces—is almost certain to fail. The US and its allies must take every possible step to pressure Iraq to join international and regional arms control regimes that can bring stability to the Gulf. At the same time, the West must organize to develop tight controls on transfers of military and dual-use technology to Iraq, focusing on the risks posed by the transfer of both conventional technologies and those for weapons of mass destruction.

Such limits on trade and technology transfers may or may not be part of arms control regimes and formal embargoes. One point, however, must be kept clearly in mind. Some arms control regimes stress equity to all signatories or tend to penalize moderate states that sign and honor such agreements while extremist states do not. "Fairness" is not the issue in dealing with Iran and Iraq. Security is the issue and will best be achieved by understanding that weakening or limiting Southern Gulf and moderate Arab states is scarcely a way of avoiding future conflicts in the Gulf.

The worst possible path that outside nations could follow would be to treat Iraq as an open market for arms, or to return to the Cold War struggle for influence in the northern Gulf. The US and the heirs of the former Soviet Union need to recognize that their past efforts to make either Iran or Iraq into allies or strategic "pillars" have been dismal failures. The US never benefited from its military support of Iran, and indeed was forced to intervene against Iran during 1987–1988. The former Soviet Union never obtained any meaningful form of strategic advantage or support from its arms transfers to Iraq.

The ultimate answer to dealing with Iraqi military capabilities, however, will be a continued military alliance between the US, Britain, and the Southern Gulf states. No deal with Iraq is likely to last longer than the West's military presence in the Gulf, or be any stronger than a combination of Southern Gulf military forces and US and British power projection capabilities. Diplomacy will at best be an extension of force by other means. As is the case with Iran, the threat from Iraq can ultimately only be contained or countered by war fighting capability.

Prospects for Political Change

The choice of a strategy for dealing with Iraq's regime and the issue of sanctions involves far harder choices. Saddam is still in power and his demise has been predicted so often that, as one senior Ba'athist official put it: "... waiting for Saddam to go is like waiting for Godot to arrive."[563] Further, there are no good options for pursuing a new leadership within either the existing "center" of the Iraqi politics, or within the "periphery" of Kurdish groups, Shi'ite factions, and opposition political parties. Each approach has powerful liabilities.

Iraq's complex political and socioeconomic situation has created conditions where outside powers can only have an indirect influence on whether Saddam goes and who succeeds him. The West and Southern Gulf can back opposition movements but these have little influence and chance of success. They can back Kurdish and Shi'ite groups but these can, at best, trigger civil conflict, and present serious risks in terms of Kurdish separatism and its impact on Turkey and Shi'ite ties to Iran. Such options are only marginally better alternatives than the present reliance on the race between the lifting of sanctions and the collapse of Saddam's regime.

Saddam Remains in Power

Any strategy towards Iraq must take explicit account of the possibility that Saddam will remain in power. Saddam is scarcely secure. The previous analysis has shown that Saddam's regime face declining support in the Sunni heartland, family defections, worsening economic situation and poor agricultural harvest. Although Iraq's acceptance of UN Security Council Resolution 986 has provided the regime with limited relief, the remaining sanctions are still firmly in place,

At the same time, Saddam Hussein has shown an extraordinary resilience for nearly a quarter of a century. He survived the Iran-Iraq war despite repeated claims by Ayatollah Khomeini that the bloodshed will only end with the demise of Saddam. He survived his humiliating defeat during Desert Storm; he defeated two rebellions, and remained in power in spite of more than five years of severe sanctions.

Saddam's opponents face many problems and Saddam is a master conspirator who is one of the few world leaders whose early political career focused exclusively on matters of intelligence and security. He began by providing security for the Ba'ath party when it was out of power, and then by ensuring the security of the Ba'ath regime once it had seized power in 1968. Saddam was and remains a man of action. His experience has given him an almost uncanny ability to detect and swiftly nip in the bud any threats to his security. Saddam also has single-mindedly practiced Mao Zedong's maxim: "People are not chives, when you cut their heads they do not grow new ones." He has neutralized opponents and rivals from within the system by the simple expedient of killing them, in stark contrast to previous Iraqi regimes who allowed their opponents to live or to go into exile and then to come back and haunt them.

As a result, the continuation of the Saddam regime now seems to depend largely on either the random success of some coup or assassination attempt by some unknown element of the "center," and the cumulative political and economic impact of sanctions on the support Saddam can obtain from the "center" and the Iraqi people. Saddam would be most likely to survive if the UN gradually removed the restraints retained in Resolution 986 and lifted sanctions with minimal or no conditions. The internal psychological, political, social, and economic impact of such a lifting of sanctions on Iraqi domestic politics would be tremendous, as would the external impact. Such a lifting would be seen as a major victory by Saddam and his regime.

Any major further relief from the UN sanctions seems unlikely in the immediate future. Many senior Iraqi government officials—possibly including Tariq Aziz—are convinced that there is little prospect that oil sanctions will be lifted further until well after the US presidential elections of November 1996.[564]

Saddam has, however, found other ways of improving his position which have a powerful internal and regional impact. For example, his decision to make the Iraqi people vote on a referendum on whether he should stay on as president for another seven years on October 15, 1995, may seem farcical by Western standards. The government "predicted" that Iraq's voters would fully support Saddam's continuation as president long in advance of the vote, and the result was clearly manipulated by the state.[565] However, it is dangerous to dismiss the symbolism involved by the referendum or the amount of power the regime demonstrated.

Saddam can always act on his promises of further liberalization as a temporary tactic. He can then reverse them when this becomes convenient or even make good on such promises with little risk of losing power. Iraq has no experience with representative government. Political activity has been limited to members of the Ba'ath Party—estimated at about eight percent of the population—and this political activity consists almost solely of a bureaucratic jockeying for power and efforts to obtain power, promotion, and privilege by supporting the government.

If Saddam does remain in power, the West and the Southern Gulf have few options other than to pursue the military containment as long as possible, find ways of defusing some of the economic and humanitarian concerns over other sanctions and extend them as long as possible, and continuing to attempt to isolate Iraq politically and diplomatically. However, it is increasingly unlikely that West and Southern Gulf states will pursue such a policy with any unity. Britain, US, Kuwait, Saudi Arabia, and the US may pursue such a policy, but many other countries are likely to seek political accommodation and economic advantage.

Saddam Falls from Power

It seems extraordinarily unlikely that Saddam will leave power voluntarily, or leave as part of some orderly transfer of power. This makes it likely that the next "president" of Iraq will be "elected" by putting a bullet into Saddam—and bullets into many of his supporters—or by a bloody coup. The only question is likely to be when this coup occurs and whether it occurs at the palace level or through broader fighting.

If the West and the Southern Gulf are lucky, such a "centrist" coup or assassination will occur soon and produce some benefits. There are several different types of leaders that might replace Saddam under these conditions:

- *Saddam the lesser:* Another leader from within the present Ba'ath elite might replace Saddam who has somewhat similar beliefs and ambitions. Such a leader will almost certainly lack Saddam's charisma and authority, but might well be able to convince other nations to lift sanctions and recognize his regime as legitimate. He is likely to be quietly revanchist, but may well act pragmatically as long as this results in the lifting of sanctions and the restoration of Iraq's oil trade and ability to import. There is no way to predict whether such a leader will become a quiet pragmatist, but such a figure could pursue many political paths. These could range from a slow move towards moderation to the covert rebuilding of Iraq's weapons of mass destruction and creating an Iraq which pursued a subtler and more effective pattern of hostility towards Iraq's neighbors and the West.
- *Saddamism without Saddam* could emerge from within the ranks of Saddam's closest associates, likely from within the ruling elite, or from within the list of other Takritis. Several come to mind: Barzan al-Takriti who is still the head of the Iraqi UN mission in Geneva, Hussein Rashid al-Takriti, army chief-of-staff during the Kuwait invasion and currently a special military advisor to Saddam, General Muzahem Sa'ab al Takrit, former head of the air force, General Hamid Sha'aban al Takriti, commander of the air force during the Iran-Iraq, Nameq al Takriti, commander of the Special Guards, Abdel Sattar Ibrahim al Takriti, commander of the Republican Guards, and Kamal Mustafa al Takriti, currently joint commander with Qusay

Hussein—Saddam's younger son—of Special Security and the brother-in-law of Hussein Kamel Hasan.[566] If Saddam disappears 'violently' this may well open the floodgates to a violent and protracted power struggle between competitors for power, a struggle which is likely to involve the opposition groups and the military.

- *An authoritarian moderate:* A coup might be led be a centrist authoritarian without Saddam's revanchist and militarist tendencies. While Iraq may lack the structure to move towards democracy in the near term, it is possible that the initial violence of any effort to overthrow Saddam could be followed by a leader willing to focus on Iraq's internal economic development, the need to accommodate its Shi'ite and Kurdish factions, and restoring Iraq's relations with other states. Iraq does have a strong class of highly educated technocrats and this class might provide powerful support for such a leader. It would be hard for such a new ruling elite to ignore the pressures for revanchism, but there are strong incentives to concentrate on development, to heal Iraq's sectarian and ethnic divisions, and reach a settlement with Iraq's neighbors that will free it of the problem of reparations.

Unfortunately for the West and the Southern Gulf, this political situation makes it difficult to pursue a "centrist" strategy. "Centrist" assassins or coup planners may seek outside support, but it is unlikely that either a Western or Southern Gulf state will be able to exercise much control over who is involved, their political character, or their actions if they achieve power. A "centrist" coup or assassination may lead to many initial promises or claims of moderation, liberalization, and political change, but the reality is most likely to be very different. Any efforts to overthrow Saddam within the present ruling Sunni elite are likely to be followed by continuing repression of the Shi'ites and Kurds, the arrest and execution of many rivals and supporters of Saddam, and the eventual arrest and execution of other opponents.

The most the West and the Southern Gulf can do under such conditions is to create strong incentives and disincentives to influence the action of the new leader. The lifting of sanctions, debt relief, forgiveness of reparations, and immunity to war crimes trials all provide an important combination of carrots and sticks. The question is whether the West and the Southern Gulf have the unity to use such tools effectively. A rush to "forgive and forget" is not the right strategy, but it is far more likely than effective diplomacy.

A Man on 'Tank-Back'

The main alternative to a "centrist" coup or assassination is an independent military coup. This prospect seems unlikely, but a military officer or group of military officers might still emerge at any time who differ in attitude and policy from Saddam Hussein and his supporters.

There is no way to determine whether such a leadership would pursue the interests of some new Sunni faction, follow the path of "Saddam the lesser" or move towards "authoritarian moderation." A reform-driven military coup seems unlikely. The Iraqi military has never been an effective agent of development and modernization, and Iraqi military rule has never succeeded in implementing effective political and socioeconomic programs. The Iraqi military has also long been riddled by factionalism. It does not matter whether one strong officer or a collective junta emerges, it is likely that such a regime will become mired in intra-factional strife.

This contingency again makes it difficult to pursue a "centrist" strategy. The military officers involved might seek outside support, but it is again unlikely that any Western or Southern Gulf state will be able to exercise much control over who is involved, their political character, or their actions if they achieve power.

It is somewhat more likely, however, that such a military government could be encouraged to incorporate Shi'ites and Kurds into its leadership, to create a national provisional government, and to rule in cooperation with civilian technocrats. The West and the Southern Gulf might be more effective in offering incentives and disincentives, and in using the lifting of sanctions, debt relief, forgiveness of reparations, and immunity to war crimes trials as carrots and sticks. There might also be less risk of divisions within the West and the Southern Gulf over such a policy, since it would not involve forgiveness of centrist political leaders involved in the invasion of Kuwait, or with such direct responsibility for attacks on the Kurds and Shi'ites.

A Takeover by the Opposition

A takeover by Iraq's opposition parties seems extremely unlikely. It stretches credulity to believe that the 60–90 exiled opposition groups, including those under the umbrella organization of the Iraq National Council, could take over. The most credible groups in this mix of opposition groups are the Kurds, the Shi'ites of various hues—including liberal democrats and secularists, moderate Islamists and Islamic fundamentalists, and Sunni Arab nationalists. All were severely weakened by the events of August–September 1996, and they could only succeed if they formed a lasting coalition that would constitute a dramatic break with Iraq's 70 year long history of domination by the center and Sunni Arabs.

If such a contingency did occur, political power would probably shift in favor of the Shi'ites, although the center of political gravity would probably still be the geographic center of Iraq where Baghdad is located. The Sunni Arabs would still play an important political role, given their predominance in the administration, politics and military establishment. The Kurds who are 20–22% of the population would constitute a powerful pressure bloc in such a new system but would not be able to dominate it the way Iraq's Sunni Arabs—who are roughly 20% of the total population—did for 70 years.

The Kurds can never dominate Iraq. They have no meaningful strength in the armed forces and are a minority in an overwhelmingly Arab (75%) country. The Kurds have also long been distrusted by both Sunni and Shi'ite Arabs, who fear that they are secessionist and who feel they take advantage of any Iraqi weakness to put forward autonomy claims.

It is difficult to envision what such a provisional regime composed of a coalition of opposition groups would do in matters of domestic and foreign policy. It is possible to speculate based on evidence from past Iraqi history and the pronouncements of contemporary opposition groups.[567] If such opposition groups can be taken seriously, they would support reform and a constitutionalist approach to government. They would end the one-party state system, and the Ba'ath would become one competing party among many. They would dismantle the vast national-security apparatus associated with the Saddam regime since 1979 and would reduce the size of the army.

Unfortunately, its both fashionable and necessary for most opposition groups to advocate such moderation while they are in opposition. It is far from clear what would happen if most actually achieve power, and whether the end result would be reform or a struggle to produce a new authoritarian leader. Many opposition groups may be far less moderate in power than in opposition.

Western and Southern Gulf efforts to create such a contingency are likely to be futile, regardless of the scale of overt or covert support. It may be worth providing limited, quiet support to the Iraqi opposition simply to keep the possibility alive and to embarrass the Ba'ath regime, but there are obvious risks in supporting one opposition faction over another. Further, a major support effort not only is likely to be a waste of money, it is likely to end up in corruption and labeling the opposition as a tool of outside interests.

If such a contingency does occur, however, it would be the ideal contingency for Western and Southern Gulf use of incentives and disincentives. Lifting of sanctions, debt relief, forgiveness of reparations, and immunity to war crimes trials could be used as carrots with only minimal concern for sticks. There would be far less risk of divisions within the West and the Southern Gulf over such a policy.

The Fragmentation of Iraq

The merciless, ruthless manner with which Saddam has treated the Kurds and Shi'ites creates some prospect that a coup in the Sunni leadership could trigger ethnic and sectarian civil war. Such a conflict might well end with a Sunni defeat of the Kurdish and Shi'ite factions—as the uprisings did in 1991. It also, however, might create a divided Iraq or even shatter the country—with a new Kurdish and/or Shi'ite mini-state.

This, however, seems an increasingly unlikely prospect, and one that has probably triggered far more Western and Southern Gulf concern than is really justified. The Kurds would probably settle for valid autonomy if this was coupled to a reasonable share of Iraq's oil resources. Iraq's Shi'ites have exhibited little wish to split the Iraqi state or follow in the path of Iran. What they have sought is political and economic power that is commensurate with their demographic size.

If this contingency offers a lesson for the West and the Southern Gulf, it is that they should intervene quickly in the event of any coup or civil conflict in Iraq to encourage the kind of reform that will give the Kurds an incentive to stay in Iraq, and Sunnis and Shi'ites an incentive to cooperate. Once again, the key tools are lifting of sanctions, debt relief, and forgiveness of reparations. The US, in particular, however, should be ready to offer concrete proposals to resolve the Kurdish issue and should not leave this issue to chance. This also scarcely involves a great deal of political creativity. As the previous chapters have shown, the basic outlines of an autonomy or federalist agreement have been discussed for more than three decades. The problem is to give such an agreement momentum at the proper opportunity.

There may also be a case for strategy towards Iraq that would advance concrete proposals for a federal solution to stabilizing a post-Saddam Iraq. Under such proposals, Iraq would do away with the traditional, highly centralized state structure which has been in the hands of one ethno-sectarian group since the founding of the state. In its place, Iraq would create a non-centralized state with the various ethnic and confessional communities having greater say in their local affairs. This could be guaranteed in a written constitution agreed upon by the central government and the constituent polities and which would not be subject to unilateral change by the central authorities. Such a federal agenda has been endorsed by King Hussein of Jordan who believes that in a post-Saddam Iraq, a federal solution would save the territorial integrity of Iraq.

Iran and Iraq: The Risk of a "Devil's Bargain"

There is one more contingency which the West and Southern Gulf must consider. While there seems to be little immediate prospect that Iran and

Iraq would join together in such a "devil's bargain," policies change and often do so suddenly and with unpredictable motives. Serious Iranian and Iraqi cooperation in using military force would radically alter the military balance in the Gulf, and a combination of Iranian and Iraqi military forces could put far more military pressure on any combination of Western and Southern Gulf forces. It would also be far harder for the Southern Gulf states to resist a combination of Iranian and Iraqi intimidation short of war. In many cases, Southern Gulf states would be likely to compromise or accommodate Iran and Iraq as long as this did not affect a major strategic interest.

Even a limited Iranian and Iraqi political alliance could rapidly escalate into a very different and far more serious war. Miscalculation, miscommunication, misperceptions, and different values are more the norm in military history than the exception, and this has certainly been true of the recent actions of Iran and Iraq. Iran's failure to accept a favorable cease-fire in the Iran-Iraq War in 1985 is a good case in point.

Given these uncertainties, it is clear that the West and the Southern Gulf need to provide any new regime with incentives to pursue other policies, and must act to limit Iran and Iraq's present and future war fighting options. Once again, such military containment would involve four interrelated sets of measures: arms control, limits on the transfer of technology and equipment, strengthening the deterrent and defensive capabilities of Southern Gulf forces, and building up Western power projection capabilities.

Such measures should be taken in concert. Focusing on one type of measure—such as arms control or efforts to strengthen Southern Gulf forces—is almost certain to fail. The West must take every possible step to pressure Iran and Iraq to join international and regional arms control regimes that can bring stability to the Gulf. At the same time, the West must organize to develop tight controls on transfers of military and dual-use technology to Iran and Iraq, focusing on the risks posed by the transfer of both conventional technologies and those for weapons of mass destruction.

The Problem of Sanctions

It is increasingly clear that the West and the Southern Gulf need to begin treating economic sanctions as a different issue from seeking changes in Iraq's regime and military containment. Support for economic measures whose net impact is to punish the Iraqi people is steadily eroding, as is support for efforts to the terms of the cease-fire that call for reparations and war crimes trials. Such measures unquestionably weaken Saddam Hussein and Iraq's current ruling elite, but they have a high humanitarian cost, and it is far from clear that they can force a change in Iraq's government. They are clearly dividing Western and Arab nations over their policies towards Iraq, they almost certainly are making Iraq's population more hostile to the West and other moderate Arab states, and their long-term cost may well exceed any short-term benefits.

The answer, however, is not to go suddenly go from the restrictive terms of UN Resolution 986 and lift all economic sanctions. It is certain that any peace between Iraq and Kuwait will not be an easy one. The UN should not only insist that Iraq accept the UN Security Council resolutions that will prevent Iraq from rapidly recovering its capability to deliver weapons of mass destruction, the UN should insist on obtaining firm Iraqi recognition of Kuwait's sovereignty and new border. Similarly, the UN needs to press for a clear autonomy arrangement that protects Iraq's Kurds. Trading Iraqi agreement on the Kuwait border issue and acceptance of Kurdish autonomy for an end to economic sanctions, an end to the threat of war crimes trails, and more realistic proposals regarding reparations and debt repayments is one alternative. It seems likely to produce far more mid and long-term stability in the Gulf than continuing to try to win a far more sweeping victory after the Gulf War than the UN chose to win during it.

As has been discussed in Chapter 5, there are no good or easy options for accomplishing these goals. There may, however, be better options than the status quo and options that could be exploited in pursuing either a "centrist" or "peripheral" strategy. These options include:

- Reaching a clear decision as to whether sanctions are or are not tied to the survival of Saddam and his coterie, and making this clear to Iraq. The present US, British, Kuwaiti, and Saudi position seems to be a de facto attempt to remove Saddam, but it is all stick and no carrot. It does not make it clear that Iraq would benefit if it does so, or what kind of new government would be acceptable.
- Offering forgiveness of debt and reparations for a new "centrist" or "peripheral" regime with an acceptable character and composition.
- Alternatively, setting forth exact conditions for changes in the behavior of the current regime in return for a step by step lifting of sanctions and/or easing of debt and reparations. Key conditions could be continued under UNSCOM operation, full and unconditional recognition of the new border with Kuwait (including a personal speech by Saddam), an autonomy agreement with the Kurds, a halt to military operations in southern Iraq, and an arms import limitation agreement.
- Shifting the burden of blame for sanctions to Saddam Hussein by offering massive shipments of humanitarian aid without compensa-

tion—effectively limiting what Iraq can import and defusing the human problem.

Once again, it must also be stressed that Kuwait and Saudi Arabia need to come fully to grips with their demands for repayment of debt and reparations and the West needs to abandon unrealistic demands for war crimes trials and instant democracy and humans rights. There are disturbing parallels between the kind of peace the UN has enforced on Iraq in terms of sanctions, potential war crimes trails, reparations, and loan repayments and the kind of peace the allies forced on Germany after World War I. Once again, the West and the Southern Gulf need to remember that it is more important to make history than remember it. Not every tragedy has to have a second act.

Sources and Methods

This volume is part of a series of volumes on each of the Gulf states which has been developed by the Center for Strategic and International Studies as part of a dynamic net assessment of the Middle East. This project has had the sponsorship of each of the Southern Gulf states as well as US sponsors of the CSIS, and each text has been widely distributed for comment to experts and officials in each Southern Gulf country, to US experts and officials, and to several international agencies and institutions, and various private experts.

Sources

The authors have drawn heavily on the inputs of outside reviewers throughout the text. It was agreed with each reviewer, however, that no individual or agency should be attributed at any point in the text except by specific request, and that all data used be attributed to sources that are openly available to the public. The reader should be aware of this in reviewing the footnotes. Only open sources are normally referred to in the text, although the data contained in the analysis has often been extensively modified to reflect expert comment.

There are other aspects of the sources used of which the reader should be aware. It was possible to visit each Southern Gulf states at various times during the preparation of this book and to talk to local officials and experts. Some provided detailed comments on the text. Interviews also took place with experts in the United States, United Kingdom, France, Switzerland and Germany. Portions of the manuscript were circulated for informal review by European officials and diplomats in some cases. Once again, no details regarding such visits or comments are referenced in the text.

Data from open sources are deliberately drawn from a wide range of sources. Virtually all of these sources are at least in partial conflict. There is no consensus over demographic data, budget data, military expenditures and arms transfers, force numbers, unit designations, or weapons types.

While the use of computer data bases allowed some cross-correlation and checking of such source, the reporting on factors like force strengths, unit types and identities, tactics often could not be reconciled and citing multiple sources for each case was not possible because it involved many detailed judgments by the author in reconciling different reports and data.

The Internet and several on-line services were also used extensively. Since such the data bases are dynamic, and change or are deleted over time, there is no clear way to footnote much of this material. Recent press sources are generally cited, but are often only part of the material consulted.

Methods

A broad effort has been made to standardize the analysis of each country, but it became clear early in the project that adopting a standard format did not suit the differences that emerged between countries. The emphasis throughout this phase of the CSIS net assessment has been on analyzing the detailed trends within individual states and this aspects of the analysis has been given priority over country-to-country consistency.

In many cases, the authors adjusted the figures and data use in the analysis on a "best guess" basis, drawing on some thirty years of experience in the field. In some other cases, the original data provided by a given source were used without adjustment to ensure comparability, even though this leads to some conflicts in dates, place names, force strengths, etc. within the material presented—particularly between summary tables surveying a number of countries and the best estimates for a specific country in the text. In such cases, it seemed best to provide contradictory estimates to give the reader some idea of the range of uncertainty involved.

Extensive use is made of graphics to allow the reader to easily interpret complex statistical tables and see long-term trends. The graphic program used was deliberately standardized, and kept relatively simple, to allow the material portrayed to be as comparable as possible. Such graphics have the drawback, however, that they often disguise differences in scale and exaggerate or minimize key trends. The reader should carefully examine the scale used in the left-hand axis of each graphs.

Most of the value judgments regarding military effectiveness are made on the basis of American military experience and standards. Although the principal author has lived in the Middle East, and worked as a US advisor to several Middle Eastern governments, he believes that any attempt to create some Middle Eastern standard of reference is likely to be far more arbitrary than basing such judgments on his own military background.

Mapping and location names presented a major problem. The authors used US Army and US Air Force detailed maps, commercial maps, and in some cases commercial satellite photos. In many cases, however, the place names and terrain descriptions used in the combat reporting by both sides, and by independent observers, presented major contradictions that could not be resolved from available maps. No standardization emerged as to the spelling of place names. Sharp differences emerged in the geographic data published by various governments, and in the conflicting methods of transliterating Arabic and Farsi place names into English.

The same problem applied in reconciling the names of organizations and individuals—particularly those being transliterated from Arabic and Farsi. It again became painfully obvious that no progress is being made in reconciling the conflicting methods of transliterating such names into English. A limited effort has been made to standardize the spellings used in this text, but many different spellings are tied to the relational data bases used in preparing the analysis and the preservation of the original spelling is necessary to identify the source and tie it to the transcript of related interviews.

Notes

Chapter 1

1. CIA, *World Factbook*, 1995, "Iraq."
2. CIA, *World Factbook*, 1995, "Iraq."
3. Energy Information Administration, *International Energy Outlook, 1995*, Washington, DOE/EIA, June 1995, p. 29.

Chapter 2

4. *Economist*, August 23, 1991, p. 36; *New York Times*, June 3, 1991; June 11, 1991, p. A-10; November 3, 1991, p. 4; *Washington Post*, July 19, 1991, p. A-16.

Chapter 3

5. CIA, *World Factbook*, 1995, "Iraq."
6. Besides Sunni Arab and Christian Arabs, the center includes a large population of Iraqi Shi'ites and Iraqi Kurds who have lived there for generations and whose economic and political fortunes are tied to the center.
7. Quoted in *The Economist*, April 6, 1991, p.40.
8. "Profile: President Saddam Hussein of Iraq," *MidEast Report*, volume 23, number 16, August 15, 1990, pp. 1–5; *Wall Street Journal*, August 27, 1990, p. 1; Ofra Bengio, "Iraq," in Ami Ayalon (ed.), *Middle East Contemporary Survey, 1993*, Volume XVII, Boulder, Westview Press, 1995, pp. 378–380.
9. *Christian Science Monitor*, April 24, 1991, pp. 1–2; for an extensive analysis of the regime's 'commitment' to change as portrayed by Tariq Aziz—Deputy Prime Minister in the aftermath of the war—see *Washington Post*, May 3, 1991, pp. A1, A23.
10. Economist Intelligence Unit, "Iraq, Country Report," No. 4, 1991, p. 10.
11. Saddam Hussein did eventually bring Hammadi back as a as a Presidential "adviser." This position had not real influence, however, and Saddam's "rehabilitation" of Hammadi seems to have been part of a broader series of attempts to rebuild support from Shi'ites and other leaders in the Ba'ath Party that were not part of Saddam's immediate coterie.
12. See *Guardian*, May 30, 1994, p. 6.
13. Quoted in *The Middle East*, March 1993, p. 11.
14. For more details on this patrimonial system of governance see Charles Tripp, "The Future of Iraq and of Regional Security," in Geoffrey Kemp and Jan-

ice Gross Stein, *Powder Keg in the Middle East: The Struggle for Gulf Security*, Washington, DC: American Association for the Advancement of Science, 1995, pp. 133–159.

15. *The Sunday Times*, April 18, 1993, p. 19; discussions with Amatzia Baram.

16. *The Times*, June 16, 1994, p. 5.

17. *Arabies*, July–August 1994, p. 7.

18. *Arabies*, nos. 103–104, July–August 1995, p. 12.

19. For extensive details of these inter-Takriti clashes see *Le Monde*, September 6, 1990, p. 6.

20. Experts differ sharply on the details of these changes. See *Washington Post*, September 14, 1991, p. A-31; November 7, 1991, p. A-46, November 14, 1991, p. A-47, December 14, 1991, p. A-15; *Wall Street Journal*, November 11, 1991, p. A-10, December 26, 1991, p. A-10 ; *Jane's Defense Weekly*, November 16, 1991, p. 926, July 13, 1991, p. 61; *The Estimate*, November 22–December 5, 1991, p. 1; *Washington Times*, November 26, 1991, p. A7; New York Times, November 7, 1991, p. 3; Los Angeles Times, November 14, 1991, p. 4; Michael Eisenstadt, "Recent Changes in Saddam's Inner Circle: Cracks in the Wall?" *Policywatch*, Number 22, November 22, 1991, pp. 1–2; *Baltimore Sun*, June 21, 1991, p. 7.

21. *New York Times*, December 11, 1991. p. A-7.

22. Much of this analysis is based on work by Kenneth Katzman of the Congressional Research Service; *Washington Post*, November 7, 1991. p. A-46.

23. *New York Times*, November 14, 1991. p. A-15.

24. See *Iraq*, Economist Intelligence Unit, Country Report, 3rd Quarter, 1995, p. 7.

25. See *Iraq*, Economist Intelligence Unit, Country Report, 3rd Quarter, 1995, p. 7.

26. *Le Monde*, August 15, 1995, p. 2.

27. See *New York Times*, August 15, 1995, p. A-3.

28. For an extensive analysis see Amatzia Baram, "Turmoil in Iraq: The Regime's #2 Defects," *Middle East Quarterly*, December 1995, p. 16.

29. Saddam's speech on August 11, 1995 on Iraqi Television as quoted in *Foreign Broadcasting Information Service, Near East and South Asia* (henceforth *FBIS-NES*) August 14, 1995, pp. 25–26.

30. Quoted in Foreign Broadcasting Information Service, August 14, 1995, p. 38.

31. *Wall Street Journal*, August 1995, p. 1.

32. Reuters, May 8, 1996, 0654.

33. Quoted in *FBIS-NES*, March 13, 1996, p. 44.

34. *Philadelphia Inquirer*, February 28, 1996, p. A3; *Washington Post*, March 1, 1996, p. A24; *Boston Globe*, February 28, 1996, p. 5.

35. "The Purge of the Majids: What is going on in Iraq?" *The Estimate*, March 1, 1996, pp. 5–8.

36. Kamran Karadaghi, "King Hussein in Washington: View From The Iraqi Opposition," *Policywatch*, no. 188, March 6, 1996, p. 2.

37. *Wall Street Journal*, February 26, 1996, p. 8.

38. *The Daily Telegraph*, August 25, 1995, p. 15.

39. *Al-Hayat*, August 31, 1995, p. 1.

40. *Al-Hayat*, August 31, 1995, p. 6.

41. *Al-Hayat*, August 31, 1995, p. 6.

42. *Al-Hayat*, August 31, 1995, p. 6.

43. *Al-Hayat*, August 31, 1995, p. 6.

44. For an extensive analysis of Saddam Hussein's political evolution over the years see the biography by Efraim Karsh and Inari Rautsi, *Saddam Hussein: A Political Biography*, New York, The Free Press, 1991.

45. See Michael Collins Dunn, "Saddam Hussein's Family: A Guide to the Quarreling Kin, Part 2," *The Estimate*, vol. VII, no. 17, August 18–31, 1995, pp. 5–8.

46. This analysis of 'Uday's rise to power is drawn from *Washington Post*, October 22, 1995, p. A1; *Christian Science Monitor*, October 20, 1995, p. 6;

47. Quoted in *FBIS-NES*, August 14, 1995, p. 25.

48. *Middle East International*, October 20, 1995, p. 3.

Chapter 4

49. Quoted in *FBIS-NES*, March 11, 1993, p. 30.

50. Quoted in *FBIS-NES*, October 18, 1995, p. 30.

51. *New York Times*, December 11, 1991. p. A7.

52. Muhammad al-Zainy, *The Iraqi Economy under Saddam Hussein: Development or Decline*, London: Al-Rafid Publishing Company, 1995 (in Arabic).

53. See Tables I and II in ACDA, *World Military Expenditures and Arms Transfers, 1991, 1992*, Washington, GPO, March 1994.

54. See Table I in ACDA, *World Military Expenditures and Arms Transfers, 1991, 1992*, Washington, GPO, March 1994, various editions.

55. The author is deeply indebted to Amatzia Baram for his help in drafting this section. Also see Michael Eisenstadt, "The Iraqi Armed Forces Two Years On," *Jane's Intelligence Review*, March 1993, pp. 121–127, and *Like A Phoenix from the Ashes*, pp. 10–13; Judith Miller and Laurie Mylroie, *Saddam Hussein and the Crisis in the Gulf*, New York, Random House, pp. 48–50; Samir al-Khalil, *Republic of Fear*, New York, Pantheon, 1990, pp. 14–16, 30–31, 36–37, 133, 143–145; Adel Darwish and Gregory Alexander, *Unholy Babylon*, London, Victor Gollancz, 1991, pp. 139–140, 219–226, 257–260.

56. *Al-Sharq al-Awsat*, July 4, 1996, p. 4.

57. *The Times*, July 4, 1996, p. 15.

58. *Jane's Defense Weekly*, October 7, 1995.

59. For extensive details on civil-military relations see May Chartouni-Dubarry, "The Development of Internal Politics in Iraq from 1958 to the Present Day," in Derek Hopwood, Habib Ishow and Thomas Koszinowski (eds.), *Iraq: Power and Society*, Reading, Ithaca Press, 1993, pp. 19–36; May Chartouni-Dubarry, "La 'question irakienne' ou l'histoire d'une puissance contrariee," in Bassma Kodmani-Darwish and May Chartouni-Dubarry (eds.), *Perceptions de securite et strategies nationales au Moyen-Orient*, Paris: Masson, 1994, pp. 57–60; Shahram Chubin and Charles Tripp, *Iran and Iraq At War*, Boulder, Westview Press, 1988, pp. 114–120.

60. For more extensive background of military politics in Iraqi political life see Ali Tahir, *Irak: Aux Origines du regime militaire*, Paris: Albin Michel, 1989; Hamid

al-Shawi, "L'Intervention des militaires dans la vie politique de la Syrie, de l'Irak et de la Jordanie," *Politique Etrangere*, no. 3, 1974, pp. 343–374.

61. For further details see *Al Wasat*, June 26, 1995, p. 24.

62. *The Guardian*, November 26, 1971, p. 15.

63. Khalid Al-Ani, *The Encyclopedia of Modern Iraq, vol. III*, Baghdad: *The Arab Encyclopedia House*, n. d., pp. 518–519.

64. *Washington Post*, April 15, 1992, p. A-32, July 3, p. A-1, July 4, 1992, p. A-14, July 10, 1992, p. A-14; *New York Times*, July 4, 1992, p. A-4, July 6, 1992, p. A-6, July 7, 1992, p. A-3, July 10, 1992, p. A-3.

65. *The Sunday Times*, April 18, 1993, p. 19; discussions with Amatzia Baram.

66. *Washington Post*, October 4, 1992, p. A-35.

67. Many of the details in this analysis are based on discussions with Amatzia Baram.

68. *Baltimore Sun*, April 15, 1993, p. 6A; *Washington Times*, April 27, 1993, p. A-2.

69. *Al-Hayat*, April 16 1996, p. 5, excerpts of the interview are also in *FBIS-NES*, April 18, 1996, pp. 21–26.

70. Quoted in *FBIS-NES*, April 18, 1996, p. 24. Also see *Jane's Defense Weekly*, March 27, 1996, p. 4.

71. *Washington Times*, November 22, 1995, p. A-12; United Press, February 1, 1996, 0932.

72. On Tali' al-Duri see the exhaustive work on the Iraqi armed forces by Syrian Staff Colonel Ahmed Zaydi, *Al bina' al ma'anawi lil quwat al-musallah al-iraqiyah* (The Development of the Fighting Spirit of the Iraqi Army), Beirut: Dar al-Rawdah, 1990, pp. 336–341.

73. *Al-Hayah*, July 12, 1996, pp. 1, 6.

74. USCENTCOM map, supplied June 1996.

Chapter 5

75. Hanna Batatu, *The Old Social Classes and the Revolutionary Movements of Iraq*, Princeton: Princeton University Press, 1978, p. 13.

76. Hanna Batatu, *The Old Social Classes and the Revolutionary Movements of Iraq*, Princeton: Princeton University Press, 1978 p. 17.

77. For more analysis see the classic study of the evolution of the Iraqi polity by Hanna Batatu, *The Old Social Classes and the Revolutionary Movements of Iraq*, Princeton: Princeton University Press, 1978.

78. For extensive details of the socioeconomic evolution and changing nature of Iraq under the monarchy see Phebe Marr, *The Modern History of Iraq*, Boulder: Westview Press, 1985, esp. pp. 127–147.

79. For detailed descriptions of the evolution of Iraqi political history see Hanna Batatu, *The Old Social Classes*, and Phebe Marr, *The Modern History of Iraq*.

80. Saddam's rationale was that he did so after having quashed a "conspiracy" masterminded by Syria.

81. For more details see Ahmed Hashim, "Iraq and Post–Cold War Order," in M. E. Ahrari and James H. Noyes, *The Persian Gulf After the Cold War*, Westport, CT: Praeger Publishers, 1993, pp. 99–124.

82. CIA, *World Factbook, 1995*, "Iraq."

83. The opposition's first collective platform is detailed in Foreign Broadcasting and Information Service, *Daily Report: Near East and South Asia*, January 2, 1991, pp. 31–33.

84. *Middle East International*, March 22, 1991, pp. 11–12.

85. *International Herald Tribune*, February 28, 1882, p.1; *Middle East Economic Digest*, March 6, 1991, p. 14.

86. "Irak: cherche opposition desesperement," *Arabies*, no. 72, December 1992, pp. 6–7.

87. *Middle East International*, November 6, 1992, p. 4.

88. "Opposition in disarray," *The Middle East*, December 1994, pp. 9–10.

89. *The Guardian*, July 1, 1995, p. 44.

90. Karen Dabrowska, "The Iraqi opposition: falling apart?" *Middle East International*, October 21, 1994, pp. 19–20.

91. Quoted in *FBIS-NES*, March 2, 1993, p.26.

92. *Economist Intelligence Unit*, Iraq Country Report no. 4, 1995, pp. 11–12.

93. *FBIS-NES*, December 12, 1995, pp. 33–34.

94. *Middle East International*, December 1, 1995, pp. 11–12.

95. For King Hussein's speech see *FBIS-NES*, August 24, 1995, pp. 43–46

96. Most of this section is summarized from the *Middle East Contemporary Survey*, various years between 1976 and 1988. See also Edmund Ghareeb, Marion Farouk-Sluglett and Peter Sluglett, *Iraq Since 1958: From Revolution to Dictatorship*, London: Routledge, 1987, pp. 164–167.

97. Based on US State Department, Country Chapters on Human Rights—Iraq, Internet edition, US State Department on-line data base, accessed August 26, 1995, and March 16, 1996, and Amnesty International, *Report 1994* and other material.

98. Based on US State Department, Country Chapters on Human Rights—Iraq, Internet edition, US State Department on-line data base, accessed August 26, 1995, and March 16, 1996, and Amnesty International, *Report 1994* and other material.

99. Based on US State Department, Country Chapters on Human Rights—Iraq, Internet edition, US State Department on-line data base, accessed August 26, 1995, and March 16, 1996, and Amnesty International, *Report 1994* and other material.

100. Based on US State Department, Country Chapters on Human Rights—Iraq, Internet edition, US State Department on-line data base, accessed August 26, 1995 and March 16, 1996, and Amnesty International, *Report 1994* and other material.

101. *Washington Post*, January 24, 1991, p. A18.

102. *Washington Post*, January 24, 1991, p. A18.

103. See Vahe Petrossian, "Iraq: The Kurdish Reaction to the Gulf Crisis," *Middle East Economic Digest*, November 30, 1990, p. 13.

104. *Le Monde*, April 6, 1991, p. 4;

105. *Christian Science Monitor*, May 6, 1991, p. 2.

106. *Christian Science Monitor*, May 6, 1991, p. 3, contains an excellent analysis of why the rebellion failed as seen from the perspective of the Kurds themselves.

107. Shi'ites and Iraqi deserters fled into the Huwaizah Marshes which begin south of Amara between the Tigris and the border with Iran, and the other marsh areas along the Euphrates east of Nasirya, and extend down past the junction of the two rivers to Basra. *New York Times*, March 15, 1991, p. 1.

108. A maximum of 400,000 moved into Turkey and 300,000 moved near to the border, 800,000 moved into Iran and 700,000 moved near to the border. These estimates are high, and the true number may have only been 50%–66% as large.

109. Barzani in Al-Hayat, quoted in *Mideast Mirror* , February 24, 1992, p. 21.

110. Based on US State Department, Country Chapters on Human Rights—Iraq, Internet edition, US State Department on-line data base, accessed August 26, 1995, and March 16, 1996, and Amnesty International, *Report 1994* and other material.

111. Based on US State Department, Country Chapters on Human Rights—Iraq, Internet edition, US State Department on-line data base, accessed August 26, 1995, and March 16, 1996, and Amnesty International, *Report 1994* and other material.

112. Based on US State Department, Country Chapters on Human Rights—Iraq, Internet edition, US State Department on-line data base, accessed August 26, 1995, and March 16, 1996, and Amnesty International, *Report 1994* and other material.

113. *Middle East International*, January 20, 1995, p. 5.

114. *Al-Hayat*, August 29, 1995, p. 6.

115. Based on US State Department, Country Chapters on Human Rights—Iraq, Internet edition, US State Department on-line data base, accessed August 26, 1995, and March 16, 1996, and Amnesty International, *Report 1994* and other material.

116. *Washington Post*, March 31, 1995, p. A33.

117. *Economist*, August 23, 1991, p. 36; *Guardian*, January 14, 1992, p. 8; *New York Times*, October 9, 1991, p. A-6, October 20, 1991, p. A-1; October 27, 1991, p. A-3, August 12, 1992, p. A-1; *Baltimore Sun*, January 16, 1992, p. 7A, October 28, 1991, p. A-2; *Washington Post*, October 12, 1991, p. A-20, October 26, 1991, p. A-15, May 19, 1992, p. A-12, May 21, 1992, p. A-44, May 23, 1992, p. A-20. For a discussion of some of the history and activities involved, see Ofra Bengio, "Baghdad Between Sh'ia and Kurds," Policy Focus, No. 18, Washington, The Washington Institute for Near East Policy, February, 1992; *Turkish Times*, June 15, 1992, p. 1; *Christian Science Monitor*, June 10, 1992, p. 1.

118. Based on US State Department, Country Chapters on Human Rights—Iraq, Internet edition, US State Department on-line data base, accessed August 26, 1995, and March 16, 1996, and Amnesty International, *Report 1994* and other material.

119. Based on US State Department, Country Chapters on Human Rights—Iraq, Internet edition, US State Department on-line data base, accessed August 26, 1995, and March 16, 1996, and Amnesty International, *Report 1994* and other material.

120. Based on US State Department, Country Chapters on Human Rights—Iraq, Internet edition, US State Department on-line data base, accessed August 26, 1995, and March 16, 1996, and Amnesty International, *Report 1994* and other material.

121. Based on US State Department, Country Chapters on Human Rights—Iraq, Internet edition, US State Department on-line data base, accessed August 26, 1995, and March 16, 1996, and Amnesty International, *Report 1994* and other material.

122. Saeed Barzin, "Iran's cautious response," *Middle East International*, September 6, 1996, p. 6.

p. A-2; *New York Times*, June 26, 1992, A-19, August 19, 1992, p. A-1, August 27, 1992, p. A-14, October 19, 1992, p. A-16; *Los Angeles Times*, August 14, 1992, p. A-1, August 19, 1992, p. A-1; *Washington Times*, September 6, 1992, p. A-10, September 12, 1992, p. A-7, March 1, 1993, p. A-2, March 2, 1993, p. A-2; *Philadelphia Inquirer*, October 19, 1992, p. 1. The IISS, *Military Balance, 1993–1994*, p. 117.

146. USCENTCOM mnap, June 1996.

147. Based on US State Department, Country Chapters on Human Rights—Iraq, Internet edition, US State Department on-line data base, accessed August 26, 1995, and March 16, 1996, and Amnesty International, *Report 1994* and other material.

148. Based on US State Department, Country Chapters on Human Rights—Iraq, Internet edition, US State Department on-line data base, accessed August 26, 1995, and March 16, 1996, and Amnesty International, *Report 1994* and other material.

149. Based on US State Department, Country Chapters on Human Rights—Iraq, Internet edition, US State Department on-line data base, accessed August 26, 1995, and March 16, 1996, and Amnesty International, *Report 1994* and other material.

150. Based on US State Department, Country Chapters on Human Rights—Iraq, Internet edition, US State Department on-line data base, accessed August 26, 1995, and March 16, 1996, and Amnesty International, *Report 1994* and other material.

151. Based on US State Department, Country Chapters on Human Rights—Iraq, Internet edition, US State Department on-line data base, accessed August 26, 1995, and March 16, 1996, and Amnesty International, *Report 1994* and other material.

152. Based on US State Department, Country Chapters on Human Rights—Iraq, Internet edition, US State Department on-line data base, accessed August 26, 1995, and March 16, 1996, and Amnesty International, *Report 1994* and other material.

153. Based on US State Department, Country Chapters on Human Rights—Iraq, Internet edition, US State Department on-line data base, accessed August 26, 1995, and March 16, 1996, and Amnesty International, *Report 1994* and other material.

154. CIA, World Factbook, 1995, "Iraq."

Chapter 6

155. Based on US State Department, Country Chapters on Human Rights—Iraq, Internet edition, US State Department on-line data base, accessed August 26, 1995, and March 16, 1996, and Amnesty International, *Report 1994* and other material.

156. Based on US State Department, Country Chapters on Human Rights—Iraq, Internet edition, US State Department on-line data base, accessed August 26, 1995, and March 16, 1996, and Amnesty International, *Report 1994* and other material.

157. Based on US State Department, Country Chapters on Human Rights—Iraq, Internet edition, US State Department on-line data base, accessed August 26, 1995, and March 16, 1996, and Amnesty International, *Report 1994* and other material.

158. Based on US State Department, Country Chapters on Human Rights—Iraq, Internet edition, US State Department on-line data base, accessed August 26, 1995, and March 16, 1996, and Amnesty International, *Report 1994* and other material.

159. Based on US State Department, Country Chapters on Human Rights—Iraq, Internet edition, US State Department on-line data base, accessed August 26, 1995, and March 16, 1996, and Amnesty International, *Report 1994* and other material.

123. *Reuters*, September 11, 1996; *Washington Post*, September 8, A28.

124. Peter Feuillherade, "Iraq agrees oil for food deal with UN, *East*, July–August, 1996, pp. 9–10.

125. *Reuters*, September 11, 1996.

126. *Reuters*, September 11, 1996.

127. *Reuters*, September 13, 1996.

128. *Middle East Economic Survey*, September 9, 1996, pp. C1–C2.

129. *Middle East Economic Survey*, September 9, 1996, p. C1.

130. *Middle East Economic Survey*, September 9, 1996, p. C2.

131. *Middle East Economic Survey*, September 9, 1996, p. C2.

132. *Middle East Economic Survey*, September 9, 1996, p. C3.

133. *Middle East Economic Survey*, September 9, 1996, p. C3.

134. *Reuters*, September 13, 1996.

135. *Reuters*, September 16, 1996.

136. CIA, *World Factbook, 1992*, p. 162.

137. For more on the activities of the militant Shi'ite groups see Antoine Jalkl "L'Opposition Irakienne dans tous ses etats," *Arabies*, no. 51, March 1991, pp. 16–21.

138. This description of the Shi'ite rebellion relied on Antoine Jalkh, "L'Opposition irakienne dans tous les etats," *Arabies*, no. 51, March 1991, pp. 16–21; Phebe Marr, "Iraq's Future: Plus ca change . . . or something better," mimeo.; Pierre Martin, "Les chiites d'Irak de retour sur la scene politique," *Maghre-Machrek*, no. 132 April–June 1991; and *Iraq*, Economist Intelligence Unit Country Report, nos. 1–4, 1991.

139. Shi'ites and Iraqi deserters fled into the Huwaizah Marshes which begin south of Amara between the Tigris and the border with Iran, and the other marsh areas along the Euphrates east of Nasirya, and extend down past the junction of the two rivers to Basra. *New York Times*, March 15, 1991, p. 1.

140. *New York Times*, March 15, 1991, p. 1.

141. *New York Times*, March 15, 1991, p. 1.

142. Based on US State Department, Country Chapters on Human Rights—Iraq, Internet edition, US State Department on-line data base, accessed August 26, 1995, and March 16, 1996, and Amnesty International, *Report 1994* and other material.

143. Based on US State Department, Country Chapters on Human Rights—Iraq, Internet edition, US State Department on-line data base, accessed August 26, 1995, and March 16, 1996, and Amnesty International, *Report 1994* and other material.

144. Anti-Ba'ath groups claimed up to 10,000 armed rebels and 100,000 civilians were present in the marshes but these estimates seem sharply exaggerated. Washington Post, April 30, 1992, p. A-37, July 2, 1992, p. A-32, July 24, 1992, p. A-32, August 12, 1992, p. A-23, August 17, p. A-1; *New York Times*, August 12, 1992, p. A-6; *Washington Times*, August 9, 1992, p. A-10; *Economist*, August 8, 1992, p. 36; *Jane's Defense Weekly*, June 6, 1992, p. 967; *US News and World Report*, May 25, 1992, p. 53.

145. *Washington Post*, September 7, 1992, p. A-19, November 21, 1992, pp. A-16 and A-21, June 29, 1993, p. A-14, July 24, 1993, p. A-18, October 18, 1993, p. A-1; *Baltimore Sun*, December 8, 1992, p. 4A; *Philadelphia Inquirer*, November 21, 1992,

160. Based on US State Department, Country Chapters on Human Rights—Iraq, Internet edition, US State Department on-line data base, accessed August 26, 1995, and March 16, 1996, and Amnesty International, *Report 1994* and other material.

161. Based on US State Department, Country Chapters on Human Rights—Iraq, Internet edition, US State Department on-line data base, accessed August 26, 1995, and March 16, 1996, and Amnesty International, *Report 1994* and other material.

162. Based on US State Department, Country Chapters on Human Rights—Iraq, Internet edition, US State Department on-line data base, accessed August 26, 1995, and March 16, 1996, and Amnesty International, *Report 1994* and other material.

163. Based on US State Department, Country Chapters on Human Rights—Iraq, Internet edition, US State Department on-line data base, accessed August 26, 1995, and March 16, 1996, and Amnesty International, *Report 1994* and other material.

164. Based on US State Department, Country Chapters on Human Rights—Iraq, Internet edition, US State Department on-line data base, accessed August 26, 1995, and March 16, 1996, and Amnesty International, *Report 1994* and other material.

165. Based on US State Department, Country Chapters on Human Rights—Iraq, Internet edition, US State Department on-line data base, accessed August 26, 1995, and March 16, 1996, and Amnesty International, *Report 1994* and other material.

166. Based on US State Department, Country Chapters on Human Rights—Iraq, Internet edition, US State Department on-line data base, accessed August 26, 1995, and March 16, 1996, and Amnesty International, *Report 1994* and other material.

167. Based on US State Department, Country Chapters on Human Rights—Iraq, Internet edition, US State Department on-line data base, accessed August 26, 1995, and March 16, 1996, and Amnesty International, Report 1994 and other material.

168. Based on US State Department, Country Chapters on Human Rights—Iraq, Internet edition, US State Department on-line data base, accessed August 26, 1995, and March 16, 1996, and Amnesty International, *Report 1994* and other material.

169. Based on US State Department, Country Chapters on Human Rights—Iraq, Internet edition, US State Department on-line data base, accessed August 26, 1995, and March 16, 1996, and Amnesty International, *Report 1994* and other material.

Chapter 7

170. IMF International Financial Statistics, and International Energy Agency, *Middle East Oil and Gas*, Paris, IEA/OECD, 1995, p. 247.

171. IMF International Financial Statistics, and International Energy Agency, *Middle East Oil and Gas*, Paris, IEA/OECD, 1995, p. 247. These statistics portray a sharper drop than the US government estimates provided by ACDA in *World Military Expenditures and Arms Transfers, 1994–1995*, Washington, GPO, 1996, Table I.

172. CIA on-line Internet country data base, "Iraq." Accessed January 31, 1996.

173. IMF International Financial Statistics, and International Energy Agency, *Middle East Oil and Gas*, Paris, IEA/OECD, 1995, p. 247.

174. See "Gulf Economies VIII: Iraq," *Gulf States Newsletter*, vol. 19, no. 498, October 31, 1994, p. 8; Thierry Brun, "Sous la tutelle de la faim," *Le Monde Diplomatique*, December 1991, p. 14; Elizabeth Picard, "Le regime Irakien et la crise: Les ressorts d'une politique," *Maghreb-Machrek*, no. 130, October–December 1990, p. 25.

175. IMF International Financial Statistics, and International Energy Agency, *Middle East Oil and Gas*, Paris, IEA/OECD, 1995, pp. 2555–257.

176. See Helen Chapin Metz (ed.), *Iraq: a country study*, Washington, DC: Federal Research Division, Library of Congress, 1990, pp. 145–146; Makram Sader, "Le developement industriel de l'Irak," *Maghreb-Machrek*, no. 92, April–June 1981, pp. 25–30; Economist Intelligence Unit, *Iraq: Country Profile, 1994–1995*, pp. 25–26.

177. See John Townsend, "Industrial Development and the Decision-Making Process," in Tim Niblock (ed.), *Iraq: The Contemporary State*, London: Croom Helm, 1982, p.258.

178. Makram Sader, "Le developement industriel de l'Irak," pp. 34–37.

179. John Townsend, "Industrial Development and the Decision-Making Process," in Tim Niblock (ed.), *Iraq: The Contemporary State*, London: Croom Helm, 1982, pp. 257–258.

180. Arab Ba'ath Socialist Party, *The Central Report of the Ninth Regional Congress*, June 1982, Baghdad, 1983, p. 124.

181. Arab Ba'ath Socialist Party, *The Central Report of the Ninth Regional Congress*, June 1982, Baghdad, 1983, p. 124.

182. Arab Ba'ath Socialist Party, *The Central Report of the Ninth Regional Congress*, June 1982, Baghdad, 1983, p. 124.

183. Arab Ba'ath Socialist Party, *The Central Report of the Ninth Regional Congress*, June 1982, Baghdad, 1983, p. 124.

184. Arab Ba'ath Socialist Party, *The Central Report of the Ninth Regional Congress*, June 1982, Baghdad, 1983, pp. 125–126.

185. Jonathan Crusoe, "Ambitious plans for Iraqi industry," *Middle East Economic Digest*, March 31, 1989, pp. 2–3.

186. Jonathan Crusoe, Iraq: *MEED Profile*, February 1989, p. 44.

187. Cited in Jonathan Crusoe, Iraq: *MEED Profile*, February 1989, p. 45.

188. Yezid Sayigh, *Arab Military Industry: Capability, Performance, and Impact*, London: Brassey's, 1992, p. 103.

189. For more detail on Iraq's military industries see the various chapters on the military of this book; and the following sources: Yezid Sayigh, *Arab Military Industry*, pp. 103–130; Jonathan Crusoe, *Iraq: MEED Profile*, February 1989, p. 47; George Willis, "Open Sesame: Baghdad show reveals Iraqi military-industrial capabilities," *International Defence Review*, no. 6, 1989.

190. *Los Angeles Times*, January 28, 1992, p. C-1.

191. World Bank estimates, World Resources Institute, and *Middle East Economic Digest*, January 26, 1996, p. 7.

192. Cited in Alan Richards and John Waterbury, *A Political Economy of the Middle East: State, Class, and Economic Development*, Boulder: Westview Press, 1990, p. 147.

193. This section on the evolution of Iraqi agriculture relies on, Helen Chapin Metz (ed.), *Iraq: a country study*, Federal Research Division, Library of Congress, Washington, DC, 1990, pp. 153–162; Jonathan Crusoe, Iraq, *Middle East Economic Digest Profile*, February 1989, pp. 54–64; Phebe Marr, *The Modern History of Iraq*, Boulder: Westview, 1985, pp. 131–132; Tariq Y. Ismael and Jacqueline S. Ismael, "Iraq's Interrupted Revolution," *Current History*, January 1985, pp. 30–31; Alan Richards and John Waterbury, *A Political Economy of the Middle East*, pp. 151–152.

194. Phebe Marr, *The Modern History of Iraq*, pp. 131–132.

195. Quoted in Jonathan Crusoe, "Economic Outlook: Guns and Butter, Phase Two?" in Frederick Axelgard (ed.), *Iraq In Transition: A Political, Economic, and Strategic Perspective*, Center for Strategic and International Studies, Boulder: Westview Press, 1986, p. 44.

196. IMF *International Financial Statistics*, and International Energy Agency, *Middle East Oil and Gas*, Paris, IEA/OECD, 1995, p. 247.

197. CIA, *World Factbook, 1991*, pp. 148–149.

198. Arab Ba'ath Socialist Party, *The Central Report of the Ninth Regional Congress*, June 1992, Baghdad, 1983, pp. 128–135.

199. Arab Ba'ath Socialist Party, *The Central Report of the Ninth Regional Congress*, June 1992, Baghdad, 1983, pp. 128–135.

200. For extensive analyses of Iraq war and home front strategies see Shahram Chubin and Charles Tripp, *Iran and Iraq At War*, Boulder: Westview Press, 1988, pp. 108–122; Arab Ba'ath Socialist Party, *The Central Report of the Ninth Regional Congress*, June 1982, Baghdad 1983, for an Iraqi assessment; Jonathan Crusoe, "Economic Outlook: Guns and Butter, Phase Two?" Frederick Axelgard (ed.), *Iraq In Transition: A Political, Economic, and Strategic Perspective*, Boulder: Westview Press, 1986, pp. 33–58.

201. Helen Chapin Metz (ed.), *Iraq: A Country Study*, Federal Research Division, Library of Congress, Washington, DC, 1990, p. 123.

202. The estimates in this Chart are little more than rough indicators of the scale of Iraq's problems. No one outside the Ba'ath regime has a clear picture of: The exact extent of Iraq's debt, the breakdown of the amount Iraq owed to its various creditors, the ratios between civil and military debt, and the breakdown of loans authorized but never disbursed from loans authorized and disbursed. Most of the figures provided in the following analysis for the debt up to the period 1990 and cited by numerous other sources have come from international financial and economic institutions: the OECD states, the Bank of International Settlements, the Economist Intelligence Unit, and the International Monetary Fund.

203. For example, see Helen Chapin Metz (ed.), *Iraq: A country Study*, 124, yet two pages later she mentions that the total debt was between $50 billion and $80 billion; Jonathan Crusoe, *Iraq: MEED Profile*, February 1989, p. 13; *Financial Times*, October 10, 1989, p. 4.

204. Phebe Marr, "Iraq in the 1990s: Growth Dependent on Oil Revenues, Debt, Spending Priorities," *Middle East Executive Reports*, June 1990, pp. 11–15.

205. *Financial Times*, October 10, 1989, p. 4.

206. *FBIS-NES*, August 24, 1995, p. 35.

207. The obsessive secrecy of the Ba'athist regime concerning economic statistics and economic indicators has been remarked upon by a number of analysts who study Iraq's political economy, e.g., see Benoit Parisot, "La situation economique et financiere de l'Irak a la mi-1990," p. 36; John Townsend, "Industrial Development and the Decision-Making Process," where he says: "Any serious study of contemporary Iraq is hampered by the lack of information, and particularly statistical information, on all aspects of economic development. Much official published material tends to be more of a public relations exercise than an attempt to give precise facts," p. 271.

208. For a similar assessment see The Economist Intelligence Unit, *Iraq Country Report* No. 2, 1991, p. 15.

209. "Report of the United Nations Mission To Assess Humanitarian Needs in Iraq, March 10–16, 1991, led by Martti Ahtisaari, Under-Secretary-General for Administration and Management, excerpts in Middle East Report, May–June 1991, p. 12.

210. For surveys of post–Gulf War reconstruction see the extensive analyses in, *inter-alia, Sunday Times* (London), October 4, 1992, p. 6; *Middle East International,* May 15, 1992, pp. 8–9; *Le Monde,* August 24, 1994, p. 1, 16; *Washington Post,* November 8, 1992, p. A-41; *International Herald Tribune,* January 25, 1993, p. 1, 4.

211. A description of the situation in the south can be found in *The Guardian,* February 6, 1993, p. 4.

212. Economist Intelligence Unit, *Iraq,* no. 2, 1992, p. 14.

213. *Le Monde,* February 4, 1993, p. 4.

214. Amer al-Roubaie and Wajeeh Elali, "The Financial Implications of Economic Sanctions Against Iraq," *Arab Studies Quarterly,* vol. 17, no. 3, Summer 1995, p. 58.

215. These figures are cited by Dr. Fadhil Chalabi, "Iraq's Oil: The Economic and Political Constraints," *Middle East Economic Survey,* April 17, 1995, p. D7.

216. Reuters, February 1, 1996, 2057.

217. Once again hard statistical evidence is difficult to come by. The analysis that follows is overwhelmingly based on the first-hand experiences and observations of journalists, analysts and aid officials that have visited Iraq over the past five years and which is to be found in the following sources: *Le Monde,* February 4, 1993, p. 4; *Middle East International,* February 5, 1993; *Times* (London), October 23, 1994, p. 5; *International Herald Tribune,* October 26, 1994, p. 1, 6; *Le Monde,* November 11, 1994, p. 1, 5; *Boston Globe,* July 23, 1995, p. 1; Roddy Scott, Miriam Shahin and Kirk Albrecht, "Saddam's Fate in the balance?" *The Middle East,* October 1995, pp. 5–11.

218. *Financial Times,* September 11, 1995, p. 4.

219. *Times* (London), October 23, 1994, p. 6.

220. *Al Hayat,* July 9, 1995, p. 10.

221. Cited in Amer al-Roubaie and Wajeeh Elali, "The Financial Implications of Economic Sanctions Against Iraq," *Arab Studies Quarterly,* vol. 17, no. 3, 1995, p. 63.

222. *Le Monde,* February 4, 1993, p. 4.

223. *Middle East Economic Digest,* January 12, 1996, p. 11.

224. *Washington Times,* January 21, 1996, p. A-11.

225. The Economist Intelligence Unit, *Iraq Country Report No. 3, 1992,* pp. 18–19.

226. The Economist Intelligence Unit, *Iraq Country Report No. 2, 1993,* p. 18.

227. Peter Feuilrehade, "Iraq: Privatization in desperation," *The Middle East,* November 1993, p. 27.

228. *Financial Times,* May 6, 1993, p. 4.

229. *Le Monde,* February 4, 1993, p. 4.

230. *New York Times,* December 1, 1995, p. A-9; *Washington Times,* October 24, 1995, p. A-1.

231. *Washington Times,* October 24, 1995, p. A-1.

232. *Wall Street Journal,* February 5, 1996, p. C-1.

233. Reuters, January 22, 1996.

234. *Middle East Economic Survey,* October 24, 1992, p. A-10.

235. *Financial Times,* September 13, 1996, p. 4.

236. *International Herald Tribune,* February 16, 1995, p. 1.

237. *Le Monde,* November 11, 1994, p. 4.

238. For extensive analyses of the social ills besetting Iraq see *Christian Science Monitor,* October 30, 1995, p. 1; *Le Monde,* 11 October 1994, November 7, 1995, p. 5; *International Herald Tribune,* July 25, 1994, p. 1, 5.

239. On the rise of crime and the breakdown of social discipline in a country that was once lauded as the "Prussia of the Middle East" see the extensive analysis in *Sunday Times,* January 31, 1993, p. 5.

240. Andrew North, "Iraq: In a state of limbo," *The Middle East,* April 1993, pp. 14–15; Economist Intelligence Unit, *Iraq,* no. 3, 1994, p. 19.

241. *FBIS-NES,* September 26, 1995, pp. 32–33.

242. *Le Monde,* October 11, 1994.

243. Figures are cited in *Middle East International,* May 15, 1992, p. 9.

244. *Middle East International,* April 2, 1993, pp. 9–10.

245. Cited in Peter Feuillrehade, "Iraq: Privatization in desperation," *The Middle East,* November 1993, p. 27.

246. Reuters, January 13, 1994; AP Worldstream, January 8, 1994.

247. A summary of these views are contained in a journal that is hardly sympathetic to the Saddam Hussein regime, see "Iraq: Down but not out," *The Economist,* April 8, 1995, pp. 21–23.

248. *Washington Post,* February 11, 1995, p. A-20.

249. Figures are cited in *Christian Science Monitor,* October 30, 1995, p. 1.

250. *Christian Science Monitor,* June 28, 1995, p. 10.

251. Fergus McLeod, "Babylon By Bus: A Personal Glimpse Inside Saddam Hussein's Iraq," NatWest Washington Analysis, March 23, 1995, p. 1.

252. *Washington Post,* July 26, 1993, p. A-1, A-14.

253. *Christian Science Monitor,* October 30, 1995, p. 1.

254. Quoted in *Le Monde,* November 7, 1995, p. 5.

255. See *Le Monde,* November 7, 1995, p. 5; Anne-Marie Johnson, "Iraq: Life under sanctions," *Middle East International,* October 22, 1993, pp. 20–22.

256. See the comments of Tariq Aziz in *FBIS-NES,* January 24, 1992, p. 36.

257. Cited in *Middle East International,* May 15, 1992, p. 9.

258. *Middle East Economic Survey,* January 23, 1995, p. A-4.

259. *Middle East Economic Survey,* January 6, 1992, pp. A1–A2.

260. *Middle East Economic Survey,* November 11, 1991, p. A-6.

261. Quoted in *Middle East Economic Survey,* December 9, 1991, p. A-2.

262. *FBIS-NES,* October 3, 1991, pp. 13–14.

263. *Middle East Economic Survey,* April 24, 1995, pp. A1–A2.

264. "Iraq says it wants to negotiate with UN on humanitarian oil sales," Energy Wire, NatWest Securities, January 16, 1996; Wall Street Journal, May 23, 1996, p. A-11.

265. *Boston Globe*, February 4, 1996, p. 6.

266. Quoted in Walid Khadduri, "MEES Interview with Iraqi Oil Minister," *Middle East Economic Survey*, November 27, 1995, p. D-4.

267. Quoted in Walid Khadduri, "MEES Interview with Iraqi Oil Minister," *Middle East Economic Survey*, November 27, 1995, p. D-4.

268. *Middle East Economic Survey*, November 27, 1995, p. D-4.

269. See *Middle East Economic Survey*, November 20, 1995, p. A-4.

270. *Middle East Economic Survey*, January 15, 1996, p. A-5; Washington Times, February 8, 1996, p. A-13.

271. ACDA print out of May 14, 1996, and discussions with US experts.

272. Reuters, January 2, 1996.

273. Cited in *Middle East Economic Survey*, January 8, 1996, p. A-8.

274. Cited in *Middle East Economic Survey*, January 8, 1996, p. A-8.; Also see Reuters, January 22, 1996.

275. Reuters, January 1, 1996.

276. *New York Times*, February 6, 1996, p. A-6, February 7, 1996, p. A-9; *Washington Post*, February 7, 1996, p. A-16; *Boston Globe*, February 7, 1996, p. 9; *Wall Street Journal*, February 5, 1996, p. C-1

277. Quoted in *Middle East Economic Survey*, January 22, 1996, p. A-2; Reuters, January 18, 1996, 0305.

278. *Washington Post*, February 20, 1996, p. A3.

279. *Middle East Economic Survey*, March 25, 1996, pp. A2–A3.

280. See Robert Copaken, "Iraq's Return to the Oil Market: Timing and rationale," *Geopolitics of Energy*, Issue 18, no. 3, March 1996, pp. 5–6; *Washington Post*, February 20, 1996, p. A3.

281. For more details see *Middle East Economic Survey*, March 25, 1996, pp. A4–A5; *Washington Post*, March 12, 1996, p. A9; *Washington Times*, March 12, 1996, p. A13; *Middle East International*, March 15, 1996, pp. 11–12.

282. *Middle East Economic Survey*, March 4, 1996, pp. A1–A2.

283. Quoted in *FBIS-NES*, March 13, 1996, p. 43.

284. *Reuters*, April 4, 1996

285. *Baltimore Sun*, May 21, 1996, p. 1-A; *Los Angeles Times*, May 24, 1996, p. A-1; *Philadelphia Inquirer*, May 25, 1996, p. C-7; *Wall Street Journal*, May 21, 1996, p. A-3, May 28, 1996, p. A-12; *Washington Times*, May 21, 1996, p. A-1, May 27, 1996, p. A-13.

286. *Middle East Economic Survey*, April 29, 1996, pp. A1–A4.

287. *Le Monde*, May 22, 1996, p. 2.

288. Cited in Reuters, July 10, 1995.

289. Quoted in *Middle East Economic Survey*, August 5, 1991, p. A-5.

290. Cited in *FBIS-NES*, January 24, 1992, p. 36.

291. *Boston Globe*, July 23, 1995, p. 1.

292. *Le Monde*, November 12, 1994, p. 3.

293. Quoted in *Middle East International*, February 5, 1993, p. 10; see also *Times* (London), October 23, 1994, p.

294. *Wall Street Journal*, May 23, 1996, p. A-11.

295. For the whole report see *Middle East Economic Survey*, May 13, 1991, pp. D-6 to D-9.

296. Chalabi, April 17, 1995.

297. *Middle East Economic Survey*, May 13, 1991, pp. D-6 to D-9.

298. World Bank, *World Population Projections, 1994–1995*, Washington, World Bank, 1994; *Middle East Economic Digest*, July 28, 1995, p. 11; CIA *World Factbook, 1995*, "Iraq."

Chapter 8

299. *Oil and Gas Journal*, September 23, 1991, p. 62.

300. Petroleum Economist, Petroleum Finance Company, and Congressional Quarterly, *The Middle East*, 7th Edition, Washington, Congressional Quarterly, 1990, p. 195.

301. International Energy Agency, *Oil, Gas, and Coal Supply Outlook*, Paris, IEA, 1995, pp. 55–57.

302. *Oil and Gas Journal*, December 30, 1991, pp. 43–49; Other estimates indicate that Iran has 100 billion barrels of proven reserves and 45 billion barrels of probable reserves. See Joseph P. Riva, Jr. of the Congressional Research Service, writing in the *Oil and Gas Journal*, September 23, 1991, p. 62.

303. International Energy Agency (IEA), Middle East Oil and Gas, Paris, IEA/OECD, 1995, pp. 137–138.

304. *Oil and Gas Journal*, December 30, 1991, pp. 43–49.

305. For a typical industry estimate, see NatWest Securities, *Strategic Assessment: Major Oils; Identifying Value from a Global Perspective*, London, NatWest Securities (Mobil, Total, Shell and BP), 1995, p. 60.

306. Department of Energy, Energy Information Agency, *International Energy Outlook 1995*, Washington, Energy Information Agency, June 1995, pp. 27–29.

307. International Energy Agency (IEA), *Middle East Oil and Gas*, Paris, IEA/OECD, 1995, pp. 137–138.

308. International Energy Agency (IEA), *Middle East Oil and Gas*, Paris, IEA/OECD, 1995, pp. 137–138.

309. Department of Energy, Energy Information Agency, *International Energy Outlook 1995*, Washington, Energy Information Agency, June, 1995, pp. 36–37; *Oil and Gas*, Vol. 92, No. 52, December 25, 1994, pp. 42–43.

310. International Energy Agency (IEA), *Middle East Oil and Gas*, Paris, IEA/OECD, 1995, pp. 137–138.

311. International Energy Agency, *Oil, Gas, and Coal Supply Outlook*, Paris, IEA, 1995, pp. 110–111.

312. This section is based on reporting by DOE/EIA and the IEA and the following works: Fadhil Chalabi, "Iraq's Oil: The Economic and Political Constraints," *Middle East Economic Survey*, April 17, 1995, pp. D4–D10; Nirou Eftekhari, "Le Petrole dans l'economie et la societe irakiennes 1958–1986," *Peuples Mediterraneans*, no. 40 July–September 1987, pp. 43–78; Phebe Marr, "Iraq In the '90s: Growth Dependent on Oil Revenues, Debt, Spending Priorities," *Middle East Executive Reports*, June 1990, pp. 11–15; David Mangan, "Iraq's Likely Oil Policy: A New Conservatism," *Middle East Executive Reports*, May 1989, pp. 11–16; Benoit Parisot, "La situation economique et financiere de l'Irak a la mi–1990," *Maghreb-*

Machrek, no. 130, October-December 1990, pp. 36–44; *Iraq: A Country Study*, Washington, DC: USGPO, 1990, pp. 133–142.

313. International Energy Agency, *Oil, Gas, and Coal Supply Outlook*, Paris, IEA, 1995, pp. 256–257.

314. International Energy Agency, *Oil, Gas, and Coal Supply Outlook*, Paris, IEA, 1995, pp. 256–257.

315. Reuters, January 26, 1996, 1534.

316. International Energy Agency (IEA), *Middle East Oil and Gas*, Paris, IEA/OECD, 1995, pp. 151–152; International Energy Agency, *Oil, Gas, and Coal Supply Outlook*, Paris, IEA, 1995, pp. 56–57.

317. International Energy Agency (IEA), *Middle East Oil and Gas*, Paris, IEA/OECD, 1995, pp. 141–144; International Energy Agency, *Oil, Gas, and Coal Supply Outlook*, Paris, IEA, 1995, pp. 56–57.

318. *Wall Street Journal*, February 7, 1996, p. A-8. Associated Press, February 8, 1996, 1906.

319. Associated Press, February 8, 1996, 1906; International Energy Agency (IEA), *Middle East Oil and Gas*, Paris, IEA/OECD, 1995, pp. 141–144; International Energy Agency, *Oil, Gas, and Coal Supply Outlook*, Paris, IEA, 1995, pp. 56–57.

320. *Los Angeles Times*, May 24, 1996, p. A-1.

321. International Energy Agency (IEA), *Middle East Oil and Gas*, Paris, IEA/OECD, 1995, pp. 145–147.

322. International Energy Agency (IEA), *Middle East Oil and Gas*, Paris, IEA/OECD, 1995, pp. 145–147.

323. International Energy Agency (IEA), *Middle East Oil and Gas*, Paris, IEA/OECD, 1995, pp. 150–151.

324. International Energy Agency (IEA), *Middle East Oil and Gas*, Paris, IEA/OECD, 1995, pp. 150–151.

325. *Middle East Economic Digest*, January 19, 1996, pp. 9–14; *Wall Street Journal*, February 5, 1996, p. C-1; *Philadelphia Inquirer*, February 6, 1996, p. C-1.

326. For typical estimates, see *New York Times*, January 25, 1996, p. A-1.

Chapter 9

327. *Washington Post*, January 17, 1995.

328. Alfred B. Prados, "Iraq and Kuwait: Conflicting Historical Claims," Congressional Research Service, 91-34F, January 11, 1991, p. 4.

329. *American Arab Affairs*, Fall 1989, p. 30; *Los Angeles Times*, December 2, 1990, pp. M-4 and M-8; Theodore Craig, "Kuwait: Background, Restoration, and Questions for the United States," Congressional Research Service, 91-288F, May 21, 1992, p. 9.

330. *Washington Post*, December 19, 1987, p. A-27.

331. Department of Defense, *Conduct of the Persian Gulf War; Final Report to Congress*, Washington, Department of Defense, April 1992, pp. 6–7.

332. Department of Defense, *Conduct of the Persian Gulf War; Final Report to Congress*, Washington, Department of Defense, April 1992, pp. 3–4.

333. Department of Defense, *Conduct of the Persian Gulf War; Final Report to Congress*, Washington, Department of Defense, April 1992, pp. 3–4.

334. Alfred B. Prados, "Iraq and Kuwait: Conflicting Historical Claims," Congressional Research Service, 91–34F, January 11, 1991, p. 4.

335. *FBIS NES–90–138*, July 18, 1990, p. 21; Theodore Craig, "Kuwait: Background, Restoration, and Questions for the United States," Congressional Research Service, 91-288F, May 21, 1992, p. 8; Department of Defense, *Conduct of the Persian Gulf War*; Final Report to Congress, Washington, Department of Defense, April 1992, pp. 2–10.

336. *Jane's Defense Weekly*, February 22, 1992, p. 274, March 7, 1992, p. 375, August 1, 1992, p. A-10, August 4, 1992, p. A-14, August 8, 1992, p. 6, August 15, 1992, p. A-15; *Defense News*, September 9, 1991, p. 1, November 18, 1991, p. 3, February 17, 1992, p. 3, June 15, 1992, p. 26; *Stars and Stripes*, March 3, 1992, p. 8; *London Financial Times*, July 8, 1991, p. 3; *Washington Post*, August 28, 1991, p. A-7, September 6, 1991, p. A-24, August 15, 1992, p. A-15; *Washington Times*, December 6, 1991, p. A-2, August 5, 1992, p. A-1; *Aviation Week*, September 9, 1991, p. 21.

337. The border was laid out relatively quickly by a single British agent, Major John More, and no follow-up effort was made to create a formal survey or border markings. *Economist*, February 29, 1992, p. 45; *Philadelphia Inquirer*, February 20, 1992, p. A-16; *Wall Street Journal*, December 5, 1991, p. A-1.

338. Department of Defense background briefing, October 20, 1994 (Federal News Service); Department of Defense handouts of October 11, 1994 and October 12, 1994; *Jane's Defense Weekly*, October 22, 1994, p. 4, December 17, 1994, p. 7; US Army briefing sheet (undated) October 1994; Congressional Research Service, *Iraq Crisis, A Chronology*, October 1994, 94-808F, October 24, 1994.

339. New York Times, January 30, 1996, p. A-6.

340. *Defense News*, April 18, 1995, p. 10; Wall Street Journal, June 27, 1995, p. A-10.

341. *Defense News*, April 18, 1995, p. 10; Wall Street Journal, June 27, 1995, p. A-10.

342. CIA, *World Factbook, 1992*, pp. 161–163.

343. US State Department, Country Reports on Human Rights Practices, 1994, on-line Internet edition, June 24, 1995.

344. *Washington Times*, September 14, 1994, p. A-14.

345. *Washington Post*, July 1, 1993, p. A-18.

346. *Jane's Defense Weekly*, September 4, 1993, p. 27.

347. *Washington Post*, July 1, 1993, p. A-18.

348. *Washington Times*, October 26, 1994, p. A-12, November 7, 1994, p. A-16; *New York Times*, November 7, 1994, p. A-6.

349. *New York Times*, February 21, 1995, p. A-9; *Washington Times*, February 22, 1995, p. A-14, May 26, 1995, p. A-18, June 11, 1995, p. A7, June 12, 1995, p. A-13, June 14, 1995, p. A-19.

350. United Press, July 18, 1995, 0807; *Washington Times*, July 11, 1995, p. A-15.

351. Reuters, July 31, 1995, 0914.

352. Reuters, August 8, 1995, 0730.

353. United Press, January 30, 1996, 1151.

354. Peter Feuillherade, "Keeping the hostility alive," *The Middle East*, April 1993, p. 16.

355. For more extensive details on Iraqi-Jordanian relations over the years see Amatzia Baram, "Baathi Iraq and Hashemite Jordan: From Hostility to Alignment," *Middle East Journal*, vol. 45, no. 1, Winter 1991, pp. 51–70; Lauri Brand, *Jordan's Inter-Arab Relations: The Political Economy of Alliance Making*, New York: Columbia University Press, 1994, pp. 196–241.

356. *Wall Street Journal*, March 15, 1996, p. A-7.

357. *Middle East Economic Digest*, January 26, 1996, p. 7; World Bank data.

358. John King, "Syria and Iraq: Paving the way for closer relations," *The Middle East*, July–August 1996, pp. 14–15.

359. "Arabs Slam New Israel-Turkey Accords," *The Middle East*, June 1996, pp. 12–14.

360. John Battersby, "Israel Wins New Friends, And Isolates an Old Enemy," *Christian Science Monitor*, April 17, 1996, p. 6.

361. *Reuters*, August 18, 1996.

362. Alan George, "Syria and Iraq call a tactical truce," *Jane's Intelligence Review*, June 1996, pp. 262–263.

363. Cited in Daniel Pipes, "Turkey, Iraq, and Mosul," *Middle East Quarterly*, September 1995, p. 66.

364. Quoted in *Middle East Economic Survey*, October 7, 1991, p. A2.

365. Antoine Jalkh and Hachem Al-Ali, "Le Qatar rebelle et vulnérable," *Arabies*, April 1995, p. 29.

366. *FBIS-NES*, July 6, 1995, p. 46.

367. *FBIS-NES*, September 11, 1995, pp. 28–30.

368. *FBIS-NES*, September 21, 1995, p. 33.

369. *FBIS-NES*, September 21, 1995, p. 33.

370. *FBIS-NEA*, September 6, 1995, p. 31.

371. *Jane's Defense Weekly*, October 7, 1995, p. 4.

372. *FBIS-NES*, January 19, 1996, p. 25; *Wall Street Journal*, February 5, 1996, p. C-1.

373. *FBIS-NES*, October 17, 1995, pp. 46–47.

374. *Foreign Broadcasting Information Service, Central Eurasia* (henceforth *FBIS-SOV*), September 8, 1994, p. 13.

375. *FBIS-SOV*, September 8, 1994, p. 13.

376. Quoted in Joint Publications Research Service, Near East and Africa, August 20, 1991, p. 2.

377. *Arab Oil and Gas*, vol. XXV, no. 584, January 16, 1996, p. 30.

378. *FBIS-SOV*, September 9, 1994, pp. 12–13.

379. *FBIS-SOV*, September 9, 1994, p. 12.

380. *FBIS-SOV*, April 4, 1995, p. 12.

381. *FBIS-SOV*, July 12, 1995, p. 5.

382. Clauder Anyeli and Stephanie Mesnier, *Notre Allie Saddam*, Paris, Olivier Orban, 1992.

383. "Saddam's armor reveals crack in alliance," *International Defence Review*, no. 12, 1994, pp. 6–7.

384. *International Herald Tribune*, January 7–8, 1995, p. 1.

385. Cited in *FBIS-NES*, January 31, 1996, p. 16.

386. *Washington Times*, January 18, 1996, p. A13.

Chapter 10

387. Arms Control and Disarmament Agency (ACDA), *World Military Expenditures and Arms Transfers, 1993–1994*, Washington, GPO, 1995, p. 67.

388. Arms Control and Disarmament Agency (ACDA), *World Military Expenditures and Arms Transfers, 1989*, Washington, GPO, 1990, p. 51; US Department of Defense, *Conduct of The Persian Gulf War, Volume I*, Washington, Department of Defense, 1992, p. 4.

389. Arms Control and Disarmament Agency (ACDA), *World Military Expenditures and Arms Transfers, 1989*, Washington, GPO, 1990, Table I; Arms Control and Disarmament Agency (ACDA), *World Military Expenditures and Arms Transfers, 1994–1995*, Washington, GPO, 1996, Table I.

390. IISS, *Military Balance*, 1990–1991 and 1991–1992 editions.

391. CIA, *World Factbook, 1991*, pp. 148–149; US Department of Defense, *Conduct of the Persian Gulf War, Volume I*, Washington, Department of Defense, 1992, p. 4.

392. Richard F. Grimmett, *Conventional Arms Transfers to the Third World, 1983–1990*, Washington, Congressional Research Service, CRS-9 1-578F, August 2, 1991.

393. US Air Force, "Reaching Globally, Reaching Powerfully: The United States Air Force in the Gulf War," Washington, USAF, September 1991, pp. 3–4.

394. Arms Control and Disarmament Agency (ACDA), *World Military Expenditures and Arms Transfers, 1989*, Washington, GPO, 1990, p. 117.

395. Richard F. Grimmett, *Conventional Arms Transfers to the Third World, 1985–1992*, Washington, Congressional Research Service, CRS-93-656F, July 19, 1993, pp. CRS-56, 57, 58, 59.

396. Richard F. Grimmett, *Conventional Arms Transfers to the Third World, 1985–1992*, Washington, Congressional Research Service, CRS-93-656F, July 19, 1993, pp. CRS-67, 68, 69, 70; Kenneth Katzman, "Iraq's Campaign to Acquire and Develop High technology," Congressional Research Service, CRS-92-611F, August 3, 1991. US reporting on this subject is inconsistent. Arms Control and Disarmament Agency (ACDA), *World Military Expenditures and Arms Transfers, 1990*, Washington, GPO, 1992, p. 133. indicates that Iraq imported a total of $22,750 million worth of arms during 1985–1989, including $13,000 million from the Soviet Union, $1,700 million from France, $20 million from the UK, $1,600 million from the PRC, $90 million from West Germany, $2,900 million from other Warsaw Pact countries, $1,500 million from other European countries, $420 million from other Middle Eastern countries, $20 million from other East Asian states, $1,300 million from Latin American, and $200 million from other countries in the world.

397. Author's estimate based on interviews, EIU reports, the IISS, *Military Balance, 1993–1994*, and CIA, *World Factbook, 1992*.

398. *Washington Times*, May 2, 1993, p. A-8.

399. There are major uncertainties in these data. An alternative set of estimates is shown below:

Arms Sales to Iran by Year (in Millions of Current Dollars)

	Deliveries		Agreements	
Year	Dollar Value	Rank in Third World*	Dollar Value	Rank in Third World*
1989	—	—	1,290	5
1990	2,860	3	1,400	4
1991	1,900	4	1,500	3
1992	300	10	—	—
1993	—	—	600	7

*Out of top 10 buyers. Not shown if rank is more than tenth.
Source: Data in sections A & B are adapted from Richard F. Grimmett, *Conventional Arms Transfers to the Third World, 1986–1993*, Congressional Research Service, 94-612F, pp. 57. The annual data in part C are taken from various annual editions of Grimmett's work.

400. Germany was Iraq's largest supplier. Iraq imported $4.243 billion worth of equipment during 1985–1989, with $2.4 billion worth of heavy machinery and transportation equipment, $1.3 billion worth of manufactured goods. $425 million worth of chemicals, and $114 million worth of controlling instrument.

401. The analysis of Iraqi procurement networks and industries in this section draws heavily on Kenneth R. Timmerman, "Iraq Rebuilds Its Military Industries," House Foreign Affairs Subcommittee on International Security, International Organizations, and Human Rights, Washington, DC June 29, 1993; *Jane's Defense Weekly*, July 10, 1993, p. 9; *London Sunday Times*, October 4, 1992, p. 16; *Philadelphia Inquirer*, November 7, 1992, p. A-5; *Washington Times*, March 18, 1992, p. A-2 *New York Times*, July 15, 193, p. A-3; *Newsweek*, February 1, 1993, pp. 48–50; *Wall Street Journal*, January 19, 1999, p. A-16. June 29, 1993, p. A-6.

402. Quoted in *Jane's Defense Weekly*, October 21, 1995, p. 5.

403. Interviews; Reuters, January 28, 1996, 0438, 1058.

Chapter 11

404. Department of Defense, *The Conduct of the Persian Gulf War: Final Report*, Washington, Department of Defense, April 1992, p. 411.

405. Department of Defense, *The Conduct of the Persian Gulf War: Final Report*, Washington, Department of Defense, April 1992, p. 355.

406. Department of Defense, *The Conduct of the Persian Gulf War: Final Report*, Washington, Department of Defense, April 1992, p. 355; Dr. Eliot A. Cohen, draft text of executive summary of Gulf War Air Power Study dated April 28, 1993, p. 43. Losses include withdrawals and some systems temporarily inoperable. Total losses actually killed or captured are estimates to be 76% of tanks, 55% of APCs,

and 90% of artillery. Republican Guards units, however, only lost 50% in these categories.

407. Michael R. Gordon and General Bernard E. Trainor, *The General's War: The Inside Story of the Conflict in the Gulf*, Boston, Little Brown, 1994, pp. 429–439.

408. *Washington Post*, November 7, 1991, p. A-46, November 14, 1991, p. A-47; *Wall Street Journal*, November 11, 1991, p. A-10; *Jane's Defense Weekly*, November 16, 1991, p. 926, July 13, 1991, p. 61; *The Estimate*, November 22–December 5, 1991, p. 1; *New York Times*, November 7, 1991, p. 3; *Los Angeles Times*, November 14, 1991, p. 4; Michael Eisenstadt, "Recent Changes in Saddam's Inner Circle: Cracks in the Wall?" *Policywatch*, Number 22, November 22, 1991, pp. 1–2; *Baltimore Sun*, June 21, 1991, p. 7.

409. General H. Norman Schwarzkopf, *It Doesn't Take a Hero*, pp. 488–489.

410. *Washington Post*, July 16, 1991, p. 14, November 7, 1991, p. A-46, November 14, 1991, p. A-47; *Wall Street Journal*, November 11, 1991, p. A-10; *Jane's Defense Weekly*, November 16, 1991, p. 926, July 13, 1991, p. 61; *The Estimate*, November 22–December 5, 1991, p. 1; *New York Times*, November 7, 1991, p. 3; *Los Angeles Times*, November 14, 1991, p. 4; Michael Eisenstadt, "Recent Changes in Saddam's Inner Circle: Cracks in the Wall?" *Policywatch*, Number 22, November 22, 1991, pp. 1–2; *Baltimore Sun*, June 21, 1991, p. 7; *Daily Telegraph*, July 11, 1991, p. 9; *London Times*, October 4, 1991, p. 12; Washington Times, September 4, 1991, p. A7.

411. *New York Times*, August 8, 1991, p. A-12.

412. Estimate provided by USCENTCOM in June 1996.

413. In addition to the sources listed at the start of the Iraq section, the author has drawn on interviews with various US and foreign experts in March, April, October, and November 1993, and IISS, *The Military Balance, 1993–1994*, IISS, London, 1993, pp. 115–117; USNI Data Base. Military Technology, *World Defense Almanac: The Balance of Military Power*, Vol. XVII, Issue 1-1993, ISSN 0722-3226, pp. 139–142; Kenneth Katzman, Iraq: Future Policy Options," Congressional Research Service, CRS 91-596F, December 12, 1991, pp. 23–30; *FBIS*, October 13, 1991; Michael Eisenstadt, "The Iraqi Armed Forces Two Years On," *Jane's Intelligence Review*, pp. 121–127. March 1993, and RUSI Working Notes, August 1992–September 1993.

414. See the detailed history of the attack on Republican Guard units and the resulting losses by name in Department of Defense, *The Conduct of the Persian Gulf War: Final Report*, Washington, Department of Defense, April 1992, pp. 93–95, 104–113, 355, 401. Also references in the April 15, 1993 draft of the US Air Force *Gulf War Air Power Survey*, pp. 9–10.

415. In addition to the sources listed at the start of the Iraq section, the author has drawn on interviews with various US and foreign experts in March, April, October, and November 1993, and IISS, *The Military Balance, 1993–1994*, IISS, London, 1993, pp. 115–117; USNI Data Base. Military Technology, *World Defense Almanac: The Balance of Military Power*, Vol. XVII, Issue 1-1993, ISSN 0722-3226, pp. 139–142; Kenneth Katzman, Iraq: Future Policy Options," Congressional Research Service, CRS 91-596F, December 12, 1991, pp. 23–30; FBIS, October 13, 1991; Michael Eisenstadt, "The Iraqi Armed Forces Two Years On," *Jane's Intelligence*

Review, pp. 121–127. March 1993, and RUSI Working Notes, August 1992–September 1993.

416. Most estimates now indicate a strength of one Special Republican Guards division. Some experts feel that there are two division equivalents.

417. USCENTCOM map, June 1996.

418. USCENTCOM map, June 1996.

419. Based on US State Department, *Country Chapters on Human Rights—Iraq*, Internet edition, US State Department on-line data base, accessed August 26, 1995 and March 16, 1996, and Amnesty International, Report 1994 and other material.

420. Based on US State Department, *Country Chapters on Human Rights—Iraq*, Internet edition, US State Department on-line data base, accessed August 26, 1995 and March 16, 1996, and Amnesty International, Report 1994 and other material.

421. Based on US State Department, *Country Chapters on Human Rights—Iraq*, Internet edition, US State Department on-line data base, accessed August 26, 1995 and March 16, 1996, and Amnesty International, Report 1994 and other material.

422. Based on US State Department, *Country Chapters on Human Rights—Iraq*, Internet edition, US State Department on-line data base, accessed August 26, 1995 and March 16, 1996, and Amnesty International, Report 1994 and other material.

423. These estimates are based primarily on interviews with various experts. The 1993 IISS data show only 2,200 tanks, but this count does not track with the intelligence data the US has declassified in its studies of the Gulf War or the estimates of other experts. It may represent an attempt to count fully operational tanks, but this is unclear.

424. The IISS estimates 4,200 OAFVs, including 1,500 BTR-50, BTR-60, AML-60, AML-90, EE-9, and EE-3 reconnaissance vehicles; 700 BMP-1 and BMP-2 armored fighting vehicles; and 2,000 BTR-50, BTR-60, BTR-152, OT-62, OT-64, MTLB, YW-531, M-113A1/A2, Panhard M-3, and EE-11 armored personnel carriers. A few experts estimates Iraq only had about 2,000–2,300 operational other armored vehicles. Additional sources include interviews in London, December 1991 and April 1993, in Switzerland and Israel, January 1992, in Switzerland, January 1993, IISS data, and the views of various experts as of May and June, October and November 1993; *Jane's Defense Weekly*, February 22, 1992, p. 284; *Jerusalem Post*, January 25, 1992, p. 9; *Washington Times*, January 20, 1992, p. 10, January 17, 1992, p. A-1; *Wall Street Journal*, November 11, 1991, p. A-10; *Jane's Defense Weekly*, November 16, 1991, p. 926, February 22, 1992, pp. 284; *The Estimate*, November 22–December 5, 1991, p. 1; Michael Eisenstadt, "Recent Changes in Saddam's Inner Circle: Cracks in the Wall?" *Policywatch*, Number 22, November 22, 1991, pp. 1–2; *Defense News*, February 24, 1992, p. 1; *Washington Post*, November 7, 1991, p. A-46, March 13, 1992, p. A-19, August 6, 1992, p. A-39; *Jane's Defense Weekly*, August 8, 1992, p. 8., and

425. Sources in addition to those cited at the start of this section include interviews in London, December 1991 and April 1993, in Switzerland and Israel, Jan-

uary 1992, in Switzerland, January 1993, IISS data, and the views of other experts as of May, June, October, and November 1993; The IISS estimate is similar to the author's. Also see *Jane's Defense Weekly*, February 22, 1992, p. 284; *Jerusalem Post*, January 25, 1992, p. 9; *New York Times*, March 12, 1992, p. A-10; *Washington Times*, January 20, 1992, p. 10; *Washington Post*, November 7, 1991, p. A-46, November 14, 1991, p. A-47, March 13, 1992, p. A-19; *Wall Street Journal*, November 11, 1991, p. A-10; *Jane's Defense Weekly*, November 16, 1991, p. 926, February 22, 1992, pp. 284; *The Estimate*, November 22–December 5, 1991, p. 1; Michael Eisenstadt, "Recent Changes in Saddam's Inner Circle: Cracks in the Wall?" *Policywatch*, Number 22, November 22, 1991, pp. 1–2; Defense News, February 24, 1992, p. 1.

426. The IISS estimates 500. It is doubtful that this many are operational.

427. Many of the details in this analysis are based on discussions with Amatzia Baram.

Chapter 12

428. The author's estimate of aircraft lost to Iran is discussed in the section on the Iranian Air Force.

429. *FBIS NES 92-054*, March 19, 1992, p. 16.

430. *Jane's Defense Weekly*, November 18, 1995, p. 16.

431. IISS, *The Military Balance, 1993–1994*, IISS, London, 1993, pp. 115–117; USNI Data Base. Military Technology, *World Defense Almanac: The Balance of Military Power*, Vol. XVII, Issue 1-1993, ISSN 0722-3226, pp. 139–142; and working data from the Jaffee Center for Strategic Studies.

432. The IISS estimates are similar.

433. In addition to the sources listed at the start of the Iraq section, see Kenneth Katzman, Iraq: Future Policy Options," Congressional Research Service, CRS 91-596F, December 12, 1991, pp. 23–30; FBIS, October 13, 1991; *Washington Times*, August 2, 1991, p. B-5; *London Financial Times*, October 4, 1991, p. 4; AP AM cycle, June 12, 1991; *New York Times*, March 25, 1991, p. A-1.

434. Department of Defense, *Conduct of the Persian Gulf War: Final Report*, Department of Defense, April 1992, pp. 13–15; Slides to US Air Force presentation of the April 15, 1993 draft of the Gulf War Air Power study; Brigadier General Robert H. Scales, *Certain Victory: The United States Army in the Gulf War*, Washington, Office of the Chief of Staff, US Army, 1993, pp. 115–116.

435. Some estimates show 129–130 sites in Iraq.

436. See Dr. Eliot A. Cohen, Director, *Gulf War Air Power Survey, Volume V*, Washington, GPO, 1993, pp. 218–219; Department of Defense, *Conduct of the Persian Gulf War: Final Report*, Department of Defense, April 1992, pp. 13–15; Slides to US Air Force presentation of the April 15, 1993 draft of the Gulf War Air Power study; Brigadier General Robert H. Scales, *Certain Victory: The United States Army in the Gulf War*, Washington, Office of the Chief of Staff, US Army, 1993, pp. 115–116. These estimates were projected by different sources and the launcher or fire unit counts seem to be either rounded or based on standard Soviet battery holdings. According to Palowski, Iraq had the following radar order of battle:

Early Warning and Surveillance

Spoon Rest D/P-12M	USSR (147–161 MHz)
Flat Face A/P-15	USSR (800–900 HHz)
Squat Eye/P-15M	USSR (800–900 HMz)
Bar Lock/P-35/37	USSR (2,695–3,125 MHz)
Tall King/P-14	USSR (160–180 MHz)
TRS-2215 (mobile)	FR (E/F)
TRS-2230	FR (E/F)
AN/TPS-32 (3D)	US (2,905–3,080)
AWACS (IL-76)	FR

Surface-to-Air Missile Systems

SA-2	Fansong/Guideline
SA-3	Low Blow/Goa
SA-5	Square Pair/Gammon
SA-6	Straight Flush/Gainful
SA-7	Grail (IR Hand Held)
SA-8	Land Roll/Gecko
SA-9	Gaskin (IR Vehicle Mounted)
SA-13	Gopher (IR Vehicle Mounted)
SA-14	Gremlin (IR Hand Held)
SA-15	Track with Tube Launched Missiles (not confirmed)
SA-16	(not confirmed)
SA-19	Mounted on 2S6 Gun-Track (not confirmed)
ROLAND	
HAWK	
ASPEDITE	

London Financial Times, April 29, 1989, p. 11, July 26, 1989, p. 20; *Jane's Defense Weekly*, May 13, 1989, p. 837; April 22, 1989, p. 687, August 12, 1989, p. 255, September 30, 1989, p. 674, *Defense News*, May 8, 1989, p. 6; *International Defense Review*, 6/189, pp. 835–841.

437. Brigadier General Robert H. Scales, *Certain Victory: The United States Army in the Gulf War*, Washington, Office of the Chief of Staff, US Army, 1993, pp. 115–116.

438. The Iraqis were on alert after reports that Israel might attack Iraqi chemical and nuclear facilities. *Washington Post*, April 29, 1989, p. 16.

439. The reader should be aware that these estimates are extremely uncertain and are based largely on expert estimates of the estimated losses during the Gulf War. There is a sharp difference of opinion among some US experts as to the size of Iraq's losses during the conflict.

440. The SAM launcher estimates are based on discussions with an Israeli expert and are highly uncertain. Iran's decision was reported in the *New York Times*, July 31, 1992, p. 6.

441. *Wall Street Journal*, August 19, 1992, p. A-3.

442. Michael Eisenstadt, "The Iraqi Armed Forces Two Years On," *Jane's Intelligence Review*, pp. 121–127. March 1993.

443. Based on interviews with British, US, and Israel experts. *Washington Times*, January 16, 1992, p. G-4; *Washington Post*, February 1, 1992, p. A1, February 2, 1992, pp. A1 and A25, February 5, p. A-19; *Financial Times*, February 6, 1992, p. 4; *Christian Science Monitor*, February 6, 1992, p. 19; *Defense News*, February 17, 1992, p. 1.

Chapter 13

444. This analysis draws heavily on US Naval Institute, *The Naval Institute Guide to the Combat Fleets of the World, 1993, Their Ships, Aircraft, and Armament*, Annapolis, Naval Institute, 1993; *Jane's Fighting Ships, 1992–1993*; IISS, *The Military Balance, 1993–1994*, IISS, London, 1993, pp. 115–117; USNI Data Base. Military Technology, *World Defense Almanac: The Balance of Military Power*, Vol. XVII, Issue 1-1993, ISSN 0722-3226, pp. 139–142.

445. *Military Technology*, 2/92, pp. 97–98; *Jane's Defense Weekly*, November 4, 1995, p. 3.

446. *Military Technology*, 2/92, pp. 97–98; *Jane's Defense Weekly*, November 4, 1995, p. 3.

447. *Defense News*, May 8, 1989, p. 6.

448. These and other army strength estimates are based upon Interviews in London, December 1991, in Switzerland and Israel, January 1992; *Jane's Defense Weekly*, February 22, 1992, p. 284; *Jerusalem Post*, January 25, 1992, p. 9; *Washington Times*, January 20, 1992, p. 10; *Washington Post*, November 7, 1991, p. A-46, November 14, 1991, p. A-47; *Wall Street Journal*, November 11, 1991, p. A-10; *Jane's Defense Weekly*, November 16, 1991, p. 926, February 22, 1992, pp. 284; *The Estimate*, November 22–December 5, 1991, p. 1; Michael Eisenstadt, "Recent Changes in Saddam's Inner Circle: Cracks in the Wall?" *Policywatch*, Number 22, November 22, 1991, pp. 1–2; *Defense News*, February 24, 1992, p. 1.

Chapter 14

449. Washington Post, ; New York Times, May 26, 1993, p. A-8, June 24, 1992, p. A-3, July 17, 1993, p. A-14, Agence France Presse, April 12, 1993, May 15, 1993, July 19, 1993, BBC ME/1664/A, April 16, 1993, ME/1721/A, June 22, 1993; Armed Forces Journal, July 1992, p. 23; Christian Science Monitor, ; Financial Times, May 26, 12993, p. 6; Washington Times, April 12, 1993, p. A-2, Baltimore Sun, May 24 ,1993, p. 5-A.

450. US Department of State, Patterns of Global Terrorism, 1992, Washington State Department Press, April 1993; Wall Street Journal, June 28, 1993.

451. New York Times, June 27, 1993, p. A-1; Washington Post, June 27, 1992, p. A-1; November 22, 1993, p. A-14. For an article challenging Iraq's role in the plot, see Seymour M. Hersh, "A Case Not Closed," New Yorker, November 1, 1993, p. 80.

452. US State Department, 1994 and 1994 reports on terrorism, Internet on-line edition, accessed August 29, 1995.

453. US State Department, 1994 and 1994 reports on terrorism, Internet on-line edition, accessed August 29, 1995.

454. US State Department, 1994 and 1994 reports on terrorism, Internet on-line edition, accessed August 29, 1995.

455. US State Department, 1994 and 1994 reports on terrorism, Internet on-line edition, accessed August 29, 1995.

Chapter 15

456. *Arms Control Today*, April 1993, p. 29.

457. *Jane's Intelligence Review*, March 1995, p. 115.

458. *Washington Post*, November 27, 1993, p. A-20.

459. United Nations Special Commission, "Report to the Security Council-S/1995/494," 20 June 1995, p. 10.

460. United Nations Special Commission, "Report to the Security Council-S/1995/864," 11 October 1995, p. 7.

461. United Nations Special Commission, "Report to the Security Council-S/1995/864," 11 October 1995, pp. 7–8.

462. United Nations Special Commission, "Report to the Security Council-S/1995/864," 11 October 1995, p. 8.

463. United Nations Special Commission, "Report to the Security Council-S/1995/864," 11 October 1995, pp. 8–10.

464. These comments are based on Ambassador Rolf Ekeus's speech to the Washington Institute on November 26, 1995, and *Policywatch*, Number 175, November 20, 1995.

465. United Nations Special Commission, "Report to the Security Council-S/1995/864," 11 October 1995, p. 11.

466. United Nations Special Commission, "Report to the Security Council-S/1995/864," 11 October 1995, p. 9.

467. *Jane's Defense Weekly*, January 3, 1996, pp. 17–18; United Nations Special Commission, "Report to the Security Council-S/1995/864," 11 October 1995.

468. *Washington Post*, December 15, 1995, p. A-30; *Jane's Defense Weekly*, January 3, 1996, pp. 17–18.

469. *Jane's Defense Weekly*, May 13, 1995, p. 5.

470. *Jane's Defense Weekly*, May 6, 1995, p. 15.

471. *Washington Post*, April 6, 1995, p. 1.

472. *Washington Post*, March 28, 1996, p. A-28; *Jane's Defense Weekly*, April 10, 1996, p. 15.

473. Office of the Secretary of Defense, *Proliferation: Threat and Response*, Washington, Department of Defense, April 1996, pp. 17–24.

474. *Washington Post*, July 26, 1991, p. A-1; "Ambassador Rolf Ekeus, Unearthing Iraq's Arsenal," *Arms Control Today*, April 1992, pp. 6–9.

475. The UN refused to name the facilities at the time of this declaration, because it feared Iraq would move some of the equipment and missiles located at those sites.

476. *Washington Post*, February 14, 1992, p. A-33; *Washington Post*, January 15, 1992, p. A-18.

477. *New York Times*, February 28, 1992, p. 28; *Washington Times*, February 11, 1992, p. 1, November 6, 1992, p. A-7.

478. Reuters Ltd., July 20, 1995; *Jane's Defence Weekly*, July 29, 1995, p. 13.

479. *The Atlanta Constitution*, January 6, 1992, p. 1; *New York Times*, February 28, 1992, p. A-28, November 5, 1992, p. A-10; *Washington Times*, February 11, 1992, p. 1, November 6, 1992, p. A-7; *Washington Post*, January 27, 1993, p. A-16, July 7, 1993, p. A-28; *Philadelphia Inquirer*, March 16, 1993, p. E-1; *Arms Control Today*, December 1992, p. 7.

480. United Nations Special Commission, "Report to the Security Council-S/1995/864," 11 October 1995, pp. 14–15.

481. *New York Times*, August 26, 1995, p. 3.

482. UN Security Council, Note by the Secretary General, S/1995/864, 11 October, 1995, p. 15; *Jane's Defense Weekly*, January 3, 1996, pp. 3, 15–19.

483. United Nations Special Commission, "Report to the Security Council-S/1995/864," 11 October 1995, pp. 14–15.

484. United Nations Special Commission, "Report to the Security Council-S/1995/864," 11 October 1995, pp. 14–15.

485. Associated Press, October 14, 1995; *Washington Post*, October 14, 1995, p. A-1.

486. *New York Times*, December 22, 1995, p. A-18; *Washington Times*, December 28, 1995, p. A-13; UN Security Council, Note by the Secretary General, S/1995/864, 11 October, 1995, p. 15; *Jane's Defense Weekly*, January 3, 1996, pp. 3, 15–19.

487. *Jane's Defence Weekly*, November 11, 1995, p. 4; UN Security Council, Note by the Secretary General, S/1995/864, 11 October, 1995.

488. *Christian Science Monitor*, January 23, 1992, p. 1; *Jane's Intelligence Review*, December 1995, p. 559.

489. *New York Times*, August 26, 1995, p. 3; *Washington Post*, August 26, 1995, p. A-1.

490. Office of the Secretary of Defense, *Proliferation: Threat and Response*, Washington, Department of Defense, April 1996, pp. 17–24.

491. *Washington Post*, October 14, 1995, p. A-1; *Policywatch*, Number 175, November 20, 1995.

492. *Washington Post*, January 15, 1992, p. A-18; *Washington Times*, September 12, 1991, p. A-8, March 5, 1992, p. 1; *US News and World Report* published an article claiming that Iraq might have an underground factory and some 800 missiles on February 10, 1992 (p. 22). General Colin Powell later indicated that he had seen no evidence of any underground facility and that Iraq's maximum holding might be about 250 missiles. *Albany Times Union*, February 5, 1992, p. 7.

493. *Jane's Intelligence Review*, March 1995, p. 116.

494. Michael Eisenstadt, *Like A Phoenix from the Ashes*, Washington, Washington Institute Policy Paper No. 36, pp. 36–37.

495. Michael Eisenstadt, *Like A Phoenix from the Ashes*, Washington, Washington Institute Policy Paper No. 36, pp. 36–37.

496. Michael Eisenstadt, *Like A Phoenix from the Ashes*, Washington, Washington Institute Policy Paper No. 36, p. 37.

497. *Washington Post*, December 8, 1995, p. A-13, December 15, 1995, p. A-30; *Washington Times*, December 8, 1995, p. A-17; Reuters, December 22, 1995, 0240.

498. The US is considering modifying its own drones to use GPS to achieve such accuracies. *Defense Week*, January 3, 1994, p. 1.

499. *Jane's Defence Weekly*, January 30, 1993, pp. 20–21; *Defense Electronics and Computing*, IDR press, September 1992, pp. 115–120; *International Defense Review*, May 1992, pp. 413–415; *Jane's Remotely Piloted Vehicles 1991–1992*; Keith Munson, *World Unmanned Aircraft*, London, Jane's 1988; *Air Force Magazine*, March 1992, pp. 94–99, May 1992, p. 155.

500. Office of the Secretary of Defense, *Proliferation: Threat and Response*, Washington, Department of Defense, April 1996, pp. 17–24.

501. There is no evidence of forward deployment of chemical weapons, but the author visited many Iraqi command sites which still had extensive instructions and orders relating to the use of chemical weapons.

502. *Jane's Intelligence Review*, December 1995, pp. 556–560.

503. See the description in Anthony H. Cordesman, *Iran and Iraq, The Threat from the Northern Gulf*, Boulder, Westview, 1994; *Jane's Intelligence Review*, Vol. 4, No. 9, pp. 413–415, and December 1995, pp. 556–560

504. *Jane's Intelligence Review*, December 1995, pp. 556–560.

505. DF-2 and cyclohexanol, and isopropanol were stored separately and had to be hand loaded into the munitions.

506. Department of Defense, *Conduct of the Persian Gulf War: Final Report*, Department of Defense, April 1992, p. 207.

507. *New York Times*, November 12, 1991, p. A-3; *Christian Science Monitor*, January 23, 1992, p. 1; *Jane's Defense Weekly*, December 14, 1991, pp. 1144–1145; Associated Press, December 12, 1991, PM cycle.

508. *Jane's Intelligence Review*, December 1995, pp. 556–560.

509. *Jane's Defense Weekly*, November 11, 1995, p. 4.

510. UN Security Council, Note by the Secretary General, S/1995/864, 11 October, 1995, pp. 17–19; *Policywatch*, Number 175, November 20, 1995.

511. United Nations Special Commission, "Report to the Security Council-S/1995/864," 11 October 1995, pp. 18–19.

512. Department of Defense, *Conduct of the Persian Gulf War: Final Report*, Department of Defense, April 1992, pp. 16–18; "Ambassador Rolf Ekeus, Unearthing Iraq's Arsenal," *Arms Control Today*, April 1992, pp. 6–9; *Christian Science Monitor*, January 23, 1992, p. 1; *The Atlanta Constitution*, January 16, 1992, p. 1; *Jane's Defense Weekly*, December 14, 1991, pp. 1144–1145; Associated Press, December 12, 1991, PM cycle. The UN found nearly 100 metal working machines for chemical weapons at the plant during a raid on November 20, 1991.

513. United Nations Special Commission, "Report to the Security Council-S/1995/864," 11 October 1995, p. 19.

514. *Washington Times*, December 28, 1995t, p. A-13.

515. The technical content of this discussion is adapted in part from the author's discussion of the technical aspects of such weapons in *After the Storm: The Changing Military Balance in the Middle East*, Boulder, Westview, 1993; working material on biological weapons prepared for the United Nations, and from

the Office of Technology Assessment, *Proliferation of Weapons of Mass Destruction: Assessing the Risks*, United States Congress OTA-ISC-559, Washington, DC, August, 1993; Kenneth R. Timmerman, *Weapons of Mass Destruction: The Cases of Iran, Syria, and Libya*, Simon Wiesenthal Center, Los Angeles, August, 1992; Dr. Robert A. Nagler, *Ballistic Missile Proliferation: An Emerging Threat*; Systems Planning Corporation, Arlington, 1992; and translations of unclassified documents on proliferation by the Russian Foreign Intelligence Bureau provided to the author by the staff of the Government Operations Committee of the US Senate.

516. The technical content of this discussion is adapted in part from the author's discussion of the technical aspects of such weapons in *After the Storm: The Changing Military Balance in the Middle East*, Boulder, Westview, 1993; working material on biological weapons prepared for the United Nations, and from the Office of Technology Assessment, *Proliferation of Weapons of Mass Destruction: Assessing the Risks*, United States Congress OTA-ISC-559, Washington, DC, August, 1993; Kenneth R. Timmerman, *Weapons of Mass Destruction: The Cases of Iran, Syria, and Libya*, Simon Wiesenthal Center, Los Angeles, August, 1992; Dr. Robert A. Nagler, *Ballistic Missile Proliferation: An Emerging Threat*; Systems Planning Corporation, Arlington, 1992; and translations of unclassified documents on proliferation by the Russian Foreign Intelligence Bureau provided to the author by the staff of the Government Operations Committee of the US Senate.

517. Office of the Secretary of Defense, *Proliferation: Threat and Response*, Washington, Department of Defense, April 1996, pp. 17–24.

518. *Arms Control Today*, April 1993, p. 29.

519. Eliot Cohen, ed., *Gulf War Air Power Survey*, Volume II, Part II, p. 327.

520. United Nations Special Commission, "Report to the Security Council-S/1995/864," 11 October 1995, p. 20; *Washington Post*, July 6, 1995, p. A-17.

521. United Nations Special Commission, "Report to the Security Council-S/1995/864," 11 October 1995, p. 22.

522. United Nations Special Commission, "Report to the Security Council-S/1995/864," 11 October 1995, p. 23.

523. United Nations Special Commission, "Report to the Security Council-S/1995/864," 11 October 1995, pp. 25–26.

524. United Nations Special Commission, "Report to the Security Council-S/1995/864," 11 October 1995, pp. 23–24.

525. United Nations Special Commission, "Report to the Security Council-S/1995/864," 11 October 1995, pp. 24–25.

526. United Nations Special Commission, "Report to the Security Council-S/1995/864," 11 October 1995, p. 25.

527. United Nations Special Commission, "Report to the Security Council-S/1995/864," 11 October 1995, p. 26.

528. United Nations Special Commission, "Report to the Security Council-S/1995/864," 11 October 1995, pp. 26–27.

529. *Jane's Defense Weekly*, January 3, 1996, p. 19.

530. Interviews with UN personnel and UN Security Council, Note by the Secretary General, S/1995/864, 11 October, 1995.

531. *New York Times*, August 26, 1995, p. 3; *Washington Post*, August 26, 1995, p. A-1.

532. *Policywatch*, Number 175, November 20, 1995; UN Security Council, Note by the Secretary General, S/1995/864, 11 October, 1995.

533. UN Security Council, Note by the Secretary General, S/1995/864, 11 October, 1995.

534. *Jane's Defense Weekly*, November 11, 1995, p. 4.

535. UN Security Council, Note by the Secretary General, S/1995/864, 11 October, 1995, p. 27.

536. *Washington Times*, August 30, 1995, p. A-10.

537. *Reuters Ltd.*, October 11, 1995.

538. Interviews with UN personnel.

539. United Nations Special Commission, "Report to the Security Council-S/1995/864," 11 October 1995, pp. 27–28.

540. *Washington Post*, July 6, 1995, p. A-17.

541. *Jane's Defense Weekly*, April 10, 1996, p. 15.

542. Confirmed by interviews with UN and US State Department personnel. Also see UN Security Council, Note by the Secretary General, S/1995/284, April, 1995.

543. *Washington Post*, August 26, 1995, p. A-1.

544. *The Atlanta Constitution*, January 16, 1992, p. 1.

545. Calculated based on estimates from the Office of Technology Assessment as cited in *Newsweek*, September 4, 1995, p. 34, and figures provided by the Pentagon as cited in *Time*, September 4, 1995, p. 41.

546. The technical content of this discussion is adapted in part from the author's discussion of the technical aspects of such weapons in *After the Storm: The Changing Military Balance in the Middle East*, Boulder, Westview, 1993; working material on biological weapons prepared for the United Nations, and from the Office of Technology Assessment, *Proliferation of Weapons of Mass Destruction: Assessing the Risks*, United States Congress OTA-ISC-559, Washington, DC, August, 1993; Kenneth R. Timmerman, *Weapons of Mass Destruction: The Cases of Iran, Syria, and Libya*, Simon Wiesenthal Center, Los Angeles, August, 1992; Dr. Robert A. Nagler, *Ballistic Missile Proliferation: An Emerging Threat*; Systems Planning Corporation, Arlington, 1992; and translations of unclassified documents on proliferation by the Russian Foreign Intelligence Bureau provided to the author by the staff of the Government Operations Committee of the US Senate.

547. UN and US experts commenting on the evidence to date. No clear documentation is available to define the scope of Iraqi release authority.

548. For detailed descriptions of the Iraqi effort see Anthony H. Cordesman, *Iran and Iraq: The Threat From the Northern Gulf*, Boulder, Westview, 1994; *After the Storm*, Boulder, Westview, 1993; and *Weapons of Mass Destruction in the Middle East*, London, Jane's/RUSI, 1992; and

549. *Jane's Intelligence Review*, December 1992, pp. 554–555.

550. *Washington Times*, January 29, 1996, p. A-15; *New York Times*, January 26, 1996, p. A-8.

551. Office of the Secretary of Defense, *Proliferation: Threat and Response*, Washington, Department of Defense, April 1996, pp. 17–24.

552. International Atomic Energy Agency, "Report to the Security Council-S/1995/844," 6 October 1995, p. 4; *Jane's Intelligence Review*, December 1992, p. 556.

553. Reuters Ltd., November 7, 1995, December 18, 1995, 0342; *New York Times*, December 22, 1995, p. A-18.

554. For very different views, see Peter D. Zimmerman, *Iraq's Nuclear Achievements: Components, Sources, and Stature*, Washington, Congressional Research Service, 93-323F, February 18, 1993; Gary Milhollin, "The Iraqi Bomb," *New Yorker*, February 1, 1993, pp. 47–55, and Diana Edensword and Gary Milhollin, "Iraq's Bomb-an Update," *New York Times*, April 26, 1993, p. A-17.

555. *Jane's Defence Weekly*, March 11, 1995, pp. 28–29.

556. *Washington Times*, August 30, 1995, p. A-10.

557. *Washington Times*, October 14, 1995, p. A-10.

558. Reuters, January 30, 1996, 1227; *Jane's Defense Weekly*, January 3, 1996, p. 19

559. See Kenneth Katzman, "Iraqi Compliance with Cease-Fire Agreements," Congressional Research Service, IB92117, March 25, 1994; and Note by the Secretary General, S/26584, November 5, 1993; Note by the Secretary General, S/26825, December 1, 1993; Note by the Secretary General, S/26910, December 21, 1993; Note by the Secretary General, S/1994/31, January 14, 1994; Report on the Twenty Second IAEA Inspection, 1–15 November, 1993; Note by the Secretary General, S/1994/341, March 24, 1994; and Note by the Secretary General, S/1994/355, March 25, 1994.

560. Associated Press, October 14, 1995; A full post-war list has never been published. A US government list published after the Gulf War is contained in the Federal Register, Volume 56, Number 64, April 3, 1991, pp. 13584 to 13589.

Chapter 16

561. Department of Defense background briefing, October 20, 1994 (Federal News Service); Department of Defense handouts of October 11, 1994, and October 12, 1994; *Jane's Defense Weekly*, October 22, 1994, p. 4, December 17, 1994, p. 7; US Army briefing sheet (undated) October 1994; Congressional Research Service, *Iraq Crisis, October 1994, A Chronology*, 94-808F, October 24, 1994.

562. Author's estimate using $1991 figures from US Arms Control and Disarmament Agency (ACDA), *World Military Expenditures and Arms Transfers, 1991–1992*, Washington, GPO, 1994, pp. 67 and *, and converting into 1995 dollars using OMB conversions.

563. Iraqi Ba'athist official quoted in *The Guardian*, October 29, 1994, p. 13.

564. See *Middle East Economic Survey*, vol. 39, no. 1, October 1995, p. A5.

565. *Washington Times*, October 16, 1995, p. A1, A22; *Washington Post*, October 16, 1995, p. A15.

566. Saleh Kallab, "Irak et 'voisins': La Roulette Russe," *Arabies*, no. 106, October 1995, p. 18.

567. See also Jamal al-Attiya, "Irak: L'Apres-Saddam," *Arabies*, no. 50, 1991, pp. 12–15.

About the Book and Authors

This volume provides analysis of the state of Iraq's security and of current Western policy toward the country in the wake of the Gulf War. It also examines the political, economic, and security impact of sanctions, Iraq's future role as an oil exporter, the U.S. policy of "dual containment" in relation to Iraq, and options for dealing with Iraq in the future.

Anthony H. Cordesman has served in senior positions in the office for the secretary of defense, NATO, and the U.S. Senate. He is currently a senior fellow and Co-Director of the Middle East Program at the Center for Strategic and International Studies, an adjunct professor of national security studies at Georgetown University, and a special consultant on military affairs for ABC News. He lives in Washington, D.C. **Ahmed S. Hashim** is a fellow in Political-Military Affairs and the Middle East Program at the Center for Strategic and International Studies in Washington, D.C., where he specializes in strategic issues. Previously, he was a research associate at the International Institute for Strategic Studies in London. He lives in Virginia.